D1067226

Rosemary Ingham is a costume designer, costume technician, writer, and teacher. Her work has been seen at the Long Wharf Theatre, the Alley Theatre, the Dallas and Utah Shakespearean Festivals, TheatreVirginia, and others. She has written, with Liz Covey, *The Costumer's Handbook, The Costume Technician's Handbook, The Costume Designer's Handbook,* and *The Pattern Development Handbook,* and appears on *The Pattern Development Video,* produced by Theatre Arts Video Library. She attended the Yale Drama School and currently teaches at Mary Washington College in Fredericksburg, Virginia.

Liz Covey is a free-lance costume designer whose work has been seen at America's leading theatres from coast to coast. Born and educated in England, she received her training at the Leicester College of Art and worked at many of London's most prestigious theatres before moving to the United States. She is a member of the faculty of the Theatre Department at Barnard College, Columbia University, and also teaches at Bennington College, Bennington, Vermont. Ms. Covey lives in Manhattan.

THE
Costume

Designer's HANDBOOK

*A Complete Guide for Amateur
and Professional Costume Designers*

*Rosemary Ingham
Liz Covey*

Second Edition

HEINEMANN EDUCATIONAL BOOKS, INC. • PORTSMOUTH, NH

Heinemann
A division of Reed Elsevier Inc.
361 Hanover Street   Portsmouth, NH 03801-3912
Offices and agents throughout the world

© 1992 by Rosemary Ingham and Elizabeth Covey. Originally © 1983 by Prentice-Hall, Inc.
All rights reserved.

No part of this book may be reproduced in any form or by electronic or mechanical means, including
information storage and retrieval systems, without permission in writing from the publisher, except by
a reviewer, who may quote brief passages in a review.

Every effort has been made to contact copyright holders for permission to reprint borrowed material
where necessary, but if any oversights have occurred, we would be happy to rectify them in future
printings of this work.

Library of Congress Cataloging-in-Publication Data
Ingham, Rosemary.
    The costume designer's handbook : a complete guide for amateur
and professional costume designers / Rosemary Ingham, Liz Covey.–2nd ed.
      p.   cm.
    Includes bibliographical references.
    ISBN 0-435-08607-3
    1. Costume design. 2. Costume. I. Covey, Liz. II. Title
TT507.T46 1992
792'.026—dc20
                                             92–15238
                                               CIP

Cover photograph: Monica Bell as Lady Macbeth in the Utah Shakespearean Festival production of
    Macbeth. Costume design by Rosemary Ingham. Photograph by Michael Schoenfeld, courtesy
    of the Utah Shakespearean Festival.
Interior design by Maria Carella.
Cover design and color insert design by Wladislaw Finne.
Prepress production services by Camden Type 'n Graphics.
First published by Prentice-Hall, Inc. as "A Spectrum Book" and reissued in a Prentice-Hall Press Edition.

Printed in the United States of America.

94 95 96 9 8 7 6 5 4 3

Contents

Foreword, vii / Acknowledgments, viii

Designing

1

The Playscript

5

2

The Production

32

3

Costume Research

49

4

Preliminary Sketching
And Color Layout

69

5

Final Sketches

88

6

The Pre-Production Period

124

7

The Production Period

158

8

The Costume Design Business

188

Reference

Selected Painters
for Costume Research

215

Bibliography

226

Booksellers

254

Useful Publications

256

Useful Addresses

257

Costume Societies

258

Shopping Guide:
New York City   259
*Elsewhere in
the United States*   268
Canada   278

Index

281

Foreword

My joy in the theatre is collaboration. I began my artistic life as a writer, but I couldn't bear the loneliness: the quiet room, the blank piece of paper in the typewriter, the desperate hope that the phone would ring. I am cut out for the frantic energy of the rehearsal hall and for the complex interweaving of sensibilities that mark a fruitful design conference. The designer supplements me more profoundly than anyone else in the production process, for my visual skills have had to be developed consciously over the years, and my teachers have been the fine design artists who have taken me in hand. None was more influential or more persuasive in the early years of my career than one of the authors of this invaluable book.

Rosemary Ingham helped teach me color, and certainly line, but more importantly how to enlist the actor's best instincts in reaching vital costume decisions. I have no patience with costume designers who view actors as pliable dolls on which to drape fabric. There comes a time in nearly every rehearsal period when a good actor will know certain things about the character to be played that neither the director, the designer, nor even the writer can possibly know. If asked to wear clothes that violate his or her own deep sense of reality, the actor will remain an actor in a costume for the run of the show. A bit of breath will have been knocked out of the character, and breathing—*life*—is what the theatre is all about.

Of course, a sensitive designer can guide the actors toward that very discovery of a character's inner nature, provided the director and the designer have between them a true, if sometimes unspoken, bond of understanding. I can't always speak to a designer in specific visual terms, although I have learned with the years a much larger visual vocabulary than I had when I started. Nevertheless, I have found that visual specifics are not necessarily the material of my most productive design dialogues. I must work with designers who have a genuine concern for text and for meaning, and who can express themselves in those terms. They must delight in the discoveries of rehearsal and be as flexible in their ideas as I try to be in mine. An admirable design is meaningless if the actor cannot wear it with conviction and if the director cannot help the actor find some grains of the character's identity in the clothes.

Relaxation is, for me, the key to all good work in the theatre, and I hope for the same ease in the costume shop or the fitting room that I attempt to preserve in the rehearsal hall. No one has to deal more with actor tension than the costume designer, and his or her ego must be securely in place in order not to exacerbate a moment of fury or despair. I like designers who are strong and confident enough to hang onto one of their most precious tools, a sense of humor, when someone may be trying to grab it out of their hands.

So the designers who function best with me are those with a sense of the whole, a sense of humor, and a sense of self. Of course, taste and visual genius don't hurt a bit. That's a lot to find in one person, but it's just such a confluence of remarkable individuals who can exult in sharing that provides me with the true excitement of collaboration in the theatre.

ARVIN BROWN
Artistic Director
Long Wharf Theatre

Acknowledgments

Janet Addis
Frances Aronson
Susan Ashdown
Mark Avery
Whitney Blausen
Veronica Ann Brady
Rita Brown
Mary Aiello Bruce
Robert Bruyr
Richard Bryant
Pat Cavins
Bob Chambers
Martha Christian
Hillary Derby
James Glavan
Susan Griffin
Rosalind Heinz
Richard Ingham
Robert E. Ingham
Stephen Ingham
Nagle Jackson
Barbara Joyce
Jeffrey Lieder
Susan Medak
Mark Rasdorf
Jennifer Smith-Windsor
John Stephano
Carol Wells-Day

Arena Stage
The Costume Collection
Hartford Stage Company
Long Wharf Theatre
McCarter Theatre
Milwaukee Repertory Theater
TheatreVirginia
Utah Shakespearean Festival

And a special thanks to the designers who allowed us access to their portfolios and professional lives:

Keith Belli
Michael J. Cesario
Susan B. Cox
Laura Crow
Lowell Detweiler
Susan Hilferty
Ann Hould-Ward
Arnold S. Levine
Andrew B. Marlay
David Murin
Colleen Muscha
Beth Novak
Carol Oditz
Susan Rheaume
Susan Tsu
Jennifer Von Mayrhauser
Ann Wallace

The Costume Designer's Handbook

1
The Playscript

Each element has its own particular relation to the drama and plays its own part in the drama. And each element—the word, the actor, the costume—has the exact significance of a note in a symphony. Each separate costume we create for a play must be exactly suited both to the character it helps to express and to the occasion it graces.

ROBERT EDMOND JONES
The Dramatic Imagination

Plays are crafted. A playscript is an artificial construct, not a slice of life. It is structured experience, not random experience. However artless it may appear to be, a play is wholly artful. It is created, contrived, crafted, and shaped by its writer.

Plays are both more than life and less than life. Dramatic actions are packed with more meaning and more significance than most random life events. Plots organize dramatic actions into complete structures with beginnings, middles, and ends. Every dramatic event, no matter how small, influences and shapes play structure; in contrast, routine real-life occurrences seem to have little effect on the sprawling human story. On the other hand, dramatic characters are far less complex than living people, and dramatic dialogue is a contrived arrangement of words, usually composed to sound like human speech but selected only to articulate the play.

Even when a play seems most realistic, when its characters appear to speak real conversation, sit on real sofas in real rooms and drink real coffee, it is not like life, only life-*like*. A play has far more in common with a painting, a sonnet, or a sonata than it does with life.

When you compare a play to a piece of music you can speak of its notes, its themes, its harmonies. When you say it's like a painting you can point to the elements of design within it—line, shape, color, texture, pattern—and the principles of composition with which these elements are combined—unity, variety, balance, emphasis, rhythm, proportion. Like sonnets, plays are shaped both by external and internal forms. They are closed systems, formal and interdependent, and they rely upon surprising combinations of familiar elements for their interest and power.

A playwright is a craftsperson, and a play may be said to be designed and built, unit by unit, action by action, word by word. Each play has a finite number of units, even when the multiplicity and complexity of the units seem to be infinite and to defy analysis.

FIGURE 1-1. A play has far more in common with a painting, a sonnet, or a sonata than it does with life. *The Ascent of Mount Fuji* by Chingiz Aitmatov and Kaltai Mukhamedzhanov at Arena Stage. *Set design by Ming Cho Lee. Photo by George de Vincent.*

Because plays are constructed from units you can examine, they are open to analysis. You may search for the nature and structure of a play by correctly identifying its parts and by perceiving the patterns in which the playwright has arranged the parts. But, because plays are creations of the human imagination, which is capable of combining dramatic events in an infinite number of patterns, each playscript analysis will require a different process and each play will contain a unique collection of facts and will have a unique structure.

How to Read and See Plays

Good theatre designers must be good play readers. This is not a skill that comes naturally to everyone. Children seldom encounter plays in their early reading experience. By the time a play does appear in a sixth- or seventh-grade literature anthology, the habits acquired from reading continuous prose narrative are well ingrained. Some of these habits may inhibit good play reading.

Plays make different demands on their readers than stories or essays do. Because you are given less information, every piece of which is vital to the structure, you must pay close attention to every word. You may not skim through passages that seem to stray from the theme or plot because plays do not allow for digression. You must not expect plays to describe or elaborate or reflect because plays are nothing but action. Plays exist in the present tense; therefore, the reader must learn to perceive the actions *as happening* rather than *as happened*.

Exercise Your Imagination

It's difficult to learn to read plays well if you have not seen many plays performed on stage. When you are reading a play well, you are seeing it in your mind's eye. There is an environment, there are characters, and there is movement. Only in live performance can you discover the means by which dramatic events in the playscript are brought to life by actors and by design elements. As you watch, you build up a store of staging and setting possibilities with which to fuel and excite your own imagination. You can practice applying these possibilities as you read plays.

Especially valuable experience can be gained when you see the same play in different productions with different sets and different actors. Even when the playscript is not altered at all, you will see how different choices in emphasis, color, rhythm, etc., make each production unique. You will realize that the goal of production is not doing the play *right* but making it *coherent*. You will begin to understand how to read the playscript as the blueprint rather than the description of a production.

Films and Television

Watching a filmed or televised play is not the same experience as seeing a play on stage. Film and television scripts are different from playscripts in two very important ways:

1. The most important structural element in the filmscript is the camera; and
2. A film or television script is intended to become a record of what has happened, not of what is happening (except in the almost extinct "live" television dramas).

In all filmed and televised play productions, the camera shapes the experience for the audience by selecting what is seen in contrast with what is heard. The audience has no choice; the selection is absolute. The larger scene, the other characters, the broader action, are simply eliminated from the picture and the viewers are carried through the story seeing precisely what the writer and the director want them to see.

Focusing Attention Without the Camera

When dramatic events occur on stage, there is no way to make the rest of the setting, or other characters in the scene, disappear. There is no mechanism for zooming the audience's attention in on significant glances or gestures. Focus, which in film or television is imposed by the camera, must, in the theatre, be created and maintained by the combined efforts of playwright, director, actors, and designers. It is their task to make sure the audience is attracted to the right place at the right time in order to experience the significant event.

Playwrights manipulate focus through their choice of words and events and by the way in which they arrange them. A gifted playwright can capture the audience's attention by contrasting sounds or dialogue rhythms, by an entrance, by ringing the telephone, or by introducing an unexpected piece of information at just the right moment. Directors support and clarify the playwright's choices by staging and orchestrating the events in ways that make it difficult for an audience to miss their significance. Actors find physical and emotional ways to command focus at the correct times. Designers contribute to focus through their selections of set and costume elements, through area illumination and the use of evocative color. Creating consistent stage focus for the audience is the greatest challenge faced by those who work in live theatre.

Young theatrical designers whose main experience with drama has been through the media of film and television often have difficulty manipulating focus in their designs. They are used to seeing everything in detail, up close and selected for them. Their sets and costumes may, therefore, have too many areas of interest to allow for any focusing of attention or they may be uniformly bland. Such designs seem to be waiting for an outside eye, a camera, to select from them. The best way to solve this design problem is to see live

FIGURE 1-2. Designers contribute to focus through their selections of set and costume elements, area illumination, and evocative color. The Follet family in *All the Way Home* at the McCarter Theatre. *Costume design by Jennifer von Mayrhauser. Photograph by Cliff Moore.*

performances and notice all the ways by which your attention is directed. You will be surprised how often design elements figure directly in both successful and unsuccessful focusing of stage action.

Plays Happen Now

Stage focus is affected by the fact that plays happen in present time. Even though the production has been designed, built, rehearsed and "set" prior to its opening to the public, each performance is *now* and subject to change. Designs and performances must, therefore, be flexible enough to allow for a certain amount of variation from performance to performance. While a film director may do fifty "takes" of a scene until the needs of his or her visual structure are fulfilled, a stage director must seek ways of doing each scene that will be effective despite the changes in audience, atmosphere, temperature, and in the delicate emotional balance between characters that will

inevitably vary from night to night. Designs must be, as Robert Edmond Jones called them, environments in which the play may live rather than decorative backgrounds that illustrate one static view of the play. A film is the same every time you see it, selected, spliced, and sealed in a can. No two performances of a play are ever identical.

If you have seen many more films than plays, you will probably visualize any playscript you are reading as if it were a filmscript. As you read, notice that you are perceiving most action in medium and close shots. If this is your way of visualizing, try to change it by taking a few moments at the beginning of the play to set the whole stage in your mind's eye. Furnish it, plant trees, erect walls. Place the characters firmly in the set, and every time you are inclined to zoom in on one or two faces for an intimate bit of dialogue, recall the set you have imagined and listen to the dialogue from the middle of the house with the whole stage visible. Learn to read playscripts as plays and not as movies.

The First Reading

Even though you're reading a play because you've been asked to design it, read it the first time for pleasure only. Try not to take note of what the play will eventually demand of you. Be the audience. Read to find out who falls in love with whom, which character murdered the king, and whether or not the young couple ends up happily ever after. Try not to make notes and, if possible, read the whole play at a single sitting.

When you have finished the first reading, stay put for a moment and experience your response completely. One of the basic tenets of good playscript analysis is the ability to suspend judgment and examine the text in objective terms, not through a haze of likes and dislikes. But, since all play readers, including designers, respond personally to the plays they read, make

sure you have an opportunity to register your feelings about the play immediately after your initial encounter with it. Designers can do good work whether they like the play they're working on or not. Quality design does not depend on personal taste and feelings. But, if you allow your feelings free rein for a few moments in the beginning of the process, it will be easier for you to put them aside later on in order to proceed with the objective part of the work.

These are the goals of the first reading: discover what the play's about and what happens, meet the characters, and respond to the play as personally as possible. Having done so, accept the play on its own terms, without prejudice (prejudging), and prepare to find out what it's made of and how it works.

Additional Readings

Most designers will read a play straight through at least once or twice more in order to become thoroughly familiar with everything that happens. These readings are important steps in the process of establishing the play as a construct, an ordered system of parts. They often excite the first visual images that suggest the play's environment.

Choose a pleasant surrounding in which to read. Some people like music in the background while others prefer silence. Some read late at night and others early in the morning. The important thing about a surrounding is that it allow the reader to achieve a state of maximum concentration with minimum interference.

During the last of these general readings it is helpful to be armed with a transparent yellow marker, or "highlighter," with which to mark costume and character references in the script as well as entrances and exits if the play has a complicated movement pattern. These highlighted areas can be spotted quickly when you settle down to make charts and lists.

A Designer's Analysis

As soon as you feel satisfied that you understand what appears to be going on in the play, it's time to turn your attention to the process of *analysis*. In this process, you must examine the play in order to distinguish its component parts, separately and in their relation to the whole. Everything that is said in the play, everything that happens in the play, and everything that is described by the playwright must be scrutinized. The first part of the process is to correctly identify these script facts, and the second part is to discover how each fact functions within the whole play.

For many theatre designers, analyzing a text is a frustrating task, a necessary evil to be gotten through as quickly as possible. Their approach generally consists of gathering a few obvious facts about time, place, and number of characters, possibly drawing a rough chart to follow the characters through the action, and maybe making a few vague notes about atmosphere and feeling. Thus armed, these design-ers put away their scripts, attend production meetings, listen to and talk with the director, and, without consulting the script again, begin to draw and build.

Designers who work this way misunderstand the unique nature of plays and divorce themselves early from their most reliable and evocative source of information *and* inspiration, the script.

On the other hand, a designer who recognizes that the text should be central to the design process develops methods of using the playwright's words to discover how the play works and what its environment looks like.

Playscript analysis would be easy if each play were a simple construct with a single interpretation and only a few parts, clearly discerned. Such a play would make easy visual demands and require only one production to illuminate the script completely. But, if this were true, if plays were so simple and transparent, the theatre would have lost its vitality centuries ago. The fact is that even the smallest and most straightforward play is a construct of many meanings and, depending upon the angle from which it is viewed, many faces. It can be acted, directed, and designed in many ways and from many angles without departing from the text. One of the endless fascinations of a great and complex play, such as *Hamlet,* is the sheer density of its structural elements and layers. One of the greatest problems in producing *Hamlet* is choosing which face, or faces, of the play to show on the stage at any given time.

You must remember, however, that even in *Hamlet* the number of possibilities for production is not infinite. *Every play,* whether it is relatively simple or highly complex, *does have an inherent structure.* The playwright built the structure, for better or for worse, and it is as basic to the play as your genetic structure is to you. The structure is the play's potential; it tells you what it is capable of being and what it cannot be.

Limitations and Possibilities

Playscript analysis for designers functions in two ways which sometimes appear to be contradictory but are, in fact, complementary: 1. You discover many design possibilities within the script; and 2. You discover the limitations the script imposes on design choice. On the one hand you find information that allows you to see a character in many different guises, inhabiting several sorts of landscapes, all of which are allowed or indicated by the words of the text. On the other hand you find a structure in the play that imposes a set of guidelines you may use for choosing suits, hats, and architectural detail. In the process, you learn that many things will work for this play but not everything.

None of this discussion is meant to suggest that designers should limit their participation in the collaborative process or ignore the ideas of directors. This analysis is part of the designer's pre-conference preparation, and the primary aim of the analysis is to help designers be more active collaborators. Designers, more than any other members of the production team, need to discover the largest number of possibilities in every script and find many visual statements that are true to the play so they can absorb and assimilate all the ideas the director, actors, and other designers have about the play. The more complete a designer's analysis of the script is before the collaborative process begins, the more flexible that designer can be in the process of creating the physical production.

Fact Finding

The first step in playscript analysis is to move from an understanding of the play in terms of what appeared to be happening in the early readings to a rigorous examination of the facts that are contained in the play, facts that are there to tell you precisely what is happening. In your search for script facts, collect only what is there. Don't make assumptions. That is to say, don't add to the given or expand upon it. This is particularly important when you are dealing with plays set in well-known historical periods. A designer may know more about the period than the playwright does. It is usually counter-productive to add facts to a play when the playwright, either out of ignorance or because he or she was consciously limiting the scope of the play's world, didn't include them. It is not, for example, at all helpful to add what is now known about the good aspects of King Richard III of England's character to a production of Shakespeare's

Richard III. Such facts may be true but they are not true of Shakespeare's play.

Remember that a play is the sum of all its facts and no fact is, ultimately, more important than another. One may take up more stage time, another may be more interesting to discuss, and yet another may be more accessible to you, but the success of the play in production depends upon the balance created between all the parts within the whole.

FIGURE 1-3. Shakespeare's *Richard III* at the Long Wharf Theatre with Carolyn Coates and Richard Venture. *Costume design by John Conklin. Photograph by William Smith.*

Analysis for the
Imagination and Intellect

The creative act is not merely a mechanical manipulation of matter into form.

BERNARD BECKERMAN

Design in the theatre is intellectual and imaginative, practical and poetic, mechanical and magical. For playscript analysis to have broad application to theatre design it must feed both the imagination and the intellect. It is not enough to use analytical tools to discover only what physical things the play requires: How many doors must the set have? Will the windows be practical? What historical period should the swords and shields convey? Which characters in the ball scene wear masks? You must, of course, know these things; and yet it is of equal importance to discover visually informing bits and pieces within the script which translate from the verbal to the visual in ways that always seem mysterious even to those who repeatedly engage in such translating.

No one can describe the process of creating images or perceptions or explain why each one is unique to the imagination that creates it. (And, of course, no one has the vaguest notion why some imaginations contribute to works of genius while others foster works of smaller scope.) Yet, unpredictable as it is, you must as theatre designers possess a responsive and well-exercised imagination. It is as vital to your work as your ability to read and think logically.

Imagination seldom approaches problems in a sequential manner. Instead it produces images, perceptions, and emotional responses which may, on the one hand, present themselves as fragments which seem to have little connection with one another or, on the other hand, spring forth whole and intact like Venus in the myth. These imaginative products don't seem bound to ordinary reality, and yet they may illuminate a given design choice more brilliantly than "real" facts, shedding entirely new light on all that you have previously known.

Both the intellect and the imagination are stimulated by facts discovered in the script. The intellect uses these facts to define and solve practical problems related to place, use, and historical accuracy. Imagination uses the same facts to reflect and evoke sensoral response and to support psychological and emotional forces. The intellect and the imagination work interdependently to create the play's visual environment. The two processes illuminate and check up on each other. A design that is all intellect may only serve the play in mechanical ways while one that is all image may be perfect for one moment in the first act but wrong for all the rest.

Combining Intellect and Imagination

Fully realizing that examples are always simplistic, here are three isolated facts from three well-known plays and a brief consideration of the intellectual and imaginative responses they might evoke:

1. Big Daddy is dying of cancer.
2. James Tyrone is a stingy man in the eyes of his family.
3. Horatio describes the beard of Hamlet's Ghost "as I have seen it in his life, /A sable silvered."

Your intellect will make note of these facts, place them in groups with related and substantiating facts, and assign them to help solve the following problems:

1. What does Big Daddy look like?
2. What does James Tyrone's house look like?
3. How "ghostly" is Old Hamlet's Ghost?

You will be led to ask additional questions, some of which can't be answered in the script—What does a man dying of cancer really look like? What color is sable?—and some which the script can answer—Which characters accuse James Tyrone of stinginess and under what circumstances? Does anyone who encounters Hamlet's Ghost have difficulty recognizing him? Consider all the questions raised by facts you discover but make it a rule of thumb to concentrate especially on the ones that can be answered in the text.

Your imagination, stimulated by the facts of Big Daddy's cancer, James Tyrone's meanness, and the sable silvered beard, is unconcerned with practicality and order; it responds at random with visual fragments, spacial constructs, sensory ideas, or with pure feeling. Because each imaginative reaction is unique and personal, it is difficult to find examples that don't seem contrived. But suppose, for the sake of this example, that the following visual images are produced by the facts discovered above:

1. Big Daddy's cancer appears to you as a body shape, drawn and lumpy with a tension in it that suggests a big man's body being drained from within.

2. You respond to James Tyrone's tight-fistedness by visualizing a bare room with only a clutch of skeletal furniture shapes crouched in the gloomy pool of light cast by a single burning light bulb.

3. Horatio's specific observation of the exact color combination in Old Hamlet's beard invokes a ghost that is vibrant, super-real, more minutely detailed and more accurate than life.

How can you integrate your intellectual and imaginative responses to the text and apply them to the choice of suits, hats, beards, ground plans, and furniture?

BIG DADDY'S CANCER

If you allow your intellectual response to Big Daddy's cancer to dominate, there is the chance that what you discover about the physically debilitating effects of the disease will inspire you to over-indicate these effects with detailed make-up and ill-fitting clothes due to weight loss. Before making that decision, consider the image your imagination produced; it was not specific but suggestive. Allow these responses to inform each other and perhaps you will come to "see" Big Daddy as a man who is dying, in fact, but whose disease must be perceived gradually by the audience and by the other characters in the play. His costume and make-up may help suggest that he is being ravaged from within; they must not illustrate it.

JAMES TYRONE'S STINGINESS

The room image created by the fact of James Tyrone's stinginess might well, if not tempered by rational questions, lead you to create a set that is far too shabby to be the summer home of a celebrated, well-to-do actor. In this case you must reassess your image in intellectual terms. James Tyrone is an ambiguous figure. Can you afford to emphasize one side over the others? To whom does he appear stingy and what exactly is the nature of that stinginess? Don't abandon the image, however, because it remains an important reaction. You may want to use it to inform the environment for the final act when father and sons are, in fact, caught in the bleak illumination of the single bulb James Tyrone will permit.

OLD HAMLET'S GHOST

Using your image of a "real looking" ghost that was stimulated by Horatio's detailed description of his beard, you can return to the script to check out the logic of such a choice. You discover that no one who encounters the Ghost has any difficulty recognizing him. No one describes him in other than human-appearing terms. You might also ask if young Hamlet is not apt to be more emotionally affected by a ghost that actually looks like his father did than by one costumed in a fearful ghostly suit? In this instance, image and intellect may illuminate and substantiate each other.

These are examples of how designers interrelate what has recently come to be called *left brain thinking* (intellectual and rational) and *right brain thinking* (spatial, intuitional, and image-producing). Both are essential. Both must be given equal weight. Both require facts to stimulate them into action.

An Outline for Playscript Analysis

The following outline will help you discover the important script facts in a relatively orderly fashion and suggest a way to examine the facts that will reveal something about the play's shape and structure. The wording of the outline and the order in which its parts appear are of little importance. Not all the questions or statements in the outline will apply to every play. When you encounter one that doesn't fit the situation, skip over it and move on. Playwrights don't write plays in order to have them fit into anybody's outline. Yet any outline for playscript analysis that is worth considering should be malleable enough to work for any play. Playscript analysis is only viable for designers if it helps them make discoveries about the play that have visual as well as verbal components. Results are far more important than slavish adherence to method.

I. Where are they?
1. Exact geographical location.
2. Note textural references and descriptions

II. When are they?
1. Day, month, year.
2. Note special significance of date or season.

III. Who are they?

1. Relationships and socio-economics.
2. Under what government?
3. In what religious environment?
4. Believing what about ethical conduct, sex, marriage, family?

IV. What happened before the play begins?

V. What do the major characters think about their world?

VI. What is the function of each character?
1. Who is the protagonist?
2. Who is the antagonist?
3. Which characters lead and which support?
4. Identify and describe stereotypical characters.
5. Identify and describe crowds.

VII. What is the Dialogue Mode?
1. Naturalistic dialogue.
2. Literary dialogue.
3. Poetic dialogue.
4. Sound and grammar.
5. Ambiguity.

VIII. What is the play's action?
1. Create an action chart.

IX. What is the play's theme?

I. Where are they?

1. Exact Geographical Location
2. Note Textural References and Descriptions

Most playwrights make a statement of place at the beginning of their scripts. These may range from a terse, "A country road. A tree." in Samuel Beckett's *Waiting For Godot* to George Bernard Shaw's detailed three-page description of St. Dominic's Parsonage in *Candida*—he identifies certain books on the shelves and tells us there is "a black japanned flower-painted coal scuttle" on the hearth. Jot down such facts (within reason!) but keep your eyes open for textual substantiation because it is usually what characters say about their surroundings that proves most evocative for designers.

At the opening of Shelagh Delaney's *A Taste of Honey*, you will read: "the stage represents a comfortless flat in Manchester and the street outside." A half-dozen lines into the first scene, Helen describes this flat:

Anyway, what's wrong with this place? Everything in it's falling apart, it's true, and we've no heating— but there's a lovely view of the gasworks, we share a bathroom with the community and this wallpaper's contemporary. What more do you want?

A few pages further on, Peter, Helen's boyfriend, sums up the neighborhood in three words: "Tenements, cemetery, slaughterhouse." These are the kinds of textural facts that excite the designer's imagination. "Comfortless flat" is too general. The more specific the fact is, the more resonant it will be.

II. When Are They?

1. Day, Month, Year
2. Special Significance of Date or Season

Note the day, month, and year if they are given. Note the time of day and the season. Make an additional note if the date has special significance. *Ah, Wilderness!* takes place on July 4, and you may be sure the playwright had reasons for making this choice.

You won't be able to discover a precise "when" for all plays. Some suggest timelessness, some project into an unspecified future, and some can be played in a variety of periods. Many of Shakespeare's plays fall into this last category, particularly the comedies.

The director usually chooses the period in which the play will be set but occasionally the costume designer will be involved in the production early enough to affect that choice. When you're reading a play that does not have a specified time, be aware of general time impressions you receive from the dialogue, small facts or an overall tone that might help locate the play in a particularly suitable period. If you are asked to design a play in a period that seems inappropriate to you, go back to your script and see if you can discover specific events or words in the text that seem to justify your response. Share these with the director. They may be things he or she has not yet discovered.

FIGURE 1-4 (above). Family dinner on the fourth of July in Eugene O'Neill's *Ah, Wilderness!* at the Long Wharf Theatre. *Costume Design by Bill Walker. Photograph courtesy of Long Wharf Theatre.*

FIGURES 1-5 & 1-6. Sir Andrew Aguecheek from *Twelfth Night* in two different centuries. Figure 1-5 (below left), designed for the Great Lakes Shakespeare Festival and Figure 1-6 (below right), for the Indiana Repertory Theatre, both by Liz Covey. Both sketches executed with technical pen and ink on heavy tracing paper. *Photograph by Frances Aronson.*

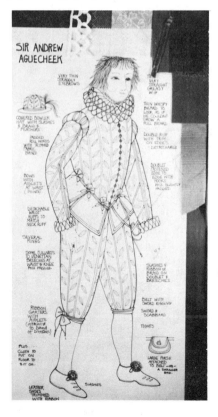

III. Who Are They?

1. Relationships and Socio-economics

2. Under What Government?

3. In What Religious Environment?

4. Believing What about Ethical Conduct, Sex, Marriage, Family?

Be certain you know who is married to whom and who their children are. Note all family relationships, however vague. Ask what economic relationships exist between the characters. Who is rich and who is poor? Are the characters coming up in the world or going down? Who has the money power? Who does not? Who is the employer and who is the employee? Who leads by birth and who leads in spite of it?

Always be aware of subtleties in social and economic relationships and remember that the playwright may be writing from a point of view and from life experiences quite different from your own. Learn to pick up clues to socio-

economic identity. A female character who remarks that she attended Radcliffe is slipping you a fact about who she is. A character who says his father was "on the dole" gives another. Sometimes a speech mannerism will indicate a lower class background when everything else about the character obscures it.

Many Americans have little or no understanding of social class in the English and European sense and therefore cannot always see the difference between economic status and social class. Remember, although the level of economic affluence may relate to social class, it doesn't always. A character is not lower class simply because he or she is low on cash. This is particularly true in countries, and in areas of this country, where class status is more closely associated with family background than with money.

It is usually important to know what form of government is in power in the play's world. Is it a monarchy, an oligarchy, or a dictatorship? Who is the leader? Is there political stability or

FIGURE 1-7. Be certain you know who is married to whom. Family and guests in Noel Coward's *Hay Fever* at the McCarter Theatre. *Costume design by Robert Morgan. Photograph by Cliff Moore.*

political turmoil? Are the characters in the play directly related to the political structure? If so, how?

The relationship between characters and government may be implied rather than stated. Absence of specific dialogue about government or politics is, in itself, not enough reason to rule out the presence of a political climate. Playwrights often assume—particularly when they are writing plays contemporary with their own lifetimes—that the current political structure is an understood part of the play's structure.

Chekhov's plays cannot be called political plays; the government is seldom mentioned. Yet, when Vershinin rhapsodizes about the future in Act III of *Three Sisters,* he is speaking in a political as well as in a philosophical and sentimental framework. The more you know about that framework, the more you know about Vershinin.

And yet, in reality, what a difference there is between what is now and has been in the past! And when a little more time has passed—another two or three hundred years—people will look at our present manner of life with horror and derision, and everything of today will seem awkward and heavy, and very strange and uncomfortable. Oh what a wonderful life that will be—what a wonderful life!

Ask also if the play takes place in the context of particular religious perspective. Is there a national religion? Do the major characters belong to a distinct religious group? Is organized religion an important social institution in the play?

A religious component, like politics and government, may be present in a play's background even though little or no specific reference is made to it. In Frank Cucci's *High Time,* a play about a 40-year-old Italian/American widow adjusting to life without a husband, the Roman Catholic church plays a major role in the woman's world even though the play has no religious theme as such. It is a fact that demands some support, however subtle, within the design scheme.

There are, of course, some plays which have nothing whatsoever to do with religion, government, or politics. Accept the absence and do not try to impose any of them on a production when they are absent in the text.

The moral stance in a play is particularly important to designers. Study the script to discover the prevailing attitudes about ethical conduct, sex, marriage, and family. How are women viewed? Is ethical conduct valued? What social institutions exist to uphold community morals?

FIGURE 1-8. Formal attire designed for the McCarter Theatre's production of *Heartbreak House* by Andrew B. Marlay. The sketch is done in pencil, watercolor, and colored pencil on watercolor paper. *Photograph by Frances Aronson.*

Social institutions are the moral guardians of any age and they set and enforce behavior. They put pressure on people to dress themselves appropriately and to furnish their homes correctly. Adhering to correct modes of dress and submitting to accepted lifestyles have been moral yardsticks since the dawn of civilization. In some periods restrictions are many, in some they are few. They are seldom absent altogether. Costume designers in particular must understand the role of social institutions in regulating fashion, and they must be able to relate contemporary mores as they are expressed in clothing to the particular play being designed.

Many playwrights write about the struggle between free spirited characters and the prevailing moral stance of their day. Costume can add important visual support to such conflicts. A character who lives comfortably within the mores of his or her time projects a very different image from one who looks on contemporary mores as constraints and struggles against the institutions that try to enforce them.

The answers to these first three questions—where, when, and who—will provide you with a bulging and unwieldy bag of facts about the play, its world, and its characters. Some of them may be contradictory, others are sure to be confusing. Try not to jump to conclusions about anything until all the facts are in and have begun to take on a shape. For the present, simply collect.

IV. What Happened Before the Play Begins?

As soon as you are familiar with the play's present, begin to discover its past. Be sure you stick to the text, however, and consider only what is revealed there. Many designers fall into the habit of making up background facts that seem reasonable but which, if incorporated into the design, may give false signals and confuse the present action. For instance, it might seem quite plausible to assume that Stanley Kowalski played football in high school. But if the costume designer gives him a school jacket to wear with an athletic letter on it, the audience may expect him to be a former high school hero who is having difficulty adjusting to adult life. Such expectations, completely unsupported by the text, can obscure what Stanley is and does in the present. It is always a temptation to "fill in" what the playwright has chosen not to present. Be wary of such impulses.

V. What Do the Major Characters Think About Their World?

Ask if the play's major characters are representative of their world or in revolt against it. Are they insiders, part of the establishment, or outsiders. If they are outsiders, do they wish they were inside or are they outside by choice?

Contrast character attitudes at the beginning of the play with attitudes at its end. Most major characters move from some form of ignorance to some form of knowledge in the course of the play. Sometimes this knowledge is acquired by the progression of present dramatic events and sometimes by the revelation of a past event which then affects the character's attitude toward the present.

Perceiving changes in attitude can be especially helpful to a costume designer. Natasha, in Chekhov's *Three Sisters*, is in awe of Andre's house and of his sisters when she makes her appearance in Act I. By the second act she is Andre's wife and familiarity has replaced awe. In Act IV she has become the undisputed mistress of her environment, plans major changes in the landscaping of the estate, and criticizes the sisters' appearances as they once criticized hers. Such clear-cut attitudinal changes in a character undoubtedly demand visual support in her choice of clothing.

VI. What Is the Function of Each Character?

Francis Hodge, in *Play Directing, Analysis, Communication and Style,* defines character as what the playwright makes and characterization as what the actor makes. This is a useful way to separate script fact from rehearsal and production fact. In the following pages, all references to character will refer to what can be found in the play's text. Characterization will mean character *plus* actor, director, and physical production.

Much of a costume designer's work involves supporting a successful union between character and characterization. It is easier for the designer to affect this union when he or she has had enough time to get acquainted with the character before actors, director, and production realities appear on the scene. (This is *not* to suggest that costumes ought to be designed before a play is cast which is risky business, not unlike designing a set without knowing anything about the stage or the theatre that will house it.)

Dramatic characters are the moving parts of the play structure, the speakers and the doers. Their words and actions are confined by the play and they have no other life than the one given them by the playwright.

You have already collected many facts about the characters in the play. You know where, when, and who they are. You know something about their backgrounds and their attitudes. Now it's time to consider characters as units of dramatic structure. Ask what each character contributes to the play and how his or her function might be visually supported. It's obvious that an on-duty policeman in a play has to wear a uniform in order to perform his function on stage. The leading man, the villain, the innocent victim, and the crowd extra also have specific tasks to perform and must be dressed in ways that will help the audience see them do what they were created to do. This is an important part of creating stage focus.

The following functional labels often overlap. Use them to examine the ways in which characters perform rather than as character definitions.

FIGURES 1-9 & 1-10. Two Kates strike characteristic poses in two unusual costumes for productions of Shakespeare's *Taming of the Shrew*. Figure 1-9 (left) is Rose Pickering in the Milwaukee Repertory Theater's version. *Costume design by Susan Tsu. Photograph by Mark Avery.*
FIGURE 1-10 (right) is Leslie Geraci at the McCarter Theatre. *Costume design by Liz Covey. Photograph by Cliff Moore.*

1. Who Is the Protagonist?

The protagonist is the leading character, the mover, the one who wants, the one who incites action. Lear is the protagonist of *King Lear,* Jimmy Porter of *Look Back in Anger,* Dolly Levi of *The Matchmaker,* and Vanya of *Uncle Vanya.* Protagonists are always wanting things, telling others what to do, hatching plots and shooting at people who displease them. Some plays may have more than one protagonist although it's unusual to have two of equal weight. The protagonist is

an important focal point for the audience who must see everything that character does.

2. Who Is the Antagonist?

This character stands in the way of what the protagonist wants. This is the adversary, the complication. In melodrama the antagonist is the villain, and in farce it may be the stupid servant who delivers the note to the wrong lady. Iago *(Othello)* is an antagonist and so is Banquo *(Macbeth).* Traditionally, antagonists take focus periodically but must be able to slip into the background at other times.

3. Which Characters Lead and Which Support?

The terms "lead" and "support" in this context do not refer to Actor's Equity Association rules which govern pay scales for actors playing lead and support roles. A lead character in playscript analysis is differentiated from a support character, not by number of lines spoken or time spent on the stage, but by the function each performs in the play.

Lead characters advance from ignorance to knowledge, they go somewhere, they learn, they come to understand, they rise and fall, and, by doing what they do, they move the dramatic action forward.

Support characters do one thing, exert one force, or express one unchanging point of view. Their stance quite literally supports the actions of the leading characters, although that support often takes the form of resistance against what the leading characters want.

In Kaufman and Hart's *The Man Who Came to Dinner*, two support characters are Mr. and Mrs. Ernest W. Stanley, the couple in whose house the play takes place. These characters, whose attitudes never change, exert a constant—and very funny—resistance to virtually everything the leading characters want.

FIGURE 1-11. Halo Wines and Mark Hammer as Miss Preen and Sheridan Whiteside in *The Man Who Came to Dinner*, produced by Arena Stage. *Costume design by Marjorie Slaiman. Photographed by George de Vincent.*

Miss Preen, in the same play, performs a lead function even though her role is a small one. Her character alters considerably as a result of her constant exposure to Sheridan Whiteside's insults. Her comic progression from ignorance to knowledge drives her to turn on Whiteside, to abandon her assignment, and to resign from the nursing profession.

It is far more useful for a costume designer to consider characters in terms of their functions than it is to think of them as big and little parts. Support characters often demand costumes that are single bold strokes, specific, to the point, and absolutely correct. Even if the character is only on stage for a moment to perform a single action, the physical appearance must support that action clearly and without ambiguity.

Lead characters are complex and multidimensional. They have many levels of personality and are capable of expressing different points of view. Even in such a relatively uncomplicated lead character as Miss Preen, there is room for some complexity. Her function is to change, and the potential for this will be part of the way she looks.

As you examine characters and their functions, make a list of the leads and one of the supports. Identify the protagonist and the antagonist. By each lead character note what change in attitudes (or actions, or whatever) occurs in the course of the play, and by each support character describe what task that character performs.

4. Identify and Describe Stereotypical Characters

Stereotype is not a derogatory word. A stereotypical character is not a character the playwright has neglected to develop completely. Playwrights depend on stereotypes and bring them on when they need to show the audience an immediately identifiable character type, using as few words of dialogue as possible. The audience recognizes them chiefly by dress and behavior: the Irish cop, the talkative New York City cab driver, the gum-chewing secretary, the salesman, and several varieties of private detective. Wordy introductions are not necessary. It is the first impression that makes the statement.

Sometimes the stereotypical character will remain just what the initial appearance showed him or her to be. At other times the stereotype will broaden into a more complex character, perhaps quite different from the stereotypical expectation.

Many costume designers, in an effort not to be thought dull and unimaginative, avoid choosing the obvious outfit for a stereotypical character: a slinky taffeta dress for the prostitute, a polyester leisure suit for the automobile salesman. They search for something more subtle, something different. Before you shun the obvious in these situations, consider the playwright's intent. If the structure of the scene depends on that character being instantly recognized by the audience, anything the costume does to delay that recognition will interrupt the flow of dramatic events. In these instances it is always best to support the character with clothes that speak louder, and more pointedly, than words.

5. Identify and Describe Crowds

The secret to costuming crowds is to perceive them as members of one functional group. A crowd is usually "the peasants," "the other inmates," "the mob." Imagine them as a single force and, without resorting to inappropriate uniformity, never permit crowd members so much individualization that their group identity will be lost.

VIII. What Is the Dialogue Mode?

Playscripts are virtually all direct discourse, which we call dialogue. Dialogue, spoken by characters, tells you everything that happens in the play and everything the playwright wants you to know about what happens. Because of the tasks it must perform, dramatic dialogue is carefully structured and therefore totally unlike most human conversation. It cannot ramble from subject to subject as most people do when they talk to someone else. Dialogue is the most artful building material in the dramatic construct and the play's most important structural element.

The first reading of a play will tell you what the dialogue says; you also learn what happens from moment to moment. An analysis of the dialogue introduces you to *how* the play says what it says.

There are three important modes of dialogue. Each one affects the way in which the audience perceives the play. In some plays dialogue is structured to imitate ordinary human speech as accurately as possible. In other plays it is much more artificial and only seems to sound like talking. Some plays are written in a dialogue mode which, when compared to ordinary conversation, is frankly fake. The choice of a dialogue mode is up to the playwright but it is strongly influenced by the historical period in which the play was written, the type of play it is, and its subject matter or theme.

1. Naturalistic Dialogue

In Paddy Chayefski's *Marty,* the dialogue closely imitates ordinary conversation. The words the characters speak seem to be exactly what you would expect to hear in reality. The mother says: "My son, Frank, he was married when he was nineteen years old. Watsa matter with you?"

Such dialogue is characterized by very careful selection of specific details, rhythms, pronunciations, particular grammatical structures. The visual worlds for plays such as *Marty,* often called naturalistic plays, are also careful selections of specifics, artfully combined to evoke a sense of reality.

2. Literary Dialogue

Literary dialogue never reads like ordinary conversation but, when it is spoken by actors, it becomes their mode of speech, fully accepted by the audience as such. George Bernard Shaw wrote masterful literary dialogue. The following example is from *Candida:*

MARCHBANKS
Misery! I am the happiest of men. I desire nothing now but her happiness. Oh, Morell, let us both give her up. Why should she have to choose between a wretched little nervous disease like me, and a pigheaded person like you? Let us go on a pilgrimage, you to the east and I to the west, in search of a worthy lover for her: some beautiful arch angel with purple wings—

MORELL
Some fiddlestick!

Playwrights who work in the literary dialogue mode create characters who are by nature verbal enough to speak in this somewhat heightened manner. It is the mode for plays of ideas and exploration. Within the literary mode the playwright is not expected to include all the conventional utterances that characterize real speech, the "uh-huhs," the "you knows," and so on. There is a freedom to allow the character to say exactly what is necessary in a highly articulate manner.

Designs for such plays are similarly freed from the demand for explicit naturalistic detail. Visual elements can be direct, suggestive rather than representational, the essence of reality rather than its imitation. *The Glass Menagerie* is a play exquisitely written in the literary dialogue mode. Look at the set design by Jo Mielziner for the original Broadway production of the play and examine the essential elements and the way they are melded into an environment for that play.

3. Poetic Dialogue

Dramatic poetry doesn't pretend to be common speech. Plays written in poetic dialogue tend to be particularly intense whether they are comic or serious. Everything the actors say is heightened by poetic devices: rhythm, rhyme, metaphor. Poetic dialogue is the richest ground in which the designer's imagination can work, cultivating visually evocative words and phrases and reaping powerful images.

JULIET
'Tis almost morning. I would have thee gone—
And yet no farther than a wanton's bird,
That lets it hop a little from his hand,
Like a poor prisoner in his twisted gyves
And wish a silken thread plucks it back again,
So loving-jealous of his liberty.

4. Sound and Grammar

Playwrights arrange sounds and manipulate grammatical structures in order to give dialogue more than simple sense meanings. Short words and uncomplicated constructions are typical of the dialogue spoken by forthright characters; sinuous sentences with a complexity of dependent clauses can reveal a sneaky nature. Short, clipped sentences and hard sounds are associated with sophisticated comedy, and romances may have dialogue with full, rounded sounds and many parallel constructions.

Most designers respond kinesthetically to sound. The feelings that are stimulated by hearing spoken words and rhythms engage the imagination in the production of visual images. Inspiration and information may come hand in hand from listening to the sounds and shapes of dialogue.

Notice, for example, that the Nurse and Juliet have a lot of direct, declarative speech in *Romeo and Juliet.*

NURSE
Will you speak well of him that killed your cousin?

JULIET
Shall I speak ill of him that is my husband?
Ah, poor my lord, what tongue shall smooth thy name
When I, thy three-hours wife, have mangled it?

In contrast, Claudius' dialogue in *Hamlet* has quite another sound and shape. Here are his opening lines in Act I, Scene ii.

FIGURE 1-12. Petie Seale as the Nurse and Valery Mahaffey as Juliet in the Milwaukee Repertory Theater's production of *Romeo and Juliet. Costume design by Susan Tsu. Photograph by Mark Avery.*

Though yet of Hamlet our dear brother's death
The memory be green and that it us befitted
To bear out hearts in grief, and our whole kingdom
To be contracted in one brow of woe,
Yet so far hath discretion fought with nature
That we with wisest sorrow think on him
Together with remembrance of ourselves.

Convoluted, dependent constructions continue for a total of twenty-four lines before Claudius can manage his first simple, declarative sentence on Line 24, "So much for him." Claudius is, of course, as slippery in action as he is in words.

Playwrights also manipulate grammar to protect information or to make points. Much dialogue is constructed in such a way that the important phrase, the actual point of the speech, is at the end. Human conversation seldom manages such precision, and information often gets lost. The playwright cannot afford to take chances; the dialogue is structured so audiences will be sure to hear the important parts.

These are George's lines in Act I of Albee's *Who's Afraid of Virginia Woolfe?*

I'm very mistrustful. Do you believe ... do you believe that people learn nothing from history. Not that there is nothing to learn, mind you, but that people learn nothing? I am in the History Department.

Not only does the important statement come at the end of the segment, but the "I am" is not contracted, adding emphasis to the sentence.

In some instances a designer may perceive the essence of a whole play through the shape of a few lines, not only through the information contained in them but also through their sound and shape. The following segments from a variety of plays may provide you with examples of the kinds of dialogue you might perceive as microcosms of the entire play.

THE CHALK GARDEN by Enid Bagnold
What I have been listening to in court is not my life. It is the shape and shadow of my life. With the accidents of truth taken out of it.

THE LADY'S NOT FOR BURNING by Christopher Frye
Poor father. In the end he walked in
Science like the densest night. And yet
He was greatly gifted.
When he was born he gave an algebraic
Cry; at one glance measured the cubic content
Of that ivory cone his mother's breast
And Multiplied his appetite by five.
So he matured by a progression, gained
Experience by correlation, expanded
Into a marriage by contraction, and by
Certain physical dynamics
Formulated me. And on he went
Still deeper into the calculating twilight
Under the twinkling of five-pointed figures
Till Truth became for him the sum of sums
And Death the long division.

HEY YOU LIGHT MAN by Oliver Hailey
Hey, Mayonnaise! Well, would you look at that. Roy Roca never let me keep mayonnaise. Never. He got sick on it once in 1947—a brand I got on sale for a dime a quart—and he never allowed it in his house again. Me, I love mayonnaise. I've missed it something awful. Not a sandwich goes by I don't think of it.

MURDER IN THE CATHEDRAL by T.S. Eliot
...living, living and partly living.

5. Ambiguity

Expository prose should be, insofar as the language will permit, clear and straightforward. Writers of books such as this one choose words because the meanings of those words are as precise as possible. Verbs should describe exact action and nouns should name specific things. Dramatic dialogue is not the same at all. Plays say many things at the same time, as you have seen. The simple conveying of information is but one aim of dialogue; other facets of meaning are equally important. Playwrights often choose words precisely because those words do not have

FIGURE 1-13. John Kani and Winston Ntshona as Vladimir and Estragon, with Bill Flynn as Pozzo, in Samuel Beckett's *Waiting for Godot*. Produced by the Baxter Theater, Cape Town and presented by the Long Wharf Theater. *Designer, Donald Howarth. Photograph by Gerry Goodstein.*

explicit meanings but are evocative of many meanings, in other words, *because* they are ambiguous. Characters are also allowed to make contradictory statements about themselves, others, and events in the play. They may be constantly guilty of saying one thing and doing another, as the following excerpt from Samuel Beckett's *Waiting For Godot* illustrates:

VLADIMIR
Well? Shall we go?

ESTRAGON
Yes, let's go.
(They do not move. Curtain.)

Meaning in plays is not simple. Listen to the following segment, also taken from *Waiting for Godot:*

ESTRAGON
So long as one knows.

VLADIMIR
One can bide one's time.

ESTRAGON
One knows what to expect.

VLADIMIR
No further need to worry.

ESTRAGON
Simply wait.

VLADIMIR
We're used to it.

Everything in the preceding passage is intentionally obscure. There is a suggestion of present tense meaning which has to do with the actual

28

dilemma faced by the characters, yet every word seems to mean more than it says. Each line may be perceived on several different levels.

Not all dramatic dialogue is this ambiguous but you must expect most dramatic characters to speak more than simple sense. Usually, what is underneath the simple sense will speak to designers in ways that stimulate visual images. In Gogo and Didi's (Estragon and Vladimir) exchange it is the underlying tone of resignation and futility that allows you to *see* the characters in their world.

Many designers in the theatre are serious music lovers whose work is profoundly affected by all the qualities of sound. Those who design for the opera, the musical theatre, and dance use music as the wellspring of their work. There are musical components in all plays which, when perceived, can inspire design work on many types of plays. Practice listening to plays until you can hear the underlying rhythms, the contrasting tones, the different keys in which different scenes are played. Listen to plays read aloud and try reading them yourself. When you can hear *how* a play speaks as well as *what* it speaks about, you are a step closer to creating its environment.

VIII. What Is the Play's Action?

Now you know enough to begin to examine the play as a whole structure, which is another way of saying that now you can discover the play's central action. Francis Hodge defines action as the "life force of the play." Action is not plot, it is the reason for plot. Action is what causes audiences to laugh and to cry.

A play's central action can usually be expressed in a few words related to the attitude changes in the leading characters. The central action of *The Matchmaker* is Dolly Levi's pursuit and capture of Horace Vandergelder. In *Romeo and Juliet* it is the two young lovers' attempt to realize their love even though their families are bitter enemies. In *The Miracle Worker*, Annie Sullivan teaches the blind, deaf, and mute child, Helen, to communicate with the outside world.

Each central action is composed of many subsidiary actions and reactions. The continuous process of action and reaction advances the play. The end comes when an equilibrium is reached, when the energy for producing reaction is momentarily still, when whatever the central action proposed to do is done, successfully or unsuccessfully.

Whenever you speak about a play's dramatic action, be sure to choose strong, active verbs that state rather than explain the action. Amanda Wingfield *imposes* her will on Laura; Regan and Goneril *betray* Lear, Didi and Gogo *wait* for Godot; Macbeth *murders* the king.

1. Create an Action Chart

This is a good time to turn all your analysis into a tangible expression, a character/scene action chart that will provide you with both practical planning facts and a means by which you can discover the play's rhythmic structure.

Lay out the action chart on a sheet of paper wide enough to allow each scene in the play approximately an inch and a half of space across the top of the page. Draw vertical lines to create a column for each scene. (Using graph paper for the chart will save time.) List each character in the play, usually in order of appearance, down the left side of the paper, and divide this list with horizontal lines. These lines will intersect the columns and form a block in each scene column for each character. (See Figure 1–14.) Following each character, from left to right on the chart, place a mark in every scene block in which that character appears. Self-adhesive, colored spot labels are specially neat and handy for marking. The position of the mark within the block can indicate the portion of the scene in which the character enters. Some designers will add a brief description of each character beside the name: the Squire, a Franciscan brother, Arkadina's son, etc. Write in the actors' names when you know them.

In the blocks designating scenes, note the location, the time of day and date, or passage of time from the preceding scene, if that is pertinent. Some plays will respond better to charting if you divide them into French scenes (a French scene begins at each major entrance or exit of a character or characters) rather than conventional act and scene breaks. In this instance use script page numbers rather than act and scene numbers.

The action chart's main analytical function is to reveal to you at a glance the individual and group movements of characters through the play. Many times these movements occur in patterns—repetitive, parallel, alternating—that identify each play's unique rhythmic structure. Similar patterns may be perceived in scene locations—an alternation between Venice and Belmont, a progression from country to city or from public place to private place—times of day, and seasons of the year. The purpose of the action chart is to organize facts you have already found into facts with a design.

FIGURE 1-14. An action chart for G.B. Shaw's *Arms and the Man*.

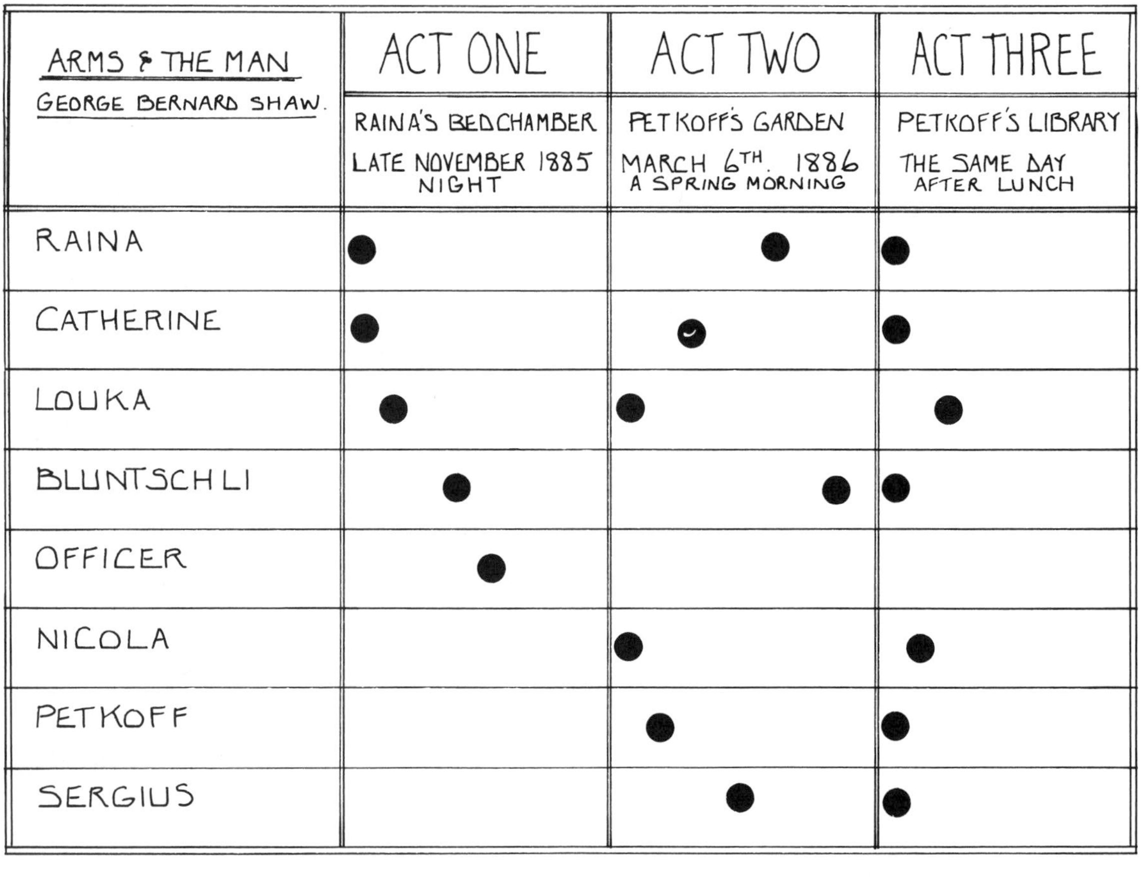

ARMS & THE MAN GEORGE BERNARD SHAW.	ACT ONE RAINA'S BEDCHAMBER LATE NOVEMBER 1885 NIGHT	ACT TWO PETKOFF'S GARDEN MARCH 6TH. 1886 A SPRING MORNING	ACT THREE PETKOFF'S LIBRARY THE SAME DAY AFTER LUNCH
RAINA	●	●	●
CATHERINE	●	●	●
LOUKA	●	●	●
BLUNTSCHLI	●	●	●
OFFICER	●		
NICOLA		●	●
PETKOFF		●	●
SERGIUS		●	●

IX. What Is the Play's Theme?

People always want to know what the theme of the play is and this is probably the most difficult of all things to discover. Few, if any, playwrights begin writing with a theme in mind. They have characters, an incident or two, and usually an idea of what central action they wish to create. But theme isn't usually present in the early stages. A play's theme emerges in the course of the writing and is fully developed only when the work is done. "How do I know what I'm thinking about until I write it?" is actually true for many writers. When the theme does emerge, particularly in a very good play, it becomes the unifying principle of the work, inseparable from every action and every word, an integral wholeness.

Designers perceive theme in a manner much like the playwright discovers it and never until all the action has unfolded and resolution has occurred. Theme results from accumulation of fact, from accretion, and from absorption. The theme of *Romeo and Juliet* , you may say, is the power of love to break down walls of hate. But you will only know this when the play has come to an end.

Theme may or may not inform design. It's difficult to make a play's theme visual since it is largely conceptual, having to do with ideas and intellectual responses. Nevertheless, you will feel that your work is more complete if you complete your analysis with a concise statement of the play's theme.

Conclusion

Analyzing playscripts using the methods described in this chapter can help designers make the leap from what is written by the playwright to its visualization on the stage.

Although it has taken a number of pages, and many words, to discuss these processes, much of the analytical work can be done in a very short time. If you have two weeks for script work prior to your first design conference, you can use it to good advantage. On the other hand, you can accomplish quite a bit in two hours if that's all the time available to you. The quality of your own concentration, which produces visual response and feeling, is what ultimately counts.

The quiet time that a designer spends with a script can be one of the most aesthetically productive parts of the design process. Cherish that time, use it sensitively, and you will be more than ready to move into the more lively world of production.

2
The Production

It is useful to consider designing for the theatre as an accumulation of discoveries which begins when the designer reads the play and ends when the complete production is revealed to the audience—oftentimes the most remarkable discovery of all! Chapter 1 dealt with discovering the play through reading and seeing and with the ways in which visual images can support and sustain the playwright's words without reiterating them, ignoring them, or overwhelming them. These first discoveries are private encounters between the designer and the script.

Chapter 2 moves the designer away from the purely personal encounter into the early phase of practical production. Other people begin to be involved, other ideas, other points of view. This is a particularly exciting phase of the process, but the designer must take care not to lose the private discoveries which were made in the initial script work to the swarm of practical realities that rise up in early design and production conferences.

Prepare to Meet with the Director

The costume designer's first design conference will often be a private meeting with the director. There are many occasions, however, when a producer will be included, and other times when the set designer and possibly the lighting designer will be present.

It is customary for directors in today's theatre to plan a production in more or less the following order:

1. Choose a script to do;
2. Begin thinking about the setting and engage a set designer;
3. Cast at least the key roles;
4. Bring in a costume designer;
5. Bring in a lighting designer.

Even when the costume and set designers begin work at the same time, the director will usually have more specific set ideas than clothing ideas in the early stages of discussion. The costume designer coming into the production discussions after the set design has begun to take shape, must take care not to suppress his or her personal responses to the script, even if they differ from the interpretation being explored. Few productions are designed from first ideas alone, and no theatre designer can afford to be passive. The creative collaboration carries with it the responsibility of sharing.

Therefore, the serious costume designer will appear at the first design conference prepared and willing to discuss the play. Useful aids for this first meeting are a list of specific questions and notes for discussion, an action chart and, perhaps, a rough costume plot. The designer who is eager to collaborate will bring neither conclusions, solutions, formulated statements about the true meaning of the play being discussed, nor costume sketches to this meeting.

No matter how well you know the play, it is difficult to keep all the movements of thirty characters in eighteen scenes in your head while you are discussing it with the director. Figure 2-1 is an action chart for *Twelfth Night* which organizes those eighteen scenes and the thirty-odd characters in a neat, orderly way. It is easy to read and will keep you from having to thumb endlessly through your script to find out exactly who is in Act I, Scene IV. The chart shows you which characters appear in which scenes and what overall movement each character has through the play. You can see at a glance which costumes will play together, a great help when you come to working out color. It also helps you anticipate difficult costume changes and avoid impossible ones.

FIGURE 2-1. An action chart for Shakespeare's *Twelfth Night*.

TWELFTH NIGHT	ACT ONE 1 ORSINO'S PALACE	2 SEACOAST OF ILLYRIA	3 OLIVIA'S HOUSE	4 ORSINO'S PALACE	5 WITHIN OLIVIA'S HOUSE	ACT TWO 1 LODGING ON SEACOAST	2 STREET NR. OLIVIA'S HOUSE	3 WITHIN OLIVIA'S HOUSE	4 WITHIN ORSINO'S PALACE	5 OLIVIA'S GARDEN	INTERMISSION	ACT THREE 1 BEFORE OLIVIA'S HOUSE	2 WITHIN OLIVIA'S HOUSE	3 A STREET IN ILLYRIA	4 OLIVIA'S GARDEN	ACT FOUR 1 BEFORE OLIVIA'S HOUSE	2 WITHIN OLIVIA'S HOUSE	3 OLIVIA'S HOUSE	5 1 BEFORE OLIVIA'S HOUSE
ORSINO – DUKE OF ILLYRIA	●			●					●										●
SEBASTIAN – BROTHER TO VIOLA						●								●		●		●	●
ANTONIO – A SEA CAPTN. FRIEND TO SEBASTIAN						●								●	●				●
A SEA CAPTAIN – FRIEND TO VIOLA		●																	
VALENTINE – ⎤ GENTLEMEN ATTENDING	●			●															
CURIO – ⎦ ON THE DUKE	●			●					●										●
SIR TOBY BELCH – UNCLE TO OLIVIA			●		●			●		●		●	●			●	●		●
SIR ANDREW AGUECHEEK			●					●		●		●	●			●			●
MALVOLIO – STEWARD TO OLIVIA					●		●	●		●					●		●		●
FABIAN – ⎤ SERVANTS										●			●		●	●			●
FESTE – A CLOWN ⎦ TO OLIVIA					●			●	●			●				●	●		●
OLIVIA – A COUNTESS					●							●			●	●		●	●
VIOLA – SISTER OF SEBASTIAN		●		●	●		●		●			●			●				●
MARIA – OLIVIA'S WOMAN			●		●			●		●		●	●		●		●		●
LORDS	●			●					●										●
A PRIEST																		●	●
SAILORS		●																●	
OFFICERS															●				●
MUSICIANS	●																		
SERVANT															●				
ATTENDANTS																			●

Perhaps you found the action chart a valuable part of script analysis. Now, as you discuss practical and aesthetic design necessities with the director, it will become an invaluable visual and organizational aid.

The Rough Costume Plot

Some designers make a rough costume plot part of the initial script work while others save this task for later when more specific information is available. The rough plot is a list, drawn from the designer's reading, of exactly what each character might be likely to wear in each scene of the play. The garments aren't described, merely listed: trousers, shirt, belt, socks, shoes, overcoat, and so on. The rough plot, like the character/scene breakdown, can help to give the designer a sense of the play's visual shape and scope. It can become, as the discoveries accumulate and the work on the production moves ahead, the official finished plot for the shop and for the wardrobe staff, noting and describing each piece of clothing worn by each character in the play.

The following costume plots, one rough and one finished, are for Noel Coward's *Private Lives*.

Rough Costume Plot
"Private Lives"

SIBYL		VICTOR	
ACT I	ACT I	ACT I	ACT I
(a)	(b)	(a)	(b)
wig	evening dress	shirt	shirt
dress	purse	tie	collar
slip	gloves	3 pc. suit or separates	tie
garter belt or girdle	shoes	suspenders	vest
stockings	jewelry	cufflinks	dinner jacket
shoes		shoes	trousers
jewelry		socks	suspenders
rings		handkerchief	cufflinks
			collar studs
ACT II	ACT III		shirt studs
hat	*same as Act* II		shoes
suit and blouse *or*	minus hat, gloves, etc.		socks
dress and jacket or coat			
purse		ACT II	ACT III
gloves		hat	*same as Act* II
shoes		shirt	
jewelry		tie	
		suit	
		suspenders	
		cufflinks	
		shoes	
		socks	
		handkerchief	

SIBYL

ACT I
(a)
wig—blonde
dress—dusty pink
    printed rayon crepe
    w/ecru collar & cuffs
slip—tea rose rayon
    crepe
girdle
    long-legged panty
    girdle
stockings—w/seams
shoes—pale beige
    leather w/strap
earrings—pearl
wedding ring
engagement ring

ACT II
hat—beige and navy
    straw
blouse—beige silk w/
    navy polka dots
skirt and jacket—navy
    crepe
purse—beige leather
    clutch
gloves—beige leather
earrings/slip/shoes from
    Act 1 (a)

ACT I
(b)
evening dress—tur-
    quoise printed
    chiffon
evening purse—pearl
    beaded
gloves—cream fabric,
    over the elbow
shoes—cream lizard
    skin sandals
earrings—pearl drop
necklace—3 rows pearls
bracelet—pearl strands

ACT III
same as Act II
minus jacket, hat,
    gloves etc.
jacket added during act.

VICTOR

ACT I
(a)
shirt—beige w/white
    stripes and french
    cuffs
tie—brown silk polka
    dot bow tie
vest—cream w/brown
    windowpane checks
trousers—cream linen
jacket—beige gabardine
    w/back belt
suspenders
cufflinks—gold
shoes—tan brogues
socks—beige
handkerchief—off-white
    cotton

ACT II
hat—light grey fedora
shirt—light grey striped
    w/french cuffs
tie—blue/grey/red silk
    paisley 4-in-hand
suit—blue/grey double
    breasted
suspenders—grey
arm garters
cufflinks—silver
shoes—black lace-up
socks—black from Act
    1 (b)
handkerchief—off-white
    cotton

ACT I
(b)
shirt—boil front even-
    ing shirt
collar—wing
tie—black bow
vest—black brocade
dinner jacket—black
evening trousers—black
suspenders—white
cufflinks—gold
collar studs
shirt studs
shoes—black patent
socks—black

ACT III
same as Act II

The First Design Conference

Working with Different Directors

It is important to note here that each director, like each designer, has a personal and unique way of working. One may present the designer with a total production scheme, complete with color preferences and accessory choices, at the first meeting. Another won't have a clue how the show might look. Designers favor the director who has strong but general feelings about how the play should be approached and what effect it will ultimately have on an audience, but who encourages the designer to share in the process of creating the total production. Some directors will express their feelings about the play in words; others will allude to the work of a specific artist or to a single painting to convey their response to the play; still others will refer the designer to a piece or type of music.

Whatever the director's manner of approaching and arriving at a production scheme, it is the designer's job to respond to and be inspired and guided by what is conveyed during the first, and subsequent, meetings. It is the director's responsibility to achieve and maintain production coherence, and it is up to the costume designer not only to help plan the production but also to make sure that each garment worn in the play contributes to this coherence.

In the early planning stage it is imperative that the designer understand what the director is saying, seeing, and feeling. If the designer thinks that a painting the director has chosen to convey his or her response to the play is antithetical to the play's spirit, then it is up to the designer to do more than feel confused or decide that the director has no visual sense. Designers are trained to look at paintings in certain ways whereas untrained people will look and respond quite differently. In this situation it is not important to judge the director's taste in art but to discover what the director's response really means in relation to the play. The designer must urge the director to keep on talking until the two reach some degree of understanding. It is not always easy to communicate on visual matters and the designer must use a great deal of tact and persistence to draw the necessary information from certain directors.

Period and Style

From the costume designer's point of view, the most important matters to be considered during the first design conference are those of period and style. Some plays dictate a specific period, while others are less specific and a period and style of production must be considered and decided upon.

FIGURE 2-2. An unusual period choice for Shakespeare's *Taming of the Shrew:* Italy just after WWII. Rose Pickering as Kate, Henry Strozier as Baptista, and Maggie Thatcher as Bianca. Produced by the Milwaukee Repertory Theater. *Costume design by Susan Tsu. Photograph by Mark Avery.*

If the period seems obvious, as in, for example, *Becket* or *A Man For All Seasons*, it can be useful for the designer to take a few clear illustrations of clothing from that period (preferably reproductions of paintings or drawings of the time) to the meeting. Directors vary enormously in their knowledge of period clothing and more than a few appreciate being shown pictures of the particular period garments under discussion. The designer should also be prepared to answer basic questions regarding manners and customs from that era or ways in which the actual garments were worn.

Many of Shakespeare's plays, particularly the comedies, can be placed quite successfully in a wide variety of periods. When a designer is discussing the choice of period with the director, it is important for the designer to find out what overall impression of the play the director wishes the audience to perceive. A formal and restrained *Much Ado About Nothing* might be well supported by choosing late 16th century lines and silhouettes while a romantic approach to the same play could be enhanced by clothing from the 1820's.

The visual style of the production will be related to period choice, but it will also reflect the play's point of view and the director's interpretation. These will, in turn, effect the way in which the designer looks at period research. For example, even though both plays may be set in the 1930's, the visual styles of Noel Coward's *Present Laughter* and Clifford Odet's *Golden Boy* will be very different.

FIGURE 2-3. Tom Hewitt as King Lear and Jeffrey Bihr as the Fool in Tadashi Suzuki's *The Tale of Lear,* a unique version of Shakespeare's *King Lear.* Produced jointly by Arena Stage, Berkeley Repertory Theatre, Milwaukee Repertory Theater, and StageWest. *Costume design by Tadashi Suzuki. Photographed by Joan Marcus.*

FIGURE 2-4.

FIGURE 2-5. John P. Connolly as the Secretary and Larry Shue as Chichikov.

FIGURES 2-4, 2-5, 2-6, and 2-7. Sketches and photographs from a production of *Dead Souls* with frankly theatrical costumes and make-up. Directed by John Dillon at the Milwaukee Repertory Theater. *Costume design by Carol Oditz. Photographs of sketches by Frances Aronson. Production photographs by Mark Avery.*

FIGURE 2-6.

FIGURE 2-7. Peggy Cowles as Sofya Ivanovna.

FIGURE 2-8. Ralph Cosham as Benjamin and Stanley Anderson as Corden in *The Piggy Bank* at Arena Stage. *Costume design by Martin Pakledinaz. Photograph by Joan Marcus.*

FIGURE 2-9. The "Family Portrait" in Christopher Durang's *The Marriage of Bette and Boo* at Arena Stage. *Costume design by Gregg Barnes. Photograph by Joan Marcus.*

Character and Script

At some point in the first design conference the discussion will turn from the overall production approach toward specific script and character considerations. The designer will have a list of questions organized in an economical way. Many of the questions will fall into the following seven categories:

1. Will characters be eliminated or added? Will actors be cast in more than a single role?

In large-cast plays, small roles are often eliminated, or two small roles amalgamated into one, in order to limit the size of the cast. Such decisions may decrease the number of costumes needed. On the other hand, certain plays, par-

ticularly history plays with battles and musicals, require crowds, or choruses, which may vary greatly in numbers. At the first meeting ask for specific numbers but always remember that crowds have a way of growing in rehearsal, particularly in those productions where extra crowd members do not require extra salaries. In such situations be on the lookout for burgeoning crowds. It is important to have in hand, as soon as possible, an accurate list of characters, both speaking and nonspeaking roles.

Character doubling is the use of a single actor to play more than one role. Doubling must be carefully worked into the production design in order to facilitate the necessary clothing changes, sometimes allowing specific garments to be used for more than one character, sometimes providing a wig or face hair to effect a change. The action chart will come in handy for checking the feasibility of doubling.

2. Will the script be cut? Will any changes be made in place or time of day?

Look at all script cuts. A cut that may enhance a scene's dramatic movement may also render a planned costume change impossible. The designer's script should include all text cuts and these should be reflected on the character/scene breakdown chart.

Location and time of day changes may effect the appropriateness of the dress in those scenes and may even add additional outfits to the production.

3. Discuss each reference in the script to specific garments, accessories, and colors.

Ask whether or not the director wishes to adhere to such references. Sometimes the specific garment or accessory will be changed because of the period choice, whereas sometimes the director simply has another preference. Quite often a line referring to a dress color may be dropped or altered because that color doesn't happen to suit the actor playing the role. In such cases the costume will be done in another more becoming color.

4. Does the director plan on using props or accessories not called for in the script?

Canes, parasols, eyeglasses, fans, etc., are often used to help the actor create his or her character. Such accessories should be included in the costume design and, many times, a rehearsal version will be required.

5. Will the actors be called upon to engage in any unusual physical activity that will effect the costumes?

This is particularly important when restricting period garments are required. Most costumes can be rigged for extraordinary movement but only if the rigging has been worked into the design and construction plans. Choice of fabric may also depend on physical activity. If, for instance, Romeo is to actually climb a rough stone wall on his way to Juliet's balcony, his doublet should probably not be built from a loosely woven, slubbed silk! Ask about sitting, rolling, or crawling on the floor in order to minimize and plan ahead for unusual cleaning.

6. Discuss each character in turn.

It is essential from the first discussion onward that the costume designer knows exactly how the director sees each character in the play. Ask the director to describe physical appearance and to assign general character traits to each. Osric, for instance, may be seen as tall and thin with long curls and a pointed goatee; he is, perhaps, a dandy, full of self-importance but rather stupid. The tall thin appearance and the dandiness can be well supported by the costume design. Polonius, on the other hand, might be perceived as portly, full-bearded, and expensively but conservatively dressed; he is secure in his position in the court, a doting father and a gossip. In this case the actor might require padding underneath his costume and a beard; his position in the court may be suggested by using rich fabrics, employing elegant lines and adding a gold chain of office.

Discuss each character in this manner. Mention age, social status, and occupation. Be as specific as possible about face hair, wigs, and padding since these will directly affect the designs. Note the possibility of any stage business requiring hidden pockets, undressing, or the use of unusual accessories.

7. Who is cast?

If the production has been cast when the first design conference takes place, much of the dis-

FIGURE 2-10. Gilbert Price as Mark Antony in the Milwaukee Repertory Theater production of *Julius Caesar. Costume design by Susan Tsu. Photograph by Mark Avery.*

cussion outlined above will be in terms of specific actors. If it has not been cast, ask the director to describe the sort of actors he or she has in mind for the roles. Whenever possible, it is both interesting and helpful for the designer to attend casting auditions, particularly call-backs. Often the designer can see what the director wants each character to be by the type of actor being auditioned.

When the actors are already cast, the costume designer should make plans with the director to see and measure them before designing the production. If the actors are unavailable and will not appear until rehearsals begin, ask for a photograph, a description, and a few measurements and sizes. Know in advance that the leading lady has a very large bust and is short-waisted and avoid designing a strapless evening dress with a high waist. When the measurement blank reveals that an actor is five feet tall and weighs two hundred pounds, the designer can choose something other than horizontal stripes for his costume.

The costume designer's work is a great deal easier when casting is completed before the designs are due. Unfortunately, this is not always possible, and often the designer has to put pencil to paper long before the actors are chosen. In this situation, the work will be based primarily on character and on the director's description of both character and type of actor desired. Inevitably, once the casting is complete, certain changes will have to be made in the designs in order to accommodate the actors. Expect and plan for such changes.

Although one might assume at this point that the first design conference could easily last for twenty-four hours, the discussion will probably be brisk and much of the pertinent information quickly shared. Some questions will have to be reserved for later meetings, although it is very important for the designer to have as many answers as possible before settling down at the drawing board. The success of the initial design meeting will depend largely on how much script preparation both the director and the designer have done and how specific the designer can be with questions.

Production Realities

Budgeting Time and Money

Next to an exciting and viable production scheme, the two most important pieces of information the costume designer must discover before approaching the drawing table are the budget allocation for materials and the costs and conditions of labor. Sometimes it is possible to get these production details from the director but often this information must come from the producer, the business manager, technical director, or costume shop manager. The costume designer must find out who to see in each situation and, once again, be prepared with specific queries.

Labor and Material Costs

It is virtually impossible to design a set of costumes outside the classroom without knowing what the budget is. Budgets will vary greatly, depending upon the affluence of the producing organization. While there is no doubt that handsome costumes can be designed and built on quite limited budgets, this can only happen if the limitation is known and accounted for in the early design process.

Always consider the total amount of the materials budget in terms of the actual number of costumes required for the production. A one-thousand dollar materials budget has one kind of reality if the production calls for fifteen costumes and quite another if there are to be fifty.

If, after some serious apportioning, the costume designer finds that the rock bottom production demands exceed the budget allotted to costumes, it is up to the designer to point this out immediately. Make up a cost estimate and bring it in for the producer and the director to examine. Never put a set of costumes into the shop if there is insufficient money to construct it.

If more money cannot be found, the designs may have to be greatly simplified or, in extreme circumstances, the production postponed or cancelled.

Costs and conditions of labor vary from one situation to another. If the costumes are to be built in a commercial shop, the designer will present the shop with finished designs and receive an estimated price for their construction. If this amount is more than the budget allotment for labor, the designer may either simplify the designs or go to another shop. Initial bids will often be sought from two or three shops in order to get the best price. It may take some time before the budget and the actual cost are in line and an agreement can be made between the designer and the shop. The arrangement will be for a specific number of garments as designed; any additions or elaborate changes will cost more.

In regional theatres, stock companies, and colleges and universities, costumes will more than likely be constructed in a resident shop staffed by the producing organization. The technicians in these shops will be responsible for building costumes for all the plays produced by the group. In these situations the designer must know the number and experience level of the technicians who will construct the costumes and the length of time that has been scheduled for building.

A wise designer will be sensitive to the skill and experience levels of the people working in the costume shop and will not design costumes far beyond their ability to construct them. This should not be looked on as an onerous restriction for the designer but as one of the many practical considerations that make up the design process. Besides, with the designer's support, even the most inexperienced costume technician enjoys a challenging problem or an experiment with a new process when time permits.

Time and Facilities

Along with assessing the skill of the techni-cians, the designer must be aware of the total building time and try not to design a set of costumes that cannot be finished by opening night. College and university costume shop crews work a limited number of hours and these work periods must fit into the overall class and study schedule. The shop staff members in most re-gional and stock theatres are paid a weekly salary for a forty to a forty-eight hour work week, usually with no provision for overtime compen-sation even though overtime work is the rule rather than the exception. The technicians may receive a few days off at the end of the produc-tion period but this, in most cases, does not adequately make up for the many hours of overtime they have devoted to finishing the costumes.

Far too many designers, particularly those who work in many different theatres on a free-lance basis, help to exploit the dedication and the good nature of costume technicians by not trying to protect them from excessive overwork in the initial design process. Careful design and thoughtful planning can play a large part in regulating the work load. There is no reason why a designer should not consider the well-being of the technicians along with budget and aesthetics.

If the designs will require more compli-cated execution than the designer feels the re-sident shop can handle, or take more time than has been allocated, it is up to the designer to talk with the producer or business manager and request additional personnel. Such requests, made in the early stages of production, can usually be accommodated. Pre-planning is always preferable to last minute scrambling.

A designer working with a resident shop should also know what equipment is available in that shop. If, for instance, there are no fabric dyeing facilities, the designer will either have to shop color carefully or allow for professional dyeing in the materials budget. The presence or absence of millinery equipment, tailor's dumm-ies, a serger, or tools for making jewelry will all effect the design process. In a shop where but-tonholes are regularly sent out to be done at a hefty cost, the designer will think twice before asking for practical buttons down the fronts of all the doublets!

Resident shops differ in the ways in which they charge stock supplies to individual shows. Some have separate general supply budgets out of which to purchase thread, tailor's chalk, tracing paper, bones, etc., and such items are not charged directly to the production materials budget. In other shops the materials budget for each pro-duction may be charged for each yard of muslin used in draping and every spool of thread pur-chased for a particular show. Before starting to work, the designer must know exactly what the materials budget is intended to cover.

The resident shop will usually have a cos-tume stock from which the designer may pull at will. The designer should go through the stock in person if at all possible or, if this is not possible, ask a shop staff member to look for specific items from the designer's list. The materials budget will go much farther if basic items such as men's shirts, tights, or petticoats can be pulled rather than purchased or built. There may also be major garments from the appropriate period that can be used with alteration and/or retrimming. However, for the most successful show, the rest of the costumes should be designed with the pulled items in mind. It is not always the best idea to try and fit pulled garments into a set of costumes that is already designed. The availability of stock items should be a very early consideration.

A cooperative relationship between the de-signer and the shop staff will help create a pleasant work period. Whether the designer is working with a particular shop for the first or the fiftieth time, a careful review of production realities will get the work off to a good start.

Talks with the Other Designers

If the set and lighting designers are not present at the initial design conference between the costume designer and the director, a separate meeting with them should be set up before the design process is too far along. In order for the production to have coherence, it is necessary for all the designers to share a similar understanding of the production scheme. Although the costume designer and the lighting designer should discuss the approach to the show and color ideas as soon as possible, the actual lighting design will not be completed until after the set and costumes are designed.

The conversation between the costume designer and the set designer, however, should cover several specific areas, particularly if the set design is already underway.

1. *Color.* All set colors affect costume fabric choices. As soon as the set designer has made any color decisions, the costume designer should have paint chips, swatches of upholstery fabric, and/or wallpaper samples.

2. *Basic Construction.* The costume designer should always know if there is to be a raked

FIGURE 2-11. Set and costumes that are obviously the result of a fruitful collaboration between designers. Chekov's *The Cherry Orchard,* produced by Arena Stage. Zelda Rubinstein as Charlotta Ivanovna and John Leonard as Yepikhodov. *Costume design by Miruna Boruzescu. Set design by Radu Boruzescu. Photograph by Joan Marcus.*

stage and, if so, the degree of the rake. A significant rake can present a difficulty for actors in floor-length garments which, although they may look too short when the actor is coming downstage, may trip the actor moving upstage. The costume designer should also know the height and width of stair treads and the height and width of doorways. High, narrow stair treads may interfere with the actor wearing a long, tight skirt or extremely high heels. Doors must be high enough to accommodate wigs and headpieces and wide enough for panniers and hoops if the production demands them.

3. *Stage Floor Surface.* Many costume budgets have been exceeded because, at the last minute, it was necessary to have dance rubber put on the bottoms of all the actors' shoes so they would not slip and fall. Costume designers should always find out

in advance what the stage floor surface will be like and make plans in accordance with that information.

4. *Furniture.* If the costumes will include wide skirts, make sure the furniture is wide enough to accommodate them and that there is sufficient walking room from one side of the stage to the other. If the furniture is to have a rough textured surface, this may effect fabric choice.

All the designers involved in a production should stay in close touch with one another's work. After the costume sketches are completed and approved by the director, the costume designer should make a set of photocopies with swatches attached for the lighting and set designer. If everyone who is working on the show continues to talk with everyone else, problems will be solved before they have a chance to become too big to handle.

The Production Book

Just before settling in to draw, many designers find it useful to set up a production book which will become the gathering place for all the information pertinent to that partiular show. Such a book, well tended, will be an invaluable aid to a busy designer, handy to grab for meetings and for shopping trips. An inexpensive loose-leaf binder will provide an excellent cover for the production book, and filler pages with reinforced holes will minimize the chances of losing sheets. The production book may be just the place for reading and research notes and, if the complexity of the script demands it, a synopsis of scenes.

More specific contents of a production book might be:

1. *Calendar.* Draw a calendar on graph paper

that covers the entire production period. Note production meetings, photo calls, and dress rehearsals, and add in other dates, such as fittings, as they are scheduled.

2. *Addresses and Telephone Numbers.* The stage manager will often compile a list of addresses and telephone numbers of all the people involved in the production which can be placed in the book. Otherwise, the designer should make such a list including cast members, director, producer, other designers and costume shop personnel.

3. *Tax Exemption Number* (if there is one). In some states tax exempt forms must also be presented. The production book is a good place to keep a supply of these forms.

FIGURE 2-12. A designer's calendar.

	S	M	T	W	T	F	S
JANUARY	3 — COST. SHOP OFF TODAY	4 — PROD. MEETING FOR "YOU NEVER CAN TELL"	5	6 — SKETCHES DUE "ARMS & THE MAN"	7	8	9
	10	11 — SHOP STARTS "ARMS & MAN"	12	13	14 — SHOW ROUGH SKETCHES "Y N C T" TODAY	15	16
	17 — COST. SHOP OFF TODAY	18	19 — 1ST REH. "ARMS & MAN" TAKE M/MENTS	20 — REST OF M/MENTS & 1ST FITTINGS "ARMS"	21 — 1ST FITTINGS "ARMS" (MUSLINS)	22 — ALL "ARMS" FABRIC DUE ★PROD. MTNG.	23
	24 — COST. SHOP OFF TODAY	25 — ALL TRIM FOR "ARMS" DUE TODAY	26	27 — 2ND FITTINGS "ARMS"	28 — 2ND FITTINGS "ARMS"	29 — PRODUCTION MEETING "ARMS"	30
FEBRUARY	31 — COST. SHOP OFF TODAY	1 — ACTORS OFF TODAY; SKETCHES DUE "YOU NEVER CAN TELL"	2 — FINAL FITTING "ARMS"	3 — FINAL FITTINGS "ARMS"	4	5 — ★PHOTO CALL "ARMS" 5:00; PRODUCTION MEETING "ARMS"	6 — DRESS PARADE "ARMS" 12:00
	7 — 1ST TECH "ARMS" (NO COSTUMES)	8 — ACTORS OFF TODAY; SHOP STARTS "YOU NEVER CAN TELL"	9 — 1ST DRESS "ARMS" 12:00 1/2 HR.	10 — 2ND DRESS "ARMS" 12:00 1/2 HR.	11 — 3RD DRESS 1ST PREVIEW 7:30 1/2 HR.	12 — 2ND PREVIEW 7:30 1/2 HR.	13 — "ARMS & THE MAN" OPENS

4. *Materials Budget Breakdown*. A necessary shopping aid!
5. *Cast List*.
6. *Action Chart*.
7. *Costume Plot*.
8. *Wig and Beard List*.
9. *Hat List*.
10. *Rental Lists*. These can be particularly valuable if, as is often the case, garments are rented from several sources. Rentals should be listed in great detail to insure their safe return at the lowest possible rental fee.
11. *Measurement Chart*. This chart is invaluable for shopping. (See Figure 2-13.) It contains all the basic measurements, drawn from the shop's measurement forms, needed for ordinary shopping. In a busy store, it is much easier to consult a single chart in the production book than it is to thumb through a great pile of measurement forms which will, inevitably, end up scattered on the floor.

Costume production book contents will vary from designer to designer. The order in which they are laid out is an entirely personal matter, although it might be wise to consider putting the measurement chart all the way in the back of the book, facing the back cover, for particularly quick reference.

FIGURE 2-13. A measurement chart for shopping.

ACTOR'S NAME	HEIGHT	WEIGHT	BUST/CHEST	WAIST	HIPS 7" 9"DOWN	BRA/INSEAM	OUTSEAM S.WAIST TO FLOOR	PIERCED EARS?	L or R HANDED	ALLERGIES	HOSE/PANTS	GLOVE	BLOUSE/SHIRT	DRESS/SUIT	HAT/HEAD C.	SHOE

Conclusion

Young and inexperienced costume designers may well view the preceding discussion with horror. All this planning does not sound like much fun compared with the excitement of actually sketching costumes. Be assured that the well-informed, well-organized costume designer will, in the long run, enjoy much more freedom to concentrate on the designs and on realizing them than the chaotic designer who, by refusing to do adequate preparation, allows a multitude of practical problems to interfere with the heart of the process. Besides, many of these initial planning steps quickly become second nature and take no time at all to accomplish. And, many of them are fun as well.

3
Costume Research

The first phase of costume research begins as soon as you have read through the script—and sometimes even during the first reading—as you start to imagine the characters in action and to dress them in historical garments pulled from your own memory. If the play is a fanciful one, you will make up appropriate costumes for nymphs or ghosts, fairies or woodchucks, sorting through all the scattered facts and bits of nonsense you have seen and read and filed away for future use.

In the second phase you set out systematically to discover new facts to add to those you already possess. A short but pertinent definition of research describes the process well: "a careful search; a close searching." The emphasis in this chapter is on historical searching but you must keep in mind that costume research also means searching for any and all sorts of design ideas. Don't be surprised if you find yourself looking through pictures of flowers, fish, animals, or insects, or examining fantasy or primitive art. Costume research can take you almost anywhere.

History is Important

The costume designer is irrevocably linked to the past as well as the present, and influenced as much by history as by the events of the contemporary scene.
Motley
*Designing and Making
Stage Costumes*

Ideally every costume designer ought to know social, cultural and political history, art history, and the basic period clothing silhouettes from Mesopotamia to your own home town. You should be able, for example, to give the dates of Queen Elizabeth I's reign in England, to remember a few facts about her character as monarch, and to *see* her silhouette. You should also know which came first, the French Revolution or the American Revolution and how one differed from the other in ideology, action, and dress, and you

FIGURE 3-1. Pencil and gouache sketch of chorus costumes for *Pacifica. Design by Ann Wallace. Photograph by Frances Aronson.*

should be able to name painters whose imaginations were captured by each struggle for freedom.

Such a background, acquired during your years in school and through independent study, is part of the basic preparation you bring to every design project you undertake (along with taste, design sense, drawing and painting skills, and the techniques of clothing construction). This knowledge makes it possible for you to research each play you design in specifics rather than in generalities. If your knowledge of history is sound, your work will have an authority that it cannot achieve otherwise.

What the Audience Sees

A performer's silhouette is the starting premise of any presentation.

BERNARD BECKERMAN
Dynamics of Drama

The first thing an audience sees when an actor is revealed or comes on stage is the outline of the figure against its background. The shape of that outline creates a strong impression of character. It also conveys historical period and social and economic status at a glance. Success with this first impression depends on the designer's ability to create an evocative silhouette in clear, crisp lines, derived from accurate sources and chosen because it conveys the appropriate information about period and character to the audience.

Except on rare occasions, costume designers in the theatre are not in the business of reproducing historical costumes in detail on the stage. Theatrical costumes create an *impression* of period. The designer who sees a period accurately knows which elements of the silhouette and which details are most evocative of that period to a contemporary audience's eyes and, therefore, which need to be emphasized in the costumes. Whenever the audience perceives a correct impression through character silhouette in the opening moments of a production, that play is off to a good start.

FIGURE 3-3.
"A performer's silhouette is the starting premise of any presentation." Laurinda Barrett as Mrs. Prest in the McCarter Theatre's production of *The Aspern Papers. Costume design by Andrew B. Marlay. Photograph by Cliff Moore.*

FIGURE 3-2. Andrew B. Marlay's costume design for Margaret Lord from *Philadelphia Story.* Pencil, watercolor, and acrylics on canvas paper; background is marker spray. *Photograph by Frances Aronson.*

Seeing Accurately

It is not an easy matter to reach the point where you can look at historical garments in paintings, tapestries, sculpture, and drawings and really see them. There is a terrible potential lurking in everyone to look at an Elizabethan dress and, by making subtle and unconscious visual adjustments to what you are seeing, perceive it in proportions that are closer to your own contemporary silhouette. You may also find yourself looking at a piece of research with a preconceived idea of what is there, which prevents you from seeing what is really there. Even designers with excellent research eyes and a good deal of experience suffer lapses in seeing that interfere with their ability to convey a period successfully.

To avoid these lapses, it is necessary for a designer who is doing costume research to look, look, and look again. And, while you are looking, recall all the facts you have about the garment: cut and construction, understructure, type of fabric, method of closing, why and under what circumstances worn. Try to perceive the garment in three dimensions and be sure you know what is hidden from view: the back, where the collar starts, how the belt stays in place, where each sleeve hangs from. Feel the garment's weight and shape and the physical limitations it imposes on the body.

Once you are able to perceive the garment in this degree of detail, it ceases to be merely a flat representation on a page. It acquires depth, volume, and a potential for movement. It becomes three-dimensional in your mind's eye, accurately proportioned and correctly trimmed.

Throughout their lives costume designers continue to sharpen their abilities to see and experience research. They never stop looking at paintings, sculpture, drawings, and photographs. Whenever they have the opportunity, they study actual historical garments, examining seams and

the way they hang, methods of stitching and finishing details.

Many of you will become collectors of research materials. You will haunt second hand shops, estate sales, vintage clothing stores, flea markets, and rummage sales for antique clothing, accessories, old magazines, old patterns, illustrations, fashion plates, movie stills, and many other items of primary research interest.

FIGURE 3-4. Laura Crow's costume design for Hypatia in the Academy Festival production of G.B. Shaw's *Misalliance. Photographed by Susan Ashdown.*

Seeing by Comparison

When you are involved in a careful search for clothing facts, it's easier to see the costumes of one period accurately if you compare them with costumes of other periods. All clothing evolves from or reacts to that which preceded it, and the best way to view the changing fashion silhouette parade is through its movement from shape to shape. The tails on men's formal coats *were longer* in 1870 *than* they were in 1845. In 1947 fashionable womens' skirts dropped suddenly in length and were, in some cases, *a foot or more longer than* they had been the year before. Comparison is also helpful when you are sorting out geographical clothing differences: An ante-bellum Southern girl usually wore *wider* hoops *than* her contemporary in Boston.

FIGURE 3-5. An afternoon dress from the early 1850's.

Here is a general description of a simple afternoon dress from the early 1850's (see Figure 3-5), using comparison to evoke a sense of the garment.

The bodice of the dress is very tight and must be worn over a corset which flattens the bosom rather than pushing the bosom up under the chin. The waistline is at the natural waist in the back and on the sides but it dips below the waist in front and into a rounded point over the abdomen. The wearer's shoulders appear to be much more sloping than women's shoulders are today because the shoulder portion of the bodice is extended beyond the natural shoulder and onto the upper arm. The armhole is much lower and smaller than anything we are used to seeing in contemporary tailoring. The neckline is at the base of the neck and the bodice fastens down the center back
with small buttons, close together. Because of restriction caused by the low, tight armholes and the placement of the closing at center back, there is no way the wearer of this dress could dress herself.

The sleeves have rows of horizontal ruching and flounces at the wrists. The skirt is in three tiers, each edged with wide lace. The skirt is supported by a small hoop, not as extreme as those that became fashionable late in the decade.

Even though this is an example of a simple dress of the period, it is still much more elaborately decorated than today's dresses; the cutting and construction are more intricate and the undergarments are certainly more complicated. Any woman would feel differently about herself and about her world in the 1850's dress than she would in her modern Anne Klein wraparound.

Reading Well

A sharp eye, trained to look at clothes that have been represented by artists throughout history, is the most important research tool any costume designer can have. Only slightly less important is the ability to read quickly, accurately, and with good retention. You should be able to scan a printed page and pick out important and interesting facts and translate a written description into a mental image.

Effective reading, just like effective seeing, takes practice. It is well worth your effort to strengthen your reading skills through individual study or by taking a short course in reading effectiveness. Designers who read slowly and laboriously will find it difficult to get into the excitement of research and they may well end up with sketchy, incomplete work.

A Research Outline

No matter how extensive your design experience or how much you know about costume history, each and every new production demands a certain amount of research. Even if you are designing costumes for a play you've done before, a different production will demand its own look. If

the play is new to you, particularly if it is set in a period with which you are unfamiliar, you may find yourself with a sheaf of problems to solve and questions to answer before you can sit down to draw.

These questions begin to emerge as you study the script, and they grow in number (and often in complexity) during meetings with the director. Before you consult resource materials,

assemble all your notes into a research guide or outline which will help you organize your search and direct your efforts.

Figure 3-6 is a set of notes with which to begin the research for a production of William Gibson's *The Miracle Worker*.

It is at this point that most of you will take pad and pencil in hand and head for the library.

FIGURE 3-6. Research notes for William Gibson's *The Miracle Worker*.

THE MIRACLE WORKER -- RESEARCH GUIDE

- SET IN THE 1880's
- COUNTRY HOME - TUSCUMBIA, ALABAMA
- PERKINS INSTITUTE FOR THE BLIND, BOSTON

  - THE KELLERS ARE GENTLEFOLK; THE HOME IS GRACIOUS & COMFORTABLE
  - NEED GENERAL SILHOUETTES & DETAILS FOR:

    1. RURAL SOUTHERN GENTRY - KELLERS
    2. RURAL SOUTHERN BLACKS - VINEY & CHILDREN
    3. RURAL SOUTHERN DOCTOR
    4. URBAN NORTHERN DOCTOR (EYE SPECIALIST)
    5. URBAN NORTHERN WOMAN, VERY POOR, ANNIE
    6. BLIND CHILDREN IN CHARITY INSTITUTION IN THE NORTH

- WHAT DOES THE SOUTHERN DOCTOR'S STETHOSCOPE LOOK LIKE?
- WHAT SORT OF FACE HAIR FOR CAPT. KELLER?
- FIND PHOTOGRAPHS OF BLACK FARM CHILDREN
- OLDER SILHOUETTE FOR AUNT EV?
- PAY ATTENTION TO CONTRAST BETWEEN CLOTHES WORN BY ANNIE & BY KATE. WHAT ARE THE SIMILARITIES IN PERIOD AND THE DIFFERENCES BETWEEN WELL-TO-DO WIFE & STRUGGLING TEACHER?
- VINEY'S DRESS? IS IT A UNIFORM?
- UNDERDRAWERS FOR ANNIE.
- LITTLE GIRL'S CLOTHES - HOMEMADE PROBABLY - FOR ANNIE

Libraries

No matter how many costume books a designer owns, a trip to the library is an integral part of almost every costume design process. Designers who have only a few costume books of their own depend almost entirely on libraries for research materials. Whether you use libraries a little or a lot, you should know what you can expect to find there and how to find it in the quickest and most efficient manner possible.

Public Libraries

Nearly all towns and cities in the United States have public libraries. You may expect to find the standard costume history works almost everywhere, although in many places books such as Davenport's *The Book of Costume* and Corson's *Fashions in Hair* will be kept in the reserve book section and not allowed to circulate. Most small public libraries have only the basic and most widely known costume books, plus a few randomly chosen volumes purchased over the years by librarians who might or might not have had any interest at all in costume study. On the other hand, big city library systems, like the New York Public Library and the Enoch Pratt Free Library in Baltimore, maintain comprehensive collections of books on clothing history, construction, fashion, and costume design.

All the resources in a public library are available to people who are taxpayers in that city or town. In addition, there is almost always some provision for people who live in adjacent towns or communities to have full library privileges upon payment of a moderate fee. If you are a visitor, you can always use public library materials on the library premises, although you cannot check them out.

College and University Libraries

Very often the best place to do costume research work is in a college or university library attached to an institution that teaches the theatre arts, especially one that emphasizes theatre design. These libraries always seem to have the widest range of books on their shelves, from standard surveys such as Lucy Barton's *Costumes for the Theatre* to quite specialized volumes like *The Quaker: A Study in Costume* by Amelia Mott Gummere and *Men's Costume 1750-1800* by Zillah Halls. And they usually purchase new books in the field as they appear on the publishers' lists. Sometimes costume books are conveniently housed in a fine arts library building and occasionally there is even a separate theatre library.

College and university libraries are primarily intended for that institution's students and faculty. Most, however, do allow circulation privileges to professional people who are living or visiting in the area and engaged in specific research projects. All you usually have to do to receive these privileges is present yourself to the proper library administration person with identification and an explanation of your work. Sometimes a fee is requested, sometimes not.

Research Libraries

A research library usually has a collection of materials limited to a single field or area of study. The collection, because of its specialization, may be much more extensive than any single subject area you can find in a comprehensive library.

Museums operate research libraries that are particularly good places for costume research work. There is a wealth of clothing information in the research library at the Smithsonian Institution in Washington, D.C., for example. Research libraries are associated with most state and local historical museums and at historical sites, such as Colonial Williamsburg, Old Salem Village in Winston-Salem, North Carolina, and Sturbridge Village in Massachusetts.

Access to research libraries is often limited, and the rules governing access vary from place to place. Always phone ahead to find out exactly what the rules are. Research library materials almost never circulate and, if they are heavily used, you may need to make an appointment well in advance of your visit. On those occasions when you need special research materials, a trip to a research library can be well worth the extra planning.

Books and What Else?

In order to take full advantage of your local library, you need to know exactly what materials and services it offers. Large public and university libraries house books, serials (including magazines and newspapers), documents, manuscripts, pamphlets, pictures, clippings, films, and maps. Small libraries have books and a selection of the other things. All libraries can provide you with a brochure listing what they have and what they can do.

Library materials are classified by author, title, and subject, either in the main card catalogue or in individual guides to specific areas. Multiple classifications allow for a great deal of flexibility in what information you must know in order to find what you need.

A special service of many big city libraries is the ready reference division, a group of specially trained librarians who can give you certain kinds of information by phone. Who wrote *The Moon is Blue*? What year did Henry VIII officially create the Church of England? What is the correct mailing address and telephone number for Western Costume Company in Hollywood, California?

The Library Catalogue

Libraries maintain catalogues of their collections to help patrons identify and locate the materials they want before venturing into the stacks. Most libraries now store catalogue information, once kept on card files, on computer database programs. You can access all available information through individual computer terminals that are usually located near the library entrance. Instructions for using the program both on the screen and in printed form will be nearby. If you are extremely timid about touching a computer keypad, a librarian will be glad to help you get started.

Computerized library catalogues are organized by the same classification systems used in file card catalogues. The two most popular, and familiar, are the Dewey Decimal System, generally used by small public libraries, and the Library of Congress System, found in most college and university libraries. Research libraries may use the Library of Congress System or a private system of their own.

Classification systems allow librarians to group books of like subject matter together and to assign each one a specific place within the system which determines where it will be shelved.

Each book has its own set of call numbers that are also called identification numbers. Call numbers are composed of two symbols. The top symbol is the *class mark*, which identifies the specific classification group into which the book's subject matter places it. Below the class mark is the *author mark*, which usually includes the author's initial and indicates where the book belongs within its classification group.

Here is an example of a Library of Congress System set of call numbers, with each portion explained:

A Handbook of Costume
    by Janet Arnold
    GT
    510
    .A75
class mark: GT
    510

    GT—the portion of the class mark that is the standard classification for all books in this subject area within the Library of Congress System.

    510—refers to the general shelf area where this book is placed in this library.

author mark: .A75

    A—Ms. Arnold's initial

    75—indicates the exact place where this book is placed within its subject classification section in this library.

You can look up library materials using a title, author, or subject. The author entry for each book is its main entry and contains the most complete information. The author's name is arranged alphabetically with the last name first: Arnold, Janet. The title entry is filed alphabetically using the first word of the title but disregarding A, An, or The. If the book covers several subjects, a subject entry will exist for each, filed alphabetically: for example, Costume—Roman, 1st C. A.D. and Roman—Costume, 1st C. A.D. Most computerized library catalogues give you general information first and specific information next. For example, when you enter *A/Arnold, Janet,* you will receive a list of all the books by Janet Arnold in that library. From that list, you can choose *A Handbook of Costume.* What comes up on the computer screen is very much like what used to be printed on individual file cards (arranged in the classification system used by the library): the call number that tells you where to find the book in the library, the edition, publisher, publication date, number of pages, number of illustrations, Library of Congress subject headings, acquisition date, etc. You may also receive information that could not have been put on a file card, for example, whether or not the book is currently available for circulation.

Much costume research begins with a subject search. Before you begin a subject search in a library that uses the Library of Congress classification system, look in *Library of Congress Subject Headings,* a reference work in several volumes that lists the precise names and correct spellings of all the subject headings under which library materials are classified. Books relevant to costume research may lurk under many headings: Costume—History; Fashion—History; Theatre—Costumes; Russia—Army—Uniforms; History—Cultural—18th Century, etc. With the help of *Subject Headings,* make a list of everything that seems relevant to your search.

A subject search in the library catalogue computer will lead you to books on the subjects you select. Most computerized library catalogues also allow you to do a key word search, which can lead you to a part of a book or a chapter that contains pertinent information, even though the book itself is on a different or broader subject. A key word search might lead you to a section on the gowns of Queen Elizabeth I in a historical biography of that fashion conscious monarch.

Open and Closed Stacks

After you have consulted the library catalogue and found the call numbers for the books you want, the job of finding them on the shelves may be up to a library employee.

If the library has *open stacks,* you proceed into the shelving area to do your own looking. Most libraries have location charts to help guide you to the proper section. Shelf units are clearly marked and, of course, each book has its call number clearly visible. Open stack libraries are a great boon to costume designers because you can browse through everything in that section and sometimes find useful and interesting books you overlooked in the library catalogue.

In a *closed stack* library, however, you must give the call numbers for the books you want to a library employee whose job it is to get them for you from the shelves. This system is fine if you know exactly what you want but it does not offer you the opportunity to browse, except, of course, through the catalogue. Because some closed stack libraries do allow serious researchers into their stacks under certain, specified conditions, you should always find out if your work makes you eligible for a stack pass.

If you must wait while books are being found and brought to you, remember that it usually takes ten or fifteen minutes for them to make the trip. Bring along a sketchpad or something to read so the waiting won't grow tedious.

Finding Books Not in the Library

Sometimes you can't find what you need in your library. Don't despair. Libraries also have excellent resources for finding out about books they don't have on their shelves. Once you know the author, title, and publisher of the book that will answer your questions, you may be able to buy it, borrow it from a friend or colleague, or even from another library. The volumes that help you locate books on specific subjects are kept in the reference section and the following standard resources are available almost everywhere:

1. *Book Review Digest* began publication in 1905. Monthly. An index to reviews of current fiction and nonfiction books published in the U.S. To be included, a nonfiction book must have had two or more reviews in a selected list of journals.

2. *Publisher's Weekly* is a listing of books as they are published in the U.S.

3. *Books in Print* appears in three versions: *Authors, Titles, Subjects*. All books in print in the U.S. are listed. (*Books in Print* for England and Canada are also usually available.)

The following reference works can be particularly helpful for looking up older books and ones no longer in print.

4. *The Cumulative Book Index*—books published in the English language from 1957 until the present.

5. *The United States Catalogue*—books published in the U.S., including many published in England and imported by American and Canadian firms—from 1898-1928.

6. *Cumulations of the Cumulative Book Index* (issued as supplements to the United States Catalogue)—books published in the U.S. from 1928-1956.

7. *American Catalogue of Books*—books published between 1876-1910, mostly American, many English.

8. For books published before 1875, look at the assorted book catalogues listed in the preface of *The United States Catalogue.*

Interlibrary Loan

If you cannot buy the book you need or borrow it from a colleague, you may want to embark on an interlibrary loan. Be warned at the outset that interlibrary loan is not a swift process; it may be anywhere from ten days to a month before you hold the book in your hands. However, if you know well in advance that you are going to need a specific work, the interlibrary loan network might be the answer. For example, as you begin to design the costumes for a production of Jack

Heifner's *Vanities,* you might find it very helpful to get a copy of the 1968 Southern Methodist University Annual through interlibrary loan and see what those co-eds really wore.

Interlibrary loans are facilitated if you can give your own librarian as much information as possible about the book you need. Be sure you have a complete citation: title, edition, author, publisher, and date of publication. You will save even more time if you already know which library has the book; you may be able to find out this information by calling your state library (usually located in the state capitol) catalogue or the catalogue at the central headquarters of the state university library system. If, however, the book is quite rare and not listed in either of these central catalogues, you will have to rely on your librarian's special skills to find the book for you, and the wait will be longer.

FIGURE 3-7. Eda Zahl, Shellie Chancellor, and Elaine Hausman as the three Texas cheerleaders from Jack Heifner's *Vanities* at the Milwaukee Repertory Theater. *Costume design by Ellen Kozak. Photograph courtesy of the Milwaukee Repertory Theater.*

Here are some things you should know about interlibrary loans:

1. Loans are made from one library to another and *not* to an individual. Therefore you must be eligible to use the library through which you make the request. Most college and university libraries will only undertake interlibrary loans for their own faculty members and graduate students.

2. Sometimes the library loaning the book will stipulate that the book not leave the library to which it is being loaned, in which case you will have to do your work in the library.

3. Lending is restricted to items not easily procurable elsewhere, is limited to one or two items, and excludes rare books or potentially perishable materials.

4. The period of the loan is usually ten days to two weeks, and the borrowing individual (not the borrowing library!) is liable for all shipping charges to and from.

A more recent alternative to interlibrary loan is photocopying. After you have located the book you need at a distant library, you can often have that library photocopy the portions necessary for your work. Most libraries offer photocopying services, and the cost may well be less than the shipping charges you would incur in interlibrary loan. Your own reference librarian can make photocopying arrangements for you.

Periodicals

Periodicals are particularly valuable resources for costume designers because so many are devoted to fashion, lifestyle, and the daily activities of ordinary people. Within this century, *Look* and *Life,* with their predominantly picture format, are endlessly useful. Other periodicals that designers turn to again and again are: *Vogue, Town and Country, The Tatler, Punch, Harper's Bazaar,* and *The National Geographic.*

The points of view expressed in periodicals are contemporary, more up-to-date, and less contemplative than those in books. They are of particular interest to costume designers whose search is for the peculiar essence of a period rather than for a generalization. A photograph in a 1942 issue of *Life* shows you precisely what one group of women wore to work in a defense plant. Such a picture can be far more informative to your work than a general description of such clothing in a costume history book.

In most libraries, current issues of periodicals are shelved in the reading room while back issues, and magazines no longer publishing, are bound and kept in the stacks. Because they are not easy to replace, periodicals almost never circulate.

The names of the periodicals a library has may be listed in the main library catalogue but a listing of the individual articles which appear in them cannot be found there. There are a number of periodical indexes, each listing the articles in a certain group of magazines. Here are some of the guides that might be of specific interest to you:

1. *Art Index*—Quarterly with annual and biennial cumulations. Began in 1930; indexes over 100 magazines and museum publications in English and foreign languages including *American Fabrics and Fashions, Design Quarterly, Journal of the Warburg and Cortauld Institutes* and *The Textile Museum Quarterly.*
2. *Readers' Guide to Periodical Literature*—monthly. Began in 1900; indexes a wide selection of popular periodicals from *Life* and *Time* to *Opera.*
3. *19th Century Readers' Guide to Periodical Literature*—fifty-one periodicals indexed from 1890-1899.
4. *Humanities Index*—quarterly. From 1974 to present. (From 1907-1974 included in *Social Sciences & Humanities Index.*) Indexes English language periodicals that specialize in: archaeology, classical studies, folklore, history, language and literature, literary and political criticism, performing arts, philosophy, religion and theology.

All periodical guides are cross-indexed under author, title, and subject; the author citation is the most informative listing.

Many libraries have computerized periodical search programs that can lead you to a wide variety of sources. Most of these programs are comprehensive guides that are not limited to the periodicals in any one library.

Newspapers, Clippings, Pictures, and Videotapes

There are some occasions when you will want to go to old newspapers to do a bit of research. Maybe you need some information about a playwright who was written up in the *New York Times* a few years ago or want to read the reviews of earlier productions of the play you're designing. Perhaps you're working on a play based on historical events within the past century and are anxious to read first hand, contemporary accounts. Fortunately, many libraries can make old newspapers available to you.

Because newspapers are bulky and printed on highly perishable paper, libraries usually store them on microfilm. When you want to read a specific issue of a newspaper, you have to request the appropriate microfilm strip and read it on the screen of a microfilm machine. Thanks to microfilm, thousands of newsprint pages can be preserved and stored in the same space formerly required by only a few hundred dried and crackling bundles of newsprint.

The only really comprehensive newspaper index is the *New York Times Index,* begun in 1851 and published semi-monthly. The *Times* index is arranged in dictionary form with many cross-references to names and related topics. Events under each main heading are listed chronologically. Reviews are conveniently listed under "Theatre Reviews."

Some libraries maintain clipping and picture files with the materials sorted and stored in envelopes or folders according to subject. Needless to say, this service can be invaluable to costume designers. The Picture Collection of the New York Public Library System on Fifth Avenue is undoubtedly one of the best. You can find pictures and prints on subjects as diverse as Welsh coal miners, debutante parties in the 1950's, and French Army uniforms in the Second World War, and, if you are a New York City resident, you can check out a number of pictures from a subject file and study them in the comfort of your own work room.

Libraries also house and provide access to pictures that move, usually in videotape form. The New York Public Library at Lincoln Center has, in addition to books and archival materials, a collection of performing arts videotapes, audiotapes, and recordings. Most libraries across the country offer taped and recorded materials to patrons; sometimes you can check them out and sometimes you must look and listen in the library.

The amount and variety of visual information available on videotape is increasing, and video viewing is an especially pleasant approach to costume research. Old movies, filmed plays, television series such as "The Six Wives of Henry VIII," travelogues, and documentaries are all available on videotape, often at your local video rental shop.

Museums

It is sad indeed that visits to museums play such a small role in actual, day-to-day costume research. The schedules under which costume designers normally work make it impossible for them to find the time to travel all the way across town, or into the city, to examine a few paintings, a piece or two of sculpture, or some original garments. It's much easier, and certainly quicker, to study pictures of these items in books and to rely on the expertise of art and clothing historians who have prepared the explanatory texts.

Yet there is no comparison between the impact of a medieval tapestry hanging on the wall of the Metropolitan Museum in New York and even the finest photograph of it. One is alive with color and texture, rich in detail; the other is flat, usually shiny and by nature diagrammatic. No doubt the photograph will give you enough information to design an accurate period costume, but a look at the real thing may inspire you to add subtle touches that will enrich your design immeasurably.

And, of course, there is no way you can really understand how a late nineteenth-century corset manipulates and shapes the body until you have examined one with your own eyes and hands. Even Norah Waugh's excellent *Corsets and Crinolines* cannot give you all the details you can discover in hands-on study.

Learn to make the time to visit museums a necessary part of your working life, sometimes to research a specific costume piece (corsets, armor plate, beadwork, uniforms), and sometimes for the simple enrichment of your own sensibilities. Go to art museums and to museums of natural history and don't ignore small town historical museums and specialized collections maintained by industries and fraternal organizations.

Where to Look

Before you set off on holiday travel, take a look at *The Official Museum Directory* in your library's reference room. This wonderful book lists museums in the United States by states and by cities, gives you addresses, phone numbers, hours, admission charges, and descriptions of what you will find on display. If, for example, your camping trip takes you through the small town of Shelby, Montana, the *Directory* can tell you about the Marias Museum of History and Art which has displays of frontier women's clothing, cowboy dress, old sewing machines, and barber shop equipment.

Look also at Irene Pennington Huenefeld's *International Directory of Historical Clothing*. This helpful book can supply you with the information that The Charlestown Museum in Charleston, South Carolina has a collection of old jockey jackets, that the Museum of History and Industry in Seattle has a display of nurses uniforms from many periods, and that the Nutley Historical Society Museum in Nutley, New Jersey has Red Cross uniforms.

Should your vacation take you to England, be sure to read Chapter 7 in Janet Arnold's *A Handbook of Costume* which describes eighty-nine costume collections in England, Scotland, and Wales. Along with the displays you can expect to find, you will also learn how to make arrangements to see stored items and go equipped with addresses and telephone numbers.

The effect of seeing the real thing is long-lasting. Once you have experienced many original works of art, examined antique dresses and jackets and a variety of accessories, and seen with your own eyes just how big a medieval broadsword really is, the book illustrations you normally turn to for research will have much more life and meaning.

Record and Document Research Information

Every designer ends up with some unique and personal method of recording and organizing sketches and notes. Whatever way you devise, you should develop a storage system that allows you to find the information in the future.

You may choose to record your work on cards. Cards can be conveniently filed, both for current and for future use, in commercially produced filing boxes (plastic, metal, or heavy cardboard), or in child-size shoe boxes. Or you may put your notes and sketches in looseleaf notebooks or in individual folders and store them in shelves or in filing cabinets. Whatever your system is, it is worth the time it takes to organize and label your research.

Include Sources

It is particularly important that you write down your sources. There is nothing more frustrating than knowing that a book you once consulted for general information on military uniforms contained a detailed description of the way helmet cords were supposed to be worn by generals in the United States Army in 1874 but, because you did not make a note or jot down a citation, you cannot find the information again.

And, as long as you are training yourself to make bibliographic citations, get in the habit of jotting down the facts in an accepted format. This way you will be sure to have all the information you need and you will also have the makings of a valuable costume bibliography that you may someday want to share with others in your profession. Here are some examples:

Bernstein, Aline. *Masterpieces of Women's Costume of the 18th and 19th Centuries*. New York: Crown Publishers, 1959.

Boehn, Max von. *Modes & Manners*. 4 vols in 2. Translated by Joan Joshua. 1932. Reprint. New York: Benjamin Blom, 1971.

Gullbert, Elsa & Paul Astrom. *The Thread of Ariadne: A Study of Ancient Greek Dress*. Studies in Mediterranean Archaeology. Goteborg, 1970.

Garren, Lois Zierk. *A Study in the Process of Aging Theatrical Costumes*. Master's Thesis. University of Virginia, 1978.

Learn to take good notes and, unless you have total recall of research facts, don't rely on your memory. Trace or make quick drawings (paying careful attention to proportion!) of clothing illustrations or, if you prefer, photocopy the appropriate pages. When you trace or draw, make sure to jot down any written facts that are there to help identify and explain the illustration. Make sure to include correct citations and page numbers.

General Historical Background

Your analysis of the script you are designing will give you most of the historical facts you need: dates, locations, climate, political leadership, major political events. An interesting book that can help you to see all these facts in connection with each other is *The Timetables of History: A Horizontal Linkage of People & Events* by Bernard Grun (New York: Simon and Schuster, 1979). In what amounts to a huge, book-length chart, this work presents the concurrent history of man in seven columns:

1. History and Politics
2. Literature and Theatre
3. Religion, Philosophy, and Learning
4. Visual Arts
5. Music
6. Science, Technology and Growth
7. Daily Life.

Locate the year of your play on the left hand side of the page and as you move across you will discover the kings, wars, writers, books, painters, paintings, composers, compositions, inventors, and others who simultaneously affected the course of history.

Before you can get to know your historical characters well enough to dress them, however, you will have to discover your own personal feeling for the time, its mood, rhythm, and peculiar style. You may be able to begin with encyclopedias and historical overviews but then you must turn to social history, popular history and biography, diaries, collections of letters, and even to novels. The following works contain portions that are of particular interest to costume designers. They have been chosen at random in order to give you an idea of the kinds of choices that exist:

Pepys, Samuel. *The Diary of Samuel Pepys*. Covers the years from 1660-1669.

Tuchman, Barbara S. *A Distant Mirror: The Calamitous 14th Century*. New York: Knopf, 1978.

Evelyn, John. *The Diary of John Evelyn*. 2 vols. Editor, William Bray. New York & London: M. Walter Dunne, 1901.

Purefoy, E. & H. *Purefoy Letters 1735-1753*. Letters written by Elizabeth and Henry Purefoy. 2 vols. Editor, G. Eland. London: Widgwick & Jackson, 1931.

Uzanne, Octave. *Fashion in Paris: The Various Phases of Feminine Taste and Aesthetics From the Revolution to the End of the XIXth Century*. Translator, Lady Mary Loyd. London: William Heinemann, 1901.

You can experience different views of life in Victorian England by reading such delightful novels as Jane Austen's *Emma* and *Northanger Abbey*, Elizabeth Gaskell's *North and South*, any number of works by Charles Dickens, and John Fowles' *The French Lieutenant's Woman*.

Primary Sources

For a close look at exactly what folks were wearing at a given time, examine primary resource materials first. Some of your primary source hunting will take you to museums and galleries. Most of the time, however, you will look at pictures of primary sources in books and in magazines. Never rely solely on costume history books in which a single illustrator has redrawn all the clothing. These books are excellent for silhouette recall and early impressions but they are not sufficient for specific production research.

What follows is an outline of basic primary sources for clothing, both to look at and to read.

Prehistoric Man
Cave paintings.

Figurines.

Surmise from study of archeological digs, tools, dwelling places, etc.

Surmise from the study of contemporary primitive societies.

Ancient Civilizations
Vase paintings.

Statuary.

Tomb artifacts.

Ancient texts: records and lists, law codes, letters.

Literature, mostly myths & legends, including the Bible.

Epics and drama, philosophy, and scientific writings after the fifth century, B.C., in the Greek world.

Wall paintings (very limited in number)

The Dark and Middle Ages in the West
Church statuary.

Religious paintings.

Manuscript illumination.

Tapestries.

Laws (especially sumptuary laws).

Heraldic emblems.

Literature.

Renaissance through Mid-Nineteenth Century
Paintings—the mediocre painter is often better for detail than the famous painter, perhaps because he has less imagination and tends more often to paint exactly what he sees, wrinkles and all.

Sculpture.

Drawings and etchings.

Dolls, after the late sixteenth century. Watch the proportions as they are not always accurate for people.

Extant clothing—Use with care. Extant garments are not usually the most typical garments of their age. Always ask why they still exist: Out of sentiment, because they were worn at a special occasion like a wedding or a funeral? Because they were never successful, didn't fit, or weren't becoming? Because they were too complicated to alter or remake? You can be sure that the favorite and most common garments from another age, worn daily, wore out ages ago.

Diaries.

Letters.

Fiction.

Travelogues.

Wills.

Household inventories.

After Mid-Nineteenth Century, Add
Photographs—not truly representative of ordinary dress until family box cameras become available and casual snapshots appear.

Fashion magazines.

In the Twentieth Century, Add
Newspaper and popular magazine photographs. Television and motion pictures.

Reliable Costume History Books

The more costume research you do, the more discrepancies you will discover. Sometimes it seems as though there are as many different ideas and interpretations as there are costume historians. Don't let yourself be confused or discouraged by conflicting names, dates, or details. Keep on looking and reading and eventually you will decide who to rely on and what to believe.

Here are a few costume history reference books which are considered particularly reliable. The list is certainly not inclusive.

Arnold, Janet. *A Handbook of Costume*. London: MacMillan, 1973.

Boucher, Francois. *20,000 Years of Fashion*. New York: H.N. Abrams, 1967.

Davenport, Milia. *The Book of Costume*. New York: Crown Publishers, 1948.

Cunnington, C. Willett, Phillis Cunnington & Charles Beard. *A Dictionary of English Costume*. London: Adam and Charles Black, 1960.

Waugh, Norah. *The Cut of Men's Clothes, 1600-1900*. New York: Theatre Arts Books, 1964.

Waugh, Norah. *The Cut of Women's Clothes, 1600-1930*. London: Faber & Faber, 1968.

Waugh, Norah. *Corsets & Crinolines*. New York: Theatre Arts Books, 1954.

Also, the *Handbook of English Costume* series by C. Willett and Phillis E. Cunnington with volumes for the sixteenth, seventeenth, eighteenth, nineteenth, and twentieth centuries.

FIGURE 3-8. Designs by Michael J. Cesario for Alley Theatre's production of *The Importance of Being Earnest* with inspiration from the work of Charles Dana Gibson. Figures are rendered with pencil, watercolor, ballpoint pen, and felt pen on charcoal paper and cut out and mounted on board. *Photograph by Frances Aronson.*

FIGURES 3-9 and 3-10. Two scenes from the Hartford Stage Company's production of Shakespeare's *Antony and Cleopatra,* inspired by the paintings of Tiepolo. *Set and costume design by John Conklin. Photographs courtesy of the Hartford Stage Company.*

Costume Research is Everywhere

Libraries and museums are not the only places you will go to research clothing for plays. Contemporary costume research may take you out into the streets to look for sources, to specific neighborhoods, parks, or shops. Costume designers have been known to spend an afternoon drinking hot chocolate in a ski lodge in order to see what people wear on and off the slopes or to visit a hospital to look at the latest nurses' uniforms.

Make it a habit always to see what the people around you are wearing whether you are at a family picnic or in the supermarket. Much of what you see in real life is far too bizarre and unbelievable for the stage but you will also collect wonderful ideas for future use.

Researching very specific costume pieces can lead you on merry chases. Religious vestments—and the correct ways of wearing them—are the subjects of many costume searches. If all the books you can find on the subject fail you—and they often will with ecclesiastical dress—call a church of the correct denomination, a theology school, or denominational headquarters to ask for help. You will usually get it.

Contact the Police Department for facts about police uniforms and the Fire Department for information about firemen's uniforms. Both agencies usually have photographs and descriptions of past as well as present uniforms. Occasionally you may even run into a fireman or a policeman who has an old uniform you can borrow.

Other places where you might be able to solve particular costume problems are foreign embassies, consulates, the headquarters of a fraternal organization, or a fox hunting club. For details about old military uniforms get in touch with the Society of Military Historians and Collectors and for current uniform regulations go to the appropriate military recruiting office.

The classified pages of your telephone book contain dozens of links between you and the answers to your most baffling research questions. Make full use of this resource.

The only things that can obstruct your ability to solve all your costume research problems are lapses in energy and imagination. If you cultivate persistance, strong legs for walking, a keen eye for seeing, and a stout finger for dialing, you'll come up with an answer every time.

Painters for Research

A list of painters whose work is particularly useful for costume research begins on page 215. It is not an exhaustive list, but one that can help get you off to a good start.

4
Preliminary Sketching
And Color Layout

By now you are well acquainted with the script. You have talked with the director and know how he feels about the play. You have settled on the exact historical period in which the play will be done. You have probably chatted with the scene designer and, if you are lucky, you have a cast list. You have a pile of research notes and a pad of research drawings. Now you are ready for the most exciting part of your work. It's time to go to the drawing board and sketch costumes.

Preliminary Sketching

Preliminary sketching, or idea sketching, serves the costume designer in two ways. First, the sketches will be your initial means of visual communication with the director. From them the director will be able to see what you want the costumes to look like. Second, but even more important to you, it is through the preliminary sketching process that most designers discover for themselves what the costumes are going to look like.

Only rarely do costume designers conjure up complete, detailed costumes in the mind and then represent them on paper. The mind is more apt to visualize fragments, bits and pieces, that illuminate character perceptions. Or it may create large inclusive images that reflect the play's mood or overall rhythm. You may have a notion that the sleeves should be long and flowing; you may see small pearl buttons down the center front; you may know that the skirt must trail on the ground. Then, when you have your pencil on the drawing paper, the individual images and notions come together into a design.

There is a great deal to discover about a script before you sit down to draw, but you should never put off sketching until you have designed everything in your head. That wait may well be in vain. The process of sketching *is* the process of designing. A sketch is not an illustration of a design, it *is* a design.

Drawing

Paintings are but research and experiment. I never do a painting as a work of art. All of them are searches. I search constantly.... .

PICASSO
to Alexander Liberman

Designers who draw easily and quickly and without any gnashing of teeth seem to those for whom drawing is laborious and slow to be particularly blessed. It is probably safe to say, however, that most costume designers, no matter how well they draw, would like to draw better than they do, not just to have their sketches look better but to facilitate the design process itself. Everyone becomes frustrated with a head full of exc iting ideas and images and hands that are not facile enough to combine and communicate them on paper.

This is not to suggest, however, that a costume sketch, either in its preliminary or its finished state, is the end product of the designer's work. (Whether or not the sketch is a work of art is absolutely beside the point.) A good costume sketch is a road map leading to the costume that will eventually be cut and stitched and worn by an actor on the stage. The costume will be judged to be successful or unsuccessful, not the sketch.

Yet, the road map is important, particularly if it suggests the quality of the landscape as well as describing the route to be taken. A satisfactory rough sketch usually indicates that the designer is well prepared both with facts and with evocative design images. Good preliminary sketching will, more often than not, lead the way to clear, direct final sketches and successful costumes.

The ability to draw with some modest degree of skill is essential for all costume designers. Fortunately, basic drawing skills are not gifts from the gods; almost everyone can learn to draw well enough to communicate visual ideas. Betty Edwards, in *Drawing on the Right Side of the Brain*, says:

...drawing is a skill that can be learned by every normal person with average eyesight and average eye-hand coordination—with sufficient ability, for example, to thread a needle or catch a baseball. Contrary to popular opinion, manual skill is not a primary factor in drawing. If your handwriting is readable, or if you can print legibly, you have ample dexterity to draw well.

Drawing People

Though the ability to draw people did not come easily to me, with constant and continual observation it did come.

PAUL HOGARTH
Drawing People

Everybody believes that drawing people is more difficult than drawing anything else, be it houses, horses, boats, books, cats, or canaries. Whether or not this belief is technically true is of no real importance since the conviction that it is true saddles most people, costume designers included, with a huge mental block when it comes to sketching human figures. Since virtually all clothing requires a body to hold it up and out and since costume designers must face the prospect of drawing bodies every time they pick up a pencil, this is one block that should be worked through as quickly as possible.

People who have successfully learned to draw know that the eye is more important to the process than the hand. What you see is what you draw. In the quote at the beginning of this section, Paul Hogarth attributes his success with drawing people to "continual observation" and not to continual drawing, although it is certain that he sketched what he observed. Training your eyes to see accurately, in correct relationships and proportions, is at the heart of learning to draw.

You can practice seeing on your own. Your brain is already alerted to keep your eyes on the lookout for interesting garments and combinations of garments as you wander the aisles of your supermarket. Decide to observe human figures as well. Look at bodies as groups of relative parts which relate to each other in fairly predictable ways. For instance, about half way down the length of most bodies, the single column divides into two legs. Most elbows, when the arms are hanging straight down, are near the waistline. The corner of the eye and the join of the ear to the head are about on a line with each other (which is what makes it possible for us to wear corrective curved lenses with a minimum of distortion). Shoulders are usually wider than hips.

When you are alone, ask yourself if you can close your eyes and see how long most arms are in relationship to upper legs, how much head most people have above and below the eyes, and what are the relative lengths of the five fingers. If you discover you cannot see these human proportion details in your mind's eye, go look at people or at yourself in the mirror.

Everyone who is actively involved in learning to draw the human figure should work to become acutely aware of his or her own body and its proportions. This is not the time to view one's own body critically—My hips are *too* big!—but analytically instead—Look how my hip joint moves both up and out when I shift my weight to that leg. Your goal is not to *define* your body, as you might do by memorizing the bones and muscles and the physiology of motion in an anatomy class, but to *see* it fully and completely, so fully and completely that you can reproduce what you have seen in a mental image and onto a sheet of drawing paper.

Some designers are so in tune with the shape and proportions of their own bodies that they tend to draw their own figures over and over again as models for their costumes. It is a good idea to guard against this propensity because altering garment proportions for individual actors is an important part of the costume design process. Get in the habit of *seeing* an actor's body

quickly and proportionately. Try to indicate outstanding differences from what we consider to be the norm (extremely long legs, short waist, no neck, narrow sloping shoulders) even in the earliest sketches. Eventually the costume will have to take all physical attributes into account, and it is well not to wait until you get to the fitting room to begin to tackle proportion problems. If time permits, some designers like to visit a few early rehearsals and make quick sketches of the actors as they work.

If your emphasis is on training the eye to see more completely, all drawing practice brings improvement. Most costume designers draw regularly in the day to day performance of their work. Many, in addition, draw on their own for pleasure, and others enjoy the stimulation of attending figure drawing classes. A surprising number of designers in New York take advantage of the modestly priced drawing classes at the Art Students' League.

The better you see bodies, the better you will see clothes and the more apt you will be to create costumes that fall or curve correctly and enhance the peculiar qualities of the human figure at rest or in motion.

Stock Figures

There are designers for whom drawing the human figure is so stressful that it robs them of the freedom to concentrate on costumes at all. These designers usually *see* the figure quite adequately and can use what they see to inform their designs, but they cannot rid themselves of the block that prevents them from drawing bodies with ease.

Designers who cannot face sketching a new figure under each costume often use stock figures which they may have drawn previously or copied from other sources. It's fairly easy to change the basic positions of stock figures and you can, to some degree, alter proportions to reflect individ-

FIGURE 4-1. Female figures.

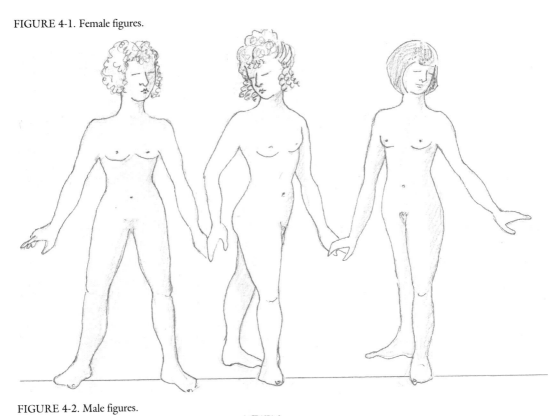

FIGURE 4-2. Male figures.

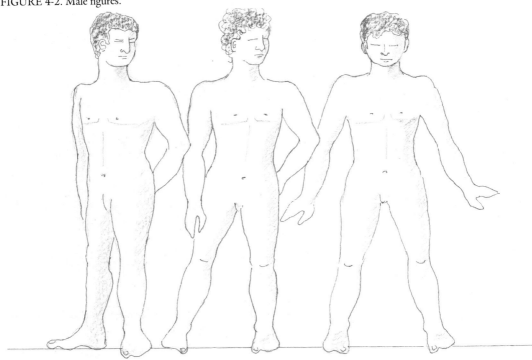

ual actors. With the aid of tracing papers, graphite or colored transfer paper, or a tracing table, you can reproduce the stock figure on your drawing paper and get on with sketching the costume.

Designers who use stock figures often keep a collection of figures in interesting poses which they have clipped from magazines and newspapers. Different periods require different poses, and some costumes rely on particular poses in order to be seen to the best advantage. A bustle dress, for example, demands a profile or three-quarter view so the bustle portion is visible. You can save time by having a good selection of possibilities available.

Figures 4-1 and 4-2 are samples of male and female figures, drawn with relatively

FIGURE 4-3. Rough pencil sketches for Jonathan in *Carnal Knowledge* for Stages in Houston, Texas. *Costume design by Keith Belli. Photograph by Rosemary Ingham.*

"normal" proportions, in poses that are useful to display some kinds of clothing. You can find other examples of normal figures in figure-drawing books. The figures in fashion design and fashion illustration books are elongated, eight or more "heads" tall. Clothing looks wonderful on fashion figures, but it can be frustrating to translate fashion-figure proportion to "normal" people.

Successful Preliminary Sketching

In order to communicate visual design ideas to a director, the preliminary sketch must show period line, accurate proportion, and appropriate detail.

LINE

A good rough sketch catches the correct period and character line with firmness and authority. The costume should not translate to the director as "sorta high-waisted" or "kinda drop-shouldered." A successful sketch makes its statement as simply and as directly as possible: This is the waistline. The puffed sleeves are that high. There is where the jacket hem is.

PROPORTION

In a discussion of costume it is almost impossible to consider line and proportion separately. The line of a garment is usually inextricably related to its proportion. The Empire line, for instance, is created by the relationship between bodice and skirt; a very short bodice, ending high above the natural waist, and a long, slim skirt. If you change this particular proportion between bodice and skirt, you change the period line. A good rough sketch indicates proportion without ambiguity, sleeves in relation to body, lapels in relation to shoulder width, etc.

Along with correct proportion within the garment, the rough sketch should also reflect correct body proportions, both for the actor (if

FIGURES 4-4 and 4-5. Rough and finished sketches for the Mother in *Ring Round the Moon*, for Heritage Repertory Theatre, Charlottesville, Virginia. The rough sketch was done with a felt marker and the finished sketch with pencil and watercolor. *Photographs by Rosemary Ingham.*

FIGURES 4-6 and 4-7. Rough and finished sketches for *Lion in Winter* by Arnold S. Levine. The rough sketch is done on bond paper with pencil. The finished sketch is watercolor wash and felt tip marker details on illustrated board. *Photographs by Frances Aronson.*

the actor is known) and for the character (no willowy Falstaffs, please!).

DETAIL

Both period and character will demand some surface detail on most costumes: striped or printed fabric, slashing, puffing, ruching, gathering, pleating, beads, bracelets, pins, hats, handbags, or swords. The rough sketch is not the place for specific details of this nature since the work is still in a preliminary stage and may change—but it is the place to suggest the necessity for detail. This area will be a brocade of some sort; there will be some kind of decoration at the neck; she will need a big hat, perhaps with feathers. Suggest these details as simply and as clearly as possible. If they are worked into the design from the beginning, there will be no chance that they will look "tacked-on" later.

If your sketch gives this information, you can be reasonably sure you know the play, the period, and the characters and can communicate your ideas to the director.

Pencil and Paper

While you are in this stage your sketches should be expendable. It should not cause you pain to crumple one up and toss it in a wastebasket, or erase it, if the images and the ideas are not working. It is seldom productive to labor unduly over a preliminary sketch. In order to encourage yourself to work freely and toss without regret, use simple, inexpensive materials for the early work.

An ordinary drawing pencil is the most versatile and expressive drawing tool available to you; it is almost always the preferred medium for preliminary sketches. Pencil lines are easy to erase and there is something about the character of pencil sketches that makes them seem far less permanent and intimidating than, say, ink sketches.

The most common papers for preliminary sketches are newsprint, butcher paper, layout or inexpensive drawing or tracing paper. All of these, except drawing paper, are available on rolls

FIGURE 4-8. Inexpensive paper for preliminary sketching. *Photograph by Colleen Muscha.*

as well as in pads. None is particularly costly; newsprint is the cheapest and tracing paper is the most expensive. (Tracing vellum is quite expensive and not the best choice for rough sketches.) Layout paper is especially versatile since it is available in a wide variety of weights and surfaces, is very white, very stout and, in most weights, can be used for tracing as well as for direct drawing.

To avoid the necessity of transferring or redrawing a sketch later, some designers do their preliminaries in a light pencil line directly on the finished sketch surface, usually watercolor paper or illustration board. Lines can be erased and changes made as the work progresses. Designers who work this way generally have a good deal of confidence in their way of working and often have some prior experience with the director.

The Whole and Its Parts

...the appearance of any element depends on its place and function in the pattern of the whole.

RUDOLPH ARNHEIM
Art and Visual Perception

At no point in the costume design process can a designer afford to concentrate solely on a single element to the exclusion of the others. Each part of a costume must relate to the whole ensemble, and each costume must relate to all the others on the stage. Scenery, lighting, the color of the actor's complexion, and the size and configuration of the stage all make specific demands on costume design. The most basic problem a costume designer faces is how to do everything at once.

FIGURE 4-9. Thumbnail sketches for Rutka Mazur and Symka Bekson in *The Wall* for the Alley Theatre. Pencil and felt tipped pen on gray charcoal paper. *Costume design and photograph by Rosemary Ingham.*

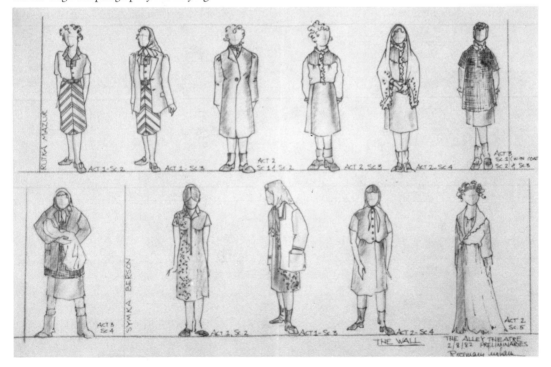

Very often when you sit down to begin preliminary sketching, it is difficult to assimilate all the discoveries and demands your script work, conferences, and research have showered upon you. A mountain of detail stands between you and your drawing paper, and it is difficult to imagine how everything you know can be translated into shirts and pants, dresses and hats.

This is the time to take a good deep breath, turn on some appropriate music, refill your coffee cup or glass of lemonade, and reflect on your earliest responses to the play, including initial production ideas. Recall your emotional response as well as your intellectual response. Allow the mountain of details to subside into your sense of the whole. Don't worry about forgetting specifics because you won't. Simply allow all the details to become part of the whole play. Breathe some more and then begin to sketch.

THUMBNAIL SKETCHES

Some designers find it easier to maintain a sense of the whole play by executing their preliminary sketches in small scale, several to a page. These are often called thumbnail sketches. Thumbnails may be four to six inch figures and they are usually grouped as they relate to each other in the play, making it easy to see at a glance how the costume shapes will interact.

Laying out several thumbnail sketches on a single sheet of paper will also make it possible for you to work on several costumes at once, first roughing in silhouettes, then adding details. Large cuffs on one gentleman's doublet may effect some bit of decoration on the lady. A striped fabric here may demand a solid surface there.

If your preliminary work is done in the same scale as the finished sketches, make it a practice to arrange the sketches around your work space so you can keep a sense of the whole as you draw. A large pin-up board adjacent to your drawing table is very convenient.

Experiment with different approaches to preliminary sketching but always make sure that you are not designing individual costumes in isolation from all the others.

The Element of Color

In a working situation, choosing costume color does not necessarily follow sketching. In all likelihood the creation of color and of shapes will move along at the same time and, in some instances, color will be chosen well before the sketching begins. It is only the demands of written organization that cause a discussion of color to follow a discussion of sketching, not a suggestion that the work be done in this order.

Many costume designers lay out a basic palette that reflects their response to the play as a whole before choosing which of the colors will be worn by which character. Others may pick out appropriate colors for leading characters and assemble a general palette for the secondary group, or groups.

A color layout, separate from costume sketches, shown to the director in the early stages of the work, can provoke especially good conversation about the play. It is always exciting to see how sensitively a play can be illuminated by color alone, how clearly forces can be opposed, lovers united, and resolutions sustained.

Although there is not space in this book for a lengthy discussion of color, the following few pages will review some basic color concepts and offer a few hints for good color use. Always remember, however, that your own personal feeling for color harmony should be your guiding principle. If you follow some of the rules you may escape choosing really awful colors but selecting distinguished color is entirely up to your own sensibilities and cannot be achieved through any prescription whatsoever.

Color and Color Perception

Color is an effect caused by the reflection of certain rays of light.

JOHN L. KING
The Art of Using Color

A detailed explanation of what color is and how it is perceived involves the sciences of physics, chemistry, and psychology and is far beyond the scope of this work. Yet it is important to convey some sense of the subject's complexity in order to suggest how potentially powerful color is. When the human eye looks at a brilliant yellow jonquil, the process by which the color is experienced involves several neurophysiological processes. Many parts of the body are affected. Minute but measurable changes occur in heart rate, respiration, and skin temperature, changes that must, it seems on reflection, contribute significantly to the simple pleasure experienced by the conscious mind when it sees a pretty yellow flower. Color indisputably involves us from head to toe.

And yet the jonquil is not even yellow. The yellow that you perceive the jonquil to be is merely a property of the light which shines on the blossom. You see yellow because of the way in which light hits the object's surface and because of the particular ability of your brain to perceive the event.

What you call light is produced by a tiny part of the electromagnetic field called the visible spectrum. Color is a natural part of the visible spectrum—a fact that Sir Isaac Newton demonstrated around 1666—and is created when light is broken down into electromagnetic vibrations, or waves, of different lengths. These wavelengths, when refracted or bent by the glass in a prism, arrange themselves into a series of colors determined by length: indigo, blue, green, yellow, orange, and red. The longest wavelength creates red, the shortest indigo. If these color wavelengths are recombined—which Newton also demonstrated—they become white light again.

The color effect occurs when light encounters a surface. The molecules that make up the surface absorb some of the wavelengths from the light and reflect others. The color you perceive is reflected wavelengths. If the surface absorbs all of the wavelengths, it is perceived as black.

Color Response

Like the notes of the basic scale when expanded into a symphony, color has seemingly unlimited variation and enormous capacity to manipulate our emotions. It is therefore one of the most powerful tools of the designer.

MARJORIE ELLIOTT BEVLIN
Design Through Discovery

If color is a natural part of all light, and human perception of color affects a significant portion of your physiological being, it is not surprising that people respond more intensely to color than they do to any other design element. Language often gives us away. Visitors to modern art galleries speak of having been "assaulted by color." Most people have colors they "love" and colors they "hate" and would agree that all human moods are to some degree affected by surrounding color.

People respond to color in many complex and interdependent ways. The society in which you live conditions you to some color responses; laws, customs, or traditions handed down from the past provide others. Associations with a specific group of people provide you with color responses you share with members of that group, and purely personal associations will inform your individual feelings about color. There is even recent investigation that suggests some color response may be purely physiological, acting directly on the nervous system without any cognition whatsoever.

Some of the following color examples fit into a single response category while others seem to overlap and involve two or more responses. In all of them you can sense the powerful role color plays in human life.

TRAFFIC LIGHT RESPONSE

As children you learn to walk across the street when you see a green light and stop when you see a red light. It is the law. In a short time the conscious concept of law is forgotten, and you and your neighbors respond directly to color as you walk on green and stop on red.

ROYALTY RESPONSE

Purple is the color of kings, and it is a rare child that doesn't give the coloring book king a royal purple robe. Once upon a time the color purple, which was then derived from a shellfish known as Murex and was very costly, was, by law, forbidden to anyone but the emperor. You don't necessarily have to know the fact in order to possess the association.

LOVE RESPONSE

Your favorite grandmother often let you make cookies with her and, to protect your dress, would wrap you in a peach-colored bib apron. Those were the happiest times. Now, grown up, whenever you are shopping for clothes, your eyes automatically fall on peach-colored garments, your favorite color.

RED AND BLUE RESPONSES

Without having any notion why, you participate to some degree in the general tendency of this culture to associate the color red with danger, blood, fire, energy, and passion; the color blue is associated with virginity, hope, and truth. Polls state that the favorite color of the vast majority of Americans of both sexes and all ages is blue. In a

related response, it has been demonstrated that a person driving an automobile in traffic will feel a much stronger urge to pass a red car than a blue car, whatever make, model, or size the car might be.

OTHER RESPONSES

People's appetites are increased in rooms where there is a great deal of orange. Agitated prisoners or hyperactive mental patients calm down in rooms where the color green predominates. Totally blind children can identify rooms that are identical in size and shape and differentiated only by one having red walls, one blue walls, and one yellow walls.

Color Response in Design

Costume designers employ general color response in order to communicate obvious information: the villain wears a black hat, the hero dons a white hat, the turncoat has a green vest on, and the adulterous woman wears a red dress. And if you are looking for more subtle communication, which is usually the case, you can apply the same color dynamic by introducing touches of the appropriate associative color: a bit of blue on a virtuous maiden's blouse or a warm brown shawl on lovable Aunt Emily. In most instances you will discover that you have chosen the psychologically correct color without conscious thought, simply because your own responses are in tune with those of your society.

It is very important, as you work with color in design, to study and explore your personal responses to hues and harmonies. Discover what excites you and use these combinations to build a personal aesthetic.

Never stop looking for new color experiences to feed your sensibilities. Collect prints and advertising layouts and photographs whose color has a strong effect on you. Visit museums just to look at color. Enjoy your ability to be surprised by new ways of using color and encourage your sensibilities to be challenged and stretched by what you see. The more sensitive you are to color, the better able you will be to affect an audience with your use of it.

Color Properties

Sometimes it seems as though there are too many colors in the world. If you look around you right now, in any direction, you will see dozens of discernible colors. The vast array of colors you meet each time you enter a fabric store may seem overwhelming. If you purchase a Pantone Color Specifier (a selection of tear-out color chips from Pantone printing inks—an excellent aid for designers) you will be faced by no less than five hundred choices, plus shades and tints. Indeed, it has been estimated that the human eye can perceive one hundred and fifty different colors and two hundred gradations of value within each of them—thirty thousand shades and tints! How, in the midst of such a variously colored world, can a designer choose a palette and compose color in such a way that it is anything but a jumble?

One answer is to begin simply. Understand the basic properties of color. Study a system of primary colors and learn how to mix them. Explore the ways in which colors alter each other in combinations. Adopt a set of terms through which you can describe color relationships to your satisfaction. Then practice using common color schemes until you feel secure enough to strike out on your own.

Color Wheel

When the band of colors that makes up the color spectrum in light is joined end to end, the result is a circle in which one color seems to flow into the next. It was this observation that led to the development of the color wheel to explore these relationships. A number of different color wheels have been devised; perhaps the simplest and most widely used resulted from the work of Herbert E. Ives. It is especially relevant to pigments.

The primary colors in Ives' color wheel are red, blue, and yellow. The theory is that these colors cannot be mixed and that all other colors can be mixed from them. This is true enough in practice to be a useful working theory.

A mixture of two *primaries* will produce a *secondary* color:

1. red + yellow = orange
3. yellow + blue = green
3. red + blue = violet

A mixture of a *primary* color and its adjacent *secondary* color produces a *tertiary* color.

1. red + orange = red/orange
2. yellow + green = yellow/green
3. blue + violet = blue/violet
4. yellow + orange = yellow/orange
5. blue + green = blue/green
6. red + violet = red/violet

Developing a color wheel gives you basic assistance in mixing color. More importantly, it provides you with a key to some of the effects colors achieve in combinations.

Colors that lie directly opposite each other on the color wheel are called *complementary* colors. Red and green are complementary; so are yellow and violet, orange and blue. Complementary colors are as different from each other as it is possible to be. They tend, when placed side by side, to intensify each other and are, as a result, quite inharmonious.

One of the most useful ways of toning down a color, however, is by mixing in a bit of that color's complement. An equal mixture of two complements will produce a *neutral* which does not have the characteristics of either.

One of the most mysterious pieces of behavior exhibited by complementaries is the phenomenon of *afterimage*. If you stare at a color intensely for half a minute or so, then look away, you will see an afterimage that is some version of the color's complement. Another attribute of afterimage is that when you place a color on a light neutral background, the neutral will acquire a tinge of the color's complement.

Although basically inharmonious in a composition, complementary colors do, however, have an affinity for each other that should not be overlooked. Many a bland costume sketch has been perked up with the addition of a necktie, bow, or flower in the color that is the complement to the main costume color—a technique that works in the same way as improving a bland soup with a dash of spice.

The relationship referred to as *split complements* involves a color and the two colors on either side of its true complement. This would combine, for example, orange with blue/violet and blue/green. Split complements tend to intensify each other and are not, by nature, harmonious.

You can also use the color wheel to explore harmonious color. The simplest route to color harmony in design is *monochromatic* color, the use of a single color with light and dark variations.

Analogous harmony joins colors that are next to each other on the color wheel, such as red/violet, violet and blue/violet.

Triad harmony combines any three colors that lie equidistant from each other on the color wheel. The three primaries form a triad and so do the three secondaries. There are two potential tertiary color triads. Triad harmonies are particularly exciting; they often call up memories of

---

FIGURE 4-10. Mixing paints.

The first time you go into an art store to purchase paints, you may have a hard time deciding which colors to buy from the scores available. And, even if you can afford to buy one tube of each, a harder decision awaits you: which color to use first when you start painting?

The following paint-mixing scheme will help you learn to mix your own. You only have to purchase six tubes, or cakes, of watercolor or acrylic paint to produce thirty-five different hues.

Colors to buy:
   I. Warm primaries:
      1. cadmium red
      2. cadmium yellow, medium
      3. ultramarine blue
  II. Cool primaries:
      A. alizarin crimson
      B. lemon yellow
      C. cerulean blue

Notice that the warm primaries are 1, 2, and 3 and the cool primaries are A, B, and C.

First, make two color wheels containing primaries, secondaries, and tertiaries—one from the warm primaries and one from the cool primaries. Remember, when mixing the tertiary colors use equal amounts of the secondary and primary colors.

If using paint in tubes, begin by squeezing out a dime-sized amount of each color and arrange each set of primaries in a triangular shape on a separate palette or surface. If using cakes, arrange them in the same manner, and moisten each cake. Try to use the same amount of pigment and water for each mixing operation and a clean brush for every mixture. Your two color wheels should look like those in Plate #1 in the color photograph section.

Now, mix the following warm and cool primaries to create nine colors:

1+A	2+A	3+A
1+B	2+B	3+B
1+C	2+C	3+C

Finally, mix the following combinations to create an additional fourteen colors:

1+2+3	A+B+C
2+A+C	B+1+3
1+B+C	A+2+3
3+A+B	C+1+2
1+2+C	A+B+3
2+3+A	B+C+1
1+3+B	A+C+2

Display both sets of primaries, and all of your mixed colors, on a single piece of white watercolor paper. This will be your own personal guide to color mixing, and it will look like Plate #2 in the color photograph section.

You can do a lot of good painting with these six tubes of paint, and, if you add Payne's gray, Hooker's green, and magenta, you might have all the colors you will ever need.

children's art and comic book illustration. When triad colors are mixed with each other, however, they form grayish or brownish hues of exceptional muddiness.

Here are a few generalizations concerning the effects colors can have on each other:

1. Dark hues appear weaker on a noncomplementary dark ground and stronger on a complementary dark ground.

2. Light colors appear weaker on a noncomplementary light ground and stronger on a complementary light ground.

3. A bright color against a dull color of the same hue will further deaden the dull color.

4. When a bright color is used against a dull color the contrast will be strongest when the dull color is complementary.

5. Light colors on non complementary light grounds are greatly strengthened if bounded by narrow bands of black or complementary colors.

6. Dark colors on noncomplementary dark grounds can be strengthened if similarly bounded by white or light colors.

Try out the following color schemes for practice. Also, make it a habit to see the color schemes in your favorite paintings, illustrations, and designs.

1. *One color* (single value and intensity), with white, gray, or black.

2. *Monochromatic* is a single hue in all desired tints and shades (with and without white, gray, or black).

3. *Modified monochromatic* is the addition of small touches of bright color in an otherwise monochromatic scheme.

4. *Analogous* colors are related to each other with a common factor. Example: orange, yellow, yellow/green; all contain the common color, yellow.

5. *Analogous with dominant hue* achieve dominance through (a) size of area, (b) its dark value against lighter ground, and (c) its light value against darker ground. The presence of the dominant hue will relieve monotony.

6. *Analogous with complementary accents* consists of the introduction of small but sometimes very intense bits of complementary color which can give surprising life to the whole.

7. *Complementary scheme* is any pleasing scheme which conspicuously introduces opposite colors. Control contrasts to avoid chaos. (*Note*: You will almost never base a color scheme on complementary colors in equal amounts if the colors are full strength. Balance the scheme with unequal amounts and/or unequal intensities.)

8. *Near or split complements* combine a color with the colors on either side of the complement. These combinations usually seem more harmonious.

9. *Triads* are color combinations that form equilateral triangles on the wheel. Triad colors will fight with each other for prominence. Choose one to dominate and veil or neutralize the others with the dominant color.

Color Vocabulary

A satisfactory color vocabulary can be a great help to you as you approach a palette. In order to be able to discuss colors, you must be able to describe their attributes. The following terms are quite commonly used although no set is universal.

Hue is the name of the color. It is synonymous with color. Red is the hue of an apple. Mixing one color with another will result in another hue.

Values are the gradations between the lightest and the darkest varieties of a color. Some refer to this attribute of color as brilliance. Values that are darker than the pure color are called *shades*; values lighter than the pure color are called *tints*.

Intensity refers to the vividness or distinctness of a hue. Some would define this as strong color versus weak color. Other words synonymous with intensity are saturation or chroma. Colors can be rendered less intense by graying them. You can change intensity without changing hue.

Warm and Cool Colors

One of the most exciting of all color properties is psychological temperature. Certain colors—red, yellow, orange—convey a sense of warmth, while others—green and blue—seem cool. There are obvious associations that help to explain this phenomenon. The warm colors are reminiscent of fire and sunlight, the cool ones of water and foliage.

In addition, every color also has warm versions and cool versions. Mixing warm and cool colors together can alter their psychological temperatures. Color combinations also affect the warmth or coolness of individual hues; you can warm up a cool color simply by placing it in a warm environment.

A good color sense is largely a product of intuition, association, and constant study.

LYNN PECKTAL
*Designing and Painting
for the Theatre*

Color and Form

The size and shape of a human silhouette against a background can be remarkably affected by color. For instance, a light figure on a dark ground appears larger than a dark figure of the same size on a light ground. Everyone knows that you can minimize the bulk of a stout figure

by dressing it in dark colors. That bulk can be minimized even more if the background is light.

Warm and cool colors in combination can also seem to alter form. Warm hues, for example, appear to advance and expand while cool hues contract and recede. If you put a red/orange circle on a blue/green background, the circle will seem to pop forward, appearing to be in front of the background rather than part of it. The opposite is also true. When a blue/green spot is placed on a red/orange ground, the background seems to come forward and the spot becomes a hole.

The effects of warm and cool colors on form probably have a physiological base. The lens in your eye has to thin out to perceive cool colors and thicken to perceive warm colors. When forced to focus and refocus on extremes of warm and cool color, the lens is in a constant shifting state which does not allow the forms to remain integrated.

Finally, both cool colors and tints seem lighter in weight and less substantial than their counterparts. Warm colors and shades appear heavier and more dense.

Color Display

Rough sketches, even if they are executed in color, are usually accompanied by some kind of color display. As soon as you begin to compose your color layout, decide what materials you want to use for it. No one material is any more correct than another, although one may be better suited to a particular project. Bright, bold costumes for a children's play might be most successfully represented with paint chips. For a set of costumes that employs a narrow range of monochromatic values for its effect, paint may be the only medium through which you can demonstrate your intent. A large show with costumes that will have many prints and subtle color relationships is best represented by fabric swatches.

USING FABRIC SWATCHES

The most common color layouts for costumes are executed in fabric swatches for some very good reasons: There seems to be an almost endless variety of possible colors. Fabric swatches are easy to come by and cost little or nothing. Fabric suggests clothing more directly than colored papers or paint chips, and fabric includes texture, which is so intimately related to color effects in design.

The presence of fabric texture and weight in swatches may be troublesome to you if you are selecting fabric pieces entirely for color and do not mean textural associations to be made. Some people find it very difficult to separate their response to texture from their response to color. A square of pale pink satin may convey exactly the correct color for a chiffon scarf. Your director may be turned off by the satin and thus reject the pink. "No," the director may say, "that's not right," without knowing where the negative response comes from.

If you are using fabric swatches to communicate only color, be very specific about your intentions. It is far better, if at all possible, to select swatches that reflect both your color and textural choices.

ATTACHING COLOR SAMPLES

There are many ways of attaching color samples for display. If you are doing a single layout, arrange the samples on a stout piece of paper or board, and glue or staple them in place. (For the paper or board on which the samples are displayed, some designers choose a color which is as near as possible to the overall set color.) Staples are the most secure; rubber cement, household cement, or spray adhesives are quite reliable. Ordinary white glue is less permanent and may give way if the layout is excessively handled.

Designers who do individual color layouts for each character rather than an overall display often staple (or glue) their color samples to 3×5

or 4×6 cards, which can be arranged and rearranged to show changing relationships and different scenes. They may be placed on the rough sketches. Later on, if the swatches are fabric pieces from the actual cloth of the costumes, the swatch cards can be attached directly to the completed sketches.

Color samples may go right on the rough sketches. Again, staples are best but glue, or even paper clips, will do. Refrain from attaching fabric swatches to sketches with straight pins since someone is bound to get stuck as sketches go from hand to hand.

Sometimes the perfect color layout presents itself in another representation, such as a painting, a tapestry, or a patterned carpet. If you can't improve on it, use it.

A Swatching Trip

Even though you may be using watercolors or paint chips to work out a color scheme for your costumes, you should take at least one trip through the shops to swatch fabric during the early stages of your work. Looking at actual fabrics may help you work out color. Also, unless you are able to have fabrics woven and dyed to your specifications—an unheard of extravagance in most theatres—you will be dependent upon the fabrics that are in the stores, so you should see what is available and collect representative samples.

There are no fixed rules of etiquette for requesting fabric swatches. Some shopkeepers welcome designers and dispense samples readily, others are very grumpy about giving away bits of cloth, and a few will not part with a thread unless you pay for it. In general, it is easier to swatch in cities where designers regularly shop for costume fabrics: New York, Los Angeles, Chicago, Washington, Milwaukee, Seattle, and so on. The shops in places where there is not much theatrical activity may not be so understanding about the

FIGURE 4-11. Supplies for a swatching trip. *Photograph by Colleen Muscha.*

way designers work. You should be careful to explain what you are doing and why, and you should tell the shopkeeper that you intend to eventually purchase cloth selected from the swatches you are considering. As with most human encounters, the more open and friendly you are, the more cooperation you are likely to receive.

Equip yourself fully for a swatching trip. Take adhesive labels or masking tape, scissors (some stores will actually let you cut your own swatches!), a ballpoint pen, and a supply of envelopes.

Stick an adhesive label or a piece of masking tape on the back of each swatch. Write the price and width of the fabric on it and also the name of the store where you got it. File the swatches in the envelopes by colors or by characters or by any other method that organizes your project.

Keep in mind the approximate yardage you will need; don't take a swatch of a cloth if there is only a yard on the bolt and the garment will require twenty. Ask, of course, if there is more of the fabric stored away or if it can be ordered. Be aware that it often takes a long time to get fabric on order; many designers have had to make a

poor second choice because delivery took longer than was expected.

If you see a bolt of fabric that you are quite certain you will want to purchase but cannot on that day, ask the store manager to hold it for you. Many will do so gladly, although they will usually give you a time limit for picking it up.

Be sensible about prices even when your designs are not complete. You already know your budget. If it is not large enough for a great many expensive fabrics, don't swatch a great many expensive fabrics; you will only be frustrated later on. At the same time, never hesitate to ask the shop if they will consider selling the fabric to you at a discount, particularly if you are shopping for a nonprofit theatre. Some shops are willing to discount prices, especially if you purchase a significant number of yards.

Many fabric stores have backrooms or basements stuffed with old or unusual fabrics that may not have much sales appeal to the general public but are infinitely appealing to costume designers. Always ask if such a storage area exists.

Keep all swatches you don't use on one project and add them to your swatch collection for future color work. Take care, however, not to become devoted to a particular swatch from your collection during the planning stages of your designs, only to discover it is one you collected five years ago and the fabric from which it was cut has long since disappeared from the store's shelves.

Incorporating Stock and Rental Costumes

If the production you are designing must include garments pulled from the theatre's stock or rented from a commercial costume rental company, it is important to have some notion of what is available to you as you work on rough sketches and compose color. Visit the stock area if it is at all possible and look carefully at all appropriate coats, vests, dresses, shoes, etc., sketching shapes and noting colors. If you are not able to go to the rental company and participate in the selection process, ask for specific descriptions, including color, of what they have.

Include pulled and rented items in your rough sketches and their colors in your color display. Integrating costumes to be built with existing costumes in these early stages of the design work can save you the unpleasant experience of having a group of unconsidered, hastily assembled servant's costumes suddenly arrive to completely destroy the harmony of your work.

Showing Rough Sketches to the Director

The day on which you are scheduled to show rough sketches to the director was probably set during a preceding conference. In some producing organizations all meetings and deadlines are pre-scheduled. At any rate, you will know about the meeting in advance, so be ready for it. One of the most counter-productive things a designer can do to the collaborative process is to turn up at a design meeting unprepared. If some emergency prevents you from completing the preliminary work by the appointed day, call and postpone the meeting, but do not, under any circumstances, come empty-handed.

Lay out the sketches in whatever manner the project demands, by scenes, by factions, or all together. Don't talk right away. Give the director a chance to look. Remember, you have been looking at the sketches for days and have probably committed them all to memory; the director has probably not seen them at all. It takes time to see.

Don't expect universal praise for every costume sketch. Even if your prior collaboration on the production has been most satisfactory, it is highly unlikely that you and the director will agree on everything. Expect some changes to be made and assume that the changes will be improvements. This is not the time to be even faintly defensive about your work.

After the period of general looking, begin to explain each sketch in turn. Comment, if you can, on the cut, the fabric, the way it might move. If color is not included in the sketch, relate the sketch to the color display. Mention trim and accessories, hairstyles and facial hair. Try to make sure that the director is seeing everything you have indicated. Discuss the costumes in the sequence in which they will appear on stage, noting all repeats and all changes, as well as any problems that might arise because of actors' doubling.

Then listen. Listen carefully to the director's response to what you have presented. Make sure you understand what is being said: which things the director finds appropriate and which things he thinks unclear. Make suggestions and take suggestions. However, if you are asked to make major changes in your work, don't decide on them until you have had time to reflect on everything that has been said. On the spot, cut-and-paste costume design is seldom successful. Go home, get back to work, and return another day with new and better sketches.

More often than not, if your preparation and the original collaboration have been sound, the director will approve the original work with few changes and additions, and you will soon be back at your drawing table ready to prepare the final sketches for the shop.

5
Final Sketches

When a work is praised for "having simplicity", it is understood to organize a wealth of meaning and form in an over-all structure that clearly defines the place and function of every detail in the whole.

RUDOLF ARNHEIM
Art and Visual Perception

All of the costume designer's research, exploration, and preliminary drawing come together in the final sketches. There are very few rectangles of paper or board anywhere else in the world that must communicate as much information, aesthetic as well as practical, as a costume sketch. A complete costume sketch conveys, among other things, line, shape, proportion and color, history, script, and character analysis. It indicates, as clearly as possible, what the actor will wear and what the audience will see. The shop technicians look at the sketch to guide draping and pattern drafting, trim arrangement, fabric dyeing, and the creation of hats and other accessories. Finally, the sketch becomes a part of the designer's work portfolio and may be examined by producers and directors as part of a job interview.

In light of all these demands it may seem ridiculous to say that simplicity is one of the chief attributes of a fine costume sketch. Yet this is true. The simple, direct sketch that manages to "organize a wealth of meaning" and say a great deal with a minimum of fuss is always the most effective. A flashy, overworked sketch, like wordy, overblown rhetoric, too often obscures the facts and confuses the issues. It is a mistake to equate good costume sketching with technical virtuosity and multi-media displays.

On the other hand, whereas simplicity is desirable in a costume sketch, a simplistic sketch that represents the costume with only a half dozen sensuous lines may be an exciting drawing yet fail as a final costume sketch. This is because it does not give significant information to the shop and to those members of the production group who only want to know what the costume will really look like.

Somewhere in between overdone and underdone lies the thoroughly professional, clear, direct, and beautiful sketch which is the goal of every serious designer. This chapter focuses on the more practical matters you will deal with every day while moving toward this goal: working habits and working materials.

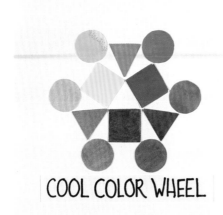

COOL COLOR WHEEL

WARM COLOR WHEEL

PLATE 1   Warm and cool color wheels.

See Figure 4-10, Mixing paints.

PLATE 2   Color mixing guide.

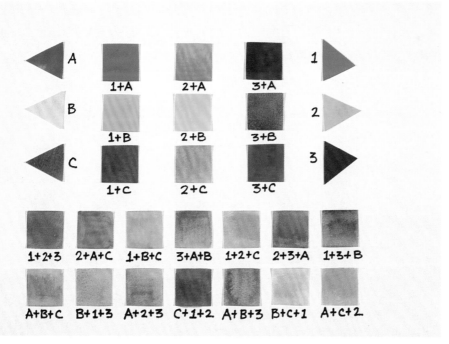

PLATE 3 Liz Covey's sketch for Ko-ko in *The Mikado* at the June Opera Festival. *Photograph by Rosemary Ingham.*

PLATE 4 Mrs. Hardcastle in *She Stoops to Conquer* at TheatreVirginia. *Costume design by Susan Tsu. Photograph by Rosemary Ingham.*

PLATE 6   Ann Hould-Ward's sketch for Louise in
Truffles in the Soup, Dan Sullivan's adaptation of
Goldoni's *Servant of Two Masters* at the Seattle Repertory
Theatre. *Photograph courtesy of Ann Hould-Ward.*

PLATE 5   Belise in *Learned Ladies*, in a production
at the Krannert Center set in the 1950s. *Sketch by Liz
Covey. Photograph by Rosemary Ingham.*

PLATE 7   Helen Ju's thumbnail sketches for a group of
characters in Gozzi's *The Blue Monster*. Third-year class project at
the Yale Drama School. *Photograph by Rosemary Ingham.*

PLATE 8   David Murin's sketch for Mrs.
Candour in *School for Scandal* at Williamstown
Theatre. *Photograph by Liz Covey.*

PLATE 9   Colleen Muscha's design for Agave in
The Bacchae. Photograph by Colleen Muscha.

PLATE 10   Production shot from *The Bacchae* at
Florida State University. *Designed and
photographed by Colleen Muscha.*

Diana LaMar as Julia and Trish Jenkins as Lucetta.

Jeffrey Guyton as Launce and
Rainn Wilson as Speed.

PLATES 11, 12, & 13   Production shots from The Acting Company's
production of *The Two Gentlemen of Verona* at Arena Stage. *Costume
design by Catherine Zuber. Photographs by Joan Marcus, courtesy of
Arena Stage.*

PLATE 14   Larry Ballard as Sir Toby Belch, Molly Mayock as Maria, Charles Dean as Sir Andrew Aguecheek, and Tony Amendola as Malvolio in the Berkeley Repertory Theatre production of *Twelfth Night*. *Costume design by Susan Hilferty. Photograph by Ken Friedman.*

PLATE 15   Gina Leishman as Inessa in the Goodman Theatre production of *Moscowteers*. *Costume design by Susan Hilferty. Photograph courtesy of Susan Hilferty.*

FIGURE 5-1. Lowell Detweiler's costume design for *Les Patineurs*. Acrylics and colored pencil on charcoal paper. *Photograph by Frances Aronson.*

FIGURE 5-2. Mexican woman in *Streetcar Named Desire*. *Costume design by Susan Tsu. Photograph by Frances Aronson.*

FIGURE 5-3. Ann Wallace's sketch for Lil in *Broadway*, done in gouache and felt pen on watercolor paper. *Photograph by Rosemary Ingham.*

Place and Time

The Work Space

Most designers are greatly affected by the atmosphere of the place where they work, its volume, its floor plan, its light source, the color of its walls, and the position of the waste paper basket. Frivolous as these concerns may seem to some, they are worth a few words if only to comfort those of you who might feel guilty because you cannot put effective paint to paper in surroundings you find unpleasant. Such failings do not indicate a lack of character.

William Faulkner, the great Southern writer, once said that if a writer was to do good work, he must find himself a "warm room." Faulkner was using these words metaphorically; one writer's warm room will be quite different from another's in the same way that the physical arrangement and decoration of one designer's work space will not resemble another's. It is true,

however, that a certain degree of individualized psychological and physical comfort must be present for most writers to write and for most designers to design.

If your work space is not as conducive to your work as you would like it to be, take a little time to see how you can improve it. Is the light satisfactory? Is your chair or stool the correct height for your drawing surface? Are your supplies conveniently arranged or must you be constantly getting up and down while you try to work?

Work spaces need not be elaborate or contain expensive furniture and equipment to be efficient and pleasant. A drawing surface, light, and a place to sit are the only necessities. Meet those needs first. Spend your money where it counts, on a chair that is kind to your own skeletal configuration, a sturdy drawing table, a moveable light source.

FIGURE 5-4. A pleasant work area. *Photograph by Colleen Muscha.*

90

YOUR DRAWING TABLE

Make sure your drawing surface is stable. Nothing irritates people more than trying to draw on a surface that rocks back and forth.

Drawing tables come in a wide variety of brands and styles; they range from extravagant models that raise, lower, and tilt at the touch of a button to more pedestrian varieties that change position through the use of hand-operated thumb screws. The size of the board itself may range from approximately 23″ × 31″ to 31″ × 42″. When you choose a drawing table, think carefully about your own needs, the available space, and your pocketbook. Shop around and be sure to investigate the possibilities of purchasing your drawing table second hand.

Some designers prefer to work on a flat table or desk with, perhaps, a portable drawing board. You can prop the board up with books, a brick, or with a set of metal brackets sold for that purpose. You can also buy a portable drawing board with legs that fold down to effect the tilt.

Whatever drawing surface you choose, make sure the area on which you draw is smooth and clean. Some designers cover their boards with a sheet of white cardboard which can be removed and replaced as necessary. An excellent material for your drawing surface is Vinyl-Flex

drawing board cover. It is sold by the yard, cuts easily with scissors or a knife, and can be fastened down with Dubl-Stik tape. One side is pale green, the other ivory, both good colors to relieve eyestrain. Vinyl-Flex is washable and resistant to nicks and cuts.

SEATING CHOICE

Choose a chair or stool that is the correct height for your work surface. Too many hours spent in a hunched-over position will result in chronic backache. You may want a back rest or support, but it is best that this be adjustable; a back rest that presses into the wrong part of your spine is worse than none at all. Don't ever purchase a work chair or stool without actually sitting on it.

FIGURE 5-6. A small drawing table with good light and a comfortable chair with good back support. *Photograph by Colleen Muscha.*

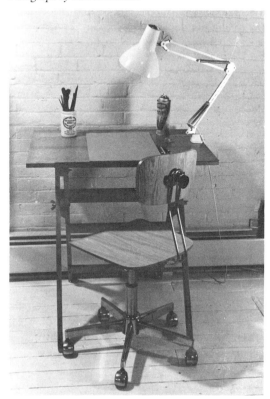

FIGURE 5-5. A tilted drawing table. *Photograph by Colleen Muscha.*

LIGHTING CHOICE

You must also have a good lamp. Ideally it should be adjustable. Jointed, flexible "architects' " lamps are popular because they are inexpensive and can be adapted to many spaces. If you use one lamp on each side of your work area and focus it correctly, you can eliminate shadows and glare. Glare is a heavy contributor to the weeping, burning eye syndrome known as eyestrain.

BE CREATIVE

Rely on imagination to help make your work area pleasant. If the faded-flower wallpaper causes discomfort, paint over it or cover it with fabric, a sheet, or even brown paper. Pin up hats on the wall if you like them, surround yourself with plants if they make you feel good or with baskets of cloth if you find that exciting. Pay attention to your needs; a work space need not follow any rules of interior decor, and you should not care how it looks to others. Indulge yourself. There are times when the best thing you can do for yourself and for your work is to purchase a beautiful stoneware pitcher that has captured your fancy and put it on your drawing table to hold brushes.

Work Hours

A costume designer's work hours are regulated only in the broadest possible sense by the production deadlines. Each day is yours to schedule; no one asks you to punch a timeclock or to report on your accomplishments at the end of each work day. You are quite free to work in fits and starts, procrastinating and postponing for several weeks and then attempting to complete all 67 final sketches in the 24 hours before the costumes must go into the shop. Some designers do this.

However, you are also free to program your work in regular, daily blocks, adjusting and readjusting your schedule to meet the changing needs of the project. Even when the amount of work seems overwhelming, you can always organize it in a way that will not leave you a basket case during dress rehearsals, the very point in the production process when you need to have your wits as sharp as possible.

Observe your work habits and figure out when you do your best work. Many times the pressure of the work will demand that you draw and paint through the night but, if you have a choice in the matter, plan your day so you are painting when you paint best. It is much easier to work with colors during the daytime hours when natural light is available. Artificial light, no matter how good the quality is, produces more strain on your eyes than natural light. Most people work more efficiently when they get an early morning start, well before telephones and the assorted cares of the day intervene.

Sketch Size

Before you go off to the art store to buy materials for final sketches, be sure you have decided what size figures you will use because this determines the amount of paper or board you will need.

It is probably a good idea to make all the figures the same size. It's easier to work out design details when your figure proportions are consistent, and the technicians, actors, and directors will certainly find the sketches easier to read. A general exception to this might be a very large costume show with many supporting or chorus characters. Designers often sketch these characters in groups with figures a third to a half of the main character sketch size.

The actual size of the figures is up to you. Some designers hit on a personally optimum size figure for all their work, others vary the size with the project. In any case, the figure should be large enough to convey the necessary information and small enough to be portable. Don't forget that you must carry the whole lot with you to meetings and to read-throughs and to the shop,

and if the sketches are too big you will have problems doing so.

Whatever the figure size, be sure that each sheet of paper or board, frame or mount, is uniform in size. There is nothing more cumbersome than trying to transport or show a lot of different sized costume sketches. If, as is often the case, they must go through the mail, it is very difficult to pack them if the outside dimensions vary.

Media

Costume designers work in many different media. Some of these are discussed individually beginning on page 94. Decide ahead of time what you want to use and what you need to purchase. If you always work in the same medium, check your supplies and make a note of additional or replacement colors you need. Many designers, however, like to try different paints and inks and methods, exploring new means to effective sketches. If you are purchasing supplies that you have had limited experience with, be sure to find out exactly what you will need to work with that medium, what papers, what additives, and what applicators.

Buy Everything at Once

Don't allow yourself to get caught at 2 AM, in a fever of inspiration, without an item you need to work with: paper, white gouache, brown ink.

FIGURE 5-7. Susan Tsu's sketch for Artimedora in *Julius Caesar* (Milwaukee Repertory Theater). Baked white glue and acrylics on a surface of heavy colored paper and plaster bandages. *Photograph by Frances Aronson.*

Before you begin any project, make a careful list of all you will need to complete it and purchase those things before you begin. If, in the course of the work, you run short of something, replace it immediately, between 9AM and 6 PM, before the shops close. Even your closest designer friends won't be happy about loaning you a bottle of ink at 4 AM and, furthermore, no one else is apt to have exactly the color or brand you hunger for.

Art Supplies and Materials

You are about to venture into your favorite—or the most conveniently located—art supply store. Whether the store is large or small, you need to know a bit about the products sold there in order to shop effectively. The multiplicity of brands and of types in every area can be bewildering. New and "improved" products appear constantly on the market, while old brands disappear without a trace. Because brands come and go, descriptions of artists' paraphernalia in this chapter are general and applicable to many different trade names. The information contained here is certainly not exhaustive; it is intended only to hit the high spots and help you chart a course through the media maze.

Pencils, Pencil Sharpeners, and Erasers

DRAWING PENCILS

Traditional, wood-encased graphite pencils have been around for quite a while—the first graphite pencil was made in 1662—and are certainly the most commonly used drawing implement. Nineteen grades of graphite are currently available and are expressed from hardest to softest as: 9H, 8H, 7H, 6H, 5H, 4H, 3H, 2H, H, F, HB, B, 2B, 3B, 4B, 5B, 6B, EB, EE. The hard grades contain more clay and the soft grades more graphite. Costume designers generally use mid-range grades, often choosing HB for general drawing and sketching and 2H and H for work with tracing paper.

FIGURE 5-8. Colleen Muscha's sketch for the Sergeant and the Recruiter from *Mother Courage and Her Children* by Brecht. A Milwaukee Repertory Theater production. Sketch rendered in ebony pencil on watercolor paper. *Photograph by Frances Aronson.*

DRAFTING OR CLUTCH LEAD PENCILS

Clutch lead pencils, or holders, are designed and manufactured for precision drafting as well as for drawing. The barrels operate with a push-button action which holds and dispenses graphite leads in the full range of grades.

Clutch holders may be of metal or plastic construction. Some people prefer the heavier weight of the metal model. If you are not familiar with pencils of this type, it is a good idea to try several varieties before deciding which one to purchase.

AUTOMATIC MECHANICAL PENCILS

A less expensive version of the drafting pencil is the automatic mechanical pencil. Most brands have a quick-click mechanism which self-feeds the leads from a storage chamber which holds about twelve extra leads. The leads come in four sizes—from thin to less thin: 0.3mm, 0.4mm, 0.5mm, 0.7mm—which do not need to be sharpened. There are only a limited number of graphite grades available, usually from 2B to 6H, and not all grades may exist in each size. These pencils are excellent for rough sketching.

SKETCHING PENCILS

Designers may prefer pencils manufactured especially for sketching. Some are soft, round, very black graphite leads; others are broad, rectangular blocks of graphite, excellent for shading drawings. Carbon pencils give a somewhat different line and texture to a sketch, and white charcoal pencils are useful for adding highlights.

PENCIL SHARPENERS AND LEAD POINTERS

All pencils, except for automatic mechanical pencils, have to be sharpened regularly. Wood-encased pencils require one sort of sharpener and leads held in a clutch holder require another.

The lead pointer, either electric or manual, sharpens all varieties of clutch drafting pencils and can produce needle-sharp points on all grades of graphite. All the pointers operate on the principle of rotating the pencil around a stationary grinder.

You can also sharpen leads on a sandpaper block, which is simply a small stack of sandpaper sheets fastened to a wooden handle.

FIGURE 5-9. An assortment of drafting and automatic pencils. *Photograph by Colleen Muscha.*

FIGURE 5-10. Sketching pencils. *Photograph by Colleen Muscha.*

FIGURE 5-11. Pencil sharpeners and lead pointers. *Photograph by Colleen Muscha.*

Ordinary school-room pencil sharpeners are satisfactory for wood-encased drawing and sketching pencils, although some very soft leads and carbon pencils don't fare so well in them; the leads tend to break. You can purchase mechanical pencil sharpeners that can be screwed down to a wall or a table as well as a suction variety that adheres to most surfaces quite well. An electric pencil sharpener is a luxury but many designers praise them to the skies. Electric pencil sharpeners come in both cord and battery-operated models.

Oddly enough, soft sketching pencils and carbon pencils sharpen best in the little plastic, hand-operated gadgets you can buy at the stationery stores. These are very inexpensive but the blade dulls quickly, so keep several on hand. Along with the usual utilitarian shapes, these sharpeners are often disguised as automobiles, Mickey Mouse characters, or spaceships. Staedtler manufactures small, efficient manual sharpeners made of metal.

ERASERS

It is said that there are designers who don't own erasers. Whoever they are, they must be either very deft or they must have an inexhaustable supply of paper. For most designers, erasing is part of the process. If you are ever inadvertently caught without an eraser on hand, don't forget that you can erase pencil lines with a ball made from bread. Bread was the original pencil erasing material. It was used for centuries before the development of all the types of erasers that are available today.

FIGURE 5-12. Erasers. *Photograph by Colleen Muscha.*

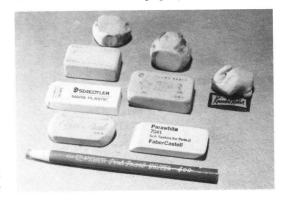

The two most popular erasers for costume design work are *putty* or *kneadable* erasers and *art* or *gum* erasers. Kneadable erasers can be moulded into any shape and are therefore good for small, detailed areas. They are soft and non-abrasive and are excellent for pencil and charcoal. Gum erasers crumble as they erase, never scratch, and almost never smudge. If you erase a large area, the crumbs you produce will make a prodigious mess. Gum erasers are particularly effective when you need to remove sketching lines from a painted sketch.

Some soft pencil erasers effectively erase graphite lines and smudge very little. Eberhard Faber's Pink Pearl is very soft and the Ruby is medium soft. Anything harder than a medium soft eraser may distress your paper surface. Plastic and ink erasers have limited use for designers. Not only is it virtually impossible to erase ink lines completely, but you could not do so without damaging the paper surface.

Pens and Inks

DRAWING PENS

The most common drawing pens combine a light-weight penholder made from aluminum, plastic, or wood and a flexible pen point which may come in a large variety of widths and types. The flexibility of the nib makes it possible for the pen line width to be varied according to the pressure placed on it by the hand. The crow quill point is extremely popular.

It takes some practice to use a drawing pen, to gauge how often it must be dipped in ink and how much pressure must be applied to maintain a steady line. (Speedball makes a fountain body for their reservoir top pens; this eliminates the need for periodic dipping.) There are advantages to using a drawing pen: it is far less temperamental than a technical pen and, for many designers, the flexible line width is highly desirable.

FIGURE 5-13. Liz Covey's sketch for Leontine in *13 Rue de L'Amour* for the Indiana Repertory Theatre. Technical pen and black ink on multimedia vellum. *Photograph by Frances Aronson.*

FIGURE 5-14. Michael J. Cesario's sketch for the Old Man in *The Chairs*. Ballpoint pen, colored pencil, watercolor wash, and enamel spray on illustration board. *Photograph by Frances Aronson.*

Some designers enjoy working with hand-cut bamboo pens. You purchase them with nibs already shaped but you can whittle the point to your own specifications with a pen knife.

FOUNTAIN PENS

Fountain pens are also made with flexible nibs which respond, although not as sensitively as drawing points, to pressure. Most are made for writing rather than drawing. Many fountain pens are designed with ink chambers that can be refilled, while others require replacement cartridges. Some are completely disposable.

TECHNICAL OR DRAFTING PENS

These pens are precision instruments designed specifically for drafting and line reduction techniques, and they are widely used for drawing. They have tubular points and cartridge ink-reservoir assemblies.

There are nine internationally recognized line widths—intended for standardized line reduction—available in all the brands. These are expressed in millimeters from smallest to largest: 0.13, 0.18, 0.25, 0.35, 0.5, 0.7, 1.0, 1.4, 2.0.

Somewhere on each nib package you will find the standardized size designations, although the individual manufacturers each market pens under their own size designations, these sizes being usually color coded somewhere on the pen casing. And, of course, each manufacturer offers more than the nine standardized nib sizes. So try not to be confused when you realize that a Castell T.G. size 3×0 is actually a finer point than a Rapidograph size 5×0. You can, if you search through the fine print, find the exact point size expressed in millimeters. Good point size choices for new users of technical pens are 0.35mm, 0.7mm, and 1.0mm.

Technical pens have either stainless steel points or jewel (sapphire) points. The jewel points are almost three times the price of the stainless steel points but they last much, much longer.

Technical pens can be temperamental and they require constant care and careful usage in order to function smoothly. Neglected or ill-used pens dry up, clog, and leak. You must always replace the pen's cap firmly after use. When starting to write, shake the pen gently in a horizontal direction, taking great care that this shaking does not occur anywhere near your

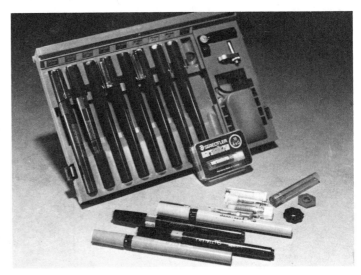

FIGURE 5-15. An assortment of technical pens. *Photograph by Colleen Muscha.*

drawing. Always draw at an angle of about 80 degrees to the horizontal and always draw in the direction of the line. Technical pens must be disassembled for cleaning, and the parts must be held under cool running water. Soak the parts periodically in water or in a commercial cleaning solution. The most effective way to clean technical pens is in a sonic cleaner with commercial cleaning solution.

There are many inexpensive technical pens on the market that require less care than the traditional types. Some of them use disposable ink cartridges, and others are completely disposable when the ink is gone.

INKS

Any brand or color, waterproof or nonwaterproof drawing ink works with a dip drawing pen. Fountain pens require inks formulated especially for them; be sure the bottle says, "fountain pen ink." Special inks are made for technical pens, although some designers feel that certain fountain pen inks work best in technical pens and clog less frequently.

Many brands and types of ink are available for technical pens; most are waterproof but some are not. These inks come in various color assortments. Black and white are opaque, and colors are, in general, translucent. Gold and silver inks are available, but the pen should be cleaned immediately after using them to prevent clogging. If the company that manufactures the technical pen you use also makes ink, it might be safest to use that one.

Any of the inks may be applied with a brush. They tend to mix and behave much like liquid watercolors, although the waterproof varieties repel other paints when dry.

FELT AND NYLON TIP PENS

There are many different brands and styles of felt and nylon tip pens on the market; most are nonrefillable. The convenience of using these pens and the fact that they require so little care often outweighs their expense and the rapidity with which they run out of ink. The inks are waterbase and may be waterproof or nonwaterproof.

FIGURE 5-16. An assortment of inks. *Photograph by Colleen Muscha.*

The line produced by felt and nylon tip pens is neither as flexible as the line you can get with a drawing or fountain pen nor as precise as a technical pen line.

DON'T OVERDO PEN AND INK LINES ON COSTUME SKETCHES

Pen and ink lines can add detail and clarity to costume sketches. However, a very heavy line, particularly if it is outlining a figure and a garment, can be misleading. Costumes on the stage are not surrounded by black outlines and must manage to stand out from the scenic background by means of color, fabric choice, and skillful use of the design elements. Keep pen lines light so you can judge what the costume will look like.

Papers and Boards

Costume designers seldom feel bound to traditional paper choices. They will apply watercolor to charcoal papers, gouache to tracing papers, and colored markers to anything. Sometimes these experiments have questionable results, but other times they are very successful. The following remarks about artists' paper and boards tend to be traditional in nature in order to give you an idea of how these materials may normally be expected to behave. Don't read them as rules or curbs to ingenuity.

PAPER WEIGHTS AND TOOTH

The number that expresses paper weight designates the weight of a standard sized ream of that paper. A ream may consist of 480 or 500 sheets; usually drawing or watercolor paper comes in reams of 480 sheets and bond or typing paper in 500 sheet reams.

Some papers are inherently heavier than others. A 70 pound watercolor paper is light

weight and a 140 pound watercolor paper is moderately heavy. In drawing papers, the light range is around 16 pounds, medium 32 pounds, and heavy 80 pounds.

Although you will probably purchase paper by how it feels to your fingers and how it reacts to your paints and other color media, it's a good idea to know the approximate weights of your favorite papers so you can save time shopping and, when it's necessary, order paper by mail.

Tooth refers to the surface textures of artists' papers. There are no standardized designations for tooth. A paper that "has tooth" possesses a surface texture and one that has little or no tooth is smooth.

FIGURE 5-17. Sketch by Ann Wallace for Mrs. Peachum in Brecht's *Threepenny Opera*. Felt pen and gouache on newspaper background. *Photograph by Frances Aronson.*

PAD SIZES

Most papers can be bought in pads with sheets either bound together or fastened in a wire spiral holder. The following is a list of normal pad sizes; specific sizes will vary slightly from brand to brand. These sizes are expressed in inches.

8½ × 11	12 × 18 (or 19)
9 × 12	14 × 17
11 × 14	18 (or 19) × 24

COLORED PAPERS

White or slightly off-white paper is always acceptable for costume sketches, but there will be times when you want to work on other colors as backgrounds. Creams, buffs, and greys are often particularly effective. Think twice before you put sketches on bright orange or green papers, and make sure your reasons for doing so are consistent with the production scheme and the effect you wish to achieve. Also beware of using dark papers since it's difficult to indicate detail accurately and have the costume resemble what it's going to look like on stage. Besides being difficult to read, sketches on dark papers are almost impossible to photocopy (a consideration which is discussed on page 122). When you work on dark papers you will usually need to add detail in a white medium: ink, pencil, or paint.

FIGURE 5-18. Colleen Muscha's sketch for Cadmus in *The Bacchae*. Watercolor and ink on watercolor paper. *Photograph by Colleen Muscha.*

GENERAL DRAWING PAPERS

All the inexpensive papers normally used for preliminary and rough sketching, as well as for research sketching, are grouped together under this heading.

Newsprint is the cheapest and most fragile of the general drawing papers and is only suitable for very rough and temporary work. It is soft and pulpy and appears in a variety of warm and cool beige tones. The surface is most appropriate to soft pencil and charcoal. A hard pencil or pen may tear the surface, and ink from felt tip markers or pens will spread. Newsprint is available in pads, sheets, and rolls and can often be bought for a very low price as end rolls from newspaper offices.

White *butcher paper* is available from craft suppliers in 36″ wide rolls. It is considerably stronger than newsprint and has a smooth, slightly hard surface. It is excellent for soft pencils, crayons, markers, inks, and gouache.

Layout papers, available in pads and on rolls, come in various weights and surface finishes. Layout is very white and normally accepts markers, pencil, charcoal, pen, and ink. Layout paper is translucent, and the sixteen-pound weight can be used for some tracing without the aid of a light board.

Most art supply shops carry a large selection of *drawing* and *sketching papers.* There are many weights and many surfaces, and you will ultimately make your choice by the way the paper feels to you. Note what is said on the front of the pad about the paper surface. Some are especially treated to accept certain media, and this information can help guide your choice.

CHARCOAL AND PASTEL PAPERS

Charcoal and pastel papers come in a wide variety of colors and qualities, in pads and by the sheet. All of them have some tooth to catch and hold color material from the charcoal or pastel stick as it passes over the surface. Most charcoal and pastel papers are available in 19″ x 25″ sheets, as well as in rolls.

TRACING PAPER AND VELLUM

Tracing paper is thin and translucent. It has a dry, crackling surface and tends to shrink up in humid conditions. Many weights and qualities of tracing papers are available, in pads and on rolls. Experiment with different papers until you find one that pleases you.

Vellum is tracing paper that has been treated with oil, causing the surface to be

FIGURE 5-19. Watercolor sketch by Rosemary Ingham for Caliban in Shakespeare's *The Tempest* at the Utah Shakespearean Festival. *Photograph by Rosemary Ingham.*

FIGURE 5-20. Tracing papers and acetate. *Photograph by Colleen Muscha.*

smoother and more substantial. Vellum is some-what more opaque than tracing paper but much less susceptible to humidity. It comes in three weights: medium, heavyweight, and extra heavy. Vellum is a sturdy durable paper, excellent for tracing costume research.

When you are showing preliminary sketches in ink or pencil on tracing paper or vellum, be sure to bring along a sheet of white paper to lay under the sketches; otherwise they may be difficult to read.

TRANSFER PAPERS

You will often need to transfer, rather than redraw, a sketch from one paper to another. This is easily done with a piece of transfer paper which acts just like the carbon sheet in multiple copy forms. Some transfer papers are coated with graphite and others an oily material not unlike that on fabric tracing papers. Both types of transfer papers leave enough oil on the copy lines to repel watercolor. It is always a good idea to press down as lightly as possible when you are making a transfer.

WATERCOLOR PAPERS

Watercolor paper is the most expensive paper regularly used by costume designers. Although every designer should experiment with many different kinds of watercolor paper, their surfaces and qualities, it is a good idea to find a middle-priced paper that satisfies you; then stick to it for the bulk of your work. Costume designs are subject to change and alteration until the production is up and running, and there is no doubt that it's easier to discard sketches if they were painted on modestly priced paper rather than on the most expensive paper.

As stated earlier, the normal weight range for watercolor paper is from 70 to 140 pounds, with very heavy weight paper at 300 pounds. A 90-pound paper is suitable for costume sketches which will be mounted or matted. A 140-pound paper is stiff enough to stand without mounting.

FIGURE 5-21. Watercolor papers and Bristol board. *Photograph by Colleen Muscha*.

Watercolor paper surface texture, or tooth, comes in three general grades: *hot press* (H.P.), which is relatively smooth; *cold press* (C.P.), which is a medium texture; and *rough* (R.), which is heavy texture.

Watercolor paper is available in pads, sheets (usually 22″ x 30″), and blocks. Sheets are less expensive than blocks, and you can cut them to whatever sizes you need. If you would like to have a soft torn edge rather than a sharp cut edge on your watercolor paper, put a straight edge down on the paper, and, with a pointed brush, paint a thin line of clear water along the edge. Give the water a few moments to be absorbed by the paper, then carefully fold and tear.

Watercolor paper tends to curl and wrinkle when you've painted on it. Watercolorists wet and stretch each sheet of paper, tape it down, and allow it to dry completely before they begin to paint. The advantage of watercolor paper sold in blocks is that it is already stretched and dried. You can paint on the top sheet of paper, let your work dry, then peel off that sheet.

Many of you will find you don't have time to stretch individual sheets of watercolor paper before you begin to work, and that watercolor blocks are too expensive for regular use. A relatively quick method to reduce the tendency of watercolor paper to warp and curl is to thoroughly wet *both sides* of the sheet by holding it under running water or by sponging it gently with a soft natural sponge dipped in water. Be careful not to scrub the paper's surface. Hang it up to drip dry. Used in a shower or bathtub, a clothespin clipped to a hanger, holding the paper by a corner, is a good hanging device. Do not put it in the sun to dry. Once the paper is dry, which takes less than an hour, it will remain relatively flat while you are working on it and, in addition, the surface will be softer and accept paint more readily.

BRISTOL BOARDS

Bristol boards are composed of lightweight sheets of permanently layered card stock. One to five layers are available; two and three are most widely used.

There are two general surfaces available: the kid or medium surface that is matte finish and slightly rough and the plate or high surface which is smooth and glossy. The kid surface will accept a wide variety of media: pencil, ink, dry brush, washes, acrylics, and markers; the plate surface is suitable for pencil or fine pen work.

Good bristol board will take a great deal of abuse. If you are careful, you can even scrape off ink or gouache with a knife or razor blade. It is available in single sheets or standard sized pads. Bristol is usually white or cream colored, but is sometimes available in other colors.

ILLUSTRATION BOARD

Illustration board is widely used for costume sketches. It is composed of a high-quality rag paper mounted on a relatively thick cardboard back which provides an excellent surface for watercolor and pen and ink, as well as several other mediums.

There are three general grades of illustration board: student grade, commercial grade, and high grade. The commercial grade is recommended for costume sketches.

Surfaces will be designated in the same manner as watercolor papers: hot press (smooth), cold press (medium texture), and rough (heavy texture). A good all-purpose board is Bainbridge 90-R (that is, a 90-pound paper on cardboard with a heavy surface texture) which comes in 20″ × 30″ and 30″ × 40″ sheets.

POSTER AND RAILROAD BOARD

Poster (showcard) board is made of thin white or colored papers mounted on lightweight, inexpensive cardboard. It comes in 28″ × 44″ sheets. The surface has an oily quality that is incompatible with most water-based media. Poster board is primarily useful for mounting sketches which you have done on lightweight papers.

Railroad board is similar. It is 6 ply board, the same on both sides, and is usually available in 22″ × 28″ sheets. Railroad board is less expensive than poster board.

MAT BOARDS

Art shop customers who don't know the difference sometimes mistake mat board (mounting card) for illustration board. It is made in a similar fashion with colored papers mounted on cardboard. The papers that are used, however, are thin and soft and will absorb water color and gouache, producing a dull and generally lifeless sketch. Acrylic paints, because they dry rapidly, work relatively well on mat board. Mat board is the material of choice for mounting and for framing, subjects that will be discussed later in this chapter.

PROTECTIVE PAPERS

It is always a good idea to cover your final sketches with some protective paper before you go shopping and drop them in the snow or before they go into the shop and have coffee spilled on them. Clear acetate in .003 or .005 thicknesses, available in sheets and rolls, makes a good covering. Plastic wrap, sold in supermarkets for food storage, is a cheap satisfactory substitute. If you are concerned about preserving your sketches, if you mount or mat them, be sure to use acid-free mat board *and* remove all acetate and plastic coverings before storing them.

RICE PAPERS

Many designers have, at one time or another, enjoyed experimenting with sketches on Japanese rice paper. There are many types, qualities, and textures. Some have very apparent fibers and others have been impregnated with wax to give the sheet translucence. Sumi papers are slightly more refined than ordinary rice papers and are made especially for printing. The soft, fibrous

FIGURE 5-22. Sketch by David Murin for the
Manhattan Theatre Club's production of
Translations by Brian Friel. Felt-tip pen,
watercolor, and marker spray on rice paper.
Photograph by Frances Aronson.

surfaces of all these papers make them unsuitable
for detailed pen work, but they are excellent for
loose brush strokes.

FROSTED OR MATTE ACETATE

Frosted or matte acetate is designed specifically
for pen and ink drawings that are to be reproduced and is not often used for costume
sketches. Some of the illustrations in this book
were prepared for the camera on frosted or
matte acetate. A similar version of the same
surface is available as *plastic vellum* or *multi-
medium vellum* (neither should be confused
with tracing paper vellum). Multi-media vellum will accept markers, pastels, and oils as well
as inks.

FIGURE 5-23. X-Acto knife blades and holders.
Photograph by Colleen Muscha.

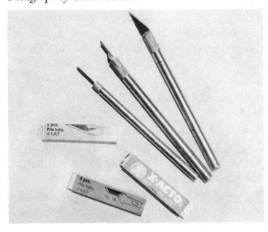

To correct ink mistakes on acetate or plastic vellum, use a sharp X-Acto knife and scratch away the ink. Remove other media carefully with a hard eraser.

Color Media

The color on costume sketches may be paints, colored inks or markers, colored pencils, or pastels. Many designers combine media for specific effects. In order to use any color medium effectively, it is helpful to know something about its composition and characteristics so that you can predict what behavior might be expected from it.

PAINTS

There are three constituents in all paints:

1. colored pigment particles;
2. the medium that carries the particles; and
3. a diluent, normally water or turpentine.

The first pigments came from the earth, from chalk, and from burnt pieces of wood. Somewhere between 2000 and 1000 BC, the Egyptians discovered mineral pigments: azurite, malachite, cinnabar, and white made from lead. The ancient Greeks added indigo, a dye, and a green called verdigris which they produced by the controlled corrosion of copper plates. The thirteenth and fourteenth centuries brought a good many new pigments to the painter's palette, and the nineteenth and twentieth centuries saw the advent of synthetic pigments developed from complex technological processes involving metals and petroleum.

Nowadays art supply stores display a wide variety of paints, ready mixed and suitable for immediate application. It's hard to realize that a century ago painters had to combine their own pigments and mediums, a tedious and time-consuming process.

OIL PAINTS

Oil paints consist of pigments in media of linseed, poppy, or walnut oils. The diluent is turpentine. Oil paints dry slowly and the dried paint takes on a particularly rich glow. The long drying time makes oil paints generally unsuitable for any design work, and costume designers almost never use them.

WATERCOLORS

Watercolors are a common color medium for costume sketches. Watercolor is made by combining very finely ground pigment with gum arabic. The gum dissolves readily in water, the diluent, and adheres firmly to paper. Most modern day watercolors also contain other additives that effect the paint's behavior.

Watercolors are transparent, a characteristic which allows the paper under the paint to play an important role in the total effect of the sketch. When you are using only watercolor, you must work from the lightest to the darkest tones.

You may choose watercolors in tubes, cakes, and jars. Tube watercolors have the consistency of a thick custard. Watercolor cakes are dry and solid, and jar water colors are liquid. Both tube and cake colors are generally available in "artist" and "student" grades with the student grade being the less expensive of the two. Insofar as your pocketbook will allow, try to always purchase artist grade watercolors; the hues and the performance are infinitely superior.

Dozens of colors are available in watercolor tubes and cakes—many more than you will ever use. Over time you will discover which colors suit your own color sense. Here are nine colors that provide a good basic palette. (See Figure 4–10, Mixing paint, in Chapter 4, and Plates #1 and #2 in the color photographs.)

cadmium red	alizarin crimson
cadmium yellow, medium	lemon yellow
ultramarine blue	cerulean blue
Hooker's green	
Payne's gray	
magenta	

FIGURES 5-24 and 5-25. Sketches by Lowell Detweiler for *Fables* at Central City Opera. Notice that the garments on the right go over those on the left. The figure on the right is created by an overlay rendered in watercolor and colored pencil on tracing paper. *Photographs by Frances Aronson.*

Liquid watercolors produce clear intense colors, often more brilliant than anything from a tube or cake. Most are available in bottles with eyedroppers. Create different color values by varying the amount of water mixed with the liquid color. Bleedproof, opaque whites are also available. Liquid watercolors mix differently with each other than do tube or cake watercolors. Experiment by mixing a sample color wheel before you begin to work on a sketch.

WATERCOLOR TECHNIQUES

There are three fundamental watercolor techniques: *wet on dry, wet into wet,* and *dry on dry.* All of these techniques aid costume designers as they strive to represent the sheen of satin, the depth of velvet, the airiness of chiffon, and the weight of stage jewelry.

Watercolor is normally laid on the paper in successive layers and the painting develops from the lightest to the darkest values. A largish expanse of watercolor is called a *wash,* which may

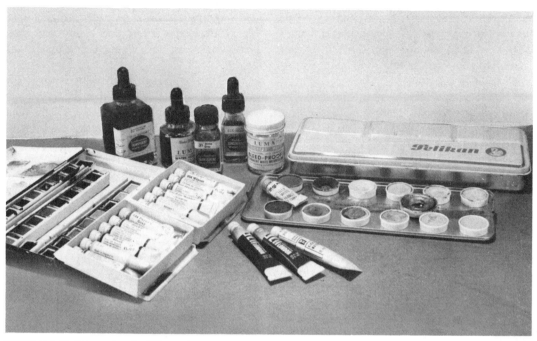

FIGURE 5-26. Watercolors in different forms. *Photograph by Colleen Muscha.*

be applied wet on dry or wet into wet. A *flat wash* is a single color; a *graduated wash* is made up of different values of the same color; and a *varigated wash* is of different colors. All washes should be applied and allowed to dry before any next step is taken. Overworking a wash can be disastrous.

Line and wash watercolor sketches are particularly suitable for representing costumes. Lines are used to draw in major shapes and features while washes amplify or unify the whole. The lines may precede the wash or be imposed over it and done with either a brush or a pen.

Other methods of applying watercolor are *stippling, scumbling,* and *dry brush application.* Stippling is putting dots of color on the paper, oftentimes on top of a dried wash. Scumbling is the application of pigment with a slight scrubbing motion. Dry brush application uses a minimum of water so the paint goes on in little feathery strokes. Practice these methods and see if you can put them to use when representing print cloth, pile textures, and fur.

Brushes are not the only vehicles for putting paint on paper. You can use small natural sponges to apply a watercolor wash and to overpaint texture in a dry on dry manner. You can also create texture in a fine spatter by scraping a kitchen knife over a toothbrush saturated with paint.

Sometimes it's necessary to completely mask off an area in the sketch. You can make an effective mask with masking tape or frisket paper, cut to size and shape, and simply stuck onto the paper. Or you can use a substance called liquid frisket, which is painted onto the paper and, when dry, seals off the area it covers. Dry frisket has a rubbery texture, like latex, and can be rolled off with a finger or eraser. If you rub your brush on a damp cake of soap before dipping it into the liquid frisket, the frisket will wash off easily when you are finished.

If, once the sketch is dry, you want to reduce the amount of color in certain places, you can do so by gently scrubbing up the excess with a sponge, blotting paper, or wad of tissues dipped in clean water. You can also scratch in highlights with a sharp-pointed knife or razor blade, working very carefully so as not to damage the surface of the paper.

GOUACHE

Gouache is also called *opaque watercolor* and *designer color*. It is most commonly available in tubes of custard-consistency paint. Tempera and poster paints are crude types of gouache prepared in liquid form and sold in jars. The pigment in gouache is coarser than the pigment in watercolor. The medium is the same, gum arabic, but it is extended with white pigment which makes the paint opaque. Dried gouache is less luminous than watercolor and has a denser surface quality. The colors are slightly chalky. Gouache is used extensively for commercial illustration, particularly for work that requires areas of flat color

FIGURE 5-27. Sketch by Ann Wallace for Nagg and Nell in Samuel Beckett's *Endgame*. Colored pencil and gouache. *Photograph by Frances Aronson.*

that will reproduce well. Gouache is highly suitable for detailed painting and is the paint most commonly used by commercial artists in air brushes.

The biggest difference between using gouache and watercolor is that, because of its opacity, gouache allows you to lay a light value over a dark value. Opaque watercolor washes are generally laid down in a middle value from which you can go both lighter and darker. A good gouache wash depends upon getting the correct consistency of paint with water. Always try your mixture before you put the wash on your sketch. Remember also that wet gouache is darker than the color will be when it's dry. If your paint lightens up too much as it dries, don't apply a second layer until the first is quite dry.

WATERCOLOR AND GOUACHE

Since watercolor and gouache contain the same medium the two paints may be used together and very often are. Many costume designers use watercolor for washes and gouache for highlights and details. Transparent watercolor technique is difficult to master completely, and the judicious assistance of opaque water colors, especially white, can simplify the process a good deal. There is nothing, however, to equal the pride you will feel when you display a delicate watercolor sketch with gleaming highlights that emanate from the paper and not from a jar or tube of opaque white.

ACRYLIC PAINT

Acrylic is the common name for a paint that combines natural and synthetic pigments with a polymerized resin binder, usually acrylic, sometimes polyvinyl acetate (PVA). The common diluent is water. Acrylics came on the market in the United States in the 1950's, although the resins were available twenty years earlier, and many artists were mixing their own paints. PVA based colors became available in the 1960's. PVA colors are less reliable and permanent than acrylic based colors.

FIGURE 5-28. Watercolor sketch for
Othello by Colleen Muscha for the Dallas
Shakespeare Festival. *Photograph by Colleen
Muscha.*

FIGURE 5-29. Acrylic paints and additives.
Photograph by Colleen Muscha.

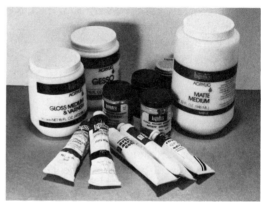

Acrylic paint dries as fast as the water in the mixture evaporates, which occurs in minutes because the porous structure of the paint allows for quick and complete evaporation. The acrylic medium is a strong adhesive that binds the paint to a great many surfaces. As a matter of fact, acrylics can be used on all surfaces except oil-based or emulsion-based grounds.

You can use acrylic paint like oil paint *and* like watercolor. You can apply it in thick layers to canvas or board with a palette knife and as a delicate wash on watercolor paper. All acrylic surfaces, when dry, are waterproof.

You can purchase acrylic paint in tubes and in jars; in both cases the paint is quite thick. In its original state it is opaque, but it can be diluted with water to transparency. Unadulterated acrylic paint in tubes dries with a low sheen while most acrylic paint in jars dries with a matte finish.

There are various additives on the market to mix with acrylic paint. Each one has a different effect on the paint's behavior. The addition of *polymer medium* provides transparency and a glaze to the finish; a *matte medium* adds both transparency and a matte surface; *modeling paste* added to the paint gives it a putty-like texture used when an artist is working the acrylic as impasto; *retarding medium* slows the drying time of the paint without changing its color; *gel medium* adds a heavy gloss finish and also retards drying; and *gesso* is a white primer which adheres to virtually all surfaces and provides a good ground for acrylic paint.

If acrylic paint is being used like oil paint, oil paint brushes are suitable; if like watercolors, watercolor brushes are the proper choice. Brushes can be cleaned with water but it must be done quickly since the paint dries so rapidly. If, by accident, a brush full of acrylic paint does harden, it can be reclaimed by soaking it in methylated spirits (ordinary or ethyl alcohol denatured with methanol) for 24 hours.

Acrylic paint has many advantages. For costume designers, it not only combines many good features of watercolor and gouache but also offers the waterproof feature which makes overpainting and the addition of detail so uncomplicated. In general, inexperienced designers find acrylic paint easier to handle than either watercolor or gouache. On the other hand, there is a certain plastic quality to the colors and few people can achieve the expressive subtleties with acrylic paint that they can with watercolor.

MARKERS

Felt composition, nylon, and fiber-tipped markers have come close to revolutionizing commercial artwork and have had a great effect on theatre design sketching as well. Markers dispense either solvent-based (permanent) inks or water-based (nonpermanent) inks of great brilliance. Water-based markers are the safest to use. Solvent-based markers that contain ethyl alcohol are safer than those based in other solvents. Read labels and use all solvent-based markers with adequate ventilation. Most brands

offer at least three nib styles: a flat angled nib, two degrees of points, and a chisel shape. Brush-type markers are also available. Markers come in a wide variety of colors.

The great advantage of using markers is that they eliminate the need for brushes, pots of water, and mixing pans. You can pick one up and apply it with no advance preparation, and it dries instantly. The main disadvantage lies in the inability to mix colors (although a certain amount of mixing can be done by applying one color over another). This means you have to buy lots of markers and, even then, accept the fact that many colors are simply impossible to achieve with markers.

Markers are also available in metallic colors, gold, silver, and bronze in both fat and thin varieties.

Markers are especially useful for quick sketches, thumbnails, and the presentation of color ideas. They are also useful in combination with acrylic paint and ink. Markers and watercolor or gouache are not always compatible.

When you're using markers it's important that you use a paper with a suitable surface in order to discourage bleed-through and spreading. Many layout papers and some drawing papers are available with surfaces specially treated

FIGURE 5-30. A variety of markers.
Photograph by Colleen Muscha.

FIGURE 5-31. Colleen Muscha's sketch for Joe in David Mamet's *Lakeboat*. Produced at the Milwaukee Repertory Theater's Court Street Theatre. Drawing pen and brush in gray inks.*Photograph by Frances Aronson.*

to accept markers. This information will be on the pad cover.

COLORED INKS

You can use colored inks the same way you use liquid watercolors, thinning them with water to alter value. The major difference is that most inks contain shellac, are waterproof, and therefore permanent when dry. Colored inks are especially effective in line and wash sketches. Ink types and brands were discussed earlier.

PASTELS

Sometimes, for a change of pace or for a particular effect, it's interesting to use a medium that is not commonly used for costume sketches. Pastels may be just the thing.

Pastels are combinations of powdered pigments with just enough gum or resin to bind them. They come in sticks that are either round or square; the square ones are recommended because they won't roll off your drawing surface. Pastel pencils which may be sharpened and used for fine detail are also available.

A pastel sketch combines the qualities of both drawing and painting. Colors are pure and fresh and can be worked into a variety of surface techniques. If you would like to study the pos-

FIGURE 5-32. Pastel sticks, pastel pencils, and charcoal. *Photograph by Colleen Muscha.*

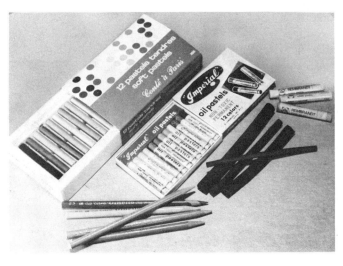

sibilities of pastels, take a look at the pastel work of the following artists: Quentin de la Tour (1704–88), Perronneau (1715–83), Chardin (1699–1779), Degas (1843–1917), and Mary Cassatt (1845–1926). You may well find yourself inspired to experiment with this medium which is often underrated and thought of as best suited for elementary school children.

Pastels are available in soft, medium, or hard varieties; they are rated according to the amount of gum in the sticks. The most brilliant colors come from the softest sticks. There are about 600 colors manufactured in pastel sticks, far more than you will ever need. A 24-color set will allow you to achieve a good deal of subtle color mixing on the page; a 48-stick set is absolutely sufficient.

Pastel costume sketches must be "fixed" in order to prevent them from smudging as they are handled. Most fixatives darken color slightly and will probably add a faint shine to the work. Two types of fixatives are available: one provides a permanent protective finish, and one is called "workable," meaning you can continue to work on the sketch on top of the fixative. *All fixative sprays contain toxic solvents. Read labels and take all necessary precautions to reduce risks to yourself and others.*

Pastel sketches should be done on the proper paper and are often especially effective on tinted papers: grays, fawns, and buffs. You may also be interested in combining pastels with watercolor or gouache.

CHARCOAL

Except for occasional rough sketches, you will seldom use charcoal in costume work except for special effects. Nevertheless, it never hurts to know something about every possible medium. If you would like to see an especially beautiful charcoal sketch, look at James McNeill Whistler's *Maude Reading.*

Charcoal is essentially burnt wood. It is available in three forms. *Stick* or *vine charcoal* is usually thin, burnt willow twigs. It is very soft and crumbly and will brush off readily. *Compressed charcoal* is burnt wood combined with a medium and formed into round or squared sticks. It is much more permanent than stick charcoal. A thin core of charcoal may also be encased in wood as a *charcoal pencil.* These are, of course, less messy to use but the range of strokes possible with them is limited. The charcoal core in pencils is available in various hardnesses. For the best results with charcoal sketches, use paper that is intended for pastels and charcoal.

COLORED PENCILS

Colored pencils are used most often in costume sketches for detail work. Occasionally a particular project might be effectively executed wholly in colored pencil, particularly light colored costumes that will be built in soft, airy fabrics.

There are two kinds of colored pencils: waterproof and nonwaterproof. The colored leads in waterproof pencils are made from a mixture of chemical pigment and kaolin and are available in a wide range of colors. The leads are relatively hard and can be sharpened into good points for drawing and for detail work. Color mixing is achieved by working one color on top of another.

FIGURE 5-33. Colored pencils. *Photograph by Colleen Muscha.*

Nonwaterproof colored pencils or watercolor pencils have soft leads. A brush full of water drawn over a line on the paper will produce a wash effect that can be very handsome.

Brushes

Good brushes are frightfully expensive and inexpensive brushes are almost always unsatisfactory in the long run. Always purchase the very best brushes you can afford; take excellent care of them and they will last for many years.

The best brushes to use with water-based pigments are called *sable*. Modern, modestly priced sable brushes are made from weasel hairs. Top quality, expensive red sable brushes are made from the tail hairs of the Siberian mink. Sable brush hairs can carry a lot of pigment from palette to paper for washes. The hairs cling together and maintain the brush shape. If they are well cared for, sable brushes will last for many years and are well worth the initial investment.

Brushes made from squirrel, bear, or pony hairs are much less expensive but much less satisfactory. It is frustrating to use brushes which hold too little paint to complete a stroke and from which hairs tend to stick out at odd angles, to say nothing of their infuriating tendency to shed hairs at the most inopportune times.

If you must purchase inexpensive brushes, try one of the white synthetic filament varieties. These brushes are soft and resilient and behave surprisingly well.

Brushes made from ox and hog hair are quite stiff and suitable for oil based pigments and acrylic paint used like oils.

Brushes come in a variety of shapes: pointed, round, flat, chisel, and fan. Pointed brushes make clean-edged strokes and are excellent for detail work. Round brushes are especially good for carrying pigment and doing washes. You can make broad single strokes with a flat brush, and the chisel shape is made especially for lettering, although it is also useful for stripes and texture on cloth. The fan brush is often called a blending brush and is used for soft details.

FIGURE 5-34. An assortment of brushes. *Photograph by Colleen Muscha.*

A typical size range for watercolor brushes is from 000 (the smallest) to 14. If you are just beginning, a good selection might be: pointed sables, numbers 2, 6, 10; round sable, number 12; and flat sable, number 14. If economy is necessary, substitute synthetic filament for the round and flat brushes. If extreme economy is called for, purchase all sizes and types in synthetic filament and plan to replace them with sable one at a time.

CLEANING BRUSHES

While you are painting, never leave brushes standing head down in water for long or you will harm their shape. Rinse the brush vigorously in a large quantity of water after each use and either return it to the brush container or lay it on paper toweling. Clean all brushes thoroughly immediately after each painting session, especially when you are using acrylic paint.

All brushes that are used with water-based paint should be washed with soap (*not* detergent) and cold water. Never use hot water because it will soften the glue that is used to hold the brush hairs in place and greatly shorten the life of the brush. Work up a gentle lather in the palm of your hand to remove all traces of pigment and rinse under running water. Shake excess water from the brushes, reshape the heads with your fingers and stand the brushes upright in a glass or jar to dry. Between periods of painting, it is all right to leave the brushes upright and in the open. If, however, they are to go unused for a long period of time, store them in a flat box with a mothball or two for added protection.

Tapes and Adhesives

Masking tape has innumerable uses. Some have already been mentioned: to mask off areas of a sketch, to help organize swatches. You will probably also use masking tape to fasten your sketch

FIGURE 5-35. Adhesives, tapes, and staplers. *Photograph by Colleen Muscha.*

to the drawing surface while you are working and to mount the sketch once it is complete.

There are actually two sorts of tape that are commonly referred to as masking tape. One is properly called drafting tape. It's thinner than actual masking tape, and slightly less sticky. It is especially designed to hold drawings, tracings, and blueprints to drawing surfaces and it lifts off of most surfaces without harm. Masking tape is a bit thicker and will adhere to more surfaces. Costume designers tend to use these two tapes interchangeably.

Scotch Magic Transparent Tape has two excellent properties combined: you can see through it and you can write on it. It is excellent for joining two pieces of paper together, almost invisibly, and irreplaceable for mocking up wig and beard patterns with plastic wrap.

Brown paper tape is the cheapest and most permanent tape for mounting and covering sketches. It comes in various widths and in both a self-adhesive variety and one that has to be moistened. If you don't enjoy licking the tape yourself, you can put a sponge in a shallow bowl, fill it with water until the sponge is saturated and a bit of water stands in the bottom of the bowl, and then pass the strips of tape over the sponge.

Rubber cement is almost as indispensible to costume designers as masking tape. Use it to mount paper onto cardboard and to attach swatches and trim to the finished sketch. It is a latex-based adhesive that is suitable for all light-weight boards and papers. Rubber cement comes in one-coat and two-coat varieties; the two-coat acts as a contact cement. Purchase a can of thinner since the adhesive tends to get too thick after a while. A rubber cement dispenser with a brush is very handy.

Rubber cement tape is an interesting and useful product. It comes with a paper backing that peels off, leaving a thin layer of adhesive.

White glue has many uses in the costume shop but not so many in the costume designer's studio. It is not the best adhesive with which to bond paper to card or to attach swatches to sketches. Papers mounted with white glue tend to buckle and wrinkle, and the glue may even show through. White glue, even when set up, may soften in warm, humid conditions and should never be considered permanent.

Miscellaneous Equipment

There is no end to the amount of equipment a costume designer can collect and use, all of it contributing in some way to getting the work done more efficiently. Once you own the basics, start saving for the treats and don't forget to let your friends and family members know what you're saving for so they can surprise you with useful gifts on holidays. What follows may help you get started on what may prove to be a lifetime of acquisition.

STAPLER

Any desk model stapling machine is adequate for tacking papers together or for fastening swatches to sketches. Keep a good supply of staples on hand and be sure to have a staple remover nearby so you won't be tempted to remove staples with your fingernail.

PAPER CUTTER

Although most art supply stores have paper cutters available for cutting your boards and papers, it is certainly convenient to have one of your own. You should not consider anything smaller than a 24″ cutter. Beware of second-hand paper cutters and test carefully before you buy. A paper cutter that doesn't cut absolutely straight is worse than none at all.

RULERS

A metal ruler will serve you both for measuring and as a straight edge for drawing lines and cutting cardboard. Twenty-four inch metal rulers

FIGURE 5-36. Paper cutter. *Photograph by Colleen Muscha.*

are particularly handy. Choose a metal ruler with a cork bottom which raises the metal edge up off the paper and prevents smudging when you use it for drawing lines. If your ruler doesn't have a cork strip, tape pennies to one side of the ruler you have to get the same effect. Plastic, see-through rulers are also very useful when you are drawing.

TRACING TABLE

Tracing tables, also called light tables or light boxes, are somewhat expensive but may be well

worth the investment if you draw slowly and are often under pressure to work quickly. A tracing table consists of a box frame, either wood or metal, a glass top, usually frosted, and fluorescent tubes inserted under the glass. The drawing to be traced is laid on the glass, and the paper on which the tracing will be drawn is placed on top of that. When the light is turned on, the lines are clearly illuminated and you can trace them onto the fresh paper with ease and accuracy. A tracing table can be a great boon when you have several drawings to redo and a short time in which to do them. It is also a helpful device for designers who use stock figures.

If you're handy with tools you can build a light table for a fraction of the cost of a commercially manufactured one. Make sure you use fluorescent fixtures because incandescent bulbs will heat up the glass so much you can't work on it.

You can create a spur-of-the-moment light table by turning a square or rectangular glass baking dish upside down over a low wattage light bulb set in a small lamp or a dime store fixture. Prop the dish up on books or bricks. The dish will eventually get too hot to work on but,

FIGURE 5-37. Tracing table. *Photograph by Colleen Muscha.*

in the meantime, you can get lots of emergency tracing done.

MAGNIFYING GLASS, REDUCING GLASS, AND MIRROR

Costume designers often find that their thumbnail sketches are better and more lively than their larger, finished sketches. Something happens in the process of enlarging the figure that makes it stiff and may even throw off its proportions. If you sometimes have this difficulty, you may find a magnifying glass a useful tool. Study the pleasing proportions in the preliminary sketch while you enlarge it by moving the glass further away from the sketch. What you see may help you to reinterpret the thumbnail accurately on a larger scale.

You may also find a magnifying glass helpful when you are examining problem areas in the sketch. Basic drawing and design problems often reveal themselves when you look at them magnified.

Examine your sketches in a mirror also. It's amazing how many flaws will show up when you see the sketch reversed and distanced. Use the mirror for looking at preliminary sketches and for checking the progress of final sketches as you work.

A reducing glass has the opposite effect of a magnifying glass; it makes things smaller. When you use it to examine a sketch you can get some notion of how the costume may look from a distance, from way up there on the stage. Carry your reducing glass with you on swatching trips. It will often help you determine if a fabric pattern will "read" from the stage.

MAT CUTTERS

These are handy little tools that greatly simplify the cutting of mats. Mat cutters come in a variety of types and prices, some with a straight-edge attached. Most will make either a straight or beveled cut.

What Information Should the Final Costume Sketch Include?

Although the costume designer will generally have the opportunity to go over all sketches with the technicians responsible for constructing the garments and accessories and will, in most instances, visit the shop regularly to attend fittings and keep up with the building progress, the designer cannot be in the shop every moment; therefore it is necessary to include certain basic information on all the sketches in order to prevent mix-ups and mistakes.

Each sketch should have the name of the play, the character, the actor, and the scene or

FIGURE 5-38. Liz Covey's sketch for Edgar in *King Lear*. Sepia ink and leather on rice paper. Note the details given on the sketch. *Photograph by Frances Aronson.*

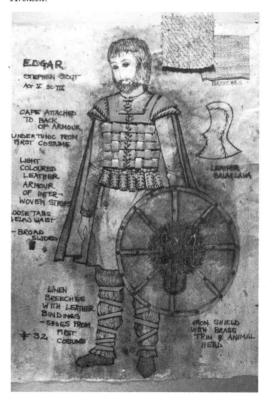

119

scenes for which the costume is intended. In a large show it is a good idea to number the sketches consecutively, and if individual characters have several costumes, to number these also. For example:

MACBETH   MACBETH
Sketch #5   Sketch #6
Lady Macbeth, Jane   Lady Macbeth, Jane
  Smith   Smith
I-5, 6, 7, & II-2   II-3
costume #1   costume #2

and so on.

Embellish the sketch as necessary with drawings of back views, decorative detail, and accessories. Write any notes and instructions that will help the technicians make correct decisions, such as pattern sources, fabric treatments, explanation of sword rigging, and the like. Describe or draw undergarments if they are necessary to the silhouette. Be sure to include any special closings the garment should have to facilitate quick changes. List unseen costume props such as a pocketwatch or a wallet (these items may also turn up on the prop list but it never hurts to have a double-check) and costume accessories like cuff links and tie pins.

It is not a good idea to put this explanatory information on the back of the sketch. Far too many notes on backs of sketches get overlooked. Devise ways of making notations on the sketch itself, ways that can be both handsome and practical. In most instances it is preferable to print or write in your own hand in a subdued ink or pencil. Fancy printing or labelling with press-on letters takes focus away from the costumed figure.

Mounting Sketches

Finished costume sketches ought to be able to stand on their own, actually as well as aesthetically. Few fitting rooms have pin-up boards and there is seldom an extra person around who can be spared for the single purpose of holding up the sketch. A sketch that wilts in the middle when you try to prop it up is maddening. Therefore, if you have not done your final sketch on very heavy paper or illustration board, it should be mounted.

The simplest way to mount a sketch is to bond it to poster board, railroad board, or mat board with rubber cement. The board may be

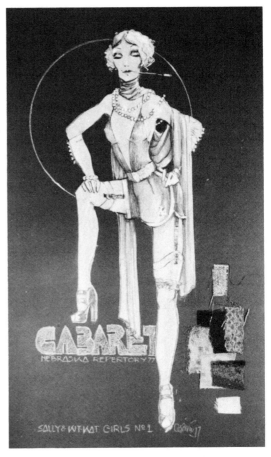

FIGURE 5-39. Michael J. Cesario's sketch for *Cabaret* produced by the Nebraska Repertory Company. Figure rendered in colored pencils on light gray paper, cut out, and flat mounted on black board. *Photograph by Frances Aronson.*

cut the same size as the sketch or a bit larger to create borders. If you are leaving a border, be sure to calculate the placement of the sketch and make pencil marks to indicate where each corner should fall.

To use rubber cement, spread a thin layer of the adhesive on the back of the sketch and on the cardboard. Allow the surfaces to dry slightly. A large sheet of tracing paper laid between the two surfaces will help you to match up your corner marks exactly. Slip the tracing paper out and press the two surfaces together. Remove any excess rubber cement with your fingers, a gum eraser, a rubber cement pick-up, or a ball of rubber cement.

WINDOW MATS

Mounting with a window mat is a bit more complicated but often much more handsome. Use mat board (mounting card) for window mats. Determine the size of the mat by adding the width of the desired borders to the size of the sketch. (Don't forget that the window has to be cut a bit smaller than the outside dimensions of the sketch paper.) Cut out the window with a sharp knife or with a mat cutter and be sure you are not cutting directly into your dining room table! Mount the sketch behind the window mat with masking tape or brown paper tape. If the sketch is on very flimsy paper, you may want to mount it on board before placing it behind the window mat.

When you are creating a border around your sketch, either by mounting it on a larger piece of board or behind a window mat, be sure to have the bottom border slightly wider than the top and sides. If all four sides are equal, the sketch will appear to be too low down and look as though it is falling out of the mat. With a window mat that is to have 3″ borders, for example, make the top and sides 3″ and the bottom 3½″. When you pin up the matted sketch, all borders will appear to be equal.

Use restraint when you are choosing a color to border a sketch. Anything that will detract from the costumed figure should be avoided.

Be aware as you are mounting your sketches that you will have to carry them around with you—don't add too much cardboard to the total weight. Borders may be of modest width. Lightweight cardboard is quite suitable for mounting, just as long as it's firm enough to stand up when it needs to.

COVERING SKETCHES

When the sketches are complete, most costume designers spray them lightly with a fixitive for protection. In addition, since costume sketches get handled so much in transit and in the shop, it is always a good idea to use one of the protective papers discussed earlier and cover them completely.

If you are mounting your sketch in a window mat, you may place a layer of protective paper behind the window before you tape down the sketch—or you may cover the whole sketch, no matter how it is mounted. Cut a sheet of protective paper two or three inches larger in all four directions than the mounted sketch. Lay the protective paper over the sketch and fold the excess to the back. Create neat corners and tape in place. Be careful when you are folding acetate; it has a tendency to crack if creased too hard.

Photocopies

Once the costumes are designed and the construction of them is underway, various people involved in the production will probably want photocopies of the sketches. A set of photocopies may go to the costume shop to be placed in the costume "bible," the book in which the construction history of that show is recorded; another set may go to the stage manager so the actors can refer to them during rehearsals; the scene designer and/or property artist may also want a set; you may even prefer to take swatched photocopies of the sketches with you on shopping trips rather than struggle under a load of cardboard.

Regular photocopies come in two sizes: 8½ × 11 and 8½ × 14. If your sketches are larger than that and if there is a photocopy center available to you, you may be able to find a machine that reduces as it copies. Drawings up to 12 × 14 can be reduced to either regular photocopy size. Since reduction is much more expensive than ordinary copying, you can save a bit by having only one set of sketches reduced and copying the other sets from the reduced set. An interesting side effect of the photocopy reduction process is that the drawings may look clearer and better in the reductions.

If there is no reducing copy machine available, you will have to copy the sketches in two halves and tape them together with Scotch Magic Transparent tape.

Color photocopies and color laser copies of sketches are expensive but very useful for shopping and in the costume shop. Laser copy color is generally more accurate than the color in photocopies.

Many theatres have their own photocopy machines and sometimes you may even encounter a copy machine with its own operator who will do the job for you.

Swatching

Before your sketches are turned over to the shop, be sure each one is accurately swatched with the actual fabrics from which the costumes will be built. Check to see that the correct side of the fabric is clearly indicated. Swatch proportionately; that is to say, if one fabric only represents a small area of color, such as a skirt border

or a necktie, put only that proportionate amount of the swatch on the sketch. Arrange swatches both attractively and sensibly, and securely. Display bits of trim, lace, and other decoration on the sketch along with the fabrics.

From the Drawing Board Into the Street

Although most of you will have been doing some shopping during the process of preparing final sketches, it is when the last sketch is complete

FIGURE 5-40. A nicely swatched sketch by Ann Wallace for Trouble-all in *Bartholomew Fayre*. Gouache on a background of brown paper bags. Brown paper bags were crumpled up, bleached, gessoed, and then varnished to board. Background painting done with watercolor in a plant sprayer. *Photograph by Frances Aronson.*

that the demands on the designer change drastically. Once all the sketches are approved by the director and are ready to go into the shop, the designer leaves the peace and quiet of reading, researching, drawing, and painting and plunges headlong into the task of purchasing everything the shop will need to build the costumes. Telephones, traffic, and shopkeepers dominate the next phase of designing costumes for the theatre.

FIGURE 5-41. Susan Tsu's sketch for Bianca in the Milwaukee Repertory Theater's production of *Taming of the Shrew*. Ready to be shopped. *Photograph by Frances Aronson.*

6

The Pre-Production Period

Ordinary clothes automatically become extraordinary on the stage or screen. The frame around the events invites intensified attention to what is being worn; we know it is there intentionally even though it represents something worn casually....

ANNE HOLLANDER
Seeing Through Clothes

The show is designed. You have sketches in hand. You are well aware that the director and the actors may make discoveries in rehearsal that will call for changes but, because you have explored the script fully and in careful collaboration with the other members of the production group, you are confident that these changes will be minimal.

Now it's time to change gears, to begin the practical pre-production work that will allow your designs to move smoothly from sketches to dresses, suits, and poke bonnets. As soon as the costume technicians have begun to cut and stitch garments, the designer must be available to oversee the work at regular intervals, to interpret drawings, answer questions, and participate in all fittings. You can accomplish all this during the production period only if you have scheduled your time well, know exactly what has to be found, pulled, rented and built, and have the bulk of the shopping done.

You may have two weeks in which to do your pre-production work or you may have two days. Some of it will inevitably spill over into the production, or building, period. Whatever time you have, do as much as you can before the shop puts scissors to cloth. This is, for example, the best time to make lists.

The following discussion is divided into four sections:

1. Planning
2. Finding, Pulling, Renting
3. Shopping and Buying
4. Recording.

The order in which they are presented is not necessarily the order in which you will be able to proceed, since each situation will determine its own order. Learn early to be flexible and don't ever wait around to complete one phase of the process before starting on the next. A time may come when you are called on to plan, pull, buy and record all at the same time in less than three days in a blinding snowstorm. If you know how to plan, how to organize your work, and how to make wise decisions quickly, you will probably succeed.

Planning

Revised Costume Plot

Many of you took a rough costume plot with you when you had your first conference with the director (discussed in Chapter 2). It was made up as part of the initial script work. This plot reflects only the needs of the text and does not include decisions made for this particular production; nor does it reflect your designs. Now is the time to update the original costume plot; in many cases you will want to write it up anew. Choose a roomy, double-spaced form in which to record the plot since there will be more changes, addi-

tions, and subtractions during the course of the production period. No costume plot is considered final until the curtain goes up on opening night.

Look at your sketches as you compose your costume plot. List every item of clothing and every accessory required by each costume. Do not overlook underwear. Include collar studs, cuff links, pocket watches, padding, handkerchiefs, and wedding rings. Don't bother to describe the items on the plot. It is enough to list them.

FIGURE 6-1. A scene from Arena Stage's production of *A History of the American Film* by Christopher Durang, a play that requires an exceptionally complicated costume plot. *Costume design by Marjorie Slaiman. Photograph by George de Vincent.*

Here are lists that include items you might put on revised costume plots for a female and a male actor.

Women
wig or hairpiece
hair decoration
corset
petticoat
understructures such as bustle, hoop skirt, pannier, etc.
dress/jacket/skirt/blouse
apron
tights
shoes or boots
belt
handkerchief
coat/cloak/cape
gloves
hat
purse
jewelry such as hat pin, brooch, ring, necklace, earrings, etc.
accessories such as parasol, umbrella, fan

Men
wig
facial hair such as beard, moustache, sideburns, mutton chops, etc.
shirt
collar
collar studs
cuff links
tie
tie pin
handkerchief
arm garters
suit/jacket/trousers/vest
suspenders
belt
socks
shoes or boots
overcoat/cape/cloak
gloves
hat

spats
jewelry such as ring, watch and chain, etc.
accessories such as cane, umbrella, etc.

When the costumes are finished—certainly by the time they are turned over to wardrobe—you can give this final costume plot to the wardrobe supervisor who will use it as a dressing list for each actor in the production. At that time you can add descriptive details to help the dressers identify individual garments.

Meet With Costume Shop Personnel

It is no secret that the relationship between a costume designer and the technicians who build the show has a great deal to do with the quality of the work that is done. A designer who treats shop personnel as automatons and does not allow them to feel involved in the work they are doing can only expect to inspire run-of-the-mill workmanship. The best work is usually done for a designer who takes the time to explain sketches, describes the effect he or she hopes the designs will have, welcomes cutting and construction advice and considers it seriously.

Treat your first official meeting with costume shop personnel as an occasion to set the stage for a good working relationship. This should be your goal even if you know the members of the staff and have worked with them before, since each building period takes on its own character. Make sure there is adequate time to go over all the sketches in detail. Remember that you have been looking at them for days; the shop technicians may be seeing them for the first time and cannot be expected to see everything at once.

Talk about each sketch. Describe how you envision it in motion, point out closings, delineate layers carefully. If fabric has not been shopped, explain what kinds of fabric you are looking for. Be as specific as possible, especially about detail and trim.

FIGURE 6-2. Frank Hamilton as Captain Shotover and Jeanne Ruskin as Ellie Dunn in the McCarter Theatre production of *Heartbreak House* by G.B. Shaw. Mr. Hamilton is wearing a false moustache, full beard, and sideburns. His own hair was bleached and treated to match. *Costume design by Andrew B. Marlay. Hair design by Paul Huntley. Photograph by Cliff Moore.*

After you have talked about the sketches, invite comments and suggestions. Listen to what is said. The shop staff will be interested mainly in how the garments are to be built and might suggest methods that may be more effective than yours. Young designers often worry that taking suggestions is tantamount to losing control of their design. Try not to take this position. All theatre is collaborative. You will never lose control of good, strong designs; sometimes they turn out even better because a draper or a craftsperson makes a valuable contribution to the work.

If you have not worked with the shop before or if there have been personnel changes since you worked there last, be sure to find out exactly how the staff is organized. Who drapes, who cuts, who stitches, and who is responsible for accessories? How many hours per day does the shop work? How are stock supplies charged and who is responsible for recording expenditures? Is there a shopper on the staff? And so on. Ask personal questions as well. If you smoke, ask for locations of designated smoking areas. Is a desk or work space provided for designers? Is a refrigerator available? Are coffee, tea, and soft drinks on hand?

A costume shop staff is a unique blend of personalities and the costume designer coming in needs to be sensitive to the individuals and to the nature of the working unit. Once you perceive the climate in a shop, you can decide how to make appropriate contributions in order to inspire the best craftsmanship possible during the time you are all working together.

Schedules and Deadlines

Now that you are acquainted with the way the shop operates, you can make a schedule for the production period and establish deadlines.

Sit down with the shop supervisor and plan the overall fitting schedule. This is particularly important if you do not live near the shop and must make periodic trips to oversee the work. Decide at the outset when you will come to the shop so the technicians can plan accordingly and be ready for your visits. Remember that a full day of fittings is exhausting for the designer and for the technicians, so try to space them to allow for rest time. In an Equity company, three separate fittings is the rule for each costume: a muslin fitting, the first fabric fitting, and the final fabric fitting. In most cases you will not see the completed costume with all its accessories until the dress parade or the first dress rehearsal.

As you make up the fitting schedule be sure you know what Actors' Equity Association regulations are in force at that theatre. Different theatres operate under different contracts with Equity, and each contract has its own rules that dictate the frequency and length of fittings as well as rules that regulate what parts of the costume the theatre is responsible for and what, if anything, is the responsibility of the actor.

If you are in doubt about Equity regulations and the shop staff cannot answer your questions, ask to talk with the stage manager or to see the theatre's Equity rule book. Should you, even inadvertently, violate an Equity rule by keeping an actor in a fitting longer than allowed, the theatre will have to compensate the actor at the overtime pay rate. Try to anticipate situations in which the normal number of hours allotted to fittings is insufficient for the work that has to be done and discuss the matter with the stage manager. Additional fitting time may be taken from rehearsal or, if this is impossible, overtime pay might be included in the budget.

On page 129 is an excerpt from the Actors' Equity Association Rule Book that applies to

contracts between Equity and the League of Resident Theatres (LORT) from September 5, 1988, through September 1, 1991. Contracts are renegotiated at regular intervals and the rules do change, so it is a good idea for costume designers to stay up to date.

If you need to contact Equity to ask about LORT contract rules or the rules that govern other types of contracts, you may write or phone any of the following offices:

NATIONAL OFFICE
165 West 46th STREET
New York, N.Y. 10036
(212) 869-8530

Fax # (212) 719-9815

BRANCH OFFICES

Chicago, Illinois 60601   Los Angeles, Calif. 90028
203 N. Wabash Ave.   6430 Sunset Blvd.
(312) 641-0393   (213) 462-2334
Fax # (312) 641-6365   Fax # (213) 962-9788

San Francisco, Calif. 94104
100 Bush Street, Suite 530
(415) 391-4301
Fax # (415) 391-1108

Many shops keep work charts on the wall that list all the costume pieces for which they are responsible; spaces are provided on the chart in which work steps can be checked off as they are completed. Such charts are supposed to reflect exactly where the work on the show is at any given time. Unfortunately, this is not usually the case—as soon as the technicians begin working at a good clip, they forget to check off the various tasks as they finish them and the chart may rapidly become useless.

In all this planning don't forget to set personal deadlines as well. Assign yourself a completion date for shopping, pick a date on which to visit the rental company, note which rehearsals you expect to attend, and schedule a meeting date with the milliner. Each production makes many, many demands on you and the only way you can meet them all is by apportioning your time carefully.

Section 12. from the Actors' Equity Association Agreement and Rules Governing Employment in Resident Theatres, September 1988 through September 1991.

12. CLOTHING AND COSTUMES

A. The Theatre shall provide all costumes and clothing except modern conventional undergarments.

B. <u>Shoes</u>. The Theatre shall also provide properly fitted footwear which, if for dancing, shall be new. All other footwear shall be clean, sanitary, and in good repair. All footwear used for dancing shall be furnished at least one (1) week prior to dress rehearsal. Such footwear shall be of suitable construction for dancing when used for Contemporary Theatre Dance Movement, i.e., classical, ballet, modern, jazz, ethnic, etc. During rehearsals, the Theatre shall furnish at least one (1) pair of toe shoes for each member of the Chorus called upon to dance in toe shoes.

C. <u>Knee Pads</u>. The Theatre shall furnish kneepads when necessary for rehearsals and/or performances.

D. <u>Make-up</u>. The Theatre shall provide all make-up except ordinary and conventional make-up. If the Actor is required to use body make-up, the Theatre shall furnish clean cloth towels for the removal of such make-up (see Rule 48(B) (4).

E. <u>Rental</u>. No Actor shall rent or lend any wardrobe to a Theatre for use in any production unless the terms of the rental, based on the schedule agreed upon in writing between and Equity and LORT, are stated in the Actor's contract of employment or in a rider thereto. The agreed upon payment shall be made to the Actor separate from but with the Actor's weekly salary.

F. <u>Cleaning</u>.

1. Costumes or clothing used in a production, shall be freshly cleaned when delivered to the Actor and cleaned thereafter whenever necessary. Spot cleaning, when required, shall be completed in time to allow at least four (4) hours for drying and airing prior to the half-hour call.

2. Stockings, shirts, and other conventional "skin parts" of costumes and/or clothes shall be laundered or cleaned for each performance. Such items may be laundered or cleaned less frequently if the Deputy and Stage Manager agree. Laundered items shall be completely dry and delivered prior to the half-hour call.

3. Costume parts that are damp due to perspiration shall be dry for each performance whenever practicable.

G. <u>Change of Hair Color</u>. The Actor may not be required to change the color of his/her hair unless he/she agrees in writing. If he/she agrees, the Theatre shall pay the expense of changing the color and of its upkeep during the run of the engagement, and of the restoration to the original color at the close of the engagement.

H. <u>Change of Hair Style</u>. The Actor may not be required to cut or change the style of his/her hair in any way, or to shave his/her head, unless he/she agrees in writing. He/she may, however, be required to let his/her hair grow, or he may be required to grow a beard provided he agrees in writing. If he/she agrees, the Theatre shall pay the original expenses and the expenses of the upkeep of said hair or hair style.

I. <u>Hairpieces and Wigs</u>. Beards and hairpieces furnished by the Theatre shall be freshly cleaned when delivered to the Actor and cleaned thereafter whenever necessary but at least once every twenty-four (24) performances. Lace on all beards, mustaches, and hairpieces shall be cleaned daily.

Structure the Budget

By now you know exactly how many dollars you have to work with. Once again, be very sure that you know exactly what the producing organization expects the budget to cover. Some items that may or may not be included in the costume budget are: wigs and facial hair, basic stitching supplies, dry cleaning, maintenance materials, transportation costs for you and for your assistant, postage or shipping, and phone calls. You must know what you are responsible for before you can structure the budget. Remember that certain items, such as muslin for draping complicated period patterns, can add up to shocking totals if you have not estimated the cost as carefully as possible. Paying for actors' haircuts or perms can also put your budget seriously out of joint during the days just before dress rehearsals if you have neglected to add in these costs from the start.

Estimate all fixed costs with the help of the shop supervisor and subtract them from the budget at the start. Next, set aside ten percent of the total budget and earmark it for tech week emergencies and last minute changes. For a show that is primarily shopped off retail racks, up this figure to fifteen percent.

FIGURE 6-3. Original budget estimate for a production of Robert Ingham's *Custer*.

```
                    Custer - budget notes

    7 uniforms

            $150 ea for materials            $1,050

    7 prs boots

            2 prs cavalry type $200 ea

            5 prs short or ordinary riding

                    boots $50 ea                 650

    3 dresses

            12 yds fabric ea @ app. $10/yd       360

    3 prs high laced, heeled ladies' boots

            $50 ea                               150

    beaded necklace for Wooden Leg                20
                                              $2,230


    silk screening process:

    photography expenses                         300

    screening supplies, equipment               400

    half-tones                                   300
                                              $1,000

                                TOTAL  $3,230
```

FIGURE 6-4. An exceptionally detailed final budget record for a production of *Biography*. A useful guide.

BUDGET BREAKDOWN -- "BIOGRAPHY"

MINNIE

Item	Amount	Subtotal
dress fabric	20.00	
collar and cuffs	5.00	25.00
shoe rental (own shoes)	12.00	37.50
dress fabric (2nd dress)	16.00	53.00
garter belt	4.99	57.99
collar fabric	6.00	63.99
3 prs. seamed stockings	6.00	69.99

SLADE

Item	Amount	Subtotal
hair appointment	50.00	
shoes	25.00	75.00
blouse fabric	22.50	97.50
girdle	7.49	104.99
gloves	6.99	111.98
gloves (2nd pair)	4.99	116.97
coat	60.00	176.97
suit fabric & interfacing	64.18	241.15
3 prs. stockings	6.00	247.15
purse	15.00	262.15
earrings	1.00	263.15
garters	2.57	265.90
coat decoration fabric	2.00	267.90
fur and fastenings	22.97	290.87

MARION

Item	Amount	Subtotal
gloves	4.99	
gloves (2nd pr.)	4.99	9.98
purse	24.99	34.97
purse (2nd one)	14.99	49.96
wig	225.00	274.96
coat fabric	79.80	354.76
muslin and lining	23.00	377.76
garter belt	4.99	382.75
girdle	4.99	387.74
shoes	39.95	427.69
smock fabric	20.00	447.69
evening dress fabric	60.00	507.69
coat lining	9.75	517.44
dress silk	60.00	574.44
draping mock-up fabric	12.50	589.94
trouser rental (own)	15.00	604.94
dress fabric (3rd dress)	67.00	671.94
coat	60.00	731.94
blouse	18.00	749.94
shoes (2nd pr.)	36.00	785.94
coat cuffs	21.00	806.94
leotard for dress base	15.50	824.44
evening gloves	7.00	831.44
3 prs. stockings	6.00	837.44
2nd leotard	17.50	854.94
shoes (3rd pr.)	62.00	916.94
jewelry	23.00	939.94
straps for evening dress	25.00	964.94
piping fabric for dress	13.00	977.94
purse (2nd one)	10.80	988.74
shoes (4th pr.)	21.00	1009.74
fur trim for coat	25.50	1035.24
trim fabric for 2nd coat	4.00	1039.24
bra	5.40	1044.64

FIGURE 6-4. (continued)

Item	Amount	Subtotal
bra (2nd one)	7.00	1051.64
purse (3rd one) & belt	14.99	1066.63
earrings	2.15	1068.78
ring	1.05	1069.83
buttons and clasp	8.00	1077.83

FEYDAK

Item	Amount	Subtotal
shoe rental (own shoes)	12.00	
suit	129.60	141.60
ties and handkerchiefs	15.99	157.59
shirts	24.90	182.49
(all other items from stock)		

WARWICK

Item	Amount	Subtotal
white gloves	3.00	
3 wing collars	13.50	16.50
wrist watch	6.00	22.50
hat rental (own hat)	6.00	28.50
shoes	37.26	65.76
(all other items from stock and borrowed free of charge.)		

KINNICOTT

Item	Amount	Subtotal
ensemble rental (actor's own)	90.00	
shirt	17.00	107.00

NOLAN

Item	Amount	Subtotal
shoe rental (own shoes)	12.00	12.00
(all other items from stock and borrowed free of charge.)		

KURT

Item	Amount	Subtotal
shoes	39.95	
shirts	24.90	64.85
(all other items from stock and borrowed free of charge.)		

MISCELLANEOUS ITEMS

Item	Amount	Subtotal
shipping for borrowed costumes	13.50	
shopping bag	.25	13.75
Tintex dyes	10.00	23.75
Xerox	.54	24.29
Ivory Snow and Tintex dyes	4.50	28.79
costume collection rental	22.00	50.79
envelopes and heel cups	7.73	58.52
Xerox	.53	59.05
phone call and Xerox	.50	59.55
costume collection refund	11.00	48.55
muslin and linings	7.50	56.06
linings	2.00	58.05
shoe dyes	16.85	74.90
Tintex dyes	2.98	77.88
tea for dipping down	1.50	79.38
hat pins	.70	80.08
dress shields	13.50	93.58
tape	2.75	96.33
hat pins	.28	96.61
Greyhound shipping	11.00	107.61
cufflinks and rings	28.85	136.46
thread or Tintex dyes	8.25	144.71
buttons	34.15	178.86
rings	3.00	181.86
barge cement and magix	10.05	191.91

MINNIE	69.99
SLADE	290.87
MARION	1077.83
FEYDAK	182.49
WARWICK	65.76
KINNICOTT	107.00
NOLAN	12.00
KURT	64.85
MISCELLANEOUS	191.91
TOTAL	2062.70

Beyond these rather obvious steps, there are no hard and fast rules for structuring a costume budget. Instinct and experience both play a large role in successful budgeting and you will get better at it every time you do it.

STARTING POINT.

For those without sufficient experience to have a starting point, begin by dividing the money that remains after you have deducted fixed expenses and the tech week emergency fund among the costumes required for the show. If you have five-hundred dollars left and there are ten costumes to produce, start off by allotting fifty dollars to each costume. What follows is a process of robbing Peter to pay Paul. The set of peasant rags will certainly cost less than the leading lady's silk dress, so you will subtract from one and add to the other. If you can pull the rags from stock, subtract even more from the cost of that costume and apply it to still another costume. Continue this juggling act until the arrangement looks sensible on paper. Remember that you should have been aware of the budget figure while you were designing the costumes and you should already have made some instinctive adjustments concerning the garments and their probable cost.

ESTIMATING.

After the initial breakdown has been established, begin to price individual items. Go through your revised costume plot and estimate, piece by piece. If specific garments or accessories have to be purchased, get on the telephone and find out exactly what you will have to spend. Don't trust memory. Prices of most things have a way of escalating; the top hat you got for sixty-five dollars three years ago might well cost ninety dollars now. If you cannot calculate the exact cost—having fabric pleated before you know exactly how many feet of pleating you will need—make a slightly higher estimate. Under-estimating leads to rude shocks.

You cannot accurately estimate fabric costs until you have worked out the yardage each garment requires. It is often a good idea to do this in collaboration with the draper. When the budget is really tight you will not want to overbuy, but you certainly don't want to run out of cloth when there are two skirt panels left to cut.

Once you have established the number of yards a costume will take, you can divide that number into the amount of money you have apportioned to it (taking out for trim, linings, buttons, etc.) in order to see what your per yard ceiling price will be. If this calculation tells you the fabric must cost no more than eight dollars per yard to fit within your budget, you will save a lot of time by not looking at more expensive choices.

Figure 6–5 contains some yardage estimates. Be sure to note fabric widths. Remember that you need extra fabric to match plaids or patterns. If the plaid or pattern is relatively regular, measure the width of one complete pattern repeat and add that amount of fabric to each yard to be purchased. One-way plaids or distant repeats may require more.

Estimate tight ruffles at a ratio of 3:1, looser ones at 2 or 2½:1. Knife pleating, such as you might use to trim an 1870's dress, is also a 3:1 ratio and eats up fabric at an amazing rate. When the fabric you are considering is silk taffeta at eighteen dollars per yard, pleating may turn out to be an extremely expensive trim; you should know this information in advance.

If, after you have finished estimating the cost of realizing the costumes you designed, you discover that the cost exceeds the budget, go back and see where corners may be cut.

1. Consider reworking certain stock garments instead of building them from scratch. Give some thought to borrowing from nearby theatres or renting, if the fee is less than the cost of building.

Note: These yardages reflect average size actors and are somewhat generous. Use them only for estimating, not for purchasing. Before purchasing actual fabrics, calculate specific yardages with the draper.

MEN

Contemporary suit (single breasted):

	45" wide fabric	54"–60" wide fabric
jacket	2³/4 yds	2 yds
trousers	2¹/4 yds	1¹/4 yds
vest fronts	³/4 yds	³/4 yds
jacket lining	1³/4 yds	

Inner structure:
   1 yd pocketing
   ¹/2 yd wigan
   4 yds stay tape
   ³/4 yd hair canvas

	45" wide fabric	54"–60" wide fabric
Long-sleeved shirt	3¹/2 yds	2³/4 yds
Frock coat, 19th C.	5 yds	3¹/2 yds
Tailcoat, 19th C.	4¹/2 yds	3 yds

WOMEN

Contemporary clothing:

	45" wide fabric	54"–60" wide fabric
Tailored jacket	2¹/2 yds	1³/4 yds
Tailored skirt	1¹/2 yds	1¹/4 yds
Trousers	2¹/2 yds	1¹/4 yds
Blouse with long sleeves	3¹/2 yds	2³/4 yds
Walking Skirt, Turn of the Century	6 yds	4¹/2 yds

Add extra for plaids, napped fabrics, and prints that must be matched.

FIGURE 6-5. Yardage estimates.

2. Think about using old fabric that the costume shop has in stock. It may not be exactly what you had in mind but a little dye and paint could transform it completely.

3. Think about using really cheap fabric and treating it with decorative techniques that will give you the look you want without the expense.

4. Reconsider using wigs and facial hair since they are particularly expensive items. As a matter of fact, you should make it a rule of thumb to avoid using a wig unless it is absolutely necessary. Unless it is a very good wig indeed, it will never look as nice as the actor's own hair. Short hair wigs for men tend to be particularly unsatisfactory.

If a wig is absolutely necessary, renting it may be cheaper than purchasing it, particularly if you can arrange to rent it from another theatre. Go through every wig and beard in the shop and see if you can make them serve, perhaps by trimming or dyeing them. Hair rinses that wash out are good solutions for wigs because the hair can be restored to its original color.

5. Scheme to save on trim by reusing braid, fringe, or appliques from old costumes. Check with the shop manager, however, before denuding stock garments. Create metallic trim by painting cotton lace and braid with bronzing powder in an FEV or lacquer solution, a process that is generally much cheaper than purchasing the real stuff.

FIGURE 6-6. Andrew B. Marlay's sketch for Lady
Utterword in the McCarter Theatre production of
Heartbreak House by G.B. Shaw. *Photograph by Frances
Aronson.*

FIGURE 6-7. Charlotte Moore wearing the costume
made from the sketch in Figure 6-6. Dress fabric
includes two antique shawls and antique lace found in
the theatre stock. *Photograph by Cliff Moore.*

FIGURE 6-8. *Cabaret* at Marriott's
Lincolnshire Theatre. The actress in this
photograph is wearing a good-looking
but very inexpensive synthetic wig.
*Costume design by Arnold S. Levine.
Photograph courtesy of Arnold S. Levine.*

FIGURE 6-9.
Katherine McGrath as Ilona Szabo in the McCarter Theatre production of Molnar's *The Play's the Thing*. Ms. McGrath wears a becoming wig, and her dress is trimmed with antique appliques. *Costume design by Robert Morgan. Photograph by Cliff Moore.*

6. Consider labor as you trim the budget. Even if the costume budget does not pay for labor directly, you must consider the number and the quality of labor hours available to you for building the costumes. Plentiful labor, even if it is semi-skilled—beginning students or the members of volunteer stitching groups which help out in many regional theatres—may supply you with hours that will save you dollars. Perhaps you can have your pleating done in the shop rather than send it out. Volunteers have been known to produce sets of hand-knit chainmail, mufflers, and masses of oversized crocheted lace. Willing shop workers with minimal skills can paint trim, add highlights to a dull brocade, and string ropes of beads. They can save you cold, hard cash if you plan the work with them in mind.

If, after all these reconsiderations, you cannot structure the cost of the show within the budget figure, go immediately to management and present your paperwork. Don't simply cross your fingers and hope it will work itself out. It probably won't, and you will save yourself a lot of grief by speaking up at this point rather than having to explain to an angry business manager why you spent more dollars than were allotted. It's easier for the producing organization to find a bit more money for costumes early on than to make up for losses later.

Make Lists

Sit down with the shop supervisor and make lists of what you propose to build, find, rent, and buy. Don't forget anything. Even if your greatest concern is finding brocades and velvets in just the right hues, you are also responsible for providing the technicians with bones, boning tape, millinery adhesive, and shoe dye. The staff shopper may purchase them but you must be sure they are on a list, complete with brand name if you have a preference. You will never be able to anticipate everything—new needs will arise in the course of building—but the more complete you can be in the beginning, the less time will be wasted later in repetitive shopping trips.

136

FIGURE 6-10. Max Wright as Balance in the Long Wharf Theatre production of Farquhar's *The Recruiting Officer*. Notice the delightful prop soldiers. *Costume and scene design by John Conklin. Photograph by William L. Smith.*

Be sure you have a list of all the property items directly related to costume which the prop shop is responsible for making, finding, or buying. You will want to okay canes and cigarette lighters and supervise weapons and weapon riggings that the property technicians are building from your designs. Make regular visits to the prop shop to look at everything that affects costume.

Finding, Pulling, Renting

Finding

Knowing what you need to find is only the first step in actually finding it. The following comments refer both to finding items you expect to acquire for free and finding extraordinary or unusual items to buy.

If you are designing a production whose run will be limited, it is often possible to borrow (for free) certain types of garments: modern policemen's uniforms, lab coats and nurses' uniforms, restaurant garb (chefs' hats and waitress uniforms), choir robes, clerical outfits, football, baseball, and basketball uniforms, academic

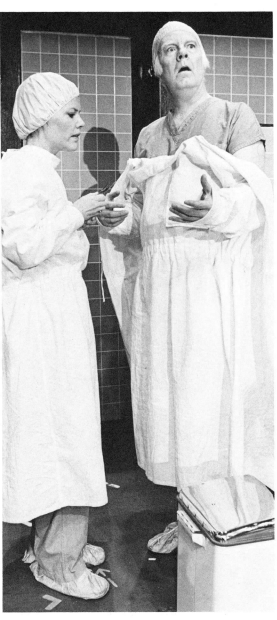

FIGURE 6-11. George Ede as Dr. Boyd and Pamela Payton-Wright as his nurse in *The National Health* by Peter Nichols at the Long Wharf Theatre. Their costumes are good examples of the kind of items costume designers must learn to find. *Costume design by Whitney Blausen. Photograph by William L. Smith.*

gowns, fur coats, and formal wear. It is easier to borrow in a city than in a small town and easiest in a medium-sized city where the local theatre is relatively well-known, respected, and has a reputation for reliability.

Never expect to find what you want to borrow on the first phone call. And don't generalize. That is to say, if one restaurant won't loan you a chef's hat, don't presume that the next one you call won't either. One young designer had the experience of calling seventeen hotels before finding one that would loan out six maid's uniforms. This designer's persistence paid off, all six uniforms were borrowed for free and the designer was therefore able to divert a large chunk of the small budget to ten yards of silk crepe for another character's evening gown.

Figuring out how to get in touch with the person who can actually loan you what you want is often a challenge. When you are contacting a hotel to inquire about borrowing, for example, you may fare better with the director of public relations than with the kitchen manager. If you are working at a regional theatre, see if there is anyone on the board of directors who can help you, a physician who can lead you to a lab coat (or provide you with one himself) or a college president who is willing to help you find an academic outfit.

Some businesses, furriers, and formal wear renters in particular, will often loan garments in exchange for free advertisement in the program. Make sure such an exchange is consistent with theatre policy before you agree to it and follow up to see that the advertisement actually appears. Some will loan items to you in exchange for a pair of tickets to a performance. Again, check theatre policy before saying yes.

Whenever you borrow, make sure the person or organization you borrow from knows exactly what use you will be making of the item and how long you will keep it. Don't promise to return a policeman's uniform on the day after strike because it will have to go to the cleaner's first.

Most established theatres carry insurance that covers loss of and damage to borrowed items. In most cases, in order for the borrowed items to be protected by the insurance, you must present management with a list of exactly what you have borrowed and what its value is—*before* the items are used. Some theatres have special insurance forms you must complete on all the props and costume pieces you borrow.

Finding the unusual, the rare, and the scarce is a task costume designers do regularly. The process can be frustrating and fascinating. There are no rules for finding what is hard to find, and the best advice is to follow every lead doggedly and don't give in to despair. Every designer has a tale of such a search. The objects searched for range from wearable World War I gas masks to turn-of-the-century fireman's boots and high button shoes for a child of 8. Such searches are made even more difficult if time and/ or money are scarce.

Always ask the shop supervisor for assistance since there is often a staff member who is good at finding things, enjoys talking with strangers on the telephone, and is not daunted by refusals. If there is, enlist that person's aid at once.

Don't put off a difficult search hoping that the object may turn up all by itself. It won't. Besides there is always the possibility that you won't find the item anywhere and must therefore allow yourself time to come up with a second best.

Pulling

Some costume designers have a genius for pulling dull, drab garments off the storage racks and reworking them into exciting costumes. This takes a special eye for seeing potential. Not everybody can imagine an ensemble created out of a skirt from one frock, a bodice from another, a cut-down jacket from a suit, and a belt sprayed just the right shade of brown. If *you* can, your small budget shows will be particularly successful.

Many designers consider pulling from stock a penance and go at it with a grumpy attitude, wishing they had the money and the labor to make everything from scratch just as they envisioned it. If you can avoid being grumpy and approach a pulled or partly pulled show as a process in which you are creating new costumes from diverse elements, you may be able to transform a burden into a challenge. It is not unusual for a costume designer to have a re-worked costume singled out for special praise in a production in which all the others were made from scratch in the shop.

If you know from the start that you will have to incorporate pulled garments in your show, you should go through stock before drawing completed sketches. It is not unusual, however, to find yourself adding more items from stock during the pre-production period either to lighten the budgetary pressure or to relieve the load on the shop.

The stocks of costumes in regional and university theatres that have been in operation for a number of years are the best hunting grounds for reusable costume pieces. These collections will probably include both old costumes and clothing donations from local people or even from small shops that have gone out of business. There will inevitably be men's shirts, ties, trousers, 1950's prom dresses, and piles of 1950's and 1960's hats. Costumes from past shows may well include some knee breeches, long skirts, shirtwaists, and vests.

Consider anything that has even the vaguest possibility for being reworked. You can conjure up some quite amazing things with the homeliest items when you add imagination and a sprinkling of inexpensive goodies. Every piece you pull from existing stock is something you will not have to purchase.

Since millinery work requires especially skillful hands and is very time consuming, get in the habit of looking at every hat in stock with an eye to reshaping, covering, spraying, and retrimming. Build hats from scratch only if there is absolutely nothing suitable to use as a base.

If you have a lot of pulling to do for a show, organize the items you are looking for in garment categories. Group suits together with notations about color and sizes, then shirts, hats, shoes, and so on. Costume storage is usually arranged by types of garments. Suits and jackets will be close together with trousers nearby. Shirts may be stored together in boxes or drawers or hung in another part of the storage area. Shoes may be at the far end of the room on shelves or in another room altogether; the same may be true of hats. You can speed up the pulling process if you are prepared to choose all the shirts at one time, all the shoes, hats, etc.

There is no such thing as a thoroughly clean costume storage area. Most are crowded,

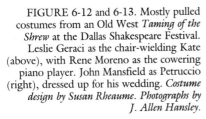

FIGURE 6-12 and 6-13. Mostly pulled costumes from an Old West *Taming of the Shrew* at the Dallas Shakespeare Festival. Leslie Geraci as the chair-wielding Kate (above), with Rene Moreno as the cowering piano player. John Mansfield as Petruccio (right), dressed up for his wedding. *Costume design by Susan Rheaume. Photographs by J. Allen Hansley.*

and the choicest things may be tucked away in hard-to-reach areas. Dress for the occasion in jeans and a sweat shirt, not in your best dress or new high-heeled shoes. Be prepared to climb ladders, rummage underneath racks, and emerge quite grubby at the end of the day.

Pulling costumes from storage takes a long time, especially if the area is not kept in good order. You may have to take many garments out to examine and measure, sometimes putting them on tailor's dummies for a really good look. You may find that three-piece suits have been split up and it will take you additional time to reassemble trousers, vest, and jacket. Make sure you allow yourself enough time to look at everything you need to see. Usually a member of the shop staff will be able to help you, a timesaver indeed. There are occasions, however, when you will want to search in solitude. If so, say so.

Before you leave the stock area in a theatre where you are designing, be sure to rehang and shelve the things you have considered and rejected. Your neatness will be noted and appreciated.

Renting

The biggest challenge in using a few rented costumes in a show is incorporating them in such a way that it doesn't look as though a strange and alien group of characters just stepped on the stage. This problem is at its most intense when you have rented sight unseen and the costumes arrive the day before first dress. Suddenly, with the intrusion of half a dozen suits and waistcoats, the subtle color range you labored on for so long over the dye pot is out the window. In most instances you have no recourse but to grin and bear it. There are a few precautions you can take to try and avert such disasters but you will probably not escape them altogether.

FIGURE 6-14. Rented uniforms for Arena Stage's production of *Sergeant Musgrave's Dance* by John Arden. *Costume design by Nancy Potts. Photograph by George de Vincent.*

Whenever you are renting from a commercial firm, make every effort to go in person to select the costumes you will use, or send a trusted associate. This is the only way to avoid surprises and, even if you don't find exactly what you want in color or in silhouette, you have a better chance of successfully incorporating it into your total scheme if you know what it looks like a month before dress rehearsal rather than a day before.

RENTAL COMPANIES

Eaves-Brooks Costume Co., Inc. (New York) and Western Costume Company (Hollywood) are currently the largest costume rental firms in the country. If you are in the midwest and can't travel to either coast, perhaps you should rent once from each in order to try them out. Western's stock comes largely from the film industry and Eaves-Brooks's from the commercial New York theatre. Rental fees are about the same, and if you are in Lincoln, Nebraska, the air freight cost is equally exorbitant from either side of the continent.

Most cities have one or more local costume rental firms. The bulk of their business is in outfitting large amateur productions—the community theatre Gilbert & Sullivan show and the annual high school musical—and in individual costume rentals for masquerade parties and Halloween, not to mention the annual traffic in Santas and elves. Local firms are not always sensitive to the needs of regional theatres and university theatre training programs and they may charge more than Western or Eaves-Brooks to rent you a single costume for a four to six week period, even when you include the cost of shipping from Western or Eaves-Brooks. If you have a talk with your local costume renter, and if the stock is broad enough to be useful to you on a fairly regular basis, you may be able to create a suitable renting relationship. There are advantages in working with a local firm, the chief one being that you can see what you're getting before you've got it.

The Costume Collection in New York City is a particularly interesting and unique costume rental organization. It is part of The Theatre Development Fund which, among other things, makes half-price tickets for Broadway shows available to people who are willing to stand in line in Times Square on the day they wish to go to the theatre. The Costume Collection serves only not-for-profit organizations which of course include all colleges and universities, most regional theatres, Off-Off Broadway, and some summer stock.

Rental fees at The Collection are considerably lower than commercial rates and you may barter for costumes. That is to say, you can trade stock garments of a sort that The Collection can use for rental credit. You must have all costumes cleaned before you return them or have a cleaning charge added to your rental bill. Even though the stock at The Costume Collection is not as comprehensive as the stocks at Western or Eaves-Brooks, there are many interesting things to be found at a cost that is easy to bear.

The best way to use The Collection is to make an appointment and select what you want to rent in person. At the time of this writing, you are allowed to take the costumes three weeks before your show opens because The Collection leaves alterations up to you. You are also welcome to make repairs and add trim although you may not cut things away, distress, or dye costumes. You can also take more garments than you actually need, try them on your actors, and make final choices. No rental charges will be made on costumes returned before your opening night, although there is a small handling fee.

According to Costume Collection Administrator Whitney Blausen, the following information must be provided by the renting organization before costumes can be taken:

1. A copy of the organization's tax-exempt certificate, IRS code 501 C-3.
2. A deposit check for fifty percent of the rental, made payable to Theatre Development Fund.
3. A letter of financial responsibility from an officer of the renting organization, on letterhead stationery written as follows:

(organization) authorizes (designer) to rent costumes in our name for (production) to be done on (dates). The seating capacity of our theatre is (_____). (organization) assumes financial responsibility for payment of the rental, cleaning costs, and for any loss, damage or late return of the costumes. We are aware that late fees of $12.00 per costume per week are charged if costumes have not been cleaned and returned by the due date in the contract and The Collection has not been notified of extenuating circumstances.

*(signed by the officer and
his or her title)*

Whenever you rent long distance from a commercial firm, be sure to send them as much information as possible about what you want: complete and accurate measurements, clear photocopies of your sketches with any notes necessary to explain them, and a range of swatches. Always phone ahead to make sure that what you want is available and to settle on a rental fee.

RECIPROCAL RENTALS

Many regional and university theatres rent costumes to and from each other either on a cash or reciprocal basis. The practice is more lively between groups within the same general area. A free-lance costume designer who works in many regional theatres will get to know what stock is where and may even begin work on a show with a specific item in mind to rent.

When designers rent costumes from other theatres, they assume the responsibility of

FIGURE 6-15. Storage racks at the Costume Collection.
Photograph by Janet Beller, Courtesy of Theatre Development Fund.

making sure those costumes are returned at the end of the run, a job often neglected simply because the designer is off working on another show at another theatre. Unless you are absolutely certain that the shop staff *never* forgets to return rentals promptly, note on your calendar the date the production closes and phone to make sure the things are being sent back. Renting or borrowing from another theatre is usually such a financial boon to your budget that you should make every effort to keep the process as simple and as business-like as possible. It goes without saying that costumes rented from another theatre should be cleaned before they are returned.

When you rent, be sure to calculate costs other than rental fees. There is shipping. Because some companies have a limit on package size, a large costume rental may have to be shipped by air freight, which is more expensive than parcel shippers like United Parcel Service. If the rental is local you may still incur gas and mileage expenses when picking up and returning the costumes. And remember cleaning costs if you are renting from The Collection or from another theatre.

Shopping and Buying

As a costume designer, you will have to buy such things as fabric, notions and trims, old clothing, and new, modern clothing. By the time you have produced the costumes for half a dozen productions in any city, you will have explored more byways than thoroughfares, poked about in a variety of curious shops, and met many interesting and unusual people. Your copy of the telephone company's yellow pages will be well thumbed and your city map will be coming apart at the folds. The work that began in solitude at your drawing board takes you far afield indeed.

Fabric

Fabric is the basis for most costumes and, like automobiles, ranges from silks and wools with the exquisite performance of a Rolls Royce or a Mercedes Benz to the sturdy cottons and cotton/synthetic blends which, like Volkswagen Rabbits and Toyota Corollas, do their jobs well but without a lot of flair. Fabric costs range as widely as the price tags on cars. You may pay forty-five dollars for a yard of silk and eighty dollars for the same amount of a wool and cashmere blend. Cotton broadcloth may, on the other hand, be tagged at three dollars and ninety-eight cents per yard and a cotton/polyester gauze at one dollar and ninety-eight cents per yard. How you choose between the extremes, and from every possibility in between, will be determined by your budget and by everything you know about fabric performance. Car purchasers don't expect a Toyota to perform like a Rolls. Costume designers have to know that polyester chiffon will not behave the way silk chiffon does. An important part of every costume designer's background is a thorough study of the fibers from which fabrics are created and the ways in which these fibers are made into yarns and the yarns woven, knitted, or pressed into pieces. Silk cloth is not desirable only because it is expensive. You want it for what it will do, for its drape and lustre. If your costume doesn't require silk performance, you won't choose silk no matter what your budget is.

Your first task, then, is to choose the fabrics that are appropriate for the garments you have

FIGURE 6-16. Rosemary Ingham's sketch of Annelle's costumes in *Steel Magnolias* for TheatreVirginia. *Photograph by Rosemary Ingham.*

FIGURE 6-17. Willi Burke, K. Strong, Trish Hunter, Marge Carroll, and Stanja Lowe in a scene from *Steel Magnolias* at TheatreVirginia. Many of these costumes were bought rather than built, and all the women wore wigs. *Photograph courtesy of TheatreVirginia.*

designed. The second consideration, often as important as the first, is to find those fabrics in the colors you want. It is with these two goals in mind that you set out to buy cloth.

Insofar as it is possible for you to do so, try never to pay a full, retail price for a yard of fabric. Virtually every city in the country has discount fabric shops, and in cities where garments are manufactured you will find shops selling both mill ends and factory ends. If you must buy from the most expensive fabric store in town, request a discount for the theatre. You may well get it.

New York City is, of course, the mecca for fabric shopping. If you know where to go and how to look, you can sometimes save enough on your cloth to pay for a round trip airplane ticket between New York and Lincoln, Nebraska.

At the end of this book is a list of New York fabric shops, grouped according to their locations in the city. However, because fabric shops constantly close, move, and change owners, it is always a good idea to check on their existence before you visit. Some of these shops will charge purchases to the institution you are shopping for if you arrange for this service in advance (important when you are buying for a college or university theatre department). Others deal only in cash. In those shops where you may be able to practice the fine art of bargaining, always make sure you have cash in hand.

FIGURE 6-18. Unique fabric choices for the young men of Verona. Shakespeare's *Romeo and Juliet* at the Milwaukee Repertory Theatre. *Costume design by Susan Tsu. Photograph by Mark Avery.*

If cost is the most exasperating part of fabric shopping, the most bewildering part for the young designer is training your eyes to see the one piece of cloth you want when it is wrapped on a bolt, jammed on a table with dozens of other bolts, sitting in the midst of a room lined, hung, and draped with fabrics of every color, weight, description, and fiber content. Learning to see well takes practice, but here are a couple of hints that may help you in the early stages.

When you first come into a shop in which fabric blossoms in unkempt profusion, revealing no order of color, content, or cost, take a little while to walk slowly around the store. Don't look for anything. Decline offers of help from the shopkeeper and simply allow your eyes to take in the territory. Soon you will discover that you are able to look past the things you don't want to see and isolate cloth you might want for your show. Choose a few for closer inspection, feel them, hold them up to see how they drape. The whole process is one of learning to block out the wrong things so you can see the right ones.

Don't forget that most fabric shops have fluorescent lighting which distorts color, particularly blues and pinks, and makes everything look duller than it will under stage lights. Take your possibilities to the front of the store and look at them in natural light before you make up your mind.

Also, don't be lured by a print that's too small. Examine the fabric with squinted eyes, from a distance or with a reducing glass. Unless you choose a print only to alter color or add a slight overall texture, stick with relatively clear, large-scale prints that can be seen from your particular stage.

Even when you have definitely decided to buy a certain fabric, shop around a little more. Chances are, especially in New York, that you may find that fabric in three different shops—for three different prices!

If your costumes require linings, make sure you get them at the same time. Purchase underlinings and interfacings if they are not supplied by the shop.

Sometimes you will depend upon assistants to do your shopping for you. This may happen when you're doing two shows at almost the same time or when the theatre you're working for employs a design assistant to work with all guest designers. You may choose to do your own swatching during the design phase of your work and then send the assistant to purchase yardage for you. Or you may have the assistant swatch within the color, weight, and texture limits you designate. Since it is usually difficult to make final choices from swatches alone, you should try to see the fabrics on the bolts or, if your budget permits, have the assistant buy a quarter or a half yard of the fabrics so you can handle them before making up your mind.

Not every costume fabric you acquire will be new and off a bolt. Sometimes you may discover exactly the right thing in an old tablecloth, curtain, or slipcover. These items are available in most thrift shops and tend to be inexpensive. Bedspreads and sheets have also been pressed into costume service as well as mattress pads and spinnaker cloth from a set of sails. Make it a habit to consider every possibility you can think of in your quest for interesting and workable fabrics.

Wrapping and Shipping Fabrics

If you shop in one city for a show being done in another, you face all the complexities of shipping. The easiest way, of course, is to have the store do it for you, and there are many fabric shops that will comply with this request, charging you little more than the actual cost of sending the packages. Most understand that you need the goods quickly and send them out as soon as possible.

FIGURE 6-19. Sometimes you may discover exactly the right thing in an old tablecloth. Larry Ballard as Chrysalde and Michael Santo as Arnolphe, in Moliere's *School for Wives* at the Intiman Theatre. *Costume design by Susan Tsu. Photograph by Chris Bennion.*

Many times, however, you have assembled your fabrics from a variety of shops that cannot ship for you, leaving you on your own to box, wrap, tape, and deliver the parcels to the appropriate carrier.

Box fabric as though you expected the worst possible handling. Fill cartons snugly so things won't shift around and work their way out. If your fabrics don't come to the top of the box, add crumpled papers; they make an excellent filler without adding lots of additional weight.

You may decide to wrap your fabric without putting it in a box. If you do this, be sure you are using at least two layers of very stout brown paper. (Top quality grocery store bags make excellent wrapping paper for small and middle-sized parcels.) Sometimes the most convenient way to ship a large quantity of fabric is on the roll or tube it came on. You can wrap two or more tubes together or roll several lengths of fabric onto a single tube. Fabrics shipped on tubes will be free of creases, which more than makes up for the work it takes to separate the layers. You can purchase special paper sacks to cover fabric roles.

Tape your packages with brown Kraft tape or with strapping tape. Masking tape is *not* stout enough for shipping, and the U.S. Post Office will no longer accept parcels with masking tape on them. Modern package sorting machines have made the use of twine unacceptable.

Always put a label with your address inside the parcel in case the outside label comes off in transit. An inside label can be your most important means of recovering a lost package.

SHIPPING SERVICES

United Parcel Service (UPS) is the most inexpensive and reliable transport for medium weight and medium size parcels. Packages cannot weigh more than fifty pounds or be more than one-hundred-twenty inches around the four longest surfaces. It isn't easy to carry a package larger than these limitations so they aren't usually a problem. UPS will pick up and deliver. They can tell you exactly how long it will take for the parcel to make the trip. UPS also offers overnight and two-day delivery services to most places, which are, of course, more expensive. If you are using UPS to ship to an organization—a theatre, college, or university—you can ship collect. Make sure you inform the receiving group how much money they must have on hand when the parcel is delivered.

The U.S. Post Office parcel post service is a bit more expensive than UPS but it is very convenient to be able to drop packages off at your local Post Office. If you do much shipping through parcel post, get a copy of the official instructions that tell you how to package and wrap and what the size and weight regulations are.

Interstate bus companies transport packages, often sending them out on the next bus if you pay a small surcharge. Your goods will arrive in the length of time it takes the bus to make the trip but someone at the other end will have to pick them up at the bus station. Be sure to put a contact phone number on the outside of any packages you send by bus. Shipping by bus is expensive, but it is fast and particularly useful to send items to out-of-the-way places.

Many other air freight and express shipping companies exist, most of which are quite dependable but generally more expensive than UPS or the Post Office. Check your yellow pages for the names of local and national shippers.

The most important thing to remember when shipping fabrics, trims, and other materials is to insure the packages at a real value rate. Each shipper offers a basic value insurance; if the contents of the package are more valuable than the company's base rate, declare the actual value and pay the extra charge. It is a small price for a lot of protection. When shipping through the Post Office, use priority mail, special handling, or special delivery to speed up the process and add additional protection. You may also request a receipt of delivery. All of these special services will add to the shipping costs.

If you will not be in the shop when your packages arrive, be sure you have labelled the contents of each package carefully. Attach notes saying which costume the fabric is to be used for, which side will be used if this is not obvious, whether or not it needs to be washed or dyed before it is cut. Careful instructions will prevent serious mistakes being made in your absence.

Notions and Trim

Most designers combine notion and trim shopping with fabric shopping so items can be matched up on the spot. Sewing notions, such as zippers, thread, tape, etc., are usually part of the stock items provided by the shop. You will, however, be responsible for purchasing buttons, decorative clasps, and any braid, lace, or appliques called for in your designs. Before you shop, don't forget to go through all the trim tucked away in the theatre shop's stock, including that on old costumes.

Shopping for trim anywhere outside New York City or Los Angeles can be extremely frustrating. Small selections and high prices are the rule in places where trim is not sold in large quantities. You will often be forced to dye, paint, combine, or simply create the trim you need from bits. If you are able to shop trim in New York, you might, if your budget can stand it, purchase a bit more yardage than you need so it can be added to the shop stock. Perhaps you will be lucky enough to find it again when you return to that theatre to do another show.

Old Clothes

Shopping for old garments can be both tedious and lots of fun. Every town and city in the country has thrift shops and often one or two that carry vintage clothing as well. Stores run by Goodwill, Salvation Army, Volunteers of America, the Saint Vincent DePaul Society and similar organizations are good places to start shopping for ordinary old clothes of contemporary vintage.

Shops that sell high-quality second hand clothes are often run on a consignment basis, and it is in places of this sort that you might be lucky enough to stumble upon a slightly out-of-date mink coat that can be altered for your leading lady, a comfortably worn Harris tweed jacket for your leading man, and, possibly, a nearly new designer frock for yourself. Consignment shops are particularly rich hunting grounds for good shoes, men's ties, purses, belts, and shirts.

Most vintage clothing shops price their garments just as high as the traffic will bear. They cater to particular customers who will pay what seems to be outrageous sums for well-padded gabardine suits and broad-shouldered crepe gowns from the forties. When you are shopping in vintage clothing shops always explain that you are looking for theatrical costumes and don't be too shy to suggest a lower price. The shop owner may be willing to part with pieces that have hung on the rack for several months for an amount considerably less than the one on the tag.

Check antique garments for wearability before purchasing them. Examine seams and tug slightly at the cloth (not, however, hard enough to produce great rips in a dress you have not yet purchased!). Make sure there are no areas where the color has faded noticeably. Beware dresses that were designed to have matching belts and don't. Unless there is enough hem allowance to make a new belt, you may have a hard time finding something to match.

Visit flea markets and rummage and garage sales for all kinds of old clothes at rock bottom

FIGURE 6-20. Andrew B. Marlay's sketch for Tracy Lord in *Philadephia Story* produced by the Pennsylvania Stage Co. The dress was purchased from an antique clothing shop. *Photograph by Frances Aronson.*

FIGURE 6-21. Mildred Dunnock, Frank Langella, and Michael Higgins in the last act of Eugene O'Neill's *Long Day's Journey into Night* at the Long Wharf Theatre. Robe and wedding dress purchased from an antique clothing shop. *Costume design by Rosemary Ingham. Photograph courtesy of Long Wharf Theatre.*

prices. Many designers go regularly to such sales to look at and sometimes buy interesting items, knowing they will turn out to be useful sooner or later.

New Clothes

It often seems to be an unwritten law in theatre that contemporary plays requiring costumes bought off the rack are set in the season opposite the one you are in. You find yourself trying to buy ear muffs in July and sun dresses in December. About the only thing you can do is announce your problem to store managers and owners who may, if it is possible, allow you to examine whatever out-of-season clothing they have in stock. Remember also that cities with garment factories are producing garments two or three seasons ahead. A sympathetic sales manager may make it possible for you to buy half a dozen wool skirts long before they will appear in the shops.

Sometimes you are lucky enough to be shopping in season, and off you go to your local department store or any number of small men's and women's shops. Most of them will allow you to take several garments out for fitting and approval. It is often easier to show your choices to your leading lady or leading man in the theatre fitting room rather than in the store where either may see and want something highly unsuitable for the play.

When shopping for shoes or boots you should have the actor accompany you if at all possible. You will save a lot of time and the frustration of exchanges.

Whenever you purchase anything you think may have to be returned, be sure that it can be returned, and for cash. Many shops will exchange for another size or another item in their stock. If you cannot find what you want in that store, the theatre will be left with credit and no certainty that they can use it in the near future.

Some situations require that you purchase costume pieces through catalogues. Before you order, be sure to find out exactly how long delivery will take and then add a few days more. Establishments that do mainly mail-order business require cash or a credit card number before they will ship any goods. Most catalogue companies ship promptly upon payment using standard delivery service from UPS, unless you request and pay for quicker shipping.

Wigs and Facial Hair

Wigs and facial hair are very special purchases. The most satisfactory pieces for the stage are custom-made and hand-tied, with real rather than synthetic hair. Synthetic hair wigs, which you will not always be able to avoid because of cost, never look quite as real on stage and they are not easy to re-style. An investment in well-made wigs of real hair will always be a good one

FIGURES 6-22 and 6-23. Wig sketches by Lowell Detweiler for the Hartford Stage Company production of *The Beaux Stratagem*. These sketches went to the wig maker along with the appropriate measurements. *Photographs by Frances Aronson.*

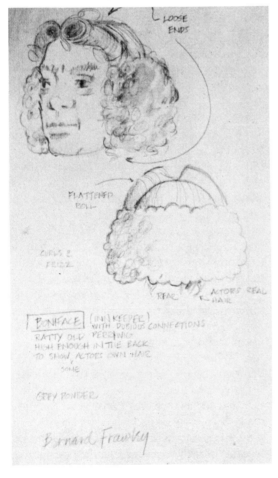

because they can be reworked and used over and over with changes in color and style.

When you are having wigs and facial hair made for a production, be sure to find out exactly how the wigmaker wants measurements taken. (This will also be true if you are renting wigs.) Carry out these instructions with care. If it is called for, send a sample of the actor's own hair for matching purposes. Send copies of your sketches showing exactly how the pieces should

be made and styled. False hair of any sort is a major investment and you want to do all you can to make sure it looks the way you want it to look.

If you have not had a great deal of experience with wigs and false beards, read Chapter 17, Beards and Moustaches, and Chapter 18, Hair and Wigs, in Richard Corson's *Stage Makeup* before you place your order.

Don't forget that the best beards and moustaches are grown by the actor on his own

FIGURE 6-24. Rachel Gurney as Hesione and Robert Nichols as Boss Nagan, in *Heartbreak House* at the McCarter Theatre. Ms. Gurney is wearing a wig, and Mr. Nichols has a false moustache and sideburns. *Costume design by Andrew B. Marlay. Photograph by Cliff Moore.*

FIGURE 6-25. Three views of the wig worn by Katherine McGrath in the McCarter Theatre production of *The Play's the Thing. Costume design by Robert Morgan. Photograph by Cliff Moore.*

face. If there is time and if he is willing, always opt for natural face hair.

WORKING WITH A HAIR DESIGNER

When you are working on a production that demands many wigs and/or fancy hairstyles and have an adequate budget, you may be able to engage a hair designer. They are usually employed on Broadway shows, and the larger resident theatres have begun to use them on occasion. The advantages for a costume designer are obvious.

The hair designer enters the production after the costumes have been designed and meets with the costume designer to go over the sketches and discuss what each actor needs in the way of wigs, styling, and face hair. Usually the hair designer will want to attend a read-through of the play and, subsequently, see each actor individually for head measurements, hair samples, etc.

Many hair designers have their own stock of wigs from which to pull. If wigs and facial hairpieces must be built or rented, the hair designer will take care of all the arrangements and oversee wig fittings that take place during the production period.

The hair designer will be present for dress rehearsal to put on wigs, dress hair, and help the actors in any way that is needed. During the dress rehearsal the hair designer will consult with the costume designer about necessary changes and execute these changes between rehearsals.

Often the hair designer will have an assistant who takes over maintenance and styling of the hair once a show has opened and who is present at every performance to assist the actors with their wigs and hairpieces.

A few of the large regional theatres employ a full-time wig and hair specialist. This person often builds wigs and hairpieces which, after their initial use, can be placed in stock. The savings inherent in building up a stock of usable wigs, having the wig and face hair stock well cared for, and avoiding the last minute emergencies for which local hairdressers must often be engaged make a strong argument in favor of employing such a specialist.

Your Shopping Spirit

The impression you make on shopkeepers when you are shopping a show reflects on you and sometimes on the theatre where you are working. Be as polite and as businesslike as you can. Make sure garments taken out on approval are returned promptly. Be certain you understand the state's requirements for tax exempt purchasing, if the theatre falls within that category, and have all the appropriate information with you, plus forms if they are required. A shopkeeper who finds you pleasant to deal with will remember you and treat you as a valued customer, and you may smooth the way for other shoppers from the theatre.

Recording

Keep Records Up-to-Date

Detailed recordkeeping along the way will eliminate hassles during the final, frantic days before the show opens.

Your costume plot appeared early in the process and has gone through a number of changes. Keep it up to date and make sure it includes everything. Your show reference book is also in progress and should be kept close at hand

CERES

MARY HOOPER

FIGURE 6-26. Swatched photocopy of a costume sketch by Keith Belli from his show reference book that is used for shopping and keeping records. The sketch is for Ceres in *The Tempest* at Stages in Houston. *Photograph by Rosemary Ingham.*

FIGURE 6-27. Costume "bible" page for a production of *Strider,* designed by Andrew B. Marlay, at the Seattle Repertory Theatre. *Photograph by Frances Aronson.*

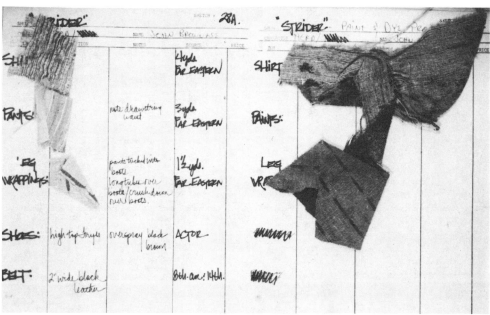

Receipt #	Date	Item/Source	Petty Cash Amount	Petty Cash Sub-Total	P.O.'s & Charges Amount	P.O.'s & Charges Sub-Total	Trans./Travel Amount	Trans./Travel Sub-Total	Combined Total Amount	Combined Total Sub-Total
1	2/5	STERN-SHIRTING/EMILIA U/SKRT	9.00						9.00	9.00
2	2/5	XEROX	.50	9.50					.50	9.50
3	2/5	TRANSP. - FARES-SHOPPING					3.00		3.00	12.50
4	2/7	LERATEX-BIANCA U/SKIRT	8.00	17.50					8.00	20.50
5	2/7	ZUPNIK-IAGO CLOAK & TUNIC	12.00	29.50					12.00	32.50
6	2/7	EUR.WOOL-RODERIGO VELVET	6.00	35.50					6.00	38.50
7	2/9	THUR-OTHELLO O/ROBE	15.00	50.50					15.00	53.50
8	2/9	PATERSON-OTHELLO LINING	10.98	61.48					10.98	64.48
9	2/9	INTERC. - BIANCA/MONTANO	21.50	82.98					21.50	85.98
10	2/9	JONAS-DES.NIGHTG./U/DRESS	8.00	90.98					8.00	93.98
11	2/9	TRANSP. - SHOPPING					3.75	6.75	3.75	97.73
12	2/9	U.P.S. SHIPPING	4.27	95.25					4.27	102.00
13	2/9	CAB TO UPS & SUBWAY					5.75	12.50	5.75	107.75
14	2/10	GLADSTONE-OTHELLO ROBE			21.50				21.50	129.25
15	2/10	B&T-DES.CAPE/CAST TUNIC	31.50	126.75					31.50	160.75
16	2/10	ART-MAX-BIANCA SLEEVES	7.25	134.00					7.25	168.00
17	2/10	C&F-GRATIANO O/GOWN/SHIRT			29.56	51.06			29.56	197.56
18	2/10	TRANSP.-FARES-SHOPPING					3.00	15.50	3.00	200.56
19	2/12	COST. ARMOUR - HELMETS			90.00	141.06			90.00	290.56
20	2/12	TRIM EX. BUTTONS & CORDING			24.21	165.27			24.21	314.77
21	2/12	OSGOOD - OTHELLO/DES/CASS.			61.00	226.27			61.00	375.77
22	2/12	TRANS. CAB TO STN.					4.25	19.75	4.25	380.02
23	2/12	ROUND-TRIP TRAIN TKT					31.50	51.25	31.50	411.52
24	2/13	CAB FROM STN .					4.50	55.75	4.50	416.02
25	2/14	XEROX	.25	134.25					.25	416.27
26	2/15	DYES	3.60	137.85					3.60	419.87
27										
28										
29										
30										

18-408 EYE-EASE LEDGER — NATIONAL — MADE IN U.S.A.

always. Never go shopping without it and use it as a repository for all bits of information that are pertinent to the production: stage manager's notes, a city map, and the name and address of a cobbler who is willing to repair a fragile pair of period shoes for you.

The shop may also be keeping a record of the show's progress. In New York workrooms and in many regional shops as well, this is called the "show bible." Show bibles contain fabric samples, fabric swatches that have been dyed and/ or painted with recipes and instructions for the dye or paint process used, records of yardages bought and actual yardages used, addresses of places where work was jobbed out and how much it cost, etc. These books are particularly valuable for productions that might be done annually (*A Christmas Carol* or *The Nutcracker*) or revived during a future season.

Keep up with your accounts. Every day after shopping, be sure to enter the monies spent. Be sure to enter charges as well as cash purchases. Charges are sneaky things that can add up quicker than the dispensing of bills. (Figure 6-28 illustrates a method of recording expenditures.) Find a recording method that works for you but remember that no system will work unless you feed it regular information. Once again, don't forget to keep a portion of your budget (ten to fifteen percent) set aside for tech week.

The action is about to begin. Your plans are made, shopping is either done or well underway, and the shop is ready to start to work. Get some rest if you can because you are about to embark on the most concentrated part of the work of a costume designer and you will need all your physical, mental, and emotional resources to cope with the days and weeks ahead.

7

The Production Period

...neither a setting nor a costume is good if the actor is uncomfortable. Part of the designer's job is to give the performer every physical and psychological, as well as visual, assistance.

JO MIELZINER
Designing for the Theatre

During this last period, the costume designer's work becomes more and more integrated into the total production effort and there will be increasing contact with the other people who are working on the show. This may be daily if you are in residence at the theatre or at regular intervals if you are not. In a university or regional theatre where shops, offices, and rehearsal spaces are normally located either in one building or in buildings that are relatively close together, it is fairly easy to keep up with everything. Other circumstances may make contact and communication difficult. If you are doing a New York show for which the set is being built on Long Island, the rehearsals taking place uptown, the production offices operating in midtown, and the costumes being built downtown, you will be hard put to stay in touch and will have to expend real effort, many taxi fares or subway tokens, and a lot of shoe leather to be every place you have to be.

The following discussion presumes you are working in a theatre where the distance between shops, stages, and offices is no great problem. If the situation is vastly different, you must find ways to adjust to it that will allow you some degree of contact with the developing production. One designer tells a story of designing costumes for a show for which the costumes were built on the East Coast while all the other activities were carried out on the West Coast. Transcontinental trips were out of the question during the production period since the designer had to be in the shop. Contact was maintained through long distance phone calls, key fittings were carried out by a West Coast assistant on garments sent back and forth by Express Mail, and runthrough rehearsals were seen on video cassettes! This was a cumbersome and expensive way to work but one which did allow the costume designer some participation in the overall process.

The production period should be the most exciting part of the process for everyone involved in it. Individual pieces of the production construct begin to fall in place. The director gets to see the acting company working together, dialogue moves from page to mouth, the

158

groundplan is taped—in scale—on the floor and real distances discovered, a painted surface becomes cloth and a brushstroke a feather. Everything that has been flat on the page, flat on the sketch and tiny on the set model comes up to life size and begins to breathe. There is nothing more exhilarating than watching all the pieces fit together, creating a total theatre experience. But between page and stage there is much to do, many seams to sew, shoes to dye, and trim to tack in place.

Much of what a costume designer does during the production period happens concurrently rather than sequentially and an actual sequence is difficult to predict. This chapter is divided into three major sections:

1. Working With Actors and Director;

2. Working With the Costume Shop; and

3. Working Through Dress Rehearsals.

There will be times during the production period when you feel as though you have too much to do, too many decisions to make, and too many people to please. It is during these times that you will be glad you have a well-read, well-researched, well-designed, and well-planned play and production scheme to follow. It is far easier for you to be flexible and to make whatever changes the production period demands if your work has been thorough.

Working With Actors and Director

Read through and Design Presentation

It is generally the custom for all designers to be present at the first rehearsal; they are often called upon to make short presentations of their work to the company. Afterwards the cast may do a relaxed, sit-down read-through of the script. This initial meeting between company members often sets the tone of the work to follow.

In regional theatres the actors may have just arrived and may be meeting their fellow actors for the first time. Introductions must be made between newcomers and permanent staff members with careful identification of people and their duties. Everybody should know members of the stage management staff, the publicity director, the business manager, and others who will have to be consulted on specific matters.

During the first meeting of a professional company, the actors will assemble privately to elect an Equity deputy who will serve as their representative to management.

After business matters have been tended to, the director often talks to the company about the play and what he hopes to achieve in the production. Some directors enjoy this opportunity to chat, others have little to say and seem eager to get on with the rehearsals. Designers' presentations usually come next.

You may be asked to pin up the costume sketches on a display board or pass them around to the company. In many situations this is the first time the actors have seen any indication of what they will wear, and it will be helpful to them if you can say something about the choices you have made—how they were made and what effects they are intended to create. Answer any questions that arise and make sure the actors know you will be available for further discussions.

FIGURE 7-1. Costume designer Liz Covey, scene designer John Jensen, actors Herb Foster and Portia Paterson examine costume sketches in the rehearsal hall at the McCarter Theatre. *Photograph by Cliff Moore.*

Remember, at this point in the process the costume designer is much further ahead in character development than the actor who has not yet started to rehearse. It's quite possible that the actor's first impressions of the character will be very different from your visual interpretation. Don't be upset if an actor takes exception with his or her costume at this point. Be tactful and wait until rehearsals get underway. As the character develops, the actor may discover the costume is absolutely appropriate. If changes do occur through rehearsals, you will make adjustments—but that comes later.

After the designers have been heard from, you may expect a short break and then the read through of the script. Most read throughs take two to three hours and you should make every effort to stay. Up to now you have only imagined the play. Hearing the play aloud, even though the actors are not yet "acting," will reveal things to you that you may not have seen in the script. One of the most common realizations designers have after hearing a script read is, "I didn't know it was so funny." Humor is particularly hard to read in on the page; it leaps out at you when spoken.

While the read through is going on, take the opportunity to study the actors' faces and bodies. Imagine them in the costumes you have designed. In most cases they will not be absolute strangers to you; at the least, you will have had photographs and measurements to work with while you were designing. But this may be the first time you have had more than a few minutes to look at them objectively. You may discover that one woman's shoulders are a bit wider than you'd thought, that another's hair looks quite limp and will probably need a perm before it accepts a style the period requires, that one of the men always slumps in his chair—you may note that you want to check his posture when he's on his feet because it will effect the way his tailcoat hangs.

Perhaps the most important effect your presence at the first rehearsal has, however, is that it lets the actors know you are concerned about the play and about them. Actors meet many costume designers who are more interested in clothes than they are in plays. By involving yourself in the actor's rehearsal process, you are identifying yourself as being part of the collaborative production process. An informal chat during coffee break on the first day can create the foundation for a friendly and productive working relationship between designer and actor.

160

FIGURE 7-2. Rehearsal in progress at the Long Wharf Theatre. Director Arvin Brown, stage manager Anne Keefe, and actors Louis Beachner, Christina Whitmore, Richard Venture, John Braden, George Taylor, and Emery Battis. *Photograph by William L. Smith.*

Measurements

The initial visit the actor makes to the costume shop, usually during the first day or two of the rehearsal period, is to have measurements taken. Preliminary measurements may have been sent ahead so the drapers could begin muslins or the actor's measurement sheet might be on file from an earlier production. Nevertheless, you will probably want to take a more complete set of measurements or update and recheck old ones. This visit also affords you and the draper another opportunity to look at the body you are costuming.

Since early rehearsal days are particularly busy ones, measurement sessions are usually brief; fifteen minutes is normal. Two people taking measurements can speed up the process; one for the tape, the other to write. In some shops the draper prefers to do all the measuring; in others, measurements are taken by whomever is free at the moment. If time is really short, the shop staff may measure two or three actors at a time.

The person who records the measurements should ask the actor for height, weight, commercial clothing sizes, presence of fiber allergies, etc.

Ask if the actor has any special physical problems that will effect costume; a request for arch supports is quite common. Notice physical irregularities such as a low shoulder or a leg or arm significantly shorter than the other. Some actors will point these things out to you but others will wait for you to notice.

Costume designers should be present for measurements, helping out if necessary. Chat with the actors and make them feel welcome in the costume shop. You can help make a sometimes tedious process more pleasant and, when an actor's body is relaxed, the measurements taken are much more accurate.

Rehearsal Clothes

Although directors work in many different ways, it is the normal procedure to get the show "on its feet" and actors "off book" within the first week or so of rehearsals. (The normal rehearsal period for New York and professional regional theatre productions is three or four weeks for a straight play and five or six weeks for a musical. Universities may rehearse for six weeks but seldom longer.) At this point in the proceedings you will be asked to provide rehearsal garments.

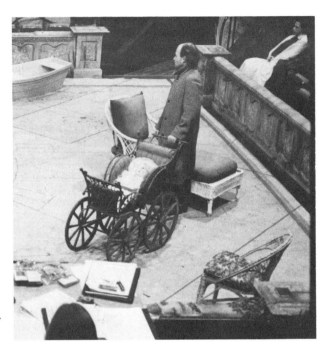

FIGURE 7-3. Actor wearing a rehearsal coat during a rehearsal of *The Three Sisters* at Arena Stage. *Photograph courtesy of Arena Stage.*

Rehearsal garments fall into two categories, both of which are very important to the actor in rehearsal. Some garments will be used to simulate restrictions, such as long skirts, boned bodices, suitcoats, high-heeled shoes. Others will help the actor work out stage business, such as handling an overcoat which has to be taken off or put on while on stage, or doffing a hat. Rehearsal fans are always a must. Try to anticipate the need for rehearsal garments so you will be prepared when the requests come.

One of the real pitfalls of providing rehearsal clothes is that the actor may become so fond of and used to the substitute hat or purse that he or she may want to use it in performance rather than the item you designed and are having built in the shop. Make sure the actors know that the pieces they are using are only for rehearsal, and always try to choose things that are not nearly so wonderful as what will appear on the day of dress rehearsal.

If the costumes have long skirts, actors should never rehearse without long skirts. Some actors have their own long rehearsal skirts which is a help to everyone and a practice to be

FIGURE 7-4. William Leach as Cyrano in the Milwaukee Repertory Theater production of *Cyrano de Bergerac*. An appropriate rehearsal costume was helpful to this actor. *Costume design by Susan Tsu. Photograph by Mark Avery.*

encouraged. If long rehearsal skirts are not available in the costume stock, you should consider finishing up the petticoats first and allowing them to be used.

Skirt understructures such as bum rolls, bustles, and panniers present special problems for the actors who must sit down and negotiate doorways in them. Approximate the shape as best you can for early rehearsals and put the real items in as soon as the shop has finished them.

Hats are especially necessary for rehearsals since they are the objects of much stage business. Men's hats are easier to find appropriate substitutes for than women's hats. This is a time to be creative with the stacks of old 1950's felts

which, when pinned up here and there, will do admirably until the perky straw number makes its appearance.

Try to allow actors ample time to break in new shoes and adjust to heel height. A week or so before dress rehearsals get underway is usually sufficient but be considerate if actors ask to wear their shoes earlier than that. If you take a moment to think about your last pair of new or unfamiliar shoes and how long it took for them to be really comfortable, and how many sore heels and toes and blisters you got in the process, you will be sympathetic to their requests. Imagine having to stand on stage trying to act when your feet are killing you!

FIGURE 7-5. Morgan Duncan as the servant, Joseph, dressed in women's clothes in *The Piggy Bank* at Arena Stage. Rehearsal costumes were vital to this transformation! *Costume design by Martin Pakledinaz. Photograph by George de Vincent.*

FIGURE 7-6. David Murin's sketch for Lucienne in *A Flea in Her Ear* produced by the Hartford Stage Company. A hat similar to this one should be available for rehearsal. *Photograph courtesy of the Touchstone Gallery, New York.*

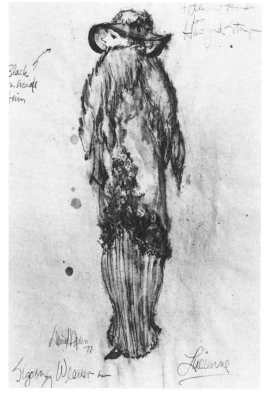

Someone on the stage management staff must take responsibility for rehearsal garments. Before a single item is issued, have a chat with that person. Explain how the garments are to be used on stage and how they should be cared for between rehearsals. Sometimes rehearsal garments are kept in cabinets in the rehearsal hall and sometimes they are returned to the costume shop after each rehearsal. It is seldom a good idea to issue a rehearsal costume directly to an actor to keep in his or her possession; actors have too many things to think about to add rehearsal costumes to the list.

If actors are using shoes, petticoats, or understructures in rehearsal that they will actually wear with their costumes, don't forget to call the items, along with the actors, for fittings.

If the show includes costume pieces that are especially difficult to get used to (straight jackets, plaster casts, or a standing ruff), plan to complete them so they can go into rehearsal early. This may eliminate a certain amount of first dress panic.

Watch Rehearsals

Whenever you can be away from the costume shop for a few minutes—when it is all right with the director—pop into rehearsals for a look at how the show is progressing. By doing so, you may be able to anticipate a potential problem and the actors will enjoy your interest. You may also find that the stimulation of seeing what is going on in the rehearsal hall increases your own excitement about the production.

Begin these visits after the first week of rehearsal and try to make them once or twice a week thereafter. In some theatres there will be periodic run throughs, either of an act or of the whole play, to which the technical staff is specifically invited. Go to these rehearsals with note pad in hand and watch closely for every bit of business and blocking that can affect costume.

Your pad will contain comments such as: "Her boned bodice will not permit her to bend that way;" "He appears to be taking something out of a pocket that doesn't exist." These rehearsals are perfect times for troubleshooting, so be alert.

Communicate with Stage Management

Once rehearsals are underway, the most important channel of communication for the costume designer is the one with stage management. In most instances this contact needs to be made on a daily basis.

Many stage managers issue a bulletin after each day's rehearsal with notes for all the design departments about that day's changes, additions, requests, and problems. Keep all these notes in your show reference book and refer to them regularly. It's easy to forget that a character needs a pocket added to the inside of his coat. It is also quite reassuring to have all this information in writing.

Good stage managers are worth their weight in gold and can make your life consistently easier. Cultivate their good will at all times.

Handling Disagreements

There will undoubtedly be times when an actor absolutely disagrees with the costume designer about what he or she should wear on stage. The structure of most theatre production in this country makes it a virtual necessity that costumes be designed, and sometimes be in the shop, before rehearsals begin. In effect, the designers and the director have already gone through a "design rehearsal process" prior to the start of the actor's rehearsal process. It would be unreasonable to suppose that differences in opinion would never arise.

As stated earlier, don't be too concerned about the exceptions an actor may take before rehearsals begin. But if, after two and a half weeks of rehearsal, the actor has strong feelings that his or her costume is wrong for the character that is developing, it's time for a conference.

You will usually sit down with the actor, director, and stage manager to talk it out. *Don't be defensive.* Your talent and ability are not in question, only the appropriateness of the costume you have designed for one character. Explain your choices and listen to the actor's objections. If you understand and perhaps even agree with the objections, you will happily set out to make whatever changes are necessary to bring actor and character into a mutually satisfactory visual relationship. If you do not understand or agree, or if you think the actor is dead wrong, the director will decide whose choice prevails.

When your choice is not supported by the director, it may be because he or she simply doesn't agree with you. It may also be because the director needs to protect a sensitive relationship with the actor, something that is often crucial to the actor's performance. If this is the case, and the director decides that the actor's feelings are more important to protect than yours, don't be bitter. You must learn to take such decisions as a part of your professional life and not as an attack on your person. Accept the new choice, work hard to fit it into the visual construct of the show, and·try to solve the problem in such a way that the shop will have a minimum of extra work.

At other times, it is the director who will ask for changes because he or she has discovered that certain choices you both made early on are not right for the show as it is being discovered in rehearsal. Once again, if you agree, your only problem is to make the changes possible. If you disagree, make sure you discuss the matter thoroughly. What you must avoid are situations in which you feel as though you have been thoughtlessly dictated to and not heard. Your opinions may not prevail in the end but, for your own mental health, make sure you express them clearly.

Always remember that theatre is a collaboration and not a place where individual artists make individual statements. All collaboration requires some degree of compromise. Remember also that there are many ways to create a single visual effect and, when one of your choices has been rejected, do everything you can to find another that will be integral, even if you never come to like it.

Working with the Costume Shop

You have begun your work with the costume shop in the best possible way: your sketches were on time, you presented them clearly and articulately, your shopping is all but complete, and you have consulted with the shop supervisor and the draper in setting up the work schedule. Now it's time for costume construction to begin in earnest and, whether you are there all the time or only at intervals, your manner in the shop, your attitudes about the work, what you do and how you do it, will have a lot to do with how successful the final product is.

Keep Your Eyes Open

Watch the work being done so you can catch mistakes early and prevent larger tasks from having to be redone. You must do this in a way that will prevent the technicians from feeling that you are breathing down their necks or being unduly critical. You can correct a mistake without allowing the person being corrected to feel that he or she is an idiot. The best way to learn to do this is to imagine yourself in the place of the person being corrected. The Golden Rule should always prevail in costume shops.

WORKING WITH THE DRAPER

In the early stages of the work, pay particular attention to the drapers and cutters. If a garment is badly patterned and/or badly cut, no amount of beautiful stitching can save it. A gifted draper, like a gifted stage manager, is worth his or her weight in gold and will not only make the garment fit accurately but will interpret your sketch with sensitivity, transferring proportions and details from the paper to the cloth in such a way that it is not just any frock coat but the very frock coat you designed.

You must not expect to find a gifted draper in every shop but you can do your best to inspire the finest work each draper is capable of producing.

Ideally, every costume designer ought to know how to drape any costume he or she designs and most do have at least a basic notion of how to proceed. The more you know, the more you will be able to participate in discussions about how garments are to be cut.

Don't dictate to the draper. If you know that you want something done in a particular way, say so, but also listen to alternative methods and try to allow the final decision to be a mutual one. Learn how to deal with different personalities and degrees of proficiency. An inexperienced draper may accept all your ideas and instructions word for word while a draper with a great deal of experience may want to fall back on his or her own familiar, tried and true ways without listening to you at all. You can, if you choose your words well, encourage the inex-

FIGURE 7-7. Costume designer Marie Anne Chiment and technician Noel Borden discuss the construction process of a costume for Arena Stage's production of *A Midsummer Night's Dream. Photograph by Joan Marcus.*

perienced draper to work out parts of the pattern independently and the less flexible one to try out a new method.

Always explain both what you want and why you want it. Thanks to your text analysis and period research, you are the resident expert on the play, the period, and the style of the costumes. Don't expect the shop technicians to know what you know. In far too many instances, they will not even have read the play! Share what you have discovered. Explain the period, tell why the doublets are cut just so and why the buttons are where they are.

If appropriate, choose authentic period patterns that may be used by the draper as guides to general shape, seam and dart positions, etc. Discourage the drafting up of period patterns verbatim since they are nearly always impossible to fit on a modern actor's body. Present knowledge of patterning and fit is far superior to what was known in the past, and it is better for the draper to begin with modern techniques and

adapt them to period shapes rather than the other way around.

DESIGN GUIDES

Be certain you have a very sure visual sense of the period silhouette you have designed since you will need it to guide you through dozens of decisions having to do with proportion, width of panniers, size of hoop, depth of cleavage, etc. You will have to make many of these decisions when the garment is being mocked up in muslin and it will take all your good sense and imagination to mentally turn that vast expanse of stiff, off-white cloth into the crisp black taffeta gown, *circa* 1876, that it will eventually become. You cannot, however, wait for the real black taffeta to be cut before you decide precisely how wide the bustle will be.

Along with your own sketches, keep research books and pictures within easy reach. Look especially at period paintings in which figures in period clothing can be compared in

FIGURE 7-8. Costume designer Doug Marmee in the costume shop at the Utah Shakespearean Festival. *Photograph by Rosemary Ingham.*

proportion to furniture, fireplaces, doorways. Recheck the proportions within the costume. Is the hoop twice as wide as the body inside it, or three times as wide? How much bodice to skirt or doublet to length of leg?

You will also take the size and scale of the stage and of the set into consideration as you guide the creation of actual silhouette and proportion in your costumes. On a tiny stage you may have to scale down a bustle or shorten a train if it threatens to get tangled up in the furniture. And always remember that actors have to fit through the set doorways—that includes their skirts, their cloaks, and sometimes their hats and parasols!

Keep an eye on general construction techniques, especially if the stitchers are relatively inexperienced. Make sure they understand the construction steps involved in each garment and why the steps should be done in a certain order.

If the draper or the shop supervisor gives a stitcher instructions with which you disagree, make sure you talk with the one who did the explaining before asking the stitcher to do it differently. Try never to say the original instructions were wrong. Always admit that there are many different ways to accomplish any stitching operation. Say firmly, however, that you dote on one particular method and would dearly love to have it done that way. If you intervene gracefully and tactfully you may even have the satisfaction of seeing your superior method adopted as standard operating procedure in that shop.

Let the stitchers know you admire skillful stitching. Try to inspire high quality workmanship without being so nit-picky that the costumes never get assembled.

Compliment Good Work

If you feel that a task has been particularly well done, say so. It could be the cut of a whole handsome garment, construction of a fabulous hat, a well-set collar, or even a neatly done continuous lap closing. Costume technicians work very hard and for modest pay. You can add immeasurably to their sense of satisfaction in work well done if you simply remember to acknowledge it.

Think Ahead

Don't ever allow the costumes to be started until you have planned for quick changes, adequate movement, and upkeep. These considerations began at your drawing board and now they should be communicated to the drapers and stitchers.

If quick changes are necessary, work out the location and nature of each closing in detail. Find out how much assistance the actor will have with the change and incorporate this into solving the problem. If a costume has to be overdressed, make sure the layers will fit on top of each other without obvious bulk. All of this should be mocked up in muslin.

If an actor wearing a tight garment has a great deal of movement, make sure to ask for gussets. Put gussets in dancers' costumes as a matter of course. If you are costuming a group of dancers, be sure to talk with the choreographer before deciding on the amount of fullness to cut into the skirts. If there are turns, the skirts will probably be very full at the bottom but gored in order to reduce bulk at the waist. Nothing on stage looks worse than a dancer doing turns in a skimpy skirt. Work out a basic formula for the full skirts and make sure all of them are cut alike, especially if more than one cutter is involved.

Anticipate maintenance problems. Ask for double-stitched seams at stress points. Make sure that collars, cuffs, and washable insets are made easily detachable so make-up can be removed from them between cleanings. Check to see that there are enough pairs of dress shields in the shop to protect all costume underarms. If a garment is to be washed during the run of the show, make sure the fabric is washed before it is cut. As a matter of fact, it isn't a bad idea to wash all washable fabrics before cutting them just in case you decide later that a costume needs to be washed or dipped down. If zippers are used in the costumes, be sure that they are sturdy metal ones. If the zipper is there for reasons of convenience and is not in period, see that the closing is contrived in such a way that the audience is spared even so much as a glint of metal teeth.

Plan for Volunteers

If the shop has the help of local volunteers, give them jobs they will enjoy and make sure their tasks are organized for them when they come in.

FIGURE 7-9. Designer Ann Hould-Ward perusing dye samples for *The Three Sisters'* costumes at Arena Stage. *Photograph courtesy of Arena Stage.*

Find out what each one can do and likes to do. A volunteer who can't stitch may really enjoy making bows, dyeing shoes, or pinning trim in place. Do your share to see that volunteers feel welcome and have a good time while they are in the shop. Happy volunteers return another day.

Be Present
and Do Your Share

Try and spend as much time as you can in the shop so you are available when needed to answer questions and make decisions. Never miss a fitting. If the shop must work late, think twice before you go off to the movies. You will be much more appreciated if you stay and help.

Between conferences, supervising, and fittings, pick out a task or two that you do well and take it for your own. It can be demoralizing for the technicians if you stand around for great chunks of the day drinking coffee. Every designer has some bit that he or she does especially well and likes to do—putting trim on hats, doing hand-rolled hems, or combing wigs. Whatever your speciality is, pitch in and do it! If you really can't do anything, at least offer to run errands or fetch the pizza for supper.

First Fitting
for a Modern or Pulled
Costume

Designing contemporary plays with costumes bought off the rack is not the piece of cake you may expect it to be. Because you have little or nothing to build, you might think you're going to get off easy. Far from it. Choosing a contemporary costume inevitably gets complicated by everybody's personal prejudices. While the costume designer can usually get away with being the expert on a period show, everybody involved with a modern play has definite opinions about what the characters should wear, especially the actors—"I would never wear a plaid skirt in the garden." "Denim makes me feel dowdy." "I think elbow patches are pretentious." "I loathe striped ties!"

Your job—and a difficult one it will be—is to keep costume conversation focused on the characters and the script and not on the actors' own likes and dislikes.

From the start, try to see that you, the actor, and the director are all looking for the same thing. Sketches that reflect the kind of dress or suit you are looking for are a great help. You won't find exactly what you've drawn but, hopefully, you'll find something that has a similar effect.

The stronger your ideas are and the more specifically they can be related to the text, the better your chances are of swinging the decisions in your direction. Tact and patience are usually required in abundance and possibly a series of first fittings before the major choices are made and everyone is pleased.

The first fitting for a contemporary production should deal only with the major garments, choosing them and working out fit and style alterations. It's a waste of time to purchase a shirt, tie, and socks before you are certain which suit will be used.

A pulled costume can be from any period and may require a great deal of reworking before it begins to look like your sketch. Make sure the actor doesn't feel like a second-class citizen if he's being put in a pulled outfit while another actor in the same production is getting three elaborate dresses made from scratch. If you are excited about the possibilities inherent in the pieces you have pulled together, you can transmit your feelings to the actor. Explain what effect you're looking for and how you plan to achieve it. Allow the actor to be involved in the process and he will happily put on and take off a half dozen pairs of trousers until you have found one with just exactly the correct amount of bagginess.

Make sure someone is present in the fitting

to take notes. This may be the design assistant or the technician who is responsible for taking measurements. Any garments that are found acceptable should immediately be tagged and put with the actor's other things. It's a pain in the neck to spend half an hour finding the best pair of trousers only to have them inadvertently returned to a rack of trousers that are all exactly the same color. Rejected costumes should be returned to stock promptly so they will not get mixed up with what is going to be used.

First Muslin Fitting

Imagine what it would be like to be pinned into a slightly scratchy, off-white dress which may or may not have the seams worn inside out, while at least three sets of eyes stare at your body, plucking now and then at the cloth and talking in a semi-foreign tongue that includes words like armscye, gusset, and bust apex. This is what it's like to be an actor at a muslin fitting: uncomfortable, ignored, and spoken of in the third person.

BE CONSIDERATE TOWARDS THE ACTOR

It's easy enough to turn this sometimes ghastly experience into a pleasant one and it is often the designer who must insist upon humane treatment for actors in fittings. Understand that few actors can tell anything about what their costume will ultimately look like when they are swathed in muslin and covered with safety pins. Bring the sketch into the fitting room, refer to it, and take time to explain which parts of the muslin refer to which parts of the sketch. If they are available, have the fabrics in the fitting room and give them to the actor to feel. Talk to—not just about—the actor and be very careful how you refer to his or her body. An actor with a short neck does not need to have it spoken of disdainfully nor will it help the dieting actor to be reminded of pudginess. Aim for a sensitive, tactful objectivity.

FIGURE 7-10. Costume designer Carol Oditz, actor Dilys Hamlett, and draper Katie Duckert in a muslin fitting at the Milwaukee Repertory Theater. *Photograph by Mark Avery.*

Show that you care about the actor's comfort and pay attention when you are told that tight armholes are cutting off circulation. Ask the actor to display some of the movements that have been blocked in rehearsal, particularly if they involve kneeling, raising the arms above the head, sitting or lying on the floor. If the fitting occurs before blocking is done, simply ask for a range of normal movements.

Muslin fittings should be attended by the draper—the draper may be responsible for actually pinning in alterations—by someone to take notes of the proceedings, and by the designer, who must see everything there is to be seen. You must make sure the muslin fits the body as snugly as the design demands but isn't pulled so tight that the costume, when cut from a bulkier fabric, will be too small. Most important of all, you must decide if the pattern pieces, the seaming, the placement of grain lines, and the proportion of all the parts—one to another—achieve the same effect on the actor in front of you as they did on the costume you sketched. You will make adjustments for a short neck, wide shoulders, and a high waist but your sketch remains the official roadmap to get to your design.

If the draper has worked closely with your sketch, the muslin will not need a radical overhaul. Few costume building schedules allow enough time to produce more than one muslin mock-up, so try to work with what is there unless it's a real disaster. If a second muslin has to be done, supervise it closely.

While you are doing all this looking, you may also be chatting with the actor and giving suggestions to the other technicians present. You may be picking out shoes and other accessories to try on after you have finished with the muslin. It is the combination of intense concentration and simultaneous activity that produces fitting room-related headaches. To prevent them, stay as relaxed as you can and do one thing at a time. Remember that your most important function in this fitting is to make decisions about the muslin

mock-up. The actual garment will be cut out of the real stuff from these adjusted muslin pieces or their paper pattern equivalents. Once the plaid silk is cut, your decisions must stand.

Ask someone to keep you informed of the passage of time throughout the fitting so you won't have to add that to your list of things to think about. If the fitting is to be thirty minutes long, you might ask to be warned at the end of ten and then twenty minutes. You cannot fit a wig, hat, and shoes in the final two minutes of the fitting and you will need to work quickly to get everything in. The more experience you have in the fitting room, the more your internal time sense will guide you and the more easily you will move through the fitting process.

Monitor the Workload and Set Priorities

Usually more time is wasted in a costume shop during the first week or ten days of a building period than at any other time and it is paid for in phenomenal amounts of overtime during the two weeks before costumes go on stage. You have already tried to avoid early time waste by having everything on hand on the day the shop begins your show. Now, while the muslins go back to the cutting tables for adjustments and transformation into real cloth, go back to your original schedule and reconsider it with the shop supervisor.

You have seen the technicians at work and can look at your original expectations in light of the staff's actual capabilities. Is your schedule realistic? Are you on schedule now? Does your schedule ask too much from the technicians on any given working day?

Request more help if you and the shop supervisor feel it is warranted. If none is available and the work load is obviously too heavy, sit down and make a list of all the shortcuts you know that can help decrease the amount of work without harming the way the costumes will look on stage. You may decide ruffles can be serged instead of hemmed and that some skirt hems can be done by machine rather than by hand. Decide to purchase preassembled hair canvas jacket fronts. Determine to set up trim early so it can all be machined. Consider the judicious use of certain adhesives.

Always be sure you are being realistic in your demands on the shop. Many of the technicians are committed to several shows in a season and it is unfair of you to ask them to do unreasonable amounts of labor on yours. Take the lead and encourage everyone to break for lunch, to go outside to eat, sit in the park, get away from the shop. Many costume shops are located in basements without windows and without a breath of fresh air or a beam of sunlight to brighten the environment. A walk outside can do wonders for morale. If there are to be evening work hours, see that everyone goes home or out for supper. Avoid "all-nighters." They might sound somewhat romantic to the newcomer, but they are times of mere drudgery during which little work actually gets accomplished. Sleep always increases efficiency. A shower, clean hair, and breakfast makes nimble fingers.

You and the shop supervisor can see to it that the schedule and the workload stay within the realm of possibility and that they provide for some free time. Within this workload and time frame, it is up to you to set the priorities and determine what gets done first and what may be left till last and what may just possibly never get done at all. Decide what is more important for the play, the actors, and for your own sensibilities and push hard to get those things done the way you want them done. Even if you adore lots of hand stitching and couturier finishes, these are things that may be dispensed with in favor of neat, sturdy closings and all the trim in place. There is usually some small something in everything you design that never gets on the stage and some dress rehearsal note that doesn't get done.

It's up to you to make sure that what doesn't get done is your decision and what the shop concentrates on doing is really priority stuff.

Dyeing

It's the rare production that won't require you to dye at least one piece of fabric to achieve a necessary color and, if the shop doesn't have a staff member who is responsible for dyeing and painting, this task will inevitably fall to you. It's not unusual for a costume designer to spend the first several days of a building period wrapped up in an apron or a smock, sweating over a hot plate, dye pot, and washing machine.

FIGURE 7-11. Sandra Yen Fong working at the dye pot at Arena Stage. *Photograph by Joan Marcus.*

Every costume designer must know the basics of fabric dyeing. Even if there is a staff dyer available, you must give advice and okay the colors. And you must know about the dye potential of various fibers so you will never present the shop with a piece of baby blue one hundred-percent polyester cloth and ask them to make it midnight blue. There is not space here to discuss dyeing processes; let it suffice to say that if you don't know about fabric dyeing, read, experiment, and learn to do it.

Make sure that fabrics are dyed and waiting when the draper is ready for them. You may find that your dyeing schedule is based on the muslin fitting schedule. As soon as a muslin is adjusted, the fabric should be ready to cut. Use your sketches to guide you. Beware of changing a color you painted and/or swatched just because you happened to mix, by accident, a color that you suddenly like better. Colors, as you recall, depend upon relationships for their effect and one change may affect the balance of the whole range.

Do test samples of your dyes before tossing in the whole piece and be sure to use the correct assistant chemicals in recommended proportions so the dye will be as permanent as possible. When you are dyeing, observe safety precautions. Protect your hands and arms with rubber gloves and your lungs with a properly filtered respirator.

Dipping a costume down is another sort of dyeing and is usually done during the later stages of the building period. White costume pieces and accessories, shirts, handkerchiefs, modesties, cuffs, and the like may be dipped to kill the glare they produce under stage lights. Commercial dye, tea, and coffee are all used to dip down costumes.

Personal taste is very much involved in toning whites; some designers seldom dip anything down while others are tormented by the mere presence of a glaring white scrap of lace flashing about in the leading lady's hand. Directors may also request that white, and other bright colors, be taken down if they feel the brightness is working against the desirable stage focus.

Start the dipping process with a light touch. After you see it on stage you may deepen the toning as necessary. The process may take several steps. Since much dipping down happens during dress rehearsals, make sure you have given the garment plenty of time to dry before the actor has to put it on again.

Second Fitting

A second fitting for the actor who is wearing contemporary or pulled garments is necessary to check on alterations and decide on accessories. It will almost always be the final fitting before dress parade or dress rehearsal. Make sure to ask the actor if you might have missed seeing any action in rehearsal that could be impeded by the costume. Explore the whole range of stage movements in the fitting room.

The second fitting for a constructed costume is the first in fabric and it may be very exciting. Your design is beginning to take shape on a real body and you should be able to see your intentions in progress. The actor also begins to understand what part the costume will play in his or her characterization and many actors spontaneously strike poses and take on attitudes that hint at a successful blending of actor, clothing, and character.

There are times when you will be disappointed in what you see. The design isn't working as you thought it would. It hangs wrong here, tucks incorrectly there, doesn't become the actor at all. Try to keep these feelings of disappointment to yourself so the actor does not perceive them. Set about to make what changes you can, keep cheerful, and save the breastbeating for later.

FIGURE 7-12. Costume designer Marie Anne Chiment fastening gauzy fabrics on a costume being modeled by intern Carl Mulert. Notice the sketch from which Ms. Chiment is working. *A Midsummer Night's Dream* at Arena Stage. *Photograph by Joan Marcus.*

Make a list of what you have to accomplish in the second fitting. Fit and style alterations come first. Check all the actor's movements and make sure they are possible. Mark hem lengths but make sure the correct shoes are on the actor's feet. Wigs, hats, and other accessories in progress should be tried on at this fitting. You may also want to discuss individual accessories with the actor since this is about the time in the rehearsal process that you will discover a purse has been cut and a handkerchief added.

Lay on trim, place bows, drape scarves, and look at everything with care. This is probably the last time you will have the actor in the costume before these things are stitched in place. Once again, don't forget to have your sketch with you in the fitting room and don't forget to consult it at every turn.

Invite the director to this fitting. Many directors enjoy seeing costumes in progress and will invite themselves. This might be a good time to chat with the director about making good use of a period costume on stage.

Actors who tend to be troublesome in fittings will often pick the second fitting to be at their worst. These actors may have suffered at the hands of thoughtless costume designers or technicians in the past. They may not have a good sense of clothing and/or be desperately concerned about the work they are doing in rehearsal. Stay calm when an ingénue in a pinned-up-the-back gown which is unfaced, unhemmed, and untrimmed tells you the dress is ugly, ill-fitting, and impossible for her character to wear on the stage. It is certainly a rude thing to say but you will gain little by pointing this out or responding in an equally rude manner. Most important of all, don't allow your own feelings to be hurt. Think of all the reasons the actor might have for taking his or her frustration out on a costume, explain what construction steps remain to be done, refer as you have done before to the sketch, and get on with your work. If you feel the situation is going to persist, ask the stage manager to set up a meeting to talk things out. Nine times out of ten the actor will return to the costume shop later to apologize for the outburst, explaining that it was the result of a particularly bad afternoon in rehearsal. Accept the apology gracefully.

Trim

Once the alterations from the second fitting have been made and before facings and closures are installed, work out and set up any trim that can be machined on. If you wait until the garment is finished, most trims have to be tacked on by hand, a time-consuming operation.

Put the costume on a tailor's dummy and pin your braids and laces in place. Move them about until you approve of the effect. If possible, do your pinning several feet from a large mirror so you can study the trim from a distance as you go along.

This is the time to decide on ruffle widths and on how many rows of lace really make up

that inset. Since all the garments being built will be reaching the first fabric fitting stage at approximately the same time, you may spend many hours ankle deep in trim.

Accessories

Actual shoes, gloves, and purses have been chosen. Now you must see that they are correctly colored. Shoes may also need heel taps or dance rubber on the soles. Some shops have the equipment for putting on their own dance rubber; others send the shoes out to a cobbler, a process which might take several days.

Make jewelry selections and see they are put in properly labeled boxes. You may have more than one choice at this point and you may not want to make up your mind until after you have seen each one on stage during dress rehearsals. Make sure all clasps are firm. Earrings should

FIGURE 7-13. Accessories are very important to Susan Tsu's costumes for the Milwaukee Repertory Theater production of *Taming of the Shrew. Photograph by Mark Avery.*

stay on without pinching and, if they are for pierced ears, be equipped to fasten securely. Check ring sizes.

Tights will have been fitted and may need to be dyed. Wash new tights thoroughly with detergent before you dye them, and leave them in the hot dye bath for the shortest possible time in order to protect their elasticity.

Make certain that actors who must wear detachable collars, ties, tie pins, clips, or collar pins know what to do with them. A surprising number do not have the foggiest notion of how to tie a bow or a Windsor knot or where to put a tie clip. Explain cheerfully and photocopy a set of instructions on the tying of ties to put up in the actor's dressing room until he gets the hang of it.

Final Fitting

Final fittings will occur close to tech week and shortly before dress parade if there is to be one.

FIGURES 7-14 and 7-15. Figure 7-14 (above) is a sketch by Carol Oditz for *Storyville* at Ford's Theatre, Washington, D.C. Trim and accessories are quite specific. Figure 7-15 (below) is a production photograph from *Storyville*. The costume at the far left was built from the sketch. *Sketch photographed by Frances Aronson. Production photograph by Richard Braaten.*

This is the time to make final adjustments, check the hem before it's put up for good (or at least until after first dress), make sure closings are neat and snug, and check that collars lie properly and sleeves hang accurately. If bodices are to be fastened to skirts, it's a good time to mark places for the hooks and bars. Check sword and dagger riggings for balance and be sure the hero's cape will stay on his shoulders. Try on the wig with the hat so the actor will get used to the feeling of being a bit top-heavy.

When the costume is all together, take the actor out into the shop for a promenade. Have the actor walk, sit, or even turn somersaults if that is part of what goes on on stage. Try to convince the young actress who is afraid of falling that she really can go upstairs without raising her skirts above her knees. Make sure the ingénue can lift her arms high enough to embrace her lover and check to see that her skirt will not be too long when she gets on the raked stage.

The director might be even more eager to see final fittings than he or she was to look at costumes in a less-finished stage.

Hopefully, the costume will be warmly praised on its first public appearance; this will be very helpful to the actor who is beginning the process of adapting to his or her sometimes quite strange garments.

There are many times when the final fittings, even if scheduled in advance, never happen because the shop is just too busy or rehearsal time is too tight. In these cases you will make the best possible use of measurements and tailor's dummies (and each other!) and do the best you can to be ready for dress parade or first dress rehearsal.

Shading, Ageing, and Distressing

Painting costumes to achieve depth or as part of an ageing or distressing process is a task that has to come last, after building and alterations are finished. Because it happens at the end, it is often done hurriedly. Some designers do it right before first dress and others wait until after first dress to check the lighting.

If ageing and distressing are vital to the look of your show, schedule your time so you can do it calmly. These processes, if well and properly done, ought to be accomplished in several steps, not in a mad rush. If you are concerned that you will go too far in breaking down a garment, treat it gently at first and plan to increase the amount of distress applied after you have seen it on stage.

There are a great many techniques for shading, ageing, and distressing stage costumes,

FIGURE 7-16. Ruby Dee, Tonia Rowe, and Jonathan Earl Peck in *The Glass Menagerie* at Arena Stage. *Costume design by Marjorie Slaiman. Photograph by Joan Marcus.*

far too many to go into here. Consult *The Costumer's Handbook* for general ideas and check the *Theatre Crafts'* Index for articles about specific production experiences.

Remember not to put permanent dirt and age spots on costumes you have rented. Use something that will clean out. If the garment is dark, try light colored make-up powders, talcum powder, or fuller's earth (a gray powdery substance sold in most drug stores). For light garments, use dark make-up powders or dry charcoal dust. A good way to apply any of these powders is to make pounce bags from squares of porous cotton fabric; put a quantity of the powder in the middle of the square and tie it up. "Pounce" the bag against the costume and the actor's skin, leaving very convincing "dirt" behind. Temporary "age" can also be added with nonpermanent hair color sprays and deodorant, in roll-on or spray applicators. All of these will readily dry-clean out.

FIGURES 7-17 and 7-18. Colleen Muscha's sketch for Fireman in David Mamet's *Lakeboat* (top left), and production photograph showing the aged, painted costume (below). Actors Victor Raider-Wexler and Paul Meacham at the Milwaukee Repertory Theater's Court Street Theater. *Photograph by Mark Avery.*

Dress Parade

Many costume designers and technicians detest dress parades and they do not occur in all theatres. They do have, however, a useful and positive side if they are well-organized and smoothly run. Under the best of circumstances a dress parade will give you the opportunity to see the costumes all assembled, individually and in groups, several days before tech week begins; this will enable you to know what you must concentrate on, what problems need solving, and what changes have to be made. The director can give voice to his concerns as well. A good dress parade can make for a more peaceful first dress.

These are the most common complaints about dress parades: 1. A dress parade means you have to get things done earlier than you would without it. 2. They are usually done in rehearsal halls with ghastly lighting. 3. The director and the designers are looking at garments up close when they were intended to be viewed at a distance; and therefore they will see problems that don't really exist. 4. Dress parades are always rushed.

Now consider an ideal dress parade. It is either being held on a theatre stage where there are no union restrictions about stage use, or management considers dress parades important enough to pay union stagehands to run it. If it is not being held on a stage it is in a large rehearsal hall where a couple of lighting instruments,

FIGURE 7-19. Bottom, played by Mark Hammer, tries out the pool that is part of *A Midsummer Night's Dream* set at Arena Stage with the assistance of technical director David M. Glenn. *Costume design by Marie Anne Chiment. Photograph by Joan Marcus.*

FIGURE 7-20. These costumes must allow for maximum movement. Gary Sloan as Tybalt and Jack Wetherall as Mercutio in the Long Wharf Theatre production of *Romeo and Juliet. Costume design by J. Allen Highfill. Photograph by William B. Carter.*

gelled and focused, illuminate the actors, who are a good distance from where the director and designers are sitting. Hand props are available as needed, particularly guns that must fit in pockets, swords that must be drawn, pocket watches, glasses, etc. There is a chair, a stool, and even a step unit in easy reach.

The stage manager has scheduled the sequence of garments carefully so the actors who have to change into second and third costumes have time to return to the dressing room while other things are being looked at. An adequate block of time has been allowed for the proceedings.

The costume crew is all on hand. The wardrobe supervisor has checked over all the costumes and is helping the actors in the dressing rooms. The shop supervisor is armed with safety pins, chalk, tape measures, and any other items thought necessary for on-the-spot chores. Another costume staff member is armed with a large note pad and pencil. Soft music would not be inappropriate.

The stage manager is in charge of the event, calls the actors in order, and keeps track of the passage of time.

Each actor has ample time to display his or her costume, turning so all sides are displayed and going through a complete repertoire of movements, including sitting, kneeling, and so on. If any part of the costume is uncomfortable the actor says so and someone from the costume shop finds out what is wrong. Many problems are simple matters of adjustment: suspenders to let down, drawstrings tied too tight, or dress shoes being worn with heavy socks. If a garment alteration is necessary, it is marked to do in the shop.

The ideal dress parade makes it possible for the actor to put the costume thoroughly through its paces. This is a better place for a seam to rip than on stage. Go through quick changes slowly, step by step, to see if there are any snags that can be cleared up before the change has to be made under pressure. Put on coats, take off hats, buckle on armor, and solve problems calmly.

Sometimes, through no one's fault, a costume simply doesn't work. The director and the costume designer usually know it at the same time. In such situations you may simply have to go back to the drawing board and come up with something new. Such occasions are certainly the exception, but isn't it better to know at dress parade that you have a new costume to create rather than several days later and much closer to opening?

If the shop has known from the first day that a dress parade was scheduled, it will be something to aim for, the first goal. Vital construction steps will be done, such as closings on quick change garments and gussets for the character who tumbles. For other than the practical necessities, the dress parade is the time to see costumes from the outside with trim in place and jewelry on. Save inside work such as linings for the days between dress parade and dress rehearsal.

After dress parade the shop staff should sit down together and go over the notes that were made. Decide how alterations and changes will be made and make assignments. Then go out to lunch or dinner, whichever is appropriate.

Working Through Dress Rehearsals

First Technical Rehearsal with Costumes

Count yourself lucky if you are working in a theatre that is able to schedule a tech rehearsal without costumes; this allows the actors to concentrate solely on getting used to the set and handling real props. In some theatres the turnaround period is so short that all design elements are added at the same time, making the rehearsal especially trying for everyone. A first tech, with or without costumes, is usually a ponderous affair that moves slowly and stops often. The actors, if they are in costume, have lots of time to sit around getting wrinkled, drinking—and maybe dripping—tea and coffee in costume, and possibly even spilling a bit of mayonnaise on their frocks in the dressing room. No amount of warning, no set of rules posted on the call board, no threats or bribes have ever been known to completely halt costume abuses under such circumstances. Be the best watchdog you can be and try especially hard to prevent mayonnaise spills which make particularly ugly stains.

Preparation for Dress Rehearsal

When costumes go into a dress rehearsal they should be completely wearable if not completely finished. The actor's work in the rehearsal won't be impeded if a bow isn't in place but he or she cannot concentrate if a hem is coming down or a sleeve is falling out.

Spend whatever time you have just before the first costume rehearsal going through the individual pieces for each actor. Perhaps the wardrobe supervisor will do this with you. Check items against your costume plot and make whatever final alterations there are in the plot. Make absolutely certain that dresses all have perspiration shields.

The stage manager has already made dressing room assignments. Help put the costumes in the dressing rooms and double check that everything is present.

An experienced wardrobe supervisor will have, in addition to the costume plot or dressing list, a list of costume pre-sets and strikes and a list

FIGURE 7-21. Electrician Jamie Gallagher and stage manager Anne Keefe in tech rehearsal at the Long Wharf Theatre. *Photograph by Bill Kelly.*

noting and describing quick changes. Duties are divided up if there are two or more people on the wardrobe staff. Check with the experienced wardrobe supervisor to see if he or she needs anything explained, then get out of the way and watch. If the wardrobe person is young and inexperienced, or, in the case of a university theatre, a rank beginner, make sure you stay close by to give a hand when it's needed, offer suggestions and, in general, be supportive.

Wardrobe should have a sewing kit containing safety pins, needles, thread, adhesive tape, and any other items that might be useful in an emergency. There should also be a pad and pencil available on which wardrobe staff members, and actors in their absence, may write down notes.

You should be backstage or near the dressing area when the actors arrive and are getting dressed for the first rehearsal with costumes. There will inevitably be questions for you. Try not to help with dressing, however, since the wardrobe staff should be doing that. Make notes of things you want to remember. Dress rehearsal

FIGURE 7-22. Actor Emery Battis prepares for a dress rehearsal of Gorky's *Summerfolk* at the Long Wharf Theatre. *Costume design by Bill Walker. Photograph by Bill Kelly.*

is certainly not a time to rely on your memory. Check each actor out when he or she is dressed and see that everything is on correctly. Wish the company and the back-stage crew good luck and make your way out into the house.

During Dress Rehearsal

Sit, at first, somewhere in the center of the house. This should be the best position for viewing the show. Later you will want to check the costumes from far back and from the very front but it is a good idea to get an average perspective first without either blurred details or sweaty faces. Make sure you are equipped to take notes (with a light if necessary) or have someone sitting by you to write down the notes you dictate.

If you are in the center of the house you will be in easy reach of the director in case you are needed while the rehearsal is going on. The set and lighting designers will have a table rigged up nearby and will be in touch with lights, sound, and stage management over headphones.

Look as hard as you can look. See the total effect first and then the details. There will be surprises. Nothing ever looks quite the way you thought it would under lights. For every costume that doesn't look quite as good, however, there will be another that looks considerably better. Don't take notes immediately. Give yourself a real chance to see.

Stage lighting can highlight your colors and sculpt the figure in the stage space or it can wash out everything and create a dull, flat picture. If you are unhappy with the gel colors or the lighting positions, don't hesitate to speak to the lighting designer about the problems you see. Be tactful but don't be shy.

Nothing in the set should be unfamiliar to you but sometimes a throw pillow or a set of curtains do unexpected battle with the leading lady's dress. The set designer will probably see the problem when you do but, if he or she doesn't, don't suffer in silence.

Now, note taking begins in earnest. Write down everything that effects the actors' movements and business. Check hemlengths and sleeve lengths. See if there are white garments which should be dipped down. Check that your shading and ageing reads properly. List everything that needs to be done. No matter that it probably all won't get done. Write it down now and assess priorities later. The shop supervisor may also be taking notes that deal with fitting adjustments. The wardrobe staff will have notes that reflect backstage incidents and actor comfort.

If the rehearsal halts to solve a costume problem, stand ready to go to the stage and assist. Practice overcomes most problems. Show the actor how far to tilt her hat and help another hang up his coat so it is easy to put on again.

Don't leave the theatre unnecessarily during the rehearsal. The director doesn't want to wait for you to be found before he can talk to you. Besides, you might miss something important. Ask someone to bring you a sandwich or a cup of coffee if you are starving, but stay in the house.

At the end of the first phase of the technical/dress marathon, the director will either have notes for you or you will be included in a general note-giving session.

Take your notes and the director's notes back to the costume shop and sit down for a session with the staff. Assemble everyone's notes and make a general work list. Assign individual costume notes to the person who is responsible for that costume, usually the draper, who will parcel out jobs to the stitchers. Make a list of things you must do and things you must shop for. When everything is in neat columns on a series of pads, go home to bed.

Between Dress Rehearsals

Before the next dress rehearsal, make sure you have gone over maintenance with the wardrobe supervisor. Tell her which costumes should be pressed for each performance and which are intentionally wrinkled and grubby. List what is washable and how often things should be washed. Ask about the dry cleaning schedule to make sure it is adequate for the show.

Attempt to solve as many of the problems listed in your notes, in order of priority, as can be handled in the hours you have before the costumes go back on the actors again. If one garment needs a lot of reworking, ask the director to allow you to keep it out of the next rehearsal so it may be complete for the one after that. Be cheerful in the shop even if you are tired. So is everyone else. Let the technicians know you are pleased with their work and proud of them. Bring in a treat, a bowl of fruit or a box of pastries, whichever is appropriate for the group.

Stop work in time for the costumes to get back to the dressing rooms well before the next rehearsal. Grab notebook and pencil and enter the darkened house for another go.

FIGURE 7-23. Dress rehearsals were important to Raye Lankford, playing Kate Hardcastle, and Allan Hickle-Edwards, as Young Marlow, as they accustomed themselves to period costumes designed by Susan Tsu for *She Stoops to Conquer* at TheatreVirginia. *Photograph by Eric Dobbs.*

Pulling It All Together

The number of dress rehearsals you have in which to pull the costumes into an integrated whole will vary from theatre to theatre. Three is average but occasionally you will run into a situation in which there is only one dress rehearsal before a preview with an audience. No matter what the front office says about a preview not being a proper performance, actors equate performance with audience no matter what, if any, ticket price the people out there are paying. Nevertheless, you may continue to take notes through preview performances and to make changes and adjustments in between. If all goes well your list will grow shorter although it may never disappear altogether.

You may be called upon to make changes during previews because the script is being cut or rewritten. If you are designing costumes for an untried musical comedy, numbers and scenes may be cut and added several times before everyone concerned is satisfied. Previews, changes in the script, and design changes may go on for many days.

However long a time you have to pull it together, do your best. Listen to good advice, ignore bad advice and hope you can tell the difference. First and foremost, learn to trust your own eyes.

On opening day it must be finished and you deserve nothing more or less than a good dinner before the performance and a good party after it.

FIGURE 7-24. A cast portrait from *Stand-Up Tragedy* at Arena Stage. *Costume design by Paul Tazewell. Photograph by Joan Marcus.*

Epilogue

In regional theatres the visiting costume designer is often due to leave for home, or for the next show, early on the morning after opening. Make sure you arrange some time to have the whole shop assembled beforehand so you can thank them for their work. Don't be afraid of sentimentality. Many costume technicians do their work devotedly; if they did, you should say so. When a designer leaves without any indication of appreciation for the work done, the shop staff is sure the designer was unhappy with what they did. Don't leave this impression if you don't mean to.

It's a nice custom to give small opening night gifts to members of the shop staff. The thought is what counts, however, and a card or a personal note will be as much appreciated as something more costly.

It always strikes costume designers as a bit sad that their work ends just as the production comes to life on stage. On opening night you may have nothing to do and you may feel, just for a moment, quite out of things. But every opening night is exciting and all the more so if the play is good, the production worthy, and the audience full of applause at the end. Be happy and proud of your work. You helped create and build what is on the stage and, if the production runs two weekends in a university theatre, six weeks in a regional theatre, or two years on Broadway, it wouldn't have been the same without you.

FIGURE 7-25. A cast portrait from the Long Wharf Theatre production of James M. Barrie's *The Admirable Crichton. Costume design by Bill Walker. Photograph by William B. Carter.*

8
The Costume
Design Business

Competition for costume design jobs is stiff, especially in New York City, in the top regional theatres, and in the film and television industries. No young designer just entering the field can expect to design a Broadway musical right away. Most of you will enter the field as a design assistant or a costume technician. All designers, until they are very well-established indeed, have to explore the job market regularly and present themselves and their work to producers and directors.

Entering The Job Market: Where, What, and How

Thanks to the significant growth of regional professional theatres in the past fifteen to twenty years, jobs for costume designers are not confined as narrowly as they once were to New York and Hollywood. You can now find design opportunities in Milwaukee, Denver, San Francisco, Atlanta, Dallas, Miami, Seattle and other large cities, as well as in a host of smaller cities and in some small towns. New York City, however, continues to be the main proving ground for theatre designers (as Hollywood is for film designers) and the place where significant reputations are made.

When you choose where you will go to begin your professional career, you must consider several things: your personality, your knowledge and experience, and your goals. Don't rush off to the Big Apple just because you think you ought to when, in reality, you would benefit from a season or two working with a regional theatre company. On the other hand, don't let fear and insecurity keep you from moving on when your abilities and ambitions begin to clamour for a larger scope.

Since the focus of this book is theatre design, this chapter concentrates on theatre de-

FIGURE 8-1. David Murin's sketch for John Barrymore for the Broadway production of *Ned and Jack*. Sketch executed in felt-tip pen, Dr. Martin's ink, and marker spray. *Photograph by Frances Aronson.*

FIGURE 8-2. Animal costumes designed by Colleen Muscha for *Frosty Escapades,* an ice-skating production for Starbuck & Shelly, Inc. *Photograph by Colleen Muscha.*

FIGURE 8-3. David Murin's sketch for Kitty in the American Stage Festival production of *The Royal Family*. Felt-tip pen, Dr. Martin's ink, and marker spray. *Photograph by Frances Aronson.*

FIGURE 8-4. Victor Raider-Wexler and Peggy Cowles in *Dance of Death* at the Milwaukee Repertory Theater. *Costume design by Pat McGourty. Photograph by Mark Avery.*

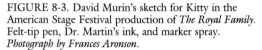

sign jobs. Many theatre designers move easily between the stage, films, and television and many of the suggestions that follow can easily be adapted to finding film and TV employment. These areas, however, are not addressed specifically.

Design teaching jobs are also outside the scope of the chapter. They require, in addition to design training and experience, advanced academic degrees and teaching ability. There is no reason to assume a good designer will be a good design teacher. Some young designers use teaching positions which include regular design assignments to gain experience before they approach the profession. This practice can be advantageous for the designer but not necessarily for the students who are being taught by someone more involved in designing than in teaching. There are, of course, many successful designers who are also brilliant teachers but, in most instances, they established their design careers before becoming teachers. On the other hand, there are brilliant design teachers who never pursued a professional design career.

Regional Theatres

Regional theatre costume shops all over the country hire several hundred costume technicians each year for work seasons that vary in length from twenty-eight to fifty weeks. Many of these positions go to young designers who are looking for opportunities to work with a full season of plays, to observe and learn from the resident or guest designers, and to earn a modest income at the same time.

If you have good draping and flat patterning skills you may well find excellent employment in this area. As stated earlier, good drapers are rare and jobs are available. Increasingly, however, the larger regional shops are hiring drapers whose profession is draping rather than drapers who are making their way into design.

Costume dyeing and painting and building costume props and accessories are particularly good jobs for young designers. Many regional theatres hire one person to carry out all these responsibilities during the season while others job in painters, dyers, and craftspeople as needed. If you are building accessories or painting costumes you will work in close contact with the designer, an optimum position for learning.

More and more regional theatres are hiring costume design assistants to work directly with incoming guest designers. In some instances design assistants are given one or two design assignments, often for the theatre's second or experimental stage. Design assistants are in a position to learn a great deal from the more experienced designers and they may be able to practice their own design skills at the same time.

You can usually create a situation in a regional costume shop in which you learn many things. Keep your eyes open all the time and always show you are willing to do a variety of tasks. Don't let yourself get stuck for long in a nonlearning job. Thirty-seven weeks of running material through a sewing machine that is stuck away in a corner may put food on the table but it won't necessarily help you toward your goal of becoming a self-supporting designer.

Very few young designers working as technicians in regional costume shops get up from their sewing machines to assume design positions and most, after a season or two, move on to another theatre and a position closer to the design process. Sooner or later an ambitious young designer has to strike out on his or her own and face the uncertainties of free-lancing. This may be a difficult transition to make and many of you will continue to do technical work for some time as you seek to establish your design reputation.

WHERE TO LOOK

There is no one central place where all regional costume shop job openings are advertised. Many appear in ArtSEARCH, a publication put out by the Theatre Communications Group, Inc., 355 Lexington Ave., New York, N.Y. 10017.

The United States Institute for Theatre Technology, Inc., commonly called USITT, also advertises design and technical job openings in its monthly publication, *USITT Sightlines*. For information about this publication and the other services offered by USITT, write to them at: 10 West 19th Street, Suite 5A, New York, NY 10011.

When you are searching for costume shop jobs in regional theatres, your best bet is to write to the theatres that interest you and send them your resume. Unless you know the name of the costume shop manager, address your correspondence to the theatre's managing director. Don't expect answers from everybody. Regional theatres tend to be understaffed and overbusy. Send inquiry letters in the early spring for work the following fall. Theatre addresses and the names of managing directors are available in the *Theatre Directory*, published each year by the Theatre Communications Group and available at the preceding address.

The following is a list of theatre companies that are members, at the time of·writing, of the League of Residents Theatres (LORT). LORT theatres are relatively well established, present a full season of plays with professional actors, and employ costume technicians. They are listed alphabetically by town or city.

Barter Theatre
Box 867
Abingdon, VA 24210
(703) 628-2281

Capital Repertory Company
P.O. Box 399
Albany, NY 12201
(518) 462-4531

New Mexico Repertory Theatre
P.O. Box 789
Albuquerque, NM 87103
(505) 243-4577

Pennsylvania Stage Company
J.I. Rodale Theatre
837 Linden Street
Allentown, PA 18101
(215) 434-6110

Alliance Theatre Company
1280 Peachtree Street N.E.
Atlanta, GA 30309
(404) 898-1119

Center Stage
700 North Calvert Street
Baltimore, MD 21202
(301) 685-3200

Berkeley Repertory Theatre
2025 Addison Street
Berkeley, CA 94704
(415) 841-6108

California Shakespeare Festival
Box 969
Berkeley, CA 94701
(415) 548-3422

Caldwell Theatre Company
P.O. Box 277
Boca Raton, FL 33432
(407) 241-7432

The Huntington Theatre Company
Boston University Theatre
264 Huntington Avenue
Boston, MA 02115
(617) 353-3320

Studio Arena Theatre
710 Main Street
Buffalo, NY 14202
(716) 856-8025

American Repertory Theatre Company
Loeb Drama Center
64 Brattle Street
Cambridge, MA 02138
(617) 495-2668

Playmakers Repertory Company
206 Graham Memorial 052A
Chapel Hill, NC 27514
(919) 962-1122

Goodman Theatre Company
200 S. Columbus Drive
Chicago, IL 60603
(312) 443-3811

Cincinnati Playhouse in the Park
P.O. Box 6537
Cincinnati, OH 45206
(513) 421-5440

Cleveland Playhouse
Box 1989
Cleveland, OH 44106
(216) 795-7010

Great Lakes Theatre Festival
1501 Euclid Avenue, Suite 250
Cleveland, OH 44115
(216) 241-5490

South Coast Repertory Theatre
Box 2197
Costa Mesa, CA 92628
(714) 957-2602

Dallas Theatre Center
3636 Turtle Creek Boulevard
Dallas, TX 75219
(214) 526-8210

Theatre Three
2800 Routh Street
Dallas, TX 75201
(214) 871-2933

Denver Center Theatre Company
1050 13th Street
Denver, CO 80204
(303) 893-4200

Goodspeed Opera House
East Haddam, CT 06423
(203) 873-8664

The North Light Rep Theatre, Inc.
600 Davis Street
Evanston, IL 60201
(708) 869-7732

Casa Manana
3101 West Lancaster
Ft. Worth, TX 76107
(817) 332-9319

The Hippodrome State Theatre
25 Southeast 2nd Place
Gainesville, FL 32601
(904) 373-5968

Hartford Stage Company
50 Church Street
Hartford, CT 06103
(203) 525-5601

North Carolina Shakespeare Festival
P.O. Box 6066
High Point, NC 27262
(919) 841-6273

Alley Theatre
615 Texas Avenue
Houston, TX 77002
(713) 228-9341

Indiana Repertory Theatre
140 W. Washington Street
Indianapolis, IN 46204
(317) 635-5266

Missouri Repertory Theatre
5100 Rockhill Road
Kansas City, MO 64110
(816) 235-1451

Clarence Brown Theatre
P.O. Box 8450
Knoxville, TN 37996
(615) 974-3447

La Jolla Playhouse
P.O. Box 12039
La Jolla, CA 92037
(619) 534-6760

Mark Taper Forum
Los Angeles Music Center
135 North Grand Avenue
Los Angeles, CA 90012
(213) 972-7384

Actors Theatre of Louisville
316-320 W. Main Street
Louisville, KY 40202
(502) 584-1265

Merrimack Regional Theatre
P.O. Box 228
Lowell, MA 01853
(508) 454-6324

The People's Light and Theatre Company
39 Conestoga Road
Malvern, PA 19355
(215) 647-1900

Coconut Grove Playhouse
P.O. Box 616
Miami, FL 33133
(305) 442-2662

Milwaukee Repertory Theater Company
108 East Wells Street
Milwaukee, WI 53202
(414) 224-1761

The Guthrie Theater
725 Vineland Place
Minneapolis, MN 55403
(612) 374-1100

Alabama Shakespeare Festival
1 Festival Drive
Montgomery, AL 36117
(205) 272-1640

Tennessee Rep
427 Chestnut Street
Nashville, TN 37203
(615) 244-4878

Crossroads Theatre Company
7 Livingston Street
New Brunswick, NJ 08901
(908) 249-5581

George Street Playhouse
9 Livingston Avenue
New Brunswick, NJ 08901
(201) 846-2895

Long Wharf Theatre
222 Sargent Drive
New Haven, CT 06511
(203) 787-4284

Yale Repertory Theatre
Box 1903A, Yale Station
New Haven, CT 06520
(203) 432-1515

Acting Company
420 West 42nd Street, 3rd Floor
New York, NY 10036
(212) 564-3510

Circle in the Square
1633 Broadway
New York, NY 10019
(212) 307-2700

Lincoln Center Theatre Company
150 West 65th Street
New York, NY 10023
(212) 362-7600

New York Shakespeare Festival
Public Theatre
425 Lafayette Street
New York, NY 10003
(212) 598-7100

The Roundabout Theatre Company
1530 Broadway
New York, NY 10036
(212) 719-9393

Virginia Stage Company
P.O. Box 3770
254 Granby Street
Norfolk, VA 23514
(804) 627-6988

Pasadena Playhouse
39 South El Molino
Pasadena, CA 91101
(818) 792-8672

Philadelphia Festival Theatre for New Plays
3900 Chestnut Street
Philadelphia, PA 10104-3105
(215) 222-5000

The Philadelphia Drama Guild
Robert Morris Building
100 North 17th Street
Philadelphia, PA 19103
(215) 563-7530

The Walnut Street Theatre
9th & Walnut Streets
Philadelphia, PA 19107
(215) 574-3550

Pittsburgh Public Theatre
Allegheny Square
Pittsburgh, PA 15212-5362
(412) 323-8200

Portland Stage Co.
P.O. Box 1458
Portland, ME 04104
(207) 774-1043

Oregon Shakespeare Co.
Portland Center of Performing Arts
1111 S.W. Broadway
Portland, OR 97205
(503) 248-4496

McCarter Theatre Co., Inc.
91 University Place
Princeton, NJ 08540
(609) 683-9100

Trinity Repertory Company
201 Washington Street
Providence, RI 02903
(401) 521-1100

TheatreVirginia
2800 Grove Avenue
Richmond, VA 23221
(804) 367-0840

Geva Theatre
75 Woodbury Boulevard
Rochester, NY 14607
(716) 232-1366

Meadow Brook Theatre
Oakland University
Rochester, MI 48309-4401
(313) 377-3300

The Repertory Theatre of St. Louis
P.O. Box 191730
130 Edgar Road
St. Louis, MO 63119
(314) 968-7340

Pioneer Theatre Company
University of Utah
Salt Lake City, UT 84112
(801) 581-4250

Old Globe Theatre
P.O. Box 2171
San Diego, CA 92112
(619) 231-1941

American Conservatory Theatre
450 Geary Street
San Francisco, CA 94102
(415) 749-2200

San Jose Repertory Company
Box 2399
San Jose, CA 95109-2399
(408) 995-0733

Asolo Theatre Company
5555 N. Tamiami Trail
Sarasota, FL 34242
(813) 351-9010

A Contemporary Theatre
Box 19400
100 West Roy Street
Seattle, WA 98119
(206) 285-3220

Fifth Avenue Musical Theatre
1308 Fifth Avenue
Seattle, WA 98101
(206) 625-1418

Intiman Theatre Company
P.O. Box 19645
Seattle, WA 98109
(206) 624-4541

Seattle Repertory Theatre
Bagley Wright Theatre
155 Mercer Street
Seattle, WA 98109
(206) 443-2210

Stagewest
Springfield Theatre Arts Assoc.
1 Columbus Center
Springfield, MA 01103
(413) 781-4470

Berkshire Theatre Festival
Main Street
Stockbridge, MA 01262
(413) 298-5536

Syracuse Stage
John D. Archbold Theatre
820 East Genesee Street
Syracuse, NY 13210
(315) 443-4008

Arizona Theatre Company
P.O. Box 1631
Tucson, AZ 85702
(602) 884-8210

Arena Stage
6th & Maine Avenue, S.W.
Washington, DC 20024
(202) 554-9066

Shakespeare Theatre
301 E. Capitol Street, S.E.
Washington, DC 20003
(202) 547-3230

Eugene O'Neill Memorial Theatre Center
National Playwrights Conf.
305 Great Neck Road
Waterford, CT 06385
(203) 443-5378

Custom Costume Shops

Young designers who have just arrived in New York City often look for work in one of the shops that build costumes on order for commercial plays, ballet, opera, films, and television. The shops vary enormously in size and quality of work but most produce beautifully built and meticulously finished costumes. Finding work in a custom costume shop will depend largely on your skill level.

The majority of the people employed by custom costume shops are members of the IL-GWU (International Ladies Garment Worker's Union) but the shops may take on non-union workers for specific periods of time, a few days or, sometimes, several weeks. If you work in a shop for any great length of time, you may be required to join the union, depending on your position.

A young designer is most apt to find work as a shopper, a milliner's assistant, a craft assistant, or an assistant to the draper. Machine stitchers are usually high-speed union employees with a great deal of experience. So are hand stitchers, although sometimes additional, less experienced hand stitchers may be jobbed in.

Shopping for a custom costume shop is excellent experience for young designers. A shopper will swatch fabrics, compare prices, and buy yardage, trim, and all manner of accessories. Being a shopper is a great way to learn where to go and what to pay. Any young designer employed as a shopper is well advised to keep a notebook of addresses and the names of people who were especially helpful.

Apply for a job in a custom costume shop by sending a letter and resume when you are settled in New York. Make sure to include a reliable phone contact number. Ask if you may visit the workroom and show examples of your work. Follow up your visit with a phone call to check on work availability. Continue to phone periodically since labor may be added at any time and you may be fortunate enough to phone on the very day the shop is hiring extra help.

Costume Rental Houses

A job as a costume rental assistant, responsible for pulling together a set of costumes for a customer, can provide useful experience for a beginning designer. There are costume rental houses all over the country. Some concentrate on operas and musicals, some on fancy dress balls, Halloween and Christmas. The former would probably be more interesting than the latter. Before you apply for a position with a rental house, take a look at the catalogue to see what sorts of costumes they rent. Send a letter and resume and follow up with a phone call.

Rental houses also hire stitchers to make alterations and, sometimes, to construct new costumes. A stitching job might turn out to be less interesting than one dealing directly with assembling a costume or a set of costumes.

The Costume Collection, a unique rental organization discussed in some detail in Chapter 6, has a full-time staff and also offers several paid internships each year to beginning designers. It is the stated hope of Whitney Blausen, administrator, that The Collection can help introduce newcomers into the costume design community.

Free-Lance Design Assistants

Assisting an established designer on a show is one of the very best ways of learning a designer's process; all young designers should have some experience assisting.

A full-time, free-lance designer will often use one or more assistants on each large project. Duties will vary greatly and may range from swatching and shopping to doing a bit of library research, shipping fabrics and accessories to an out-of-town theatre or taking charge of some fittings. Assistants may or may not attend production conferences and dress rehearsals.

When the designer is working under certain United Scenic Artists contracts, the designer's assistant must also be a union member and signed to a union contract.

Designers tend to use the same assistants over and over again. The best assistant is one with whom the designer shares basic design taste and one who can see costume choices through the designer's eyes. Once a designer finds such an assistant, that person is apt to be engaged over and over again, and a professional relationship is established that may only be broken when the assistant strikes out and begins to design on his or her own.

If you want to assist a particular designer, write and send a resume. Don't be hurt if you don't get a reply. Be sure to tell every costume designer you know and meet that you are looking for work as an assistant. Costume designers tend to know other costume designers and you may eventually be referred to someone who will hire you.

Your First Professional Design Job

Most young designers do their first professional work in regional theatre, summer stock, summer Shakespeare festivals, or Off-Off Broadway. Both fees and budgets may be minimal but this is where you get your feet wet and show what you can do.

Designing an Off-Off Broadway show will test your imagination and resources to the utmost. The budget will be small; it may even be non-existent. The backstage facilities will leave a lot to be desired and you will probably work out of your own home with little or no help. You may be called on to borrow, beg, and scavenge. You may even be limited to picking and choosing from what the actors have available in their own wardrobes.

Make the best possible use of your opportunity, however, and learn from it. Many of the plays done Off-Off Broadway are new scripts which give you a chance to design costumes for a totally uncharted and unexplored play. Every now and then an Off-Off Broadway production of a new play will excite enough interest to warrant an uptown production and, if your work has been good, you may have the opportunity to do it again—with budget, help, and a living wage!

When your first opportunity comes, no matter how remote the location or obscure the theatre, always be sure to do your very best work. The theatre community is, by comparison to most professions, very small and intricately interconnected. People with whom you work in the boondocks may be the very ones who will hire you again, in much more prestigious circumstances. You will be amazed how quickly you can acquire a reputation for doing consistently excellent work and for being a pleasant co-worker; or,

FIGURE 8-5. Costume sketch by Susan A. Cox for Shakespeare's *Much Ado About Nothing,* produced by the Alabama Shakespeare Festival. *Photograph by Frances Aronson.*

FIGURE 8-6. Jennifer von Mayrhauser's sketch for Sally Talley in *Talley's Folly* on Broadway, a show that moved to Broadway, with designer, from a smaller theatre. Sketch rendered in acrylics and Ebony pencil. *Photograph by Frances Aronson.*

for doing sloppy work and being ill-humored. Wherever you go, your reputation will precede you; make sure it's the reputation you want.

Resident Designer

Some regional theatres, usually the smaller ones, hire a full-season resident designer who is responsible for designing most, or even all, of the shows. A resident designer works closely with the costume shop and often with the same directors and actors.

Security is an important advantage of a resident design position: the security of knowing you have many shows to do from different periods, the security of a season's employment, the security of a community of people with

whom to work. A disadvantage which may surface over a long period of time is that some designers, working with the same people, may find themselves repeating their style and quality of work over and over again, not trying new approaches or experimenting with different techniques.

For some of you, a resident design job will be deeply satisfying, offering personal and geographic stability rare for theatre people. For others, it is another step toward surviving as a full-time, free-lance designer.

Free-Lance Designer

Free-lancing is being in business for yourself. Your product is your design ability and you

FIGURE 8-7. David Murin's sketch for *He Who Gets Slapped* at the Hartman Theatre. Sketch rendered in acrylics, felt-tip pen, and Dr. Martin's watercolor. *Photograph by Frances Aronson.*

Successful free-lance designers are unusually energetic people who thrive on solving problems. They enjoy meeting and working with new people in unfamiliar situations. They travel at the drop of a hat, can tolerate hotel decor, and respond readily to early morning wake-up calls. They can work anywhere. They are the people, one young designer remarked, "who have a special gleam in their eye, something that tells you they're crazy about what they do."

FIGURE 8-8. Design for an Estee Lauder print advertisement by Lowell Detweiler. Rendered in colored pencil and colored inks. *Photograph by Frances Aronson.*

market it job by job. As a free-lance designer, you have a lot of freedom and not much security. You may work wherever you want and whenever you are offered a job that fits into your schedule. You contract only for short-term responsibility and negotiate each fee individually. You neither make lengthy commitments nor do you often find yourself on a weekly payroll.

Not everybody who wants to be a free-lance designer will succeed. Some lack talent but most simply find they don't have a desire equal to the anxieties, insecurities, and frustrations of never quite knowing what the next day will bring or the stamina to keep up the hectic pace necessary to make an adequate income.

198

FIGURE 8-9. David Murin's costume design for the television series, *Ryan's Hope*. Rendered with Dr. Martin's watercolor, felt-tip pen, and marker spray. *Photograph by Frances Aronson.*

Letter and Resume

What do you say in the letter you write to inquire about design positions? To whom do you send it? What should accompany it?

The letter should be short, to the point, and appropriate to the situation. Example: You have heard from an acquaintance who is a stage manager at Theatre A that the artistic director of Theatre A is looking for a guest costume designer for production number four in the season. You ask your acquaintance if you may mention his or her name (which is the same thing as saying,

"Will you put in a good word for me?") and send off a brief letter:

Dear (director's name)
I have heard from (friend's name), a member of your stage management staff, that you are looking for a costume designer for (name of play). Please consider me for the job. I have enclosed a resume and am available at your convenience to show you my work.

That's all. State your business and stop. Don't waste words saying how great you are. Don't flatter the artistic director or the theatre. The

Example 1

Name
Street Address
City, State, Zip
Telephone #

Education

    Graduate School, Degree Granted, Date of Graduation Undergraduate School, Degree Granted, Date of Graduation

Design Experience

    Professional Theatre/Summer Stock

Play	Director	Date
		(beginning with most recent)

    Graduate School

Play	Director	Date

    Undergraduate School & Miscellaneous

Play	Director	Date

Assistant Design Experience

Designer	Play	Date

References

Name	Address	Phone Number

Example 2

Name
Street Address   Home Telephone #
City, State, Zip   Work Telephone #

EDUCATION: Degree Granted, Graduate School, Date
                  Degree Granted, Undergraduate School, Date

SKILLS:	Skill	Skill	Skill	Skill	Skill

DESIGN:

Date	Play	Theatre
	Director	

PROFESSIONAL WORK:

Date	Job Description	Theatre
	Play	

PRODUCTION WORK IN GRADUATE SCHOOL:

Date	Production	Assignment

REFERENCES:

Name	Address	Telephone Number

         Portfolio available upon request.

FIGURE 8-10. Two beginning free-lance design resumes.

letter is the polite introduction to your resume. The information in the resume—what you've done, where you've done it, and who you've done it for—will determine whether or not the director is interested enough in you to talk with you.

A general inquiry letter to a regional theatre, sent off in the spring for the following season, might read:

Dear (director's name):
I would like to be considered for a guest costume design position with your theatre next season. Enclosed is a resume. I can meet with you at your convenience and show you my work.

Don't expect too much from general inquiry letters. More than two-thirds of the time directors and producers hire designers:

1. with whom they have worked before;
2. who are recommended by a friend;
3. whose work they have seen and liked.

If you aren't famous and don't fit into any of the above categories, you may not even receive an answer to your letter of inquiry. Don't despair and don't give up writing. There is always the possibility that your letter will arrive at just the right moment, your resume will be found interesting, and you will end up landing a job. Luck should never be discounted in the theatre.

Always type job inquiry letters. Make sure your grammar is correct. Use good quality paper. When you design a professional letterhead for yourself, make sure it is simple and tasteful.

Address job inquiry letters to the appropriate person. Spell the name correctly and append the proper title. Never resort to "To Whom It May Concern." Letters so headed seldom concern anyone and usually wind up in wastecans. When you are inquiring about design jobs with a company, address your letter to the artistic director. Check the TCG *Theatre Directory* for the

name or call the theatre and ask to whom you should write.

Your resume should be arranged to fit on one page. A second page is likely to go unread. Use your design sense and lay out the resume information to your best advantage. Focus on your most impressive work.

When you're just beginning, include everything you have done that is at all relevant to the work you are seeking. Include your educational background, your student design assignments, and significant part-time jobs. Later on you will omit some of these in favor of professional design experiences. Also, in the beginning, add three or four professional references who can be contacted about your work. Be sure to check with these people and obtain their permission to be so listed. Choose people who will say positive things about you. You can't be expected to please everyone but it's foolish to solicit a reference from someone who might give you a poor report. Until you are a well-known designer, you may be sure your references will be checked.

When you first enter the design field you will not have a great deal of experience. Accept this and never be tempted to pad out or lie about what you have done. Quite frankly, the theatre community is too small for you to be able to get away with it.

Portfolios

A portfolio of your work should illustrate your process and the finished product. It is your most important advertisement. Assemble it with care; include things that you especially like and show it with pride. The following suggestions about choosing sketches and photographs for your portfolio were assembled from conversations with directors. As you might expect, there was little unanimity of opinion.

There was agreement, however, on form of presentation: Directors tend not to like slide

FIGURE 8-11. "Working men" from *A Midsummer Night's Dream* at Arena Stage. *Costume design by Smaranda Branescu. Photograph by Joan Marcus.*

FIGURE 8-12. "Working men," Jim Hillgartner, Vernon Morris, Bev Appleton, Adam Cohen, and Peter Howard from *She Stoops to Conquer* at TheatreVirginia. *Costume design by Susan Tsu. Photograph by Eric Dobbs.*

shows. Photographs are preferable, in color if possible and, ideally, alongside the original sketches.

Limit the number of sketches in your portfolio to three or four dozen at the most. Choose designs from two or three shows to make up the bulk of the work and fill in with individual sketches from other shows that illustrate different styles and a broader range of your work.

Select designs that show off your work to its best advantage, ones that are clear and easy to read. Be sure each sketch has the name of the show, the character's name, the act and scene for which it was designed and, if you wish, the actor's name. Be prepared to answer questions about the sketches, particularly questions relating to the interpretation of the play.

Select work from plays that are familiar rather than from obscure plays. It is difficult for the person looking at your work to judge the aptness of your ability to interpret character unless he or she has at least a nodding acquaintance with the script.

Whenever it is possible to do so, include photographs of the final costumes to show how the designs were realized. Point out changes that occurred during the rehearsal and in the shop. Most directors will be glad to know you are flexible enough to make changes. No matter how wonderful your sketches are, if there is no evidence of the finished product you are not presenting a complete picture of your work.

All costume designers would be well advised to take their own costume record shots or, if lacking the skills, to get a friend to do them. Photographs taken by theatre photographers seldom include exactly what you want and prints are often prohibitively expensive.

Color photocopies and color laser prints of sketches have become quite acceptable in portfolios. Make sure the copies are the best available, and the color is as accurate as possible. Laser prints, as stated earlier, are generally of better quality than color photocopies.

If you know in advance what sort of play you are being interviewed to design, adjust and rearrange your portfolio accordingly. Pick work related to the appropriate style and period. If it is a contemporary work, don't take only Elizabethan and medieval sketches. You should always show a wide range of periods but you should also alter the balance and tailor your choices to the occasion.

Interviews

First impressions are important; they may also be lasting. In an interview it is most important that you be as relaxed, as comfortable, and as natural as possible. Never put on airs or pretend to be anything you are not. You are there to present yourself, show your work, and sell your ability to do what you do as well as you know how to do it.

Dress appropriately without going to extremes. Theatre people tend to dress more casually than the business community or other professional groups. Casual is all right; sloppy is not. Most directors who were interviewed for this book said they were not very influenced by what designers wore to interviews. One did remark, however, that if he interviewed a designer who was expensively dressed, he might assume that person to be an expensive designer who would not be sufficiently budget conscious!

Some interviews are long and some are short. Some directors spend a good deal of time chatting before turning to the portfolio, others are interested in seeing your work right away. Some know a good deal about costumes and others know very little. Respond to individual situations and don't be surprised when each one is different.

It is not out of place for you to ask questions during the interview. Before you arrive, think about what you want to know. Ask about the stage, production dates, the acting company,

FIGURES 8-13, 8-14, and 8-15.
Figures 8-13 and 8-14 (above) are
sketches by Lowell Detweiler for the
Denver Center Theatre production of
Caucasian Chalk Circle. They are
rendered in ink, colored pencil, and
gouach on brown wrapping paper.
Figure 8-15 (right) is a photograph
of the two costumes. *Sketch
photographs by Frances Aronson.
Costume photograph courtesy of the
Denver Center Theatre Company.*

FIGURE 8-16. Colleen Muscha's sketch of Curley's wife from *Of Mice and Men* for the Milwaukee Repertory Theater production. Rendered in pencil and watercolor. *Photograph by Frances Aronson.*

the costume shop staff, and location. Ask for information that might influence your decision to take or not take the job if it is offered to you. Your enthusiasm for designing at that theatre may well be dampened when you discover the costume shop has two straight stitch sewing machines, one stitcher, and no cutter.

United Scenic Artists

In order to accept design jobs with some theatrical organizations, free-lance costume designers must join a union called United Scenic

Artists. USA is affiliated with the International Brotherhood of Painters and Allied Trades (IBPAT) of the AFL-CIO and is subject to the same Brotherhood constitution. In 1990 Locals 829 of New York and Los Angeles and 350 of Chicago merged. 829/350 is divided into three regions, Eastern, Central, and Western with offices in New York, Los Angeles, and Chicago. Members are registered in the region of their principal residence. Membership in USA includes costume, scenery, and lighting designers, stylists, crafts people, and scenic artists.

Membership in USA as a costume designer is usually gained by an exam and portfolio review for the beginning designer, or by a portfolio review for the more experienced designer. Exams and portfolios are reviewed by a panel of USA designers. Further information on membership can be obtained by contacting one of the regional offices:

575 8th Ave., New York, NY 10018
343 S. Dearborn, Chicago, IL 60604
540 Wilshire Blvd., Los Angeles, CA 90036

Theatrical organizations who have entered into contract agreements with United Scenic Artists may not hire a non-union costume designer except in special situations when they are also required to hire a union design supervisor. The prospect of hiring two designers for the same project usually prohibits the producing group from hiring non-union people.

Some of the large producing organizations that have hiring agreements with USA are Broadway theatres, Off-Broadway theatres, LORT theatres, ABC, NBC, and CBS television, the Metropolitan Opera, and feature film producers. Some regional and dinner theatres, some regional opera and ballet companies, and some free-lance television producers are also contracted to USA.

United Scenic Artists exists to protect the interests of designers on the job. A union contract sets minimum fees for the designs and states

FIGURES 8-17, 8-18, and 8-19. A sketch from Arnold S. Levine's union exam project in Chicago, *A Midsummer Night's Dream. Photograph by Frances Aronson.* A sketch from Colleen Muscha's union exam project in New York, *Albert Herring. Photograph by Frances Aronson.* A sketch from Helen Ju's union exam project in New York, *Follies. Photograph by Rosemary Ingham.*

that travel and out-of-pocket expenses must be reimbursed. It requires producers to pay into pension and welfare funds. It protects the designer's rights in cases of subsequent productions either of the original designs or the design concepts. It establishes rules for billing and prohibits the producing group from altering the designs after opening night without the express permission of the designer.

A union contract also clarifies the designer's responsibilities to the producer. The following broad statement describing a costume designer's duties on a production was taken from the USA 1991 Contract Information Working Rules and Rate Book:

THE COSTUME DESIGNER designs the costumes for the production and renders the following services in connection herewith:

A. Completes all necessary sketches of costumes.

B. Supplies color schemes and color sketches, or outline sketches and examples of materials to be used for each costume, and all of its ornament and detail.

C. Designs or selects or approves all costume accessories.

D. Designs or selects and supervises the coordination of all contemporary costumes, including the selection from the performer's personal wardrobe when necessary.

E. Supplies specifications for the supervision of making and painting of costumes, and the making of costume accessories.

F. Attend the dress rehearsals of the production.

G. Approves hair styling and selection of wigs, hairpieces, mustaches, beards, and of special make-ups.

H. Supplies specifications and solicits estimates for the producer from contractors mutually satisfactory to the Producer and the Costume Designer, if requested to do so by the Producer.

There are fringe benefits to union membership such as group health insurance and life insurance coverage. Perhaps the most important benefit is being part of a professional community. United Scenic Artists is a relatively small group, less than three thousand nationwide, of free-lance designers who have in their organization a means through which they can discuss and try to solve the common problems of their work.

What union membership does *not* do is find work for designers. It may protect you once you are on the job but securing that job remains entirely up to you.

Some costume designers choose to work for a long time in non-union contract situations without approaching United Scenic Artists for membership. Others rush to take the exam right away. The road to becoming a successful free-lance costume designer is about the same length for both groups. Membership in USA does not prevent you from accepting non-union design jobs yet it is no secret that the highest-paying design opportunities, especially on the East Coast, are with producing organizations that have hiring agreements with the union. Sooner or later union membership becomes a necessary step for self-supporting free-lancers.

Contracts

Designers' contracts range from the very simple to the relatively complex. Some contracts come in the form of a letter while others are set up along more formal lines. Certain points are always included while many others may or may not be present.

It goes without saying that you should always read your contract carefully and never sign it until you are satisfied with the agreement into which you are entering.

All contracts state the fee to be paid to the designer and the date on which completed costumes are expected. Beyond these two major points, a contract may state the materials budget, provisions for transportation, housing and per diem expenses, production dates, residence dates, and program billing. The contract will detail royalty terms if they apply. There may be a clause that promises the designer first refusal rights to design the production again if it moves to another theatre, an important clause in Off-Off Broadway theatre contracts.

The following contracts will give you some idea of possible variations:

Contract #1: A sample contract from a nonunion theatre
_____

Letter of agreement between _____(designer)_____ and _____(producer)_____.

This letter, when signed, will constitute an agreement between you (the "Artist") and _____ (the "Theatre") and will confirm the terms of your employment.

The Artist will be employed by the Theatre as Costume Designer for the Theatre's production of _____(name of play)_____.

The Artist agrees to the Theatre's schedule of production as follows:

1. Design conferences, to be held in _____, on _____ and _____, at mutually acceptable times.

2. Completed and approved designs, in sketch form, due in the shop by _____.

3. Photo Call for selected costumes, scheduled for _____.

4. First Dress Rehearsal, scheduled for _____.

5. First Preview performance, scheduled for _____.

For such services rendered, the Theatre agrees to compensate the Artist with a fee of _____, to be paid as follows:

1. $_____ on return of completed agreement.

2. $_____ on _____ (beginning of construction).

3. $_____ on _____ (opening performance).

The Theatre will provide two (2) round trip air fares from _____, one for the design conference, and one for the engagement. The Theatre will also provide housing for the Artist during the engagement.

Changes in this agreement may be made only by written consent of both the Artist and the Theatre.

If you accept this agreement, please sign and return two copies to the Theatre.

Contract #2: A standard United Scenic Artists/LORT contract

UNITED SCENIC ARTISTS 829/350

LOCAL 829　　　　(212) 736-4498
575 Eighth Avenue, New York City 10018

LOCAL 350　　　　(312) 431-0790
343 So. Dearborn, Chicago, Ill.　60604

COVER SHEET: *(Standard Individual Designer's Agreement)*

This Cover Sheet shall be signed in quadruplicate. Attach all riders to each copy. The Theatre shall promptly file one copy with the Union. The Designer shall not be required to furnish designs until this Cover Sheet has been executed by the Theatre.

1. AGREEMENT:

The Theatre engages the Designer to design and the Designer agrees to design the production herein described.

NAME OF THEATRE:_____

NAME OF STAGE:_____ LORT CATEGORY:_____

NAME OF DESIGNER:_____

DESIGN CATEGORY:　　SCENERY ☐　　　COSTUMES ☐　　　LIGHTING ☐

NAME OF PRODUCTION:_____

2. COMPENSATION:

The Theatre agrees to pay the Designer a fee of $_____, in thirds, according to the following schedule:

A. $_____payable on the signing by the Designer of this Cover Sheet.

B. $_____payable on the date that a full set of drawings, sketches, and/or specifications are accepted as sufficient to begin construction, in the case of scenery and costumes, and to hang instruments, in the case of lighting.

C. $_____payable on the scheduled termination date:_____ 19_____.

3. RESIDENCE:

The Designer agrees to be at the Theatre from_____ 19_____ to_____ 19_____.

4. PENSION & WELFARE:

The Theatre agrees to contribute an amount equal to eleven percent (11%) ($_____) of the above fee to the United Scenic Artists Local 829, Pension and Welfare Funds.

5. GENERAL PROVISIONS:

Both the Theatre and the Designer agree that each and every provision contained in the basic Agreement between United Scenic Artists, Locals 829 and 350, and the League of Resident Theatres shall be part of this Cover Sheet, as though set forth herein at length; and that they have read said Agreement which sets forth the minimum conditions under which the Designer may work for the Theatre. No Designer or Theatre may waive or alter any of the minimum terms and conditions of the Agreement without the written approval of the Union, except that nothing in the Agreement shall preclude a Designer from obtaining better terms and conditions than are therein provided. This provision is of the essence of the Agreement. Additional terms shall be placed in a rider attached to this Cover Sheet, and shall be deemed a part hereof.

ACCEPTED:　　　　　　　　　　　　Theatre must sign Cover Sheet first.

DESIGNER: _____　　THEATRE: _____
　　　　　(Signature)

_____　　　　By: _____
(please print name)　　　　　　　　(Signature)
Social Security Number: _____

Date: _____　　　(please print name)
　　　　　　　　　　　　　　　　Date: _____
Address: _____
　　　　　　　　　　　　　　　　Address: _____
_____
_____ Zip _____　　_____ Zip _____

Phone: (_____) _____　　Phone: (_____) _____

DUES CHECK-OFF AUTHORIZATION:

I, the undersigned member of United Scenic Artists, Local 829 or 350, affiliated with the International Brotherhood of Painters and Allied Trades, AFL-CIO, herewith authorize my employer to deduct from all monies earned my Union dues consisting of administrative dues assessed at 2% of the gross amount of all fees, and direct that such amounts so deducted be sent directly to the Financial Secretary of said Union for and on my behalf.

Signed:_____　　　　Date:_____

UNITED SCENIC ARTISTS: RECEIVED (DATE)_____ 19_____

LORT—1987

209

Contract #3: A sample letter contract
_____

Dear _____:

This letter, when signed by you, will constitute an agreement with the (name of theatre)
_____.

We hereby engage you as Costume Designer for our production of _____
_____ opening _____. For your services you will
receive a fee of _____ and a per diem of _____ for up to seven days.
We also agree to reimburse your transportation from _____ to
_____. Your fee will be payable in thirds: on receipt of a
signed agreement, on receipt of designs, and on opening. The costume budget is
_____.

Billing will be "Costumes by _____ " and will appear
with the Director in the same size and boldness.

Please sign and return the copy to me as soon as possible.
_____

No contract is carved in marble. Alteration is easy. If you have special contractual requests, make them known at the time you are hired so they can be negotiated, agreed upon, and written in. If the contract comes to you with clauses that you feel were not agreed upon, call the producer and ask for changes. When you sign a contract, you have made a legal commitment to live up to the terms of the agreement. Never enter such agreements lightly.

Many designers dislike dealing with the business side of free-lancing and/or feel that they cannot assess or negotiate a contract effectively. Some of these designers engage agents to represent them and find their services well worth the agents' percentage. Others, who find they need contract assistance only some of the time, engage a lawyer to negotiate contracts on a one-time, one-fee basis.

Taxes

As an independent business person you are responsible for running your financial affairs in an orderly and legal manner. This includes filing annual or quarterly tax returns and paying the appropriate federal, state, and social security taxes.

Some designers manage to make their way through the intricacies of Department of Internal Revenue publications on their own while others gladly pay a tax accountant to do it for them. If you opt for a tax accountant, make sure you choose one who understands the nature of your work.

Don't forget to report *all* your earnings, even if they were fees from which no withholding tax or social security contributions were withheld.

Whether you do your own tax accounting or hire someone to do it for you, you will come out better in the end and save yourself a great deal of grief if you keep all expense receipts and cancelled checks and file them regularly into appropriate categories. Some of the tax deductible expenses for free-lance costume designers are: art supplies, professional stationery, film and theatre tickets, unreimbursed out-of-town expenses, entertaining for the purpose of getting work, work-related book and magazine purchases, union dues, assistant fees paid by you, rent and utilities paid for work space. In order to deduct these expenses, however, you have to be able to substantiate the expenditures. Get in the habit of putting receipts into individually labelled envelopes or file folders. Do your sorting regularly and save yourself the horror of facing a year's worth of miscellaneous paper scraps at tax time.

A Last Word

This book began with a designer reading and analyzing a playscript; it ends with paying income tax. The progression is not incongruous. Between starting and finishing you can count on being incomparably busy as you meet with other members of the production group, haunt museums and libraries, draw, paint, shop, and work shoulder-to-shoulder with costume technicians.

You have chosen a demanding profession, the pursuit of which will require prodigious amounts of energy. It also will require you to be brave, tough, and flexible. It asks you to be both artistic and practical—usually at the same time. It insists on the presence of humor in the face of anything.

Yet few other professions offer the variety, the potential for meeting interesting and gifted people, or the many opportunities to find personal and professional satisfaction. Every play is different, every production situation is unique, and every time you set out to design costumes for the theatre you may be sure you are in for an adventure.

REFERENCE

Selected Painters for Costume Design Research

The following list of painters is organized into periods that roughly correspond with major changes in clothing silhouette. Since a painter's work may span many years, there are names that appear in more than one period. The first appearance of the painter's name is accompanied by dates and comments; subsequent appearances are limited to the name. Most dates are from:

Peter and Linda Murray, *The Penguin Dictionary of Art and Artists*, 4th ed. (Harmondsworth, Middlesex, England: Penguin Books Ltd., 1976).

1250–1350

ITALIAN

Cimabue (Cenni di Pepi) (1240–1302?)
Florentine. Believed to be Giotto's teacher.
Duccio (Duccio di Buoninsegna) (c. 1255/60–1318?)
Sienese. Blended Byzantine and Gothic elements.
Giotto (Giotto di Bordone) 1266/7–1337)
Florentine. Also sculptor and architect. Introduced, with Cimabue, a new naturalism into figures.
Martini, Simone (c. 1284–1344)
Sienese. Pupil of Duccio. Excellent sense of silhouette & good costume detail.
Orcagna, Andrea (Andrea di Cione) (c. 1308–1368)
Florentine. Also sculptor and architect.

During this period in Northern Europe artists did not sign their work and there was very little painting relevant to costume design. Sculpture from the great cathedrals such as Reims, Notre–Dame, Amiens, Naumburg, etc. offer excellent costume research. Secular manuscript illuminators appeared. The anonymously done illuminations from the *Psalter of St. Louis* (c. 1260) and those from the *Prayer Book of Philip the Fair* by Master Honoré of Paris are of particular interest.

1350–1450

FRENCH

Limbourg, Paul, Jean, and Herman de (all dead by end of 1416)
Three brothers, Flemish by birth but trained in Paris. Came under the protection of the Duke of Burgundy. Manuscript illuminators responsible for the extraordinarily beautiful *Les Tres Riches Heures du Duc de Berry* (1413) containing detailed examples of high fashion French clothing of the period.

ITALIAN

Gozzoli, Benozzo (c. 1421–1497)
His frescoes are secular in outlook.
Lippi, Fra Filippo (c. 1406–1469)
Florentine. Painted religious subjects with great attention to flowing drapery.
Masaccio, Tommaso Cassio (Tommaso di ser Giovanni di Mone) (1401–1428)
Florentine. Regarded as one of the founders of modern painting. See his frescoes in the Brancacci Chapel, especially *The Tribute Money*.
Piero della Francesca (c. 1410/20–1492)
From Tuscany. Painted strong, heroic figures. Very sensitive to clothing silhouette.
Pisanello, Antonio (c. 1395–1455/6)
Also medalist and draughtsman. His work includes costume sketches.
Uccello, Paolo (1397–1475)
Three *Battles* painted between 1454 and 1457 are of particular interest.

NETHERLANDISH

Eyck, Jan van (c. 1380?–1441)
Portraits and religious paintings with good costume detail. See particularly the *Ghent Altarpiece*. Also beautifully detailed drawings. Had a brother, Hubert, also a painter, about whom little is known.
Weyden, Roger van der (Rogier de le Pasture) (1399/1400–1464)
Settled in Brussels sometime after 1426. Painted many portraits for members of the Burgundian court. Sensitive costume detail.

1450–1550

FRENCH

Clouet, Jean II (d. 1540/1)
Court painter in France. Good costume detail especially in his portrait drawings.

Fouquet, Jehan (c. 1420–in or before 1481)
Paintings and miniatures with good costume detail.

GERMAN

Cranach, Lucas, the Elder (1472–1553)
Also etcher and designer of woodcuts. Designed propaganda woodcuts for Luther. Painted full-length portraits with fine costume detail.

Dürer, Albrecht (1471–1528)
Also produced woodcuts, engravings, drawings and watercolors. Wonderful costume detail. Good for peasant costume.

Grünewald (Mathis Neithardt–Gothardt) (c. 1470/80–1528)
Only a few paintings extant. Figures are highly dramatic with sensitively rendered clothing detail.

Holbein, Hans the Younger (1497/8–1543)
Penetratingly realist portrait painter. Settled in England and became court painter to Henry VIII. Meticulous costume detail. See drawings especially.

ITALIAN

Bellini, Giovanni (c. 1430–1516)
Venetian. Religious and mythological paintings as well as portraits. Good clothing silhouettes.

Botticelli, Sandro (c. 1445–1510)
Florentine. Favorite painter of the Medici circle. An individualist in painting style and color use. Many beautifully detailed hairstyles with classical overtones.

Carpaccio, Vittore (c. 1460/65–1523/6)
Venetian. Assistant to Giovanni Bellini. See his full-length portrait *Knight in a Landscape*.

Ghirlandaio, Domenico Bigordi (1449–1494)
Florentine. Executed religious frescoes and portraits with naturalistic detail. His son Ridolfo (1483–1561) was a portrait painter of great distinction.

Leonardo da Vinci (1452–1519)
Worked first in Milan then in Florence. The epitome of the "Renaissance man." The drawings especially have excellent clothing and hair details.

Michelangelo Buonarroti (1475–1564)
Florentine. Worked also in Bologna and Rome. Sculptor and architect. Most work heroic in nature. Drawings best for costume research.

Piero della Francesca

Raphael (Raffaello Sanzio) (1483–1520)
Born in Perugia; worked in Florence and Rome. The central painter of the High Renaissance. Exceptionally fine portraits in which both realism and idealism are present.

Signorelli, Luca (c. 1441/50–1523)
Religious frescoes and altarpieces. Vividly realistic, detailed figures.

Titain (Tiziano Vecellio, (c. 1487/90–1576)
Venetian. After Raphael's death, the most sought-after portraitist of the age. Splendid clothing detail.

NETHERLANDISH

Bruegel (Brueghel, Breughel), Pieter I (c. 1525/30–1569)
Wonderful paintings of local peasant life.

Goes, Hugo van der (d. 1482)
Highly dramatic, intricately detailed work. See *The Portinari Altarpiece* for exquisite costume details.

Memling, Hans (c. 1430/40–1494)
German-born but pure Netherlandish painter. Pupil of Roger van der Weyden. Religious paintings and fine portraits with superb costume detail. See drawings also.

1550–1625

ENGLISH

Hilliard, Nicholas (c. 1547–1619)
Goldsmith and miniaturist. Wonderful clothing detail, including footwear. See doublet with peascod belly in *A Young Man Among Roses* and several portraits of Queen Elizabeth.

Jones, Inigo (1573–1652)
Architect and designer of court masques. There are 450 extant drawings for stage scenery and costumes.

Oliver, Isaac (d. 1617)
> Miniaturist. History paintings and portraits. Student of Hilliard.

FLEMISH

Brouwer, Adriaen (c. 1605/6–1638)
> Worked in Holland. Good for realistic low life, especially sordid tavern scenes.

Gheeraerts, Marcus, the younger (c. 1561–1636)
> Huguenot refugee who settled in England. Member of a large family of painters. Full and half-length portraits, formal, heraldic, bright in color.

Rubens, Sir Peter Paul (1577–1640)
> From Antwerp. The great Baroque painter. Court painter to the Spanish Governors of the Netherlands. Early portrait work best for costume detail.

FRENCH

Clouet, Francois (d. 1572)
> Son of Jean Clouet whom he succeeded as French court painter. Specialized in portrait drawings and paintings.

ITALIAN

Bronzino, Agnolo (1503–1572)
> Florentine. Court painter to Cosimo I de Medici. One of the most important Mannerist portrait painters. Elegant clothing and fabric detail.

Caravaggio, Michelangelo (1571–1610)
> Milanese. Dramatic work. Wealth of clothing detail. Many peasant figures.

Moroni, Giovanni Battista (c. 1525–1578)
> Venetian. Quiet family portraits with good costume detail and delicate grayed colors.

Reni, Guido (1575–1642)
> Bolognese. Painter and etcher.

Tintoretto, Jacopo (1518–1594)
> Venetian. Mannerist painter of religious themes. Figures in exaggerated poses. Good garment silhouettes.

Veronese, Paolo Caliari (1528–1588)
> Trained in Verona; worked in Venice after 1553. Huge pictures crowded with fashionably dressed figures including courtiers, musicians and soldiers.

SPANISH

El Greco (Domenikos Theotocopoulos) 1541–1614)
> Cretan by birth; trained in Venice and worked in Spain. Mannerist painter. Ecstatic and passionate style. Eerie use of color and unusual clothing.

Mor, Anthonis (Antonio Moro) (c. 1517/21–1576/7)
> Portrait painter from Utrecht who became Court Painter of the Spanish Netherlands. Combined an acute sense of character with Titian-like grand style.

1625–1700

DUTCH

During this period the prosperous Dutch acquired a prodigious taste for being painted and for acquiring paintings. There is probably no other place or period where the population's appearance is so widely recorded. The most prolific of the following Dutch painters left several hundred works each.

Hals, Frans (c. 1581/85–1666)
> The great portrait painter of Haarlem. Executed both individual and group portraits of middle- and lower-class life. Painted large lively groups of Archers and Musketeers during the Dutch Wars with Spain.

Helst, Bartholomeus van der (1613–1670)
> Amsterdam. Fashionable portrait painter.

Honthorst, Gerrit van (1590–1656)
> Born and trained in Utrecht; later Court Painter at The Hague. Genre scenes and elegant portraits.

Hooch (Hoogh) Pieter de (1629–after 1689)
> Delft. Like Vermeer, his pictures are often of interiors with two or three figures engaged in some household task. Clothing rendered in sensitive detail.

Ostade, Adriaen van (1610–1681)
> Haarlem genre painter. Student of Hals. Many peasant scenes.

Rembrandt van Rijn (1606–1681)
> Leyden and Amsterdam. Enormous body of work includes etchings and drawings. Individual portraits, pairs and groups. See especially *The Night Watch* and *Staal Masters*.

Steen, Jan (1626–1679)
> Tavern keeper in Leyden. Painted humorous subjects from peasant and middle-class life. Unusual clothing details; see children's garments in *The Eve of St. Nicholas.*

Ter Borch (Terborgh, Terburg, Terborch), Gerard (1617–1681)
> Painted genre subjects and portraits, many full length. Beautiful fabric rendering. Note exquisite costume detail in the *Brothel Scene.*

Vermeer, Jan (1632–1675)
> From Delft. Painted mostly domestic interiors with figures engaged in ordinary work. Jewel-like color.

ENGLISH

Hollar, Wenceslaus (1607–1677)
> Born in Prague, worked in England. Illustrator and topographer. Etchings and watercolors of everyday, middle-class life have superb costume detail.

Jones, Inigo

Jordaens, Jacob (1593–1678)
> Born and died in Antwerp. Assistant to Rubens. Executed portraits of the House of Orange and large genre scenes of drinking bouts.

Kneller, Sir Godrey (c. 1646/9–1723)
> Born in Lubeck, trained in Amsterdam. Arrived in England around 1776 and became a leading portrait painter.

Lely, Sir Peter (1618–1680)
> Born in Germany, studied in Haarlem. Arrived in London in 1640's. Became the most influential English painter of his period and left hundreds of portraits.

FLEMISH

Brouwer, Adriaen

Rubens, Sir Peter Paul

Teniers, David II, the Younger (1610–1690)
> Predominantly genre scenes of peasant life. Over 2,000 pictures are attributed to him. His father, David Teniers, the Elder, painted religious pictures and landscapes.

Van Dyck, Sir Anthony (1599–1641)
> From Antwerp. Best work done during the nine years he lived in England executing portraits at the Court of Charles I. These are excellent costume research. See, for example, *Portrait of Charles I Hunting.*

FRENCH

Berain, Jean (1640–1711)
> Designer of court masques.

Bosse, Abraham (1602–1676)
> Illustrator, etcher and engraver. Son of a tailor. Superb source for detailed middle-class clothing.

Callot, Jacques (c. 1592/3–1635)
> Illustrator, etcher and engraver. Beautifully drawn clothing detail for the middle and upper classes.

Champaigne, Philippe de (1602–1674)
> Born in Brussels; settled in Paris in 1621. Many excellent middle-class portraits.

Largillierre (Largillière) Nicholas de (1656–1746)
> Born in Paris, trained in Antwerp. Settled in Paris in 1682. Executed portraits of the wealthy middle classes.

La Tour, Georges de (1593–1652)
> Painter of religious subjects with figures dressed in superbly detailed contemporary clothing. Wonderful use of light.

Le Brun (Lebrun), Charles (1619–1690)
> A powerful and influential artist who was chief decorator to Louis XIV. Left many drawings of interest to costume researchers.

Le Nain, Antoine (c. 1588–1648)
> Louis (c. 1593–1648)
> Mathieu (c. 1607–1677)
> Three brothers whose work is difficult to assign positively. Louis generally credited with a group of large scale paintings in cool grey tones of peasant families. See, for example, *Peasant Family* (c. 1640).

Mignard, Pierre (1612–1695)
> Lebrun's rival. Important court portrait painter. Did many allegorical portraits.

Rigaud, Hyacinthe (1659–1743)
> Principal official painter to court of Louis XIV. Also worked under Louis XV. The state portraits done with great pomp; nonofficial portraits are more natural. Particularly good for wig and hairstyle research.

SPANISH

Murillo, Bartholomé Esteban (c. 1617–1682)
> Seville. Early paintings of beggar-children are naturalistic; later ones become idealized, "fancy-dress" rags. Many religious paintings with peasant figures which tend to be sentimentalized.

Ribera, Jusepe or Jose de (1591?–1652)
> From Valencia; settled and worked in Naples.

Painted life around him with great vigor and human reality.

Velasquez, Diego Rodriguez de Silva (1599–1660)
Born in Seville. Became Court Painter in Madrid in 1623. Beautiful portraits with good costume detail.

Zubarán, Francisco de (1598–1664)
Studied and settled in Seville. Executed devotional pictures, many of saints, with figures of massive solidity and solemnity.

1700–1790

AMERICAN

Blackburn, Joseph (c. 1730–? After 1774)
Active portrait painter 1754–1763. Excellent clothing detail.

Copley, John Singleton (1738–1815)
Excellent American portraits done in the early part of his career. See, for example, portrait of *Joseph Sherburne* (1767). Spent the latter half of his life in England doing chiefly history paintings.

Feke, Robert (c. 1705–c. 1750)
New England portrait painter, both individuals and groups. Excellent examples of dress during the Colonial Period.

Peale, Charles Willson (1741–1827)
Painted the leading citizens of Philadelphia and Annapolis. Also executed excellent miniatures of Revolutionary War officers; several of George Washington.

Pratt, Matthew (1734–1805)
Portrait painter in Philadelphia and New York. Good clothing detail.

Stuart, Gilbert (1755–1828)
Painted nearly every prominent American of his day. Excellent clothing detail. The Metropolitan Museum owns 22 Stuart portraits.

Theüs, Jeremiah (c. 1719–1774)
Painted the important social and political leaders in Charleston, South Carolina.

Trumbull, John (1756–1843)
Painter of portraits and historical subjects. Of particular interest are his many portraits of Revolutionary generals.

ENGLISH

Bigg, William Radmore (1755–1828)
Genre painter. An interesting example of his work is *Shipwrecked Sailor Boy*.

Gainsborough, Thomas (1727–1788)
Regarded landscape painting as his real bent but did many portraits of great elegance. See, for example, the beautiful painting of *Mrs. Siddons*. Look out for his tendency in some portraits to costume his subject in clothing of an earlier period, such as *Blue Boy*.

Hogarth, William (1697–1764)
Also goldsmith and engraver. Great success with several series of paintings on "modern moral subjects" such as *Harlot's Progress* (1731–32), *Rake's Progress* (1735) and *Marriage a la Mode* (1733–35). The paintings and engravings in these series are full of excellent costume detail, both dress and undress.

Kneller, Sir Godfrey

Morland, George (1763–1804)
Executed picturesque rustic genre paintings. Modelled himself on Brouwer. The paintings were popularized through engravings. See particularly *Industry, Idleness* and *The Stable*.

Raeburn, Sir Henry (1756–1823)
Jeweller and miniaturist. Early portraits of local Scottish dignitaries. See, for example, the *Rev. Robert Walker Skating* (1784). Portraits after 1790 are less detailed.

Reynolds, Sir Joshua (1723–1792)
Painted almost every notable man and woman in the 2nd half of the eighteenth century. Also history works. Good costume detail, especially men. Painted some women in loose-fitting gowns especially made for use in his studio.

Romney, George (1734–1802)
Shared popularity with Reynolds and Gainsborough but artistically inferior to both. Many prosaic portraits with uninspired but accurate rendering of clothes.

Smith, Joseph R. (1752–1812)

Wheatley, Francis (1747–1801)
Early work consists of small detailed portraits. After 1884 turned to genre subjects. See, especially, *Cries of London* (1795).

West, Benjamin (1738–1812)
Born in Philadelphia but left America to study in Rome and settle in London. Maintained a long and highly profitable relationship with George III. Portraits and history paintings.

Zoffany, Johann (1725–1810)
German born, Italian trained painter who settled in England in 1761. Portraits and theatrical scenes. Several portraits of Garrick. Superb clothing and costume detail.

FRENCH

Boucher, François (1703–1770)
Began as Watteau's engraver. The most typical Rococo decorator. Painted charming mythological scenes; clothing beautiful and romantic.

Chardin, Jean–Baptiste–Siméon (1699–1779)
Best known as still-life painter. Also did small genre scenes, unsentimentalized and unidealized. Some pastel portraits.

Drouais, François–Hubert (1727–1775)
Portrait painter. Subjects included actresses and members of the royal family. Particularly successful with children.

Fragonard, Jean–Honoré (1732–1806)
Painted beautiful and sentimental subjects during reign of Louis XV. See especially the *Progress of Love* series done for Mme. du Barry. No work after the Revolution.

Greuze, Jean–Baptiste (1725–1805)
Narrative genre painting with superbly detailed middle and lower class clothing. Portraits also. No work of note after the Revolution.

Lancret, Nicholas (1690–1743)
Imitator of Watteau. Painted chiefly *fetes galantes.*

Largillierre, Nicholas de

Latour, Maurice-Quentin de (1704–1788)
With Perronneau, most celebrated 18th C. French pastellist. Vigorous portraits of French royalty and high society.

Liotard, Jean–Etienne (1702–1789)
Swiss pastellist who worked in Paris from 1725. Travelled widely as a successful portraitist.

Nattier, Jean–Marc, the Younger (1685–1766)
Painter of the ladies in Louis XV's court. Good costume detail.

Rigaud, Hyacinthe

Vigeé–Le Brun (Lebrun), Marie-Louise Elisabeth (1755–1842)
Highly successful portrait painter. Subjects included Marie Antoinette and members of the court. Fled France at the outbreak of the Revolution. Travelled widely painting excellent portraits in several countries. Her *Memoirs* are fascinating.

Watteau, Jean–Antoine (1684–1721)
His paintings of Italian comedy characters and country scenes and his beautiful crayon drawings in black, red and white are all superb costume research material.

IRISH

Buck, Adam (1759–1833)

ITALIAN

Longhi, Alessandro (1733–1813)
Well known portraitist and son of Pietro Longhi.

Longhi, Pietro (1702–1785)
Venetian genre painter. His scenes of quiet domestic life in patrician or wealthy merchant households are rich in clothing detail.

Teipolo, Giovanni Battista (1696–1770)
Venetian. Great decorator of palaces and churches. Purest exponent of the Italian Rococo.

SPANISH

Goya, Francisco Jose de (1746–1828)
Painted scenes of Spanish life and many unflattering portraits of Charles IV and his family. Graphic artist also; etched plates of the Napoleonic invasion. Good costume detail.

1790–1815

AMERICAN

Copley, John Singleton
Peale, Charles Willson
Pratt, Matthew
Stuart, Gilbert
Trumbull, John

ENGLISH

Beechey, Sir William (1753–1839)
Named Portrait Painter to the Queen in 1793. Truthful eye for detail.

Bigg, W.R.

Gillray, James (1757–1815)
Caricaturist. Good costume detail.

Hoppner, John (c. 1758–1810)
A principal follower of Reynolds. Named Portrait Painter to the Prince of Wales in 1793.

Lawrence, Sir Thomas (1769–1830)
Enormously successful portrait painter. Appointed Painter to the King in 1792. Commissioned by George IV to paint portraits of all the great personalities of the struggle against Napoleon.

Moreland, George
Opie, John (1761–1807)
    Portraits and historical subjects. Best at painting peasants, particularly children and old men.
Raeburn, Sir Henry
Romney, George
Rowlandson, Thomas (1756–1827)
    Brilliant caricaturist and graphic artist. Portrayed English life and manners with exuberance and humor.
West, Benjamin
Wheatley, Francis
Zoffany, Johann

FRENCH

Boilly, Louis–Leopold (1761–c. 1830/45)
    Printmaker and painter of genre scenes. Many grotesque or tragic pictures of the Revolution.
David, Jacques–Louis (1748–1825)
    Principal painter of French Republican virtues. Clothing beautifully rendered in all his pictures.
Gerard, Baron Francois (1770–1837)
    Student of David. Popular portrait painter during the 1st Empire.
Gros, Baron Antoine Jean (1771–1835)
    Pupil of David. Executed large pictures illustrating the Napoleonic saga. Brilliant battlepieces.
Ingres, Jean Auguste Dominique (1780–1867)
    Student of David. French portraits until 1806 when he went to Italy. Work in Italy includes wonderful drawings of visitors to Rome. Great clothing detail.
Isabey, Jean–Baptiste (1767–1855)
    Portrait painter and miniaturist.
Vigeé–Le Brun, Marie-Louise Elisabeth

IRISH

Buck, Adam

ITALIAN

Longhi, Alessandro

SPANISH

Goya, Francisco Jose de

1815–1840

AMERICAN

Ingham, Charles Cromwell (1796–1863)
    Born in Dublin, settled in New York in 1816. Elegant portraits with intricately rendered details. See full-length portrait of *Amelia Palmer* (1830).
Morse, Samuel Finley Breese (1791–1872)
    Born in Massachusetts, studied in London. Painted many portraits in New England and the South. See, for example, the full-length portrait of his eldest daughter (1835). Also inventor of, among other things, the telegraph.
Peale, Charles
Stuart, Gilbert
Sully, Thomas
Trumbull, John
Waldo and Jewett William Jewett (1795–1873) and Samuel Waldo (1793–1861)
    Two painters who produced joint portraits from 1818 to 1854. Clothing details always carefully rendered. See *The Knapp Children* painted about 1849.

AUSTRIAN

Waldmüller, Ferdinand George (1793–1865)
    Portrait and landscape painter who worked in the simple, unaristocratic Biedermeier style. Superb costume detail.

ENGLISH

Cruikshank, George (1792–1878)
    Leading caricaturist of his day, illustrator and cartoonist. Illustrated books by Charles Dickens and Harrison Ainsworth.
Beechey, Sir William
Lawrence, Sir Thomas
Raeburn, Sir Henry
Rowlandson, Thomas

FRENCH

Corot, Jean–Baptiste–Camille (1796–1875)
    Travelled widely and made many drawings to record his journeys. The late portraits are particularly strong and forthright. Many rural subjects.
David, Jacques–Louis

Delacroix, Ferdinand–Victor Eugene (1798–1863)
    Major painter of the Romantic movement in France. Subjects include scenes from North African Arab and Jewish life, battles, hunts and portraits of close friends. See his rendering of Chopin (1838). Also illustrated Byron's work.
Gros, Baron Antoine–Jean.
Ingres, Jean–Auguste–Dominique
Isabey, Jean Baptiste
Vigeé–Le Brun, Marie-Louise Elisabeth
Vernet, Emile–Jean–Horace (1789–1863)
    Paintings and lithographs include excellent battle scenes.

IRISH
Buck, Adam

1840–1865

AMERICAN
Bingham, George Caleb (1811–1879)
    Painted scenes from everyday life in the American West.
Healy, George Peter Alexander (1813–1894)
    Boston painter. Portraits include many of the great political and social figures of his time.
Ingham, Charles Cromwell
Morse, Samuel Finley Breese
Mount, William Sidney (1807–1868)
    New York painter. Portraits and genre paintings of rural life on Long Island. Exquisite clothing detail.
Nast, Thomas (1840–1902)
    Cartoonist.
Waldo and Jewett

AUSTRIAN
Waldmüller, Ferdinand George

BELGIAN
Stevens, Alfred (1828–1906)
    Also sculptor and decorator. Some good portraits and many drawings with excellent clothing detail.

ENGLISH
Burne–Jones, Sir Edward (1833–1898)
    One of the painters in the circle around William Morris and Rossetti. Dreamy romantic paintings; tapestry and stained-glass designs.
Cruikshank, George
Du Maurier, George (1834–1896)
    Caricaturist. Illustrator for *Punch.*
Frith, William Powell (1819–1909)
    Portrait painter until 1840 when he turned to costume history and genre painting. Intricate Victorian scenes. Costume of all social classes. Examine the wealth of detail in *The Railway Station.*
Hunt, William Holman (1827–1910)
    Founded the Pre-Raphaelite Brotherhood with Millais and Rossetti. His paintings in Egypt and the Holy Land have particularly interesting rustic costume detail.
Keene, Charles Samuel (1823–1891)
    Graphic artist. Many drawings in *Punch.* Pen studies of figures and landscapes.
Leech, John (1817–1864)
    Caricaturist.
Millais, Sir John Everett (1829–1896)
    Founded the Pre-Raphaelite Brotherhood with Hunt and Rossetti. Fashionable, technically brilliant painter. Portraits, costume history and genre pieces.
Morris, William (1834–1896)
    Became a painter under the influence of Rossetti. Turned to "art for use" and founded a design firm in 1861 to produce wallpaper, furniture, tapestries, stained-glass windows, carpets, etc.
Rossetti, Dante Gabriel (1828–1882)
    Poet as well as painter. Founder of the Pre-Raphaelite Brotherhood with Hunt and Millais. Highly aesthetic and self-conscious work.

FRENCH
Chassériau, Théodore (1819–1856)
    Born in the West Indies. Subject matter includes Biblical and Shakespearean illustration, scenes from North African life, religious and allegorical decorations. Pencil portraits are beautifully detailed.
Corot, Jean–Baptiste–Camille
Courbet, Gustave (1819–1877)
    Vivid naturalism. Excellent research materials in his everyday scenes from French middle-class and peasant life.

Daumier, Honoré (1808–1879)
Also lithographer and cartoonist. Strong watercolor scenes of everyday life and in the Court of Justice; straightforward and untouched by Romanticism.

Degas, Hilaire Edgar Germain (1834–1917)
Also sculptor. Early works include family portraits and history pictures in the academic manner. His own Impressionist style appears after 1860. Ballet girls, working girls, models and cabaret artists among his favorite subjects. Later work almost entirely in pastels.

Delacroix, Ferdinand–Victor Eugene

Gavarni (1804–1866)
Lithographer and caricaturist.

Manet, Édouard (1832–1883)
Early works included beautiful paintings of Spanish visitors to Paris. After 1870 adopted the Impressionist technique and palette. Always good costume detail.

Millet, Jean–François (1814–1875)
Son of a peasant. Painted genre scenes of peasants and their labors that are excellent for costume research.

PRUSSIAN

Winterhalter, Franz (1806–1873)
Painted in Paris. Portraits of royalty and aristocracy. Also genre subjects.

1865–1890

AMERICAN

Abbey, Edwin Austin (1852–1911)
Illustrator for periodicals, genre painter and watercolorist.

Bingham, George Caleb

Cassatt, Mary Stevenson (1844–1926)
Lived in Paris. Influenced by Degas. Exhibited with the Impressionists. Beautiful paintings and pastels of women and children with sensitive clothing detail.

Eakins, Thomas Cowperthwaite (1844–1916)
Also photographer. Portraits and paintings are realistic and detailed.

Healy, George Peter Alexander

Homer, Winslow (1836–1910)
Early career as magazine illustrator includes record of the Civil War with good uniform details. After 1875 devoted himself to painting American country life. Adopted a quasi-Impressionist style.

Johnson, Eastman (1824–1906)
Genre scenes. Pictures of American life, many set in New England.

Nast, Thomas

Pennell, Joseph (c. 1857/60–1926)
Printmaker and illustrator.

Pyle, Howard (1853–1911)
Popular illustrator of chivalric tales. Teacher and founder of the Brandywine School where artists like N. C. Wyeth and Maxfield Parrish studied.

Sargent, John Singer (1856–1925)
American portrait painter who settled in London and painted High Society in Edwardian and Georgian times. Huge output of work. Some larger-than-life portraits.

Whistler, James Abbott McNeill (1834–1903)
From Massachusetts. Cartographer and etcher as well as portraitist. Good costume detail.

BELGIAN

Stevens, Alfred

ENGLISH

Burne–Jones, Edward

Cruikshank, George

Du Maurier, George

Frith, William Powell

Greenaway, Kate (1846–1901)
Illustrator, painter and author of children's books. Rendered exquisite children's clothing.

Hunt, William Holman

Keene, Charles Samuel

Millais, Sir John Everett

Morris, William

Orchardson, Sir William Quiller (1832–1910)
Scottish genre and portrait painter. Painted scenes from Shakespeare.

Rossetti, Dante Gabriel

FRENCH

Béraud, Jean (1849–1935)
Genre scenes and portraits.

Cézanne, Paul (1839–1906)
One of the greatest painters of the last 100 years. Many landscapes and still lifes. Portraits have dramatic, beautifully rendered but not particularly detailed clothing.

Corot, Jean–Baptiste–Camille

Daumier, Honoré
Degas, Hilaire Edgar Germain
Doré, Gustave (1832–1883)
> Brilliant graphic artist and sculptor as well as painter. His engravings of the squalor of London life are of particular interest.

Gervex, Henri (1852–1929)
> History and genre painter. Mythological scenes.

Goubie, Jean Richard (1842–1899)
> Hunting scenes.

Manet, Édouard
Millet, Jean–François
Renoir, Pierre Auguste (1841–1919)
> One of the greatest of the painters affected by Impressionism. Early works include portraits and figure groups with nice costume details.

Tissot, James Joseph Jacques (1836–1902)
> French by birth but worked in England much of his life. Produced charming illustrations of Victorian life in paintings and etchings. Superb costume details.

Toulouse–Lautrec, Compte Henri Marie Raymond de (1864–1901)
> All his paintings, prints and drawings have lovely costume details. Subject matter reflected his own haunts: dance halls and cafes in Montmartre, cabarets, the circus, brothels.

SWEDISH

Larsson, Carl (1853–1919)
> Paintings of his own home and family provide beautiful costume research.

1890–1900

AMERICAN

Abbey, Edwin Austin
Cassatt, Mary Stevenson
Eakins, Thomas Cowperthwaite
Frost, A.B. (1851–1928)
> Illustrator. Good examples of rustic costume.

Gibson, Charles Dana (1867–1944)
> From Massachusetts. Illustrator who created the famous "Gibson Girl," an attractive, athletic, outdoor woman. His work is an excellent source for costume research.

Homer, Winslow
Johnson, Eastman
Nast, Thomas

Pennell, Joseph
Pyle, Howard
Remington, Frederic (1861–1909)
> Beautiful paintings and sculptures of life in the American West.

Russell, Charles (1864–1926)
> Genre paintings of the American West. Excellent clothing detail for both white and Indian populations.

Sargent, John Singer
Smith, Francis Hopkinson (1838–1915)
> Also novelist and engineer.

Whistler, James McNeill

BELGIAN

Stevens, Alfred

ENGLISH

Beardsley, Aubrey Vincent (1872–1898)
> Illustrator. His work is the perfect expression of Art Nouveau. Often represents highly fanciful clothing.

Burne–Jones, Edward
Greenaway, Kate
Orchardson, Sir William Quiller

FRENCH

Aublet, Albert (B. 1851)
> Also sculptor. History scenes and portraits. Great attention to costume detail.

Béraud, Jean
Bonnard, Pierre (1867–1947)
> Subjects of paintings and lithographs were usually quiet interiors with a woman bathing, dressing, or sleeping and family scenes.

Cézanne, Paul
Degas, Hilaire Edgar Germain
Gervex, Henri
Goubie, Jean Richard
Jeanniot, Pierre George (1848–1934)
> Landscapes, genre subjects and portraits.

La Touche, Gaston (1854–1913)
> Genre painter and illustrator. Favorite subject, life in Paris. See *The Casino* for evening dress.

Prinet, Rene Francois Xavier (1861–1946)
Renoir, Pierre Auguste
Tissot, James Joseph Jacques
Toulouse–Lautrec, Compte Henri de

NORWEGIAN

Munch, Edvard (1863–1944)

> Worked in German expressionist style. Graphic works and paintings are powerful. Figures have strong silhouettes but little detailed clothing.

SWEDISH

Larsson, Carl

Twentieth Century

In the twentieth century, photographs become the primary material for clothing research. Candid family pictures, newspaper and magazine photos and the work of photographic artists record exactly what people wore, when and under what circumstances. Fashion illustrators remain important sources for high fashion clothing. Painters turn, for the most part, to subjects other than the realistically rendered, clothed human form. The following artists are some of those who continue to provide useful examples of clothing well into this century.

AMERICAN

Abbey, Edwin Austin

Cassatt, Mary Stevenson

Eakins, Thomas Cowperthwaite

Flagg, James Montgomery (1877–1960)

> Illustrator. Concentrated on urban American life. Well known for his World War I posters.

Frost, A.B.

Gibson, Charles Dana

Homer, Winslow

Hopper, Edward (1882–1967)

> Foremost twentieth century American realist. Good source for everyday, ordinary dress of the thirties and forties. See drawings for greatest detail.

Leyendecker, Joseph Christian (1874–1951)

> Illustrator. Produced 321 *Saturday Evening Post* covers. In 1905 created the "Arrow Collar Man" symbol of fashionable American man-

hood. Excellent resource for well dressed men of the period.

Pennell, Joseph

Phillips, Coles (1880–1927)

> Illustrator.

Pyle, Howard

Rockwell, Norman (1894–1980)

> Noted magazine illustrator. Many examples of everyday American life, detailed and somewhat romanticized.

Russell, Charles

Sargent, John Singer

Smith, Jessie Wilcox (1863–1935)

> Painter and magazine illustrator. Did many covers for *Good Housekeeping*. Beautifully rendered women and children.

ENGLISH

Orchardson, Sir William Quiller

FRENCH

Aulet, Albert

Avy, Joseph Marius (B. 1871)

> Illustrator and painter of genre scenes. Active 1900–1941.

Barbier, George (1882–c. 1940)

> Fashion illustrator, 1910's and 1920's.

Béraud, Jean

Bónnard, Pierre

Cézanne, Paul

Erté (b. 1893)

> Fashion designer and illustrator. Associated with *Harper's Bazaar* from 1915–1935.

Gervex, Henri

Jeanniot, Pierre George

La Touche, Gaston

Prinet, Rene Francois Xavier

NORWEGIAN

Munch, Edvard

SWEDISH

Larsson, Carl

Annotated Bibliography

General Costume History

Batterberry, Michael and Ariane. *Mirror, Mirror: A Social History of Fashion*. New York: Holt, Rinehart and Winston, 1977. Monochrome and color illustrations from primary sources.

Black, J. Anderson and Garland, Madge. *A History of Fashion*. New York: William Morrow and Company, Inc., 1975. Monochrome and color illustrations from primary sources.

Boehn, Max von. *Modes and Manners*. 4 vols. in 2. Joan Joshua, trans. New York: Benjamin Blom, Inc., 1971. Reprint of 1932 edition. Covers ancient world to eighteenth century.

Boucher, Francois. *20,000 Years of Fashion*. New York: Harry N. Abrams, Inc., 1967. Monochrome and color illustrations from primary sources.

Braun and Schneider. *Historic Costume in Pictures*. New York: Dover Publications, Inc., 1975. Reprint of a 1907 German publication. 125 monochrome plates. Countries of the world from ancient times to late nineteenth century.

Broby-Johansen, R. *Body and Clothes: An Illustrated History of Costume*. New York: Reinhold Book Corp., 1968. Translated from Danish. Line drawings, monochrome and some color illustrations from primary sources. Includes chapters on primitive peoples, the Arab haik, and the Indian sari.

Contini, Mila. *Fashion from Ancient Egypt to the Present Day*. London: Paul Hamlyn, 1965. Monochrome and color illustrations from primary sources.

Cumming, Valerie and Ribeiro, Aileen. *The History of Costume*. New York: Drama Book Publishers, 1989. Comprehensive history. Monochrome and some color photographs.

Davenport, Millia. *The Book of Costume*. New York: Crown Publishers, Inc., 1948. 2 vols. Monochrome illustrations from primary sources. Ancient times to 1860s. Includes clothing, accessories, armor, and ecclesiastical vestments.

Dorner, Jane. *Fashion: The Changing Shape of Fashion Through the Years*. London: Octopus Books, 1974. Monochrome and color illustrations from primary sources.

Dunlevy, Mairead. *Dress in Ireland*. London: B.T. Batsford, Ltd., 1989. Comprehensive and scholarly survey, Bronze Age to twentieth century. Illustrations from primary sources.

Earnshaw, Pat. *Lace in Fashion: From the Sixteenth to the Twentieth Centuries*. New York: Drama Book Publishers, 1985. 200 monochrome illustrations, 4 color plates.

Ewing, Elizabeth. *Fur in Dress*. London: B.T. Batsford, Ltd., 1981. Monochrome and some color illustrations from primary sources. Early times to 1970s.

Fox, Celina. *Londoners*. New York: Thames and Hudson, 1987. All walks of life, seventeenth to early twentieth century. Valuable source for genre costume.

Ginsburg, Madeleine. *An Introduction to Fashion Illustration*. London: Victoria and Albert Museum/Owings Mills, MD: Stemmer House Publishers, Inc., 1980. Fashion illustrations from sixteenth to twentieth century.

Hansen, Henny Harald. *Costume Cavalcade: 689 Examples of Historic Costume in Colour*. London: Eyre Methuen, Ltd., 1972. 2nd edition. Originally published in Copenhagen, 1954. The color illustrations, redrawn from primary sources, are useful for quick reference.

Laver, James. *Costume and Fashion: A Concise History*. New York: Thames and Hudson, 1985. Revised edition.

Laver, James and Klepper, Erhardt. *Costume Through the Ages*. London: Thames and Hudson, 1963. Line drawings taken from primary sources. Ancient times to 1930.

Levi-Pisetzky, Rosita. *Storia del Costume in Italia*. 5 vols. Milan: Instituto Editoriale Italiano, 1964. Early times to nineteenth century. Primary source illustrations.

Marly, Diana de. *The History of Haute Couture 1850–1950*. New York: Holmes and Meier Publishers, Inc., 1980. An interesting selection of monochrome and some color illustrations.

Munro, R. W. *Highland Clans and Tartans*. New York: Crescent Books, 1977. From beginning to present day. Over 150 monochrome and color photographs. Informative.

Payne, Blanche. *History of Costume: From the Ancient Egyptians to the Twentieth Century*. New York: Harper and Row, Publishers, 1965. Line drawings, monochrome illustrations from primary sources and some scale patterns.

Racinet, Albert. *The Historical Encyclopedia of Costume*. London: Studio Editions, 1988. Originally published in the nineteenth century in 6 volumes as *Le Costume Historique*. Byzantium to 1880s.

Racinet, Auguste. *Racinet's Full-Color Pictorial History of Western Costume*. New York: Dover Publications, Inc., 1987. Reprint from nineteenth century. Middle Ages to 1800. Includes some ecclesiastical costume.

Robinson, Julian. *The Fine Art of Fashion Illustration: An Illustrated History*. New York and London: Bartley and Jensen, Publishers, 1986. Color illustrations, line drawings, and photographs. Seventeenth to twentieth century.

Scarce, Jennifer. *Women's Costume of the Near and Middle East*. London: Unwin Hyman Limited, 1987. Monochrome illustrations of primary sources. Some not-to-scale patterns.

Squire, Geoffrey. *Dress and Society 1560–1970*. New York: A Studio Book. Viking Press, 1974. Monochrome and some color illustrations from primary sources.

Tortora, Phyllis and Eubank, Keith. *A Survey of Historic Costume*. New York: Fairchild Publications, 1989. Comprehensive, well-organized text. Monochrome and color photographs of primary sources.

Victoria and Albert Museum. *Four Hundred Years of Fashion*. London: Victoria and Albert Museum in association with William Collins, 1984. Monochrome and color photographs of men's and women's costumes and accessories from the collection of the Victoria and Albert Museum. Sixteenth century to 1980s.

Walker, Richard. *Saville Row: An Illustrated History*. New York: Rizzoli International Publishers, Inc., 1989. Color and monochrome photographs of primary sources. Interesting book.

Period Catalogues

Adburgham, Alison, intr. *Victorian Shopping*: Harrod's Catalogue 1895. Reprint. Newton Abbot, Devon, England: David and Charles, 1972.

Amory, Cleveland, intr. *The 1902 Edition of the Sears Roebuck Catalogue*. Reprint. New York: Bounty Books (A Division of Crown Publishers, Inc.), 1969.

Bloomingdale Brothers. *Bloomingdale's Illustrated 1886 Catalogue: Fashions, Dry Goods and Housewares*. New York: Dover Publications, Inc., 1988.

Blum, Stella. *Everyday Fashions of the Twenties: As Pictured in Sears and Other Catalogs*. New York: Dover Publications, Inc., 1981.

———. *Everyday Fashions of the Thirties: As Pictured in Sears Catalogs*. New York: Dover Publications, Inc., 1986.

Bryk, Nancy Villa, ed. *American Dress Pattern Catalogs, 1873–1909*. Four Complete Reprints. New York: Dover Publications, Inc., 1988.

Emmet, Boris, intr. *Montgomery Ward and Company's Catalogue, Spring & Summer, 1895*. Reprint. New York: Dover Publications, Inc., 1969.

Gottwald, Laura and Janise. *Frederick's of Hollywood 1947–1973: Twenty-Six Years of Mail Order Seduction*. New York: Drake Publishers Inc., 1974.

Israel, Fred L., ed. *1897 Sears Roebuck Catalogue*. Reprint. New York: Chelsea House Publishers, 1968.

Langbridge, R. H., comp. *Edwardian Shopping: A Selection from the Army and Navy Stores Catalogues 1898–1913*. North Pomfret, VT: David and Charles, 1975.

Mirken, Alan, ed. *1927 Edition of the Sears, Roebuck Catalogue: The Roaring Twenties*. Reprint. New York: Bounty Books (A Division of Crown Publishers, Inc.), 1970.

Perelman, S. J. and Rovere, Richard, intr. *1897 Sears, Roebuck Catalogue*. New York: Chelsea House Publishers, 1968.

Schroeder, Joseph J. Jr., ed. *Sears, Roebuck & Co. 1908*. Reprint. Northfield, IL: Digest Books, Inc., 1971.

Sears, Roebuck. *Sears, Roebuck & Co. 1906*. Reprint. Secaucus, NJ: Castle Books (Division of Book Sales, Inc.), n.d.

———. *Sears, Roebuck Catalogues of the 1930s*. New York: Nostalgia Press Inc., 1978. Selections from the decade.

Antiquity

Houston, Mary G. *Ancient Egyptian, Mesopotamian & Persian Costume and Decoration*. London: Adam and Charles Black, 1954. 2nd edition.

Line drawings. Includes draping illustrations and scale diagrams of cut.

———. *Ancient Greek, Roman and Byzantine Costume and Decoration*. London: Adam and Charles Black, 1947. 2nd edition. Line drawings and color plates. Diagrams show how garments were cut and draped, including several styles of the toga. Covers 2100 B.C. to twelfth century.

Hope, Thomas. *Costumes of the Greeks and Romans.* New York: Dover Publications, Inc., 1962. Reprint from 1812. Engravings of costumes, accessories, furniture, etc.

Laver, James and Klepper, Erhardt. *Costumes in Antiquity*. London: Thames and Hudson, 1964. Monochrome plates redrawn from primary sources. Covers 3000 B.C. to sixth century A.D.

Middle Ages and Renaissance

Ashelford, Jane. *A Visual History of Costume: The 16th Century*. New York: Drama Book Publishers, 1983. Monochrome and some color illustrations.

Birbari, Elizabeth. *Dress in Italian Painting 1460–1500*. London: John Murray, 1975. Monochrome illustrations from primary sources. Line drawings of reconstructed patterns to scale.

Bentivegna, Ferruccia Cappi, ed. *Abblgliamento e Costume nella Pittura Italiana*. 2 vols. Vol. 1, *Renascimento (15th and 16th C.)* Rome: Carlo Bestetti, Edizioni d'Arte, 1962–64. Monochrome and some color illustrations from Italian paintings, all showing costume.

Cunnington, C. Willett and Phillis. *Handbook of English Mediaeval Costume*. Boston: Plays, Inc., 1969. Revised edition. Line illustrations from contemporary sources. Men, women, and children. Nineth to fifteenth century.

———. *Handbook of English Costume in the Sixteenth Century*. Boston: Plays, Inc., 1970. Revised edition. Line illustrations from contemporary sources. Men, women, and children.

Herald, Jacqueline. *Renaissance Dress in Italy 1400–1500*. The History of Dress Series. Atlantic Highlands, NJ: Humanities Press, 1981. Monochrome and color illustrations from contemporary sources.

Houston, Mary G. *Medieval Costume in England and France*. London: Adam and Charles Black, 1939. Line drawings, black and white and some color illustrations. Covers armor, ornament, religious, and academic dress and includes diagrams of cut.

Morse, H.K. *Elizabethan Pageantry: A Pictorial Survey of Costume and its Commentators from c.1560–1620*. London: The Art Book Co., 1980. Reprint of the 1934 edition. Monochrome plates and useful contemporary descriptions.

Newton, Stella Mary. *Fashion in the Age of the Black Prince. A study of the years 1340–1363*. Totowa, NJ: Rowman and Littlefield, 1980. Monochrome illustrations from primary sources. Scholarly.

Scott, Margaret. *A Visual History of Costume: The Fourteenth & Fifteenth Centuries*. New York: Drama Book Publishers, 1986. Monochrome and some color illustrations.

———. *Late Gothic Europe, 1400–1500*. The History of Dress Series. Atlantic Highlands, NJ: Humanities Press Inc., 1980. Beautiful monochrome and color illustrations from primary sources.

Vecellio, Cesare. *Vecellio's Renaissance Costume Book: All 500 Woodcut Illustrations from the Famous Sixteenth-Century Compendium of World Costume*. New York: Dover Publications, Inc., 1977. Originally published in 1598.

Seventeenth and Eighteenth Centuries

Baumgarten, Linda. *Eighteenth-Century Clothing at Williamsburg*. Williamsburg, Virginia: The Colonial Williamsburg Foundation, 1986. Monochrome and color photographs of clothing, accessories, prints, and paintings. Beautifully produced and an excellent source.

Bentivegna, Ferruccia Cappi, ed. *Abbigliamento e Costume nella Pittura Italiana*. 2 vols. Vol. 2, *Barocco—Impero (17th and 18th C.).* Rome: Carlo Bestetti, Edizioni d'Arte, 1962–64. Monochrome and some color illustrations from Italian paintings, all showing costume.

Bernier, Olivier. *The Eighteenth-Century Woman*. Garden City, New York: Doubleday and Company, Inc./The Metropolitan Museum of Art, 1981. Published in conjunction with an exhibit of the same name at the Metropolitan Museum. Monochrome and color illustrations and photographs from primary sources.

Blum, Stella, ed. *Eighteenth-Century French Fashion Plates in Full Color: 64 Engravings from "Galeries des Modes," 1778–1787.* New York: Dover Publications, Inc., 1982.

Buck, Anne. *Dress in Eighteenth Century England.* New York: Holmes and Meier Publishers, Inc., 1979. Monochrome and some color illustrations from contemporary sources.

Cummings, Valerie. *A Visual History of Costume: The 17th Century.* New York: Drama Book Publishers, 1985. Monochrome and some color illustrations.

Cunnington, C. Willett and Phillis. *Handbook of English Costume in the Seventeenth Century.* Boston: Plays, Inc., 1973. Revised edition. Line illustrations from contemporary sources. Men, women, and children. Many contemporary quotations. Good reference work.

———. *Handbook of English Costume in the Eighteenth Century.* Boston: Plays, Inc., 1972. Revised edition. Line illustrations from contemporary sources. Men's and women's clothing and accessories. Many contemporary quotations. An excellent reference work.

Daniel, Howard, ed. *Callot's Etchings.* New York: Dover Publications, Inc., 1974. 338 prints of seventeenth-century French life.

Earle, Alice Morse. *Two Centuries of Costume in America 1620–1820.* 2 vols. Rutland VT: Charles E. Tuttle Company, 1971. Reprint from 1903 edition. Monochrome illustrations from primary sources.

The Gallery of English Costume. Picture Book Number Two: *Women's Costume The 18th Century.* Manchester, England: Art Galleries Committee of the Corporation of Manchester, 1954. Monochrome photographs of clothing, underwear, and accessories from The Gallery of English Costume, Platt Hall.

Gehret, Ellen J. *Rural Pennsylvania Clothing: Being a Study of the Wearing Apparel of the German and English Inhabitants in the Late 18th and Early 19th Century.* York, PA: George R.D. Shumway, 1973. Excellent information.

The Kyoto Costume Institute. *Revolution in Fashion: European Clothing, 1715–1815.* New York: Abbeville Press, 1989. Beautiful color photographs of costumes and accessories from an exhibit.

Laver, James, *17th and 18th Century Costume.* London: His Majesty's Stationery Office, 1951.

Monochrome illustrations from primary sources.

Maeder, Edward, ed. *An Elegant Art: Fashion and Fantasy in the Eighteenth Century.* New York: Harry N. Abrams, Inc. in association with the Los Angeles County Museum of Art, 1983. Printed in conjuction with an exhibit at the Los Angeles Museum. Beautiful monochrome and color illustrations and photographs of costumes, textiles, and accessories.

Marly, Diana de. *Costume & Civilization: Louis XIV & Versailles.* London: B.T. Batsford, Ltd., 1987. Monochrome and some color photographs.

McClellan, Elisabeth. *Historic Dress in America 1607–1870.* New York: Arno Press, 1977. Reissue, 2 vols. in 1. Originally published 1904–1910, reissued in 1937 and 1968 as *History of American Costume.* Monochrome illustrations and line drawings.

Ribeiro, Aileen. *A Visual History of Costume: The 18th Century.* New York: Drama Book Publishers, 1983. Monochrome and some color illustrations.

———. *Dress in 18th Century Europe 1715–1789.* London: B.T. Batsford, Ltd., 1984. Monochrome and some color illustrations from primary sources.

Shesgreen, Sean, ed. *Engravings by Hogarth.* New York: Dover Publications, Inc., 1973. 101 plates with commentary. Wonderful for details of eighteenth-century everyday clothing.

Warwick, Edward, Pitz, Henry C., Wyckoff, Alexander. *Early American Dress: The Colonial and Revolutionary Periods.* New York: Bonanza Books, 1965. Monochrome plates and line drawings.

Nineteenth Century

Beam, Phillip. *Winslow Homer's Magazine Engravings.* New York: Harper and Row, Publishers, 1979. Covers 1857–1875. Useful for costume.

Bentley, Nicholas. *The Victorian Scene: A Picture Book of the Period 1837–1901.* New York: Spring Books, 1968. Monochrome and color illustrations of occupational and working clothes as well as fashionable dress.

Blum, Stella. *Ackermann's Costume Plates: Women's Fashions in England, 1818–1828.* New York:

Dover Publications, Inc., 1978. Monochrome and some color plates.

————, ed. *Victorian Fashions and Costumes from Harper's Bazaar 1867–1898.* New York: Dover Publications, Inc., 1974. Original fashion plates and engravings. Includes underwear, accessories, hairstyles, and children's fashions.

————, ed. *Paris Fashions of the 1890s: A Picture Source Book with 350 Designs, Including 24 in Full Color.* New York: Dover Publications, Inc., 1984. Prints of French fashions that originally appeared in *The Young Ladies Journal.* Brief descriptions, no text.

Boehn, Max von and Fischel, Max. M. Edwards, trans. *Modes and Manners of the Nineteenth Century as Represented in the Pictures and Engravings of the Time.* New York: Benjamin Blom, Inc., 1970. Reprint of 1927 edition; 4 vols. in 2. Covers 1790–1914. Illustrations from primary sources.

Bott, Alan. *Our Fathers (1870–1900): Manners and Customs of the Ancient Victorians: A survey in pictures and text of their history, morals, wars, sports, inventions & politics.* New York: Benjamin Blom, Inc., 1972. Reprint of 1931 edition. Monochrome illustrations and engravings from primary sources.

Bott, Alan and Clephane, Irene. *Our Mothers: A Cavalcade in Pictures, Quotation and Description of Late Victorian Women 1870–1900.* New York: Benjamin Blom, 1969. Reprint of 1932 edition. Monochrome illustrations and engravings from primary sources, many showing clothing.

Buck, Anne. *Victorian Costume and Costume Accessories.* Carlton, Bedford, England: Ruth Bean, 1984. 2nd revised edition of original 1961 publication with updated bibliography. Monochrome photographs, many redone for this edition.

Coleman, Elizabeth Ann. *The Opulent Era: Fashions of Worth, Doucet and Pingat.* New York: The Brooklyn Museum in association with Thames and Hudson, 1989. Published in conjunction with an exhibit at the Brooklyn Museum. Beautifully illustrated in monochrome and color.

Cunnington, C. Willet. *English Women's Clothing in the Nineteenth Century.* New York: Dover Publications, Inc., 1990. Reprint of the 1937 edition. Much more extensive coverage of women's clothing and accessories by decade than the *Handbook* below. Monochrome

plates, line drawings, and photographs of actual garments. Excellent reference.

Cunnington, C. Willett and Phillis. *Handbook of English Costume in the Nineteenth Century.* Boston: Plays, Inc., 1970. Line illustrations from contemporary sources. Men, women, and children. Clothing and accessories. Many contemporary quotations. An excellent reference work.

Daniel, Pete and Smock, Raymond. *A Talent for Detail: The Photographs of Miss Frances Benjamin Johnston 1889–1910.* New York: Harmony Books, 1974. Monochrome photographs.

Earle, Alice Morse. *Two Centuries of Costume in America 1620–1820.* 2 vols. Rutland VT: Charles E. Tuttle Company, 1971. Reprint of 1903 edition. Monochrome illustrations from primary sources.

Ford, Colin, ed. *An Early Victorian Album: The Photographic Masterpieces (1843–1847) of David Octavius Hill and Robert Adamson.* New York: Alfred A. Knopf, 1976. Monochrome photographs.

Foster, Vanda. *A Visual History of Costume: The Nineteenth Century.* New York: Drama Book Publishers, 1984. Monochrome and some color illustrations.

The Gallery of English Costume. Picture Book Number Three: *Women's Costume 1800–1835.* Manchester, England: Art Galleries Committee of the Corporation of Manchester, 1952. Monochrome photographs of clothing, underwear, and accessories from The Gallery of English Costume, Platt Hall.

————. Picture Book Number Four: *Women's Costume 1835–1870.* Manchester, England: Art Galleries Committee of the Corporation of Manchester, 1951. Monochrome photographs of clothing, underwear, and accessories from The Gallery of English Costume, Platt Hall.

————. Picture Book Number Five: *Women's Dress 1870–1900.* Manchester, England: Art Galleries Committee of the City of Manchester, 1953. Monochrome photographs of clothing, underwear, and accessories from The Gallery of English Costume, Platt Hall.

Gelman, Woody. *The Best of Charles Dana Gibson.* New York: Bounty Books, 1969. The famous "Gibson Girl" illustrations, many showing costume.

Gernsheim, Alison. *Victorian and Edwardian Fashion: A Photographic Survey.* New York: Dover Publications, Inc., 1963. Originally published as *Fashion and Reality (1840–1914).* Monochrome photographs.

Gibbs-Smith, Charles H. *The Fashionable Lady in the 19th Century.* London: Her Majesty's Stationery Office, 1969. Fashion plates for each fifth year from 1800 to 1900.

Goldthorpe, Caroline. *From Queen to Empress: Victorian Dress 1837–1877.* New York: The Metropolitan Museum of Art, 1988. Distributed by Harry N. Abrams, Inc. From an exhibit at The Costume Institute, December 1988 to April 1989.

Ginsburg, Madeleine. *Victorian Dress in Photographs.* New York: Holmes and Meier Publishers, Inc., 1983. Covers men's, women's, children's, occupational, and regional clothing with detailed explanations. 1840s to 1890s.

Jensen, Oliver. *America's Yesterdays: Images of Our Lost Past Discovered in the Photographic Archives of The Library of Congress.* New York: American Heritage Publishing Co., Inc., 1978. Many monochrome photographs.

———. *A College Album or Rah, Rah, Yesterday.* New York: American Heritage Publishing Co., Inc., 1974. Monochrome photographs.

Kunciov, Robert, ed. *Mr. Godey's Ladies: Being a Mosaic of Fashions and Fancies.* New York: Bonanza Books, 1971. Illustrations from *Godey's Ladies Book* 1830s–1870s.

Kunhardt, Dorothy Meserve and Philip B.Jr. *Mathew Brady and His World.* Alexandria, VA: Time-Life Books, 1977. Monochrome photographs 1840s–1870s.

Kyoto Costume Institute. *The Evolution of Fashion 1835–1895: Clothing that Captured the Imagination of Japan.* Kyoto, Japan: Kyoto Costume Institute, 1980. From an exhibit at The National Museum of Modern Art, Kyoto, Japan. Exquisite color and some monochrome photographs. Captions in English and Japanese.

Levitt, Sarah. *Victorians Unbuttoned: Registered Designs for Clothing, Their Makers and Wearers, 1839–1900.* London: George Allen and Unwin, 1986. Monochrome illustrations. Comprehensive.

Lucie-Smith, Edward and Dars, Celestine. *How the Rich Lived: The Painter as Witness 1870–1914.* New York: Paddington Press, Limited, 1976. Monochrome and some color illustrations of paintings, all showing costume.

Mankowitz, Wolf. *Dickens of London.* New York: Macmillan Publishing Co., Inc., 1976. Monochrome and color illustrations from contemporary sources. 1830s to 1870s.

McClellan, Elisabeth. *Historic Dress in America 1607–1870.* New York: Arno Press, 1977. Reissue, 2 vols. in 1. Originally published 1904–1910, reissued in 1937 and 1968 as *History of American Costume.* Monochrome illustrations and line drawings.

The Metropolitan Museum of Art. *The Imperial Style: Fashions of the Hapsburg Era.* New York: The Metropolitan Museum of Art/Rizzoli, 1979. Published in conjunction with an exhibit at the museum, December 1979 to August 1980.

Moore, Doris Langley and Sitwell, Sacheverill. *Gallery of Fashion 1790–1822: From Plates by Heieloff and Ackermann.* London: B.T. Batsford, Ltd., 1949. Sixteen fashion plates reproduced in color.

Museum of the City of New York. *The House of Worth: The Gilded Age in New York.* New York: Museum of the City of New York, 1982. From an exhibit at the museum.

Quennell, Peter. *The Day Before Yesterday: A Photographic Album of Daily Life in Victorian and Edwardian Britain.* New York: Charles Scribner's Sons, 1978. Monochrome photographs showing people from all walks of life including tradespeople, laborers, farm workers, etc. Useful for costume.

Ribeiro, Aileen. *Fashion in the French Revolution.* London: B.T. Batsford, Ltd., 1988. Monochrome and some color illustrations from primary sources.

Rinhart, Floyd and Marion. *Summertime: Photographs of America at Play 1850–1900.* New York: Clarkson N. Potter, Inc., 1978. Monochrome photographs.

Time-Life. *This Fabulous Century: Prelude 1870–1900.* New York: Time-Life Books, 1970. Monochrome and color illustrations and photographs of American life.

Tozer, Jane and Levitt, Sarah. *Fabric of Society.* New York: St. Martin's Press, Inc., 1984. Beautiful monochrome and color photographs of clothing from The Gallery of English Costume, Platt Hall, many showing close-ups of clothing detail and textiles.

Wilson, Angus. *The World of Charles Dickens.* New York: The Viking Press, Inc., 1972.

Paperbound edition. Monochrome and color illustrations from contemporary sources c. 1820 to 1870.

Wood, Christopher. *Victorian Panorama: Paintings of Victorian Life*. London: Faber and Faber, Ltd., 1976. Monochrome and some color illustrations of all walks of life from contemporary sources. Useful for costume.

Twentieth Century, General History

Benton, Barbara. *Ellis Island: A Pictorial History*. New York and Oxford, England: Facts on File Publications, 1985. Monochrome photographs. Good for ethnic costumes.

Blum, Stella. *Designs by Erte: Fashion Drawings & Illustrations from Harper's Bazaar*. New York: Dover Publications, Inc., 1976. Monochrome line illustrations and some color plates. 1915 to 1930s.

Byrde, Penelope. *A Visual History of Costume: The Twentieth Century*. New York: Drama Book Publishers, 1986. Monochrome and some color illustrations from primary sources.

Carter, Ernestine. *20th Century Fashions: A Scrapbook—1900 to Today*. London: Eyre Methuen, 1975. Monochrome fashion illustrations and photographs.

Clephane, Irene. *Ourselves 1900–1930*. London: John Lane The Bodley Head, Limited, 1933. Monochrome illustrations covering all walks of life.

Coleman, Elizabeth Ann. *The Genius of Charles James*. New York: The Brooklyn Museum/Holt Rinehart and Winston, 1982. Published in conjunction with an exhibit held at the Brooklyn Museum. Monochrome and color photographs and sketches of high fashion. Late 1920s to 1950s.

Cunnington, C. Willett. *English Women's Clothing in the Present Century*. London: Faber and Faber, Ltd., 1952. Line drawings, monochrome, and some color illustrations and photographs from contemporary sources. Covers 1900 to 1950 in great detail. An excellent reference.

Dars, Celestine. *A Fashion Parade: The Seeberger Collection*. London: Blond and Briggs, 1979. Monochrome photographs of high fashion, 1909–1950, taken by the Seeberger brothers who worked in Paris from the start of the century.

Erte. *Erte Fashions*. New York: St. Martin's Press, Inc., 1973. Monochrome and some color illustrations. Clothes, jewelry, and accessories. 1911 to 1972.

Ewing, Elizabeth. *History of 20th Century Fashion*. New York: Charles Scribner's Sons, 1975. Monochrome illustrations and photographs from contemporary sources reviewing women's fashion, including couture and mass production. 1900 to 1972.

The Gallery of English Costume. Picture Book Number Six: *Women's Costume 1900–1930*. Manchester, England: Art Galleries Committee of the Corporation of Manchester, 1956. Monochrome photographs of clothing, underwear, and accessories in the Gallery of English Costume, Platt Hall.

Glynn, Prudence with Ginsburg, Madeleine. *In Fashion: Dress in the Twentieth Century*. London: George Allen and Unwin, 1978. Monochrome and some color illustrations and photographs of men's and women's fashions. 1900 to 1970s.

Jensen, Oliver. *America's Yesterdays: Images of Our Lost Past Discovered in the Photographic Archives of The Library of Congress*. New York: American Heritage Publishing Co., Inc., 1978. Many monochrome photographs.

———. *A College Album*. New York: American Heritage Publishing Company, Inc., 1974. Monochrome photographs of college life in America. 1850s to 1960s.

Lewenhaupt, Tony and Claes. *Crosscurrents: Art, Fashion, Design, 1890–1989*. New York: Rizzoli International Publications, Inc., 1989. Relates fashion design to architecture, interior design, graphic design, etc. Beautiful color photographs.

Life. *The Best of Life*. New York: Avon Books, 1973. Monochrome and color photographs from *Life* magazine from 1936 to 1972, covering fashion, war, political events, sports, etc.

Mansfield, Alan and Cunnington, Phillis. *Handbook of English Costume in the Twentieth Century, 1900–1950*. Boston: Plays, Inc., 1973. Line illustrations redrawn from contemporary sources that are not as clear as the earlier handbooks, but still an excellent reference book for men's and women's clothing.

Metropolitan Museum of Art. *Fabulous Fashion 1907–67*. New York: Costume Institute, Metropolitan Museum of Art, n.d. Published in conjunction with an exhibit in Australia of costumes from the Metropolitan Museum. Monochrome and color photographs.

Milbank, Caroline Rennolds. *New York Fashion: The Evolution of American Style.* New York: Harry N. Abrams, Inc., 1989. Nineteenth century to 1980s. Each chapter covers a decade and includes a section on leading American designers.

O'Donnol, Shirley Miles. *American Costume, 1915–1970: A Source Book for the Stage Costumer.* Bloomington, Indiana: Indiana University Press, 1982. Small line drawings and monochrome photos of clothing.

Peacock, John. *Fashion Sketchbook 1920–1960.* New York: Avon Books, 1977. Line drawings of women's fashions redrawn from contemporary sources.

Robinson, Julian. *The Golden Age of Style.* New York and London: Harcourt Brace Jovanovich, 1976. Art Deco fashion illustration. Color illustrations, monochrome plates, and fashion photographs. 1901 to 1939.

Torrens, Deborah. *Fashion Illustrated: A Review of Women's Dress 1920–1950.* New York: Hawthorn Books Inc., 1975. Monochrome and color fashion illustrations and photographs from contemporary fashion magazines.

Twentieth Century, Chronological Order

Bentley, Nicolas. *Edwardian Album: A Photographic Excursion into a Lost Age of Innocence.* New York: A Studio Book. The Viking Press, 1974. Monochrome photographs showing Edwardians at work and play.

Gordon, Colin. *A Richer Dust: Echoes from an Edwardian Album.* Philadelphia and New York: J.B. Lippincott Company, 1978. Monochrome photographs.

Gersheim, Alison. *Victorian and Edwardian Fashion: A Photographic Survey.* New York: Dover Publications, Inc., 1963. Originally published as *Fashion and Reality (1840–1914).* Monochrome photographs.

Priestley, J.B. *The Edwardians.* London: Heinemann, 1970. Monochrome and color illustrations and photographs throughout.

Quennell, Peter. *The Day Before Yesterday: A Photographic Album of Daily Life in Victorian and Edwardian Britain.* New York: Charles Scribner's Sons, 1978. Monochrome photographs showing people from all walks of life including tradespeople, laborers, farm workers, etc.

Stevenson, Pauline. *Edwardian Fashion.* London: Ian Allan, Ltd., 1980. Line drawings, monochrome, and some color illustrations and photographs. Men's, women's, and children's clothing and accessories.

Thompson, Paul and Harkell, Gina. *The Edwardians in Photographs.* London: B.T. Batsford, Ltd., 1979. Monochrome photographs showing the rich and poor at work and play.

Time-Life Books. *This Fabulous Century: Volume 1 1900–1910.* New York: Time-Life Books, 1969. Monochrome and color illustrations and photographs of American life from contemporary sources.

Ishsiyama, Akira. *French Fashion Plates in Art Deco.* Tokyo, Japan: Graphic-sha Publishing Co., Ltd., 1988. Ninety-six fashion illustrations, 1908 to 1924, in color. Captions in English and Japanese.

Ridley, Pauline. *Fashion Illustration.* London: Academy Editions, 1979. Forty-eight French fashion plates, 1908 to 1925, in color.

Battersby, Martin. *Art Deco Fashion: French Designers 1908–1925.* New York: St. Martin's Press, 1974. Monochrome and color fashion illustrations.

Time-Life Books. *This Fabulous Century: Volume II 1910–1920.* New York: Time-Life Books, 1969.

Bowman, Sara. *A Fashion for Extravagance: Art Deco Fabrics and Fashions.* New York: E.P. Dutton, Inc., 1985. Many color and some monochrome photographs.

Barbier, George, et al. *Parisian Costume Plates in Full Color (1912–1914).* New York: Dover Publications, Inc., 1982. Sixty plates reproduced from *Journal des Dames et des Modes.*

Nuzzi, Cristina. *Fashions in Paris from the "Journal des Dames et des Modes" 1912–1913.* London: Thames and Hudson, 1980. Color plates of fashion illustrations including accessories.

———. *Parisian Fashion.* New York: Rizzoli International Publications, Inc., 1979. Color plates of fashion illustration from the *Journal des Dames et des Modes.* 1912 to 1914.

Le Pape, Georges, Barbier, George, et al. *French Fashion Plates in Full Color from the "Gazette du Bon Ton" (1912–1925). 58 Illustrations of Styles* by Paul Poiret, Worth, Paquin and Others. As Rendered by Georges LePape, George Barbier, et al. New York: Dover Publications, Inc., 1979.

Sann, Paul. *The Lawless Decade: A Pictorial History of a Great American Transition: From the World War I Armistice and Prohibition to Repeal and the New Deal.* New York: Bonanza Books, 1957. Monochrome photographs and illustrations from contemporary sources. 1920 to 1929.

Eckardt, Wolf Von and Gilman, Sander L. *Bertolt Brecht's Berlin: A Scrapbook of the Twenties.* Garden City, New York: Anchor Press/Doubleday, 1975. Monochrome photographs of German life.

Ginsburg, Madeleine. *Paris Fashions: The Art Deco Style of the 1920s.* New York: Gallery Books, 1989. Fashion illustrations in color from *Art-Gout-Beaute,* includes clothing, accessories, jewelry, children's clothing, and textiles.

Grafton, Carol Belanger, ed. *French Fashion Illustrations of the Twenties: 634 Cuts from "La Vie Parisienne."* New York: Dover Publications, Inc., 1987.

Hall, Carolyn. *The Twenties in Vogue.* New York: Harmony Books, 1983. Monochrome and some color photographs and illustrations from *Vogue* magazine. Fashion, social events, the arts, etc.

Jenkins, Alan. *The Twenties.* New York: Universe Books Inc., 1974. Monochrome and color illustrations and photographs of events, fashions, the arts, etc.

Laver, James. *Women's Dress in the Jazz Age.* London: Hamish Hamilton, 1964. Monochrome photographs and illustrations from contemporary sources. 1920s.

Olian, JoAnne, ed. *Authentic French Fashions of the Twenties: 413 Costume Designs from "L'Art et la Mode."* NY: Dover Publicatons, Inc., 1990. Monochrome fashion drawings.

Time-Life Books. *This Fabulous Century: Volume III 1920–1930.* New York: Time-Life Books, 1969.

Dorner, Jane. *Fashion in the Twenties and Thirties.* London: Ian Allan, 1973. Monochrome and some color plates of fashion drawings, photographs, and advertisements from contemporary publications and periodicals.

Brassai. *The Secret Paris of the 30's.* New York: Pantheon Books, 1976. Monochrome photographs of Parisian nightlife.

Hall, Carolyn. *The Thirties in Vogue.* New York: Harmony Books, 1985. Monochrome and some color photographs and illustrations from *Vogue* magazine. Fashion, social events, the arts, etc.

Horan, James D. *The Desperate Years: A Pictorial History of the Thirties.* New York: Bonanza Books, 1962. Monochrome photographs of events from the stock market crash to World War II.

Jenkins, Alan. *The Thirties.* New York: Stein and Day, 1976. Monochrome and color illustrations and photographs from contemporary sources. Literature, the arts, sports, etc.

Robinson, Julian. *Fashion in the 30s.* London: Oresko Books, Ltd., 1978. Monochrome and some color fashion illustrations and photographs from contemporary sources.

Rothstein, Arthur. *The Depression Years: As Photographed by Arthur Rothstein.* New York: Dover Publications, Inc., 1978. Monochrome photographs.

Time-Life Books. *This Fabulous Century: Volume IV 1930–1940.* New York: Time-Life Books, 1969.

Feininger, Andreas. *New York in the Forties.* New York: Dover Publications, Inc., 1978. Monochrome photographs of New York life.

Hall, Carolyn. *The Forties In Vogue.* New York: Harmony Books, 1985. Monochrome and color illustrations. The War, the arts, celebrities.

Jenkins, Alan. *The Forties.* New York: Universe Books, 1977. Monochrome and some color illustrations and photographs of people, events, the arts, sports, fashion, etc.

Lemann, Nicholas. *Out of The Forties.* New York: Simon and Schuster, Inc., 1985. A Fireside Book. Monochrome photographs, mostly small-town life in Texas.

Robinson, Julian. *Fashions in the 40s.* New York: St. Martin's Press, 1976. Monochrome and color fashion illustrations and photographs.

Time-Life Books. *This Fabulous Century: Volume V 1940–1950.* New York: Time-Life Books, 1969.

Dorner, Jane. *Fashion in the Forties and Fifties.* London: Ian Allan, Ltd., 1975. Monochrome and some color fashion illustratons and photographs. Some men's but mostly women's clothing.

Chancellor, John. *The Fifties.* New York: Pantheon Books, 1985. Monochrome photographs by well-known American photographers.

Drake, Nicholas. *The Fifties in Vogue*. New York: Henry Holt and Company, 1987. Monochrome and color illustrations. The arts, fashion, movies, etc.

Horsley, Edith. *The 1950s*. London: A Bison/Domus Book, 1978. Illustrated with monochrome and some color photographs of events, fashions, the arts, politics, etc, of the 1950s.

Lewis, Peter. *The 50s*. London: Heinemann, 1978. Monochrome photographs covering events, fashion, entertainment, and news items of the decade.

Time-Life Books. *This Fabulous Century: Volume VI 1950–1960*. New York: Time-Life Books, 1970.

Jones, Mablen. *Getting It On: The Clothing of Rock and Roll*. New York: Abbeville Press, Inc., 1987. Monochrome and color photographs of performers, musicians, costume sketches, etc. 1950s to 1980s.

Polhemus, Ted and Procter, Lynn. *Pop Styles: An A–Z Guide to the World Where Fashion Meets Rock 'N' Roll*. London, Melbourne, Sydney, Auckland, Johannesburg: Vermillion and Company, 1984. Monochrome and color illustrations.

Bernard, Barbara. *Fashion in the 60s*. New York: St. Martin's Press, 1978. Monochrome photographs and drawings of women's and some men's fashions.

Drake, Nicholas, ed. *The Sixties: A Decade in Vogue*. New York, London, Toronto, Sydney, Tokyo: Prentice-Hall Press, n.d. Color and monochrome photographs from *Vogue*. Captures the decade.

Lehnartz, Klaus. *New York in the Sixties*. New York: Dover Publications, Inc., 1978. Monochrome photographs of New York life.

Sann, Paul. *The Angry Decade: The Sixties*. New York: Crown Publishers, Inc., 1979. Monochrome photographs of people, places, and events.

Time-Life Books. *This Fabulous Century: Volume VII 1960–1970*. New York: Time-Life Books, 1970.

Hennessey, Val. *In The Gutter*. London, Melbourne, and New York: Quartet Books, 1978. Monochrome and color photographs of contemporary 1970s punk and primitive tribes as comparison.

McDermott, Catherine. *Street Style: British Design in the 80s*. New York: Rizzoli International Publications, Inc., 1987. Monochrome and color photographs of clothes, accessories, furniture, posters, etc.

Specific Countries and Cultures

AUSTRALIA

Flower, Cedric. *Duck and Cabbage Tree: A Pictorial History of Clothes in Australia 1788–1914*. Sydney, Melbourne, Singapore, London: Angus and Robertson, Ltd., 1968. Monochrome illustrations and photographs.

CHINA

Beers, Burton F. *China in Old Photographs 1860–1910*. New York: Dorset Press, 1981. Monochrome photographs.

Scott, A. C. *Chinese Costume in Transition*. Singapore, Kuala Lumpur, Hong Kong, Tokyo: Donald Moore, 1958. (Distributed by Theatre Arts Books, New York). Line drawings. Mid-nineteenth to mid-twentieth century.

Worswick, Clark and Spence, Jonathan. *Imperial China: Photographs 1850–1912*. New York: A Pennwick/Crown Book, 1978. Sepia photographs.

JAPAN

Noma, Seiroku. *Japanese Costume and Textile Arts*. New York and Tokyo: John Weatherhill, Inc., 1974. Monochrome and color illustrations and photographs of textiles and clothing.

Shima, Yukiko, trans. *A Step to Kimono and Kumihimo*. Los Angeles: Kyoto Kimono Academy, Inc., 1979. History of Japanese clothing, Kimono assemblage, and accessories. Includes a section on Japanese braided cord (Kumihimo). Line drawings and color photographs.

Sichel, Marion. *Japan*. London: B.T. Batsford, Ltd., 1987. Drawings, monochrome and some color.

Yang, Sunny and Narasin, Rochelle M. *Textile Art of Japan*. Tokyo: Shufunotomo Co., Ltd. 1989. Many color photographs of techniques, details, and garments. Chapters on the history of kimona and obi.

NATIVE AMERICAN INDIANS

Mather, Christine. *Native America Arts, Traditions & Celebrations*. New York: Clarkson N. Potter Inc., 1990. Lavishly illustrated with color and monochrome photographs.

RUSSIA

Allshouse, Robert H., ed. *Photographs for the Tsar: The Pioneering Color Photography of Sergei Mikhailovich Prokudin-Gorskii*. New York: The Dial Press, 1980. Color and some monochrome photographs of Russia and its people. Good for peasant and ethnic costume.

FitzLyon, Kyril and Browning, Tatiana. *Before the Revolution: A View of Russia Under the Last Tsar*. Woodstock, New York: The Overlook Press, 1978. Monochrome photographs of Russian life from the end of the nineteenth century to 1917. Includes hospital, military, domestic, fashionable, and lots of good peasant clothing.

Korshunova, Tamara. Translated by Inna Sorokina. *The Art of Costume in Russia: 18th to Early 20th Century*. Leningrad, Russia: Aurora Art Publishers, 1979. Revised edition, 1983. Monochrome and many wonderful color photographs of men's and women's fashionable clothing (including French couture), paintings, and accessories. Close-ups show construction details, embroidery, lace, etc. A beautiful book representing examples from the collection of costume at the Hermitage.

Lyons, Marvin. *Russia in Original Photographs 1860–1920*. New York: Charles Scribner's Sons, 1977. Monochrome photographs of all walks of Russian life, many showing good clothing detail.

Massie, Robert K. *The Romanov Family Album*. New York: The Vendome Press, 1982. Monochrome photographs of the good life in old Russia in the late nineteenth and early twentieth century from the family albums of the last Tsar.

Obolensky, Cloe. *The Russian Empire: A Portrait in Photographs*. New York: Random House, Inc., 1979. Monochrome photographs, 1850s to 1915, show clothing from all walks of life.

Onassis, Jacqueline, ed. *In The Russian Style*. New York: A Studio Book, The Viking Press, 1976. Published in conjunction with an exhibit of Russian costume at the Metropolitan Museum of Art. Monochrome and some color photographs of clothing and illustrations from contemporary sources. Seventeenth to early twentieth century.

Salisbury, Harrison E. *Russia in Revolution 1900–1930*. New York: Holt, Rinehart and Winston, 1978. Monochrome and color photographs and illustrations, some of which are useful for clothing.

Sichel, Marion. *USSR*. London: B.T. Batsford, Ltd., 1986. Line drawings, monochrome and some color.

Zaletova, Lidya, Atti, Fabio Ciofi degli, Panzini, Franco, et al. *Revolutionary Costume Soviet Clothing and Textiles of the 1920s*. New York: Rizzoli International Publications, Inc., 1989. Drawings and photographs of garments and many textile designs, monochrome and some color.

SAUDI ARABIA

Ross, Heather Colyer. *The Art of Arabian Costume: A Saudi Arabian Profile*. Fribourg, Switzerland: Arabesque Commercial SA, 1981. Color photographs and illustrations, line drawings, and patterns (not to scale). Covers history and development of clothing, jewelry, and accessories. Useful source.

———. *The Art of Bedouin Jewelry: A Saudi Arabian Profile*. Fribourg, Switzerland: Arabesque Commercial SA, 1981. Color photos of jewelry. Glossary of Arabic words and lists of technical terms. Beautiful book.

SWEDEN

Larkin, David, ed. *The Paintings of Carl Larsson*. New York: A Peacock Press/Bantam Book, 1976. Color plates of the artist's work, showing family life in Sweden 1892 to 1914, many showing clothing.

SOUTH AFRICA

Telford, A.A. *Yesterday's Dress: A History of Costume in South Africa*. Cape Town, South Africa: Purnell and Sons, Ltd., 1972. History of South African costume. Sepia and color line drawings by author. 1488 to the end of the nineteenth century.

THE AMERICAN WEST

Kauffman, Sandra. *The Cowboy Catalog*. New York: Clarkson N. Potter, Inc., distributed by Crown Publishers, 1980. Monochrome and color plates.

Reedstrom, Ernest Lisle. *Historic Dress of the Old West*. Poole, Dorset, England, New York, and Sydney: Blandford Press, 1986. Color illustrations by the author and monochrome photographs. Broad information. Excellent resource.

Sayers, Isabelle S. *Annie Oakley and Buffalo Bill's Wild West*. New York: Dover Publications, 1981. Monochrome photographs.

Time-Life. *The American West*. 26 vols. and master index. New York: Time-Life Books, 1973–76. Monochrome and color illustrations, many from primary sources.

Accessories

EYE WEAR

Corson, Richard. *Fashions in Eyeglasses From the 14th Century to the Present Day*. London: Peter Owen, 1980. (Second impression with supplement). Comprehensive and well illustrated with plates and line drawings.

Davidson, D. C. *Spectacles, Lorgnettes and Monocles*. Shire Album 227. Princes Risborough, Aylesbury, Bucks., England: Shire Publications, Ltd., 1989.

Marly, Pierre. *Spectacles and Spyglasses*. France: Editions Hoebeke, 1988. Beautifully illustrated history of eye wear from thirteenth to twentieth century.

Winkler, Wolf, ed. *A Spectacle of Spectacles*. Leipzig, Germany: Edition Leipzig, 1988. Beautifully illustrated. History of eye wear from fourteenth to early twentieth century.

FANS

Alexander, Helen. *Fans*. The Costume Accessories Series. New York: Drama Book Publishers, 1985.

Armstrong, Nancy. *The Book of Fans*. New York: Mayflower, 1978. All color illustrations.

Gostelow, Mary. *The Fan*. Dublin: Gill and Macmillan, Ltd., 1976. Illustrated with photographs.

FOOTWEAR

Atkinson, Jeremy. *Clogs and Clogmaking*. Shire Album 113. Princes Risborough, Aylesbury, Bucks., England: Shire Publications, Ltd., 1984. History and use of clogs. Small, well-illustrated, and informative paperback.

Baynes, Ken and Kate. *The Shoe Show: British Shoes Since 1790*. London: The Crafts Council, 1979. Useful, informative, and very well illustrated with monochrome and color photographs.

Dobson, Bob. *Concerning Clogs*. Clapham, N. Yorkshire, England: Dalesman Books, 1979. The use and history of clogs in England with line drawings and photographs.

Probert, Christina, comp. In Vogue Series: *Shoes in Vogue Since 1910*. New York: Abbeville Press, 1981. Illustrations, including color, from *Vogue*.

Swann, June. *Shoes*. The Costume Accessories Series. New York: Drama Book Publishers, 1982. Well illustrated.

———. *Shoemaking*. Shire Album 155. Princes Risborough, Aylesbury, Bucks., England: Shire Publications, Ltd., 1986. Roman times to twentieth century.

Wilcox, R. Turner. *The Mode in Footwear*. New York: Charles Scribner's Sons, Ltd., 1948. Line drawings.

Wilson, Eunice. *A History of Shoe Fashion*. New York: Theatre Arts Books, 1974. Line drawings. Some photographs from primary sources.

JEWELRY

Bayer, Patricia, Becker, Vivienne, Craven, Helen, Hinks, Peter, Lightbrown, Ronald, Ogden, Jack, Scaresbrick, Dina. *The Jewelry Design Source Book. A Visual Reference for all Jewelry Collectors & Enthusiasts*. New York: Van Nostrand Reinhold, 1989. Beautiful large color photographs with excellent detail.

Black, J. Anderson. *A History of Jewels*. London: Orbis Publishing, 1974. Prehistory to twentieth century.

Coles, Janet and Budwig, Robert. *The Book of Beads*. New York: Simon and Schuster, 1990. Beautiful color photographs of every bead imaginable.

Frank, Larry and Holbrook, Millard J. II. *Indian Silver Jewelry of the Southwest 1868–1930.* Westchester, PA: Schiffer Publishing, Ltd., 1990. Monochrome and color illustrations throughout. Good detail.

Hart, Harold H. *Jewelry: A Pictorial Archive of Woodcuts & Engravings.* New York: Dover Publications, Inc., 1981.

Hornung, Clarence P. *A Source Book of Antiques & Jewelry Designs.* New York: Da Capo Press, Inc., 1977.

Scarisbrick, Diana. *Jewelry.* The Costume Accessories Series. New York: Drama Book Publishers, 1985.

Wiener, Louis. *Handmade Jewelry: A Manual of Techniques.* New York: Van Nostrand Reinhold Co., 1981. Line drawings and monochrome photographs. Good process sequences.

NECK WEAR

Colle, Doriece. *Collars, Stocks, Cravats: A History and Costume Dating Guide to Civilian Men's Neckpieces 1655–1900.* Emmaus, PA: Rodale Press, Inc., 1972. Good information. Plates and line drawings. Line drawings are not always clear.

Gibbings, Sarah. *Ties: Trends and Traditions.* New York and Toronto: Barron's Educational Series, Inc., 1990. Misleading title as it covers the history of neckwear from the seventeenth century to present day. Well illustrated and informative.

Laver, James. *The Book of Public School Old Boys, University, Navy, Army, Air Force and Club Ties.* London: Seely Service and Co., Ltd., 1968. Many color plates.

Mosconi, Davide and Villarosa, Riccardo. *Getting Knotted: 188 Knots for Necks: The History, Techniques and Photographs.* Milan, Italy: Rajti, 1985.

MISCELLANEOUS

Braun-Ronsdorf, Dr. M. *The History of the Handkerchief.* Leigh-on-Sea, England: F. Lewis Publishers, Ltd., 1967. Plates of actual handkerchiefs and paintings showing them in use.

Crawford, T. S. *A History of the Umbrella.* Newton Abbot and London, England: David and Charles, 1970. Informative and well illustrated.

Cumming, Valerie. *Gloves.* The Costume Accessories Series. New York: Drama Book Publishers, 1982. Informative and beautifully illustrated.

Eckstein, E. and J. and Firkins, G. *Gentlemen's Dress Accessories.* Shire Album 205. Princes Risborough, Aylesbury, Bucks., England: Shire Publications, Ltd., 1987.

Farrell, Jeremy. *Scarves, Stoles and Shawls.* The Costume Accessories Series. New York: Drama Book Publishers, 1986.

Foster, Vanda. *Bags and Purses.* The Costume Accessories Series. New York: Drama Book Publishers, 1982.

Hague, Norma. *Combs and Hair Accessories.* Cincinnati, OH: Seven Hills Books, 1985. Small paperback with monochrome photographs. 1760 to 1940.

Johnson, Eleanor. *Fashion Accessories.* Shire Album 58. Princes Risborough, Ayelsbury, Bucks., England: Shire Publications, Ltd., 1982.

Les Accessoires du Temps. *Ombrelles Parapluies.* Paris: Paris-Musees, 1989. From an exhibit at the Musee de la Mode et du Costume. Beautiful color and monochrome photographs of primary sources.

Lester, Katherine Morris and Oerke, Bess Viola. *Accessories of Dress: An Illustrated History of the Frills and Furbelows of Fashion.* Peoria, IL: The Manual Arts Press, 1940. Monochrome plates, photographs, and line drawings. Covers accessories worn at neck, head, shoulder, waist, feet, legs, arms, wrist, and carried.

Mackrell, Jeremy. *Umbrellas and Parasols.* The Costume Accessories Series. New York: Drama Book Publishers, 1986.

Ceremonial, Academic, and Religious Dress

Arch, Nigel and Marschner, Joanna. *Splendour at Court: Dressing for Royal Occasions since 1700.* New York and Sydney: Unwin Hyman, 1987.

Clare, Rev. Wallace. *Historic Dress of the English Schoolboy.* London: The Society for the Preservation of Ancient Customs, n.d. (c.1939).

Cumming, Valerie. *Royal Dress: The Image and the Reality 1580 to Present Day.* London: B.T. Batsford, Ltd., 1989.

Dearmer, Rev. Percy. *The Arts of the Church: The Ornaments of the Ministers.* London: A. R. Mowbray and Co., Ltd., 1908. History and origins with illustrations.

Gummere, Amelia Mott. *The Quaker: A Study in Costume.* New York and London: Benjamin Blom, Inc., 1968. 1901 reprint. Quaker dress in Britain and America, seventeenth to nineteenth century.

Haycraft, Frank W. *The Degrees and Hoods of the World's Universities and Colleges.* London: The Cheshunt Press, 1923.

Jenkins, Graham. *The Making of Church Vestments.* Westminster, MD: The Newman Press, 1957. Historical information, shapes, and sizes of garments, with patterns (not to scale).

Macalister, R. A. S. *Ecclesiastical Vestments: Their Development and History.* London: Elliot Stock, 1896. Monochrome illustrations and line drawings from primary sources.

Mansfield, Alan. *Ceremonial Costume.* London: Adam and Charles Black, 1980. Monochrome illustrations, photographs, and line drawings of parliamentary dress, coronation robes, court uniforms, etc., from primary sources.

Mayer-Thurman, Christa C. *Raiment For The Lord's Service: A Thousand Years of Western Vestments.* Chicago: The Art Institute of Chicago, 1975. Published in conjunction with an exhibit at the Art Institute. Monochrome photographs of textiles and garments in the exhibit.

Mayo, Janet. *A History of Ecclesiastical Dress.* New York: Drama Book Publishers, photographs from primary sources.

Norris, Herbert. *Church Vestments: Their Origin and Development.* London: J. M. Dent and Sons, Ltd., 1949. Includes patterns, monochrome plates, and line drawings redrawn from original sources.

Rubens, Alfred. *A History of Jewish Costume.* London: Valentine, Mitchell and Co., Ltd., 1967. From antiquity, by country, with illustrations.

Scott, Stephen. *Why Do They Dress That Way?* Intercourse, PA: Good Books, 1986. Amish and Mennonite clothing. Very detailed. Monochrome plates and some line drawings.

Shaw, G. W. *Academical Dress of British Universities.* Cambridge, England: W. Heffer and Sons, 1966. Information on all major universities, with diagrams of the various hood and gown shapes.

Smith, Hugh. *Academic Dress and Insignia of the World.* Cape Town: A. A. Balkema, 1970. A definitive work in 3 volumes with line illustrations.

Tyack, Rev. Geo. S. *The Historic Dress of the Clergy.* London: William Andrews and Co., 1897. Engravings and line illustrations.

CHILDREN'S COSTUME

Cunnington, Phillis and Buck, Anne. *Children's Costume in England 1300–1900.* London: Adam and Charles Black, 1965. Contemporary quotations, primary source illustrations, and line drawings.

Ewing, Elizabeth. *History of Children's Costume.* London: B.T. Batsford, Ltd., 1977. Primary source illustrations.

Grafton, Carol Belanger. *Children: A Pictorial Archive from Nineteenth-Century Sources.* New York: Dover Publications, Inc., 1978.

Mager, Alison, ed. *Children of the Past in Photographic Portraits.* New York: Dover Publications, Inc., 1978.

Martin, Linda. *The Way We Wore: Fashion Illustration of Children's Wear 1870–1970.* New York: Charles Scribner's Sons, 1978.

Pierce, A. J. and D. K. *Victorian and Edwardian Children from Old Photographs.* London: B.T. Batsford, Ltd., 1980. Monochrome photographs of children from all walks of life.

Rose, Clare. *Children's Clothes.* New York: Drama Book Publishers, 1990. Seventeenth to twentieth century.

Hats, Hair, Wigs, and Make-up

Amphlett, Hilda. *Hats: A History of Fashion in Headwear.* Chalfont St. Giles, Bucks., England: Richard Sadler, Ltd., 1974. Line drawings.

Anlezark, Mildred. *Hats on Heads: The Art of Creative Millinery.* Berkeley, CA: Lacis. Originally published in Australia, it covers millinery techniques and trimmings in a wide variety of materials.

Arnold, Janet. *Perukes and Periwigs.* London: Her Majesty's Stationery Office, 1970. c. 1660 to 1740.

Asser, Joyce. *Historic Hairdressing*. London: Sir Isaac Pitman and Sons, Ltd., 1966. Line drawings.

Botham, Mary and Sharrad, L. *Manual of Wigmaking*. London: Heinemann, 1982. Distributed in the U.S. by David and Charles, Inc., North Pomfret, VT. 3rd edition. Clear line drawings and informative text on the art of wigmaking.

Charles, Ann and DeAnfrasio, Roger. *The History of Hair: An Illustrated Review Of Hair Fashions For Men Throughout The Ages*. New York: Bonanza Books, 1970. Line drawings, engravings, photographs, and paintings.

Clark, Fiona. *Hats*. The Costume Accesssories Series. New York: Drama Book Publishers, 1982. Beautifully illustrated.

Corey, Irene. *The Face is a Canvas: The Design & Technique of Theatrical Make-up*. New Orleans, LA: Anchorage Press, 1990. Beautifully illustrated, color and monochrome, with transparent overlays.

Corson, Richard. *Fashions in Hair: The First Five Thousand Years*. London: Peter Owen, 1965. Revised, 1971. Line drawings and engravings.

———. *Fashions in Makeup*. New York: Universe Books, 1972. Drawings, photographs, engravings, and line drawings.

———. *Stage Makeup*. Englewood Cliffs, NJ: Prentice-Hall, Inc., 1981. 6th edition.

Couldridge, Alan. *The Hat Book*. Englewood Cliffs, NJ: Prentice-Hall, Inc., 1980. Line drawings and photographs. Contemporary, but methods useful for costume.

Courtais, Georgine de. *Women's Headdress and Hairstyles in England from AD 600 to the Present Day*. London: B.T. Batsford, Ltd., 1973. Line drawings.

Dreher, Denise. *From The Neck Up: An Illustrated Guide to Hatmaking*. Minneapolis, MN: Madhatter Press, 1981. Comprehensive and detailed instructions for theatrical millinery. Line drawings, scaled patterns, engravings, and photographs.

Garsault, Mons. de. *The Art of the Wigmaker*. Reprint from 1767. London: The Hairdresser's Registration Council, 1961.

Ginsburg, Madeleine. *The Hat: Trends and Traditions*. New York and Toronto: Barron's Educational Series, Inc., 1990. History of men's and women's head coverings from Medieval times to present day.

Huggett, Renee. *Hair-Styles and Head-Dresses*. North Pomfret, VT: David and Charles, 1982. Line drawings, engravings, photographs, and paintings.

Jones, Dylan. *Haircults: Fifty Years of Styles and Cuts*. London: Thames and Hudson, Ltd., 1990. Many monochrome and some color photographs. 1940s to 1980s.

Lax, Roger and Carvainis, Maria. *Moustache*. New York, London, Tokyo: Quick Fox, 1979. Illustrations and photographs of a large variety of moustaches.

Nardi, Vincent and Fred. *How to Do Your Hair Like a Pro*. New York: Perigee Books, 1977.

Probert, Christina, comp. In Vogue Series: *Hats in Vogue Since 1910*. New York: Abbeville Press, 1981. Illustrations, including color from *Vogue*.

Severn, Bill. *The Long and Short of it: Five Thousand Years of Fun and Fury over Hair*. New York: David McKay Company, Inc., 1971. Photographs, line drawings, and engravings.

Stevens, Angela. *How to Set and Style Your Own Wig*. New York: Arco Publishing Co., Inc., 1972.

Stevens Cox, James. *An Illustrated Dictionary of Hairdressing and Wigmaking*. New York: Drama Book Publishers, 1984. Line drawings, engravings, and photographs.

Wilcox, R. Turner. *The Mode in Hats and Headdress: Including Hair Styles, Cosmetics and Jewelry*. New York: Charles Scribner's Sons, 1945. Line drawings.

Woodforde, John. *The Strange Story of False Hair*. London: Routledge and Kegan Paul, 1971. Paintings, engravings, and line drawings.

Men's Costume

Brander, Michael. *The Victorian Gentleman*. London: Gordon Cremonesi, 1975. "The manners, morals (and immorals) of our fathers and grandfathers." Not specifically on costume, but useful.

Byrde, Penelope. *The Male Image: Men's Fashions in England 1300–1970*. London: B.T. Batsford, Ltd., 1979. Well illustrated from primary sources.

Druesedow, Jean. *Jno. J. Mitchell Co. Men's Fashion Illustrations from the Turn of the Century*. New York: Dover Publications, Inc., 1990. Formal and informal fashions, 1900 to 1910.

Halls, Zillah. *Men's Costume 1580–1750*. London: Her Majesty's Stationery Office, 1970. Catalogue with photographs of costumes from the London Museum.

———. *Men's Costume 1750–1800*. London: Her Majesty's Stationery Office, 1973. More costumes from the London Museum.

Harter, Jim. *Men: A Pictorial Archive from Nineteenth-Century Sources*. New York: Dover Publications, Inc., 1980.

Keers, Paul. *A Gentleman's Wardrobe: Classic Clothes and the Modern Man*. New York: Harmony Books, 1987. Informative text with contemporary and period illustrations.

Marly, Diana de. *Fashion for Men: An Illustrated History*. New York: Holmes and Meier Publishers, 1985. Illustrations from primary sources.

Martin, Richard and Koda, Harold. *Jocks and Nerds: Men's Style in the Twentieth Century*. New York: Rizzoli, 1989. Beautiful illustrations of men from all walks of life.

Schoeffler, O. E. and Gale, William. *Esquire's Encyclopedia of 20th Century Men's Fashions*. New York: McGraw-Hill Book Company, 1973. Informative and well illustrated.

Waller, Jane. *A Man's Book: Fashion in the Man's World in the 20s and 30s*. London: Gerald Duckworth and Co., Ltd., 1977.

Occupational and Regional Costume

Barsis, Max. *The Common Man through the Centuries: A Book of Costume Drawings*. New York: Frederick Ungar Publishing Co., 1973. Line drawings, not directly from original sources.

Copeland, Peter F. *Working Dress in Colonial and Revolutionary America*. Westport, CT: Greenwood Press, 1977. Monochrome illustrations and line drawings redrawn from other sources.

Cunnington, Phillis. *Costumes of Household Servants from the Middle Ages to 1900*. New York: Barnes and Noble, 1974. Line drawings, engravings, photographs, and paintings of English servants.

Cunnington, Phillis and Lucas, Catherine. *Occupational Costume in England from the 11th Century to 1914*. London: Adam and Charles Black, 1967. Revised edition 1976. Line drawings, engravings, paintings, prints, and photographs.

———. *Charity Costumes of Children, Scholars, Almsfolk, Pensioners*. London: Adam and Charles Black, 1978. Line drawings, engravings, paintings, prints, and photographs.

Ewing, Elizabeth. *Everyday Dress 1650–1900*. London: B.T. Batsford, Ltd., 1984. Includes lots of occupational clothing for men and women from all walks of life. Monochrome illustrations and photographs from contemporary sources.

Hiley, Michael. *Victorian Working Women: Portraits from Life*. London: Gordon Fraser, 1979. Photographs of women miners, milkmaids, gymnasts, maids, etc.

Hine, Lewis W. *Women at Work: 153 photographs by Lewis W. Hine*. New York: Dover Publications, Inc., 1981. Working women 1907 to 1938.

———. *Men at Work: Photographic Studies of Modern Men and Machines*. New York: Dover Publications, Inc., 1977. Originally published in 1932.

Lansdell, Avril. *The Clothes of the Cut: A History of Canal Costume*. London: British Waterways Board, n.d. Monochrome and color illustrations and photographs.

———. *Occupational Costume and Working Clothes, 1776–1976*. Shire Album 27. Princes Risborough, Aylesbury, Bucks., England: Shire Publications, Ltd., 1977. Monochrome plates and photographs.

Lister, Margot. *Costumes of Everyday Life: An Illustrated History of Working Clothes*. Boston: Plays, Inc., 1972. Line drawings.

Marly, Diana de. *Working Dress*. New York: Holmes and Meier Publishers, Inc., 1986. Early times to twentieth century.

Masson, Madeleine. *A Pictorial History of Nursing*. Twickenham, Middlesex, England: Hamlyn Publishing, 1985. Early times to 1980s, mostly British sources.

McGowan, Alan. *Sailor: A Pictorial History*. New York: David McKay Company, Inc., 1977.

Oakes, Alma and Hill, Margot Hamilton. *Rural Costume: Its Origin and Development in Western Europe and the British Isles*. New York: Van Nostrand Reinhold, 1970. Line drawings.

Pauw, Linda Grant De and Hunt, Conover. *Remember the Ladies: Women in America 1750–1815*. New York: The Viking Press, 1976. Monochrome and color plates throughout.

Pyne, William H. *Rustic Vignettes for Artists and Craftsmen*. New York: Dover Publications, Inc., 1977. Early nineteenth century.

———. *Pyne's British Costumes*. Ware, Hertford-shire, England: Wordsworth Editions, Ltd., 1989. Reprint from 1805 with color drawings of occupational clothing.

Snowdon, James. *The Folk Dress of Europe*. New York: Mayflower Books, Inc., 1979. Monochrome and color illustrations, primary source plates, and photographs.

White, William Johnstone. *Working Class Costume 1818*. Reprint. London: The Costume Society, 1971. Eighteen plates of English rural life.

Williams-Mitchell, Christobel. *Dressed for the Job: The Story of Occupational Costume*. New York: Sterling Publishing Co., Inc., 1982. Color illustrations, engravings, prints, and photographs.

Sports Clothes

Cunnington, Phillis and Mansfield, Alan. *English Costume for Sports and Outdoor Recreation from the 16th to the 19th Centuries*. London: Adam and Charles Black, 1969. Line drawings, engravings, paintings, prints, and photographs.

Fashion Institute of Technology. *All American: A Sportswear Tradition*. New York: Fashion Institute of Technology, 1985. Published in conjunction with an exhibit at FIT. Monochrome and color illustrations from primary sources and of clothing in the exhibit.

The Gallery of English Costume. Picture Book Number Eight: *Costume for Sport*. Manchester, England: Art Galleries Committee of the Corporation of Manchester, 1963. Monochrome photographs of clothing and accessories in the Gallery of English Costume.

Green, Stephen. *Cricketing Bygones*. Shire Album 90. Princes Risborough, Aylesbury, Bucks., England: Shire Publications, Ltd., 1982.

Gurney, Gerald N. *Tennis, Squash and Badminton Bygones*. Shire Album 121. Princes Risborough, Aylesbury, Bucks., England: Shire Publications, Ltd., 1984.

Lane, Andrew. *Motoring Costume*. Shire Album 197. Princes Risborough, Aylesbury, Bucks., England: Shire Publications, Ltd., 1987.

Lee-Potter, Charles. *Sportswear in Vogue since 1910*. London: Thames and Hudson, 1984.

Lencek, Lena and Bosker, Gideon. *Making Waves: Swimsuits and the Undressing of America*. San Francisco, CA: Chronicle Books, 1989. History of swimwear in America in the twentieth century.

The Metropolitan Museum of Art. *Man and the Horse*. New York: Simon and Schuster/The Metropolitan Museum of Art, 1984. Published in conjunction with an exhibit at the Metropolitan Museum. Monochrome and color illustrations and photographs from primary sources. Early times to twentieth century.

Pilley, Phil., ed. *Golfing Art*. Topsfield, MA: Salem House Publishers, 1988. Artists' work depicting various aspects of the sport, seventeenth to twentieth century.

Probert, Christina. In Vogue Series: *Swimwear in Vogue Since 1910*. New York: Abbeville Press, 1981. Illustrations, including color, from *Vogue*.

Vandervell, Anthony and Coles, Charles. *Games & the English Landscape: The Influence of the Chase on Sporting Art & Scenery*. New York: A Studio Book, The Viking Press, 1980. Engravings, paintings, prints, and photographs. Fifteenth to twentieth century. Not specifically on costume but useful.

Underwear

Caldwell, Doreen. *And All Was Revealed: Ladies' Underwear 1907–1980*. New York: St Martin's Press, 1981. Amusing and informative. Line drawings in color.

Colmer, Michael. *Whalebone to See Through: A History of Body Packaging*. London and Edinburgh: Johnston and Bacon, 1979. Monochrome and color illustrations from primary sources.

Cunnington, C. Willett and Phillis. *The History of Underclothes*. With revisions by A.D. and Valerie Mansfield. London and Boston: Faber and Faber, Ltd. 1981. Originally published in 1951. Men and women from fifteenth century to 1950. Line drawings and primary source illustrations. Informative.

Ewing, Elizabeth. *Dress and Undress: A History of Women's Underwear*. New York: Drama Book Publishers, 1989. Partially based on *Underwear, A History*. Line drawings and monochrome illustrations from primary sources. Useful.

———. *Underwear: A History*. New York: Theatre Arts Books, 1972. Line drawings.

Fashion Institute of Technology. *The Undercover Story*. New York: Fashion Institute of Technology, 1982. Published in conjunction with an exhibit at F.I.T. Illustrations and photographs of nineteenth and twentieth century underwear in the exhibit. Useful source.

Morel, Juliette. *Lingerie Parisienne*. New York: St. Martin's Press, 1976. Fashion drawings and photographs of 1920s lingerie.

Page, Christopher. *Foundations of Fashion: The Symington Collection. Corsetry from 1856 to the Present Day*. Leicester, England: Leicester Museums, 1981.

Probert, Christina. In Vogue Series: *Lingerie in Vogue Since 1910*. New York: Abbeville Press, 1981. Illustrations, including color, from *Vogue*.

Reyburn, Wallace. *Bust-Up: The Uplifting Tale of Otto Titzling and the Development of the Bra*. Englewood Cliffs, NJ: Prentice-Hall, Inc., 1972. Amusing account with line drawings and photographs.

Rothacker, Nanette. *The Undies Book*. New York: Charles Scribner's Sons, 1976. Scale patterns, line drawings, and construction instructions for contemporary underwear including bras, slips, camisoles, panties, and girdles.

Saint-Laurent, Cecil. *The History of Ladies' Underwear*. London: Michael Joseph, 1968. Early times to 1960s. Monochrome and color illustrations from primary sources.

———. *The Great Book of Lingerie*. New York: The Vendome Press, 1986. History of underwear from 3,000 B.C. to twentieth century. Similiar to above, but enlarged and expanded.

Waugh, Nora. *Corsets and Crinolines*. New York: Theatre Arts Books, 1954. Scale patterns, line drawings, monochrome illustrations, and pertinent commentary from primary sources. Invaluable.

Uniforms, Arms, and Armor

Ashdown, Charles Henry. *British and Continental Arms and Armour*. New York: Dover Publications, Inc., 1970. Reprint from 1909. Ancient times to seventeenth century.

Barthorp, Michael. *British Infantry Uniforms Since 1660*. Poole, Dorset, England: Blandford Press, 1982. Distributed in the U.S. by Sterling Publishing Co., Inc., New York. Beautiful color plates, primary source illustrations, and photographs.

Blair, Claude. *European Armour circa 1066 to circa 1700*. New York: Crane, Russak and Co., Inc., 1972. Reprint from 1958. Line drawings and photographs from primary sources.

Blakeslee, Fred Gilbert. *Uniforms of the World*. New York: E. P. Dutton and Co., Inc., 1929. Useful source for police, army, navy, and civilian uniforms of most countries to circa 1929. Detailed descriptions, monochrome photographs.

Cassin-Scott, Jack and Fabb, John. *Ceremonial Uniforms of the World*. New York: Arco Publishing Co., Inc., 1977. Color illustrations redrawn from primary sources.

Cochrane, Peter. *Scottish Military Dress*. London: Blandford Press, 1987. Color plates redrawn from primary sources.

Davis, Brian L. *British Army Uniforms and Insignia of World War Two*. London, Melbourne, Harrisburg, PA, Capetown: Arms and Armour Press, 1983. Monochrome photographs and line drawings. Comprehensive.

———. *German Army Uniforms and Insignia 1933–1945*. New York: Arco Publishing Co., Inc., 1977. Line drawings and many monochrome photographs.

———. *German Combat Uniforms of World War Two*. Vol. I. Poole, Dorset, England: Arms and Armour Press, 1984. Monochrome and some color photographs.

———. *German Combat Uniforms of World War Two*. Vol. II. London, Melbourne, Harrisburg, PA, Cape Town: Arms and Armour Press, 1985. Monochrome and some color photographs.

Davis, Brian Leigh and Turner, Pierre. *German Uniforms of the Third Reich 1933–1945*. New York: Arco Publishing Co., Inc., 1980. Detailed color illustrations redrawn from primary sources.

Elting, John R., ed. *Military Uniforms in America: The Era of the American Revolution, 1755–1795*. San Rafael, CA: Presidio Press, 1974. Detailed color illustrations redrawn from primary sources.

———. *Military Uniforms in America*. Vol. III, *Long Endure: The Civil War Period 1852–1867*. Novato, CA: Presidio Press, 1982. Sixty-four color illustrations each accompanied by explanatory text.

Ewing, Elizabeth. *Women in Uniform Through the Centuries*. London: B. T. Batsford, Ltd., 1975. Monochrome illustrations and photographs from primary sources.

Fitzsimons, Bernard. *Heraldry and Regalia of War*. New York: Beekman House, 1973. World Wars I and II.

Fox-Davies, Arthur Charles. *A Complete Guide to Heraldry*. New York: Bonanza Books, 1978. Reprint from 1909. Comprehensive. Monochrome and some color illustrations.

Harwell, Richard. *Uniforms and Dress of the Army and Navy of the Confederate States*. New York: St. Martin's Press, Inc., 1960. First published as *Uniforms and Dress of the Army of the Confederate States* in 1861 by Charles H. Wynne, Printer, Richmond, VA.

Haythornthwaite, Philip and Chappell, Michael. *Uniforms of 1812: Napoleon's Retreat from Moscow*. Poole, Dorset, England: Blandford Press, 1982. Color and some monochrome illustrations.

Hoffschmidt, E. J. and Tantum, W. H. IV, eds. *German Army, Navy Uniforms and Insignia 1871–1918*. Old Greenwich, CT: WE, Inc., 1968. Monochrome illustrations and photographs.

Jarrett, Dudley. *British Naval Dress*. London: J.M. Dent and Sons, Ltd., 1960. Men's and women's uniforms, seventeenth to twentieth century.

Katcher, Philip. *Armies of the American Wars 1753–1815*. New York: Hastings House, Publishers, 1975. Color illustrations, monochrome plates, and photographs from primary sources.

———. *Uniforms of the Continental Army*. York, PA: George Shumway Publisher, 1981. Photographs of extant garments and accessories, primary source illustrations, and a few patterns, some to scale. Comprehensive work.

Kelly, Francis M. and Schwabe, Randolph. *A Short History of Costume and Armour 1066–1800*. Newton Abbot, Devon, England: David and Charles, 1972. Reprint from 1931. Monochrome engravings and plates from primary sources.

Knotel, Herbert Jr. and Steig, Herbert. *Uniforms of the World: A Compendium of Army, Navy and Air Force Uniforms, 1700–1937*. New York: Charles Scribner's Sons, 1980. Reprint of *Handbuch der Uniformkunde* originally published in 1937. Excellent source of information. Line drawings.

Koch, H. W. *Medieval Warfare*. London: A Bison Book, Dorset Press, 1982. Excellent monochrome and color illustrations from primary sources.

Lord, Francis A. *Uniforms of the Civil War*. Cranbury, NJ: Thomas Yoseloff, 1970. Monochrome illustrations and photographs from primary sources.

Martin, Paul. *Arms and Armour:From the 9th to the 17th Century*. Rutland, VT: Charles E. Tuttle Company, Inc., 1967. Survey. Good monochrome and some color illustrations from primary sources.

———. *European Military Uniforms: A Short History*. London: Spring Books, 1967. Originally published as *Der Bunte Rock* in 1963. Color plates and line drawings.

McGowan, Alan. *Sailor: A Pictorial History: Life aboard the world's fighting ships from the beginnings of photography to the present day*. New York: David McKay Company, Inc., 1977. Monochrome photographs.

Men-At-Arms Series. London: Osprey Publishing Co. A large series of small books. Each book has 40 pages and includes 8 pages of color illustrations redrawn from primary sources dealing with a specific military event. Includes many countries and periods. Very useful.

Mollo, Andrew. *The Armed Forces of World War II: Uniforms, Insignia, and Organization*. New York: Crown Publishers, Inc., 1981. The most comprehensive to date. Beautifully detailed color illustrations, plates of insignia, and monochrome photographs.

Mollo, Boris. *The British Army from Old Photographs*. London: J.M. Dent and Sons, Ltd., 1975. One hundred ninety-five monochrome photographs from The National Army Museum.

———. *The Indian Army*. Poole, Dorset, England, New York, Sydney: New Orchard Editions, 1981. Monochrome and color illustrations.

Mollo, Boris and Mollo, John. *Uniforms of the Imperial Russian Army*. Poole, Dorset, England: Blandford Press, 1979. Color illustrations. Peter the Great to 1917.

Mollo, John and McGregor, Malcolm. *Uniforms of the Seven Years War 1756–63*. Poole, Dorset, England: Blandford Press, 1977. Color illustrations.

———. *Uniforms of the American Revolution*. New York: Macmillan Publishing Co., Inc., 1975. Color illustrations.

———. *Army Uniforms of World War 2*. London: Blandford Press, 1973. Detailed color illustrations redrawn from primary sources.

Mollo, Andrew and Turner, Pierre. *Army Uniforms of World War I*. New York: Arco Publishing Company, Inc., 1978. Detailed color illustrations redrawn from primary sources.

North, Anthony. *An Introduction to European Swords*. Owings Mills, MD: Stemmer House Publishers, Inc., 1982. Fourteenth to nineteenth century. Monochrome and color photographs.

North, Rene. *Military Uniforms*. London: Hamlyn, 1970. Color illustrations. Brief but useful.

Pimlott, Dr. John and Gilbert, Adrian. *Military Uniforms of the World: Uniforms and Equipment Since World War II*. New York: Crescent Books, 1986. Many color illustrations, monochrome and color photographs. Excellent source.

Robinson, H. Russell. *The Armour of Imperial Rome*. New York: Charles Scribner's Sons, 1975. Comprehensive. First century B.C. to third century A.D. Numerous illustrations.

Rosignoli, Guido. *The Illustrated Encyclopedia of Military Insignia of the 20th Century. A comprehensive A-Z guide to the badges, patches and embellishments of the world's armed forces*. Secaucus, NJ: Chartwell Books, Inc., 1986.

Sachse, L. & Co. *Full-Color Uniforms of the Prussian Army: 72 Plates from the Year 1830*. New York: Dover Publications, Inc., 1981.

Saxtorph, Niels M. *Warriors and Weapons of Early Times in Color*. New York: The Macmillan Company, 1972. Illustrations based on research but not directly from primary sources.

Schick, I. T., ed. *Battledress: The Uniforms of the World's Great Armies 1700 to the Present*. London: Peerage Books, 1983. Line drawings in color, monochrome photographs, and primary source illustrations. Comprehensive.

Sietsema, Robert, *Weapons and Armor*. New York: Hart Publishing Company, Inc., 1978. Collection of monochrome pictures from public domain, shown by category.

Smith, Digby and Chappell, Michael. *Army Uniforms Since 1945*. Poole, Dorset, England: Blandford Press, 1980. Monochrome and color illustrations redrawn from original sources. includes Korea, Viet Nam, Israel, etc.

Stone, George Cameron. *A Glossary of the Construction, Decoration and Use of Arms and Armor in All Countries and in All Times, Together With Some Closely Related Subjects*. New York: Jack Brussel, 1961. Black and white illustrations within the text of alphabetical entries.

Sweeting, C.G. *Combat Flying Clothing. Army Air Forces Clothing During World War II*. Washington, D.C.: Smithsonian Institution Press, 1984. Over 150 detailed monochrome photographs. Very complete.

Tincey, John. *Soldiers of the English Civil War(2): Cavalry*. London: Osprey Publishing, 1990. Accurate, detailed drawings and information. Monochrome illustrations and photographs. Twelve color plates.

Urwin, Gregory J.W. *The United States Infantry: An Illustrated History, 1775–1918*. London, New York, Sydney: Blandford Press, 1988. Color plates, monochrome prints, maps, and photographs.

———. *The United States Cavalry: An Illustrated History*. Poole, England, New York, Sydney: Blandford Press, 1983. Thirty-two color plates, monochrome photographs, covers 1776 to 1944.

War Office. *Dress Regulations for the Army 1900*. Reprint of 1900 official edition from Her Majesty's Stationery Office. London, Rutland, VT: Charles E. Tuttle Company, 1970. Monochrome plates of photographs of uniforms, trimmings, and equipment of the British Army.

WE. *German Military Uniforms and Insignia 1933–1945*. Old Greenwich, CT: WE, Inc., 1967. Line drawings and (not very clear) monochrome photographs.

Windrow, Martin and Embleton, Gerry. *Military Dress of North America 1665–1970*. New York: Charles Scribner's Sons, 1973. Color plates, monochrome illustrations, and photographs.

Wise, Arthur. *Weapons in the Theatre*. New York: Barnes and Noble, Inc., 1968. Stage combat.

Zaloga, Steven J. *Soviet Army Uniforms in World War Two*. London: Arms and Armour Press, 1985. One hundred twenty-nine monochrome photographs of soldiers in action.

———. *Soviet Army Uniforms Today*. London, Melbourne, Harrisburg, PA, Cape Town: Arms and Armour Press, 1985. Ninety-nine monochrome photographs of soldiers in action.

Weddings and Funerals

Baker, Margaret. *Wedding Customs & Folklore*. Totowa, NJ: Rowman and Littlefield, 1977.

Cunnington, Phillis and Lucas, Catherine. *Costume for Births, Marriages & Deaths*. London: Adam and Charles Black, 1972. Medieval times to 1900. Line drawings, engravings, illustrations, and photographs from primary sources.

Felger, Donna H. comp. *Bridal Fashions: Victorian Era*. Cumberland, MD: Hobby House Press, Inc., 1986. Reprinted from fashion magazines of the period. Primarily for antique dolls, but useful.

Ginsburg, Madeleine. *Wedding Dress 1740–1970*. London: Her Majesty's Stationery Office, 1981. Sepia fashion drawings and photographs.

Lansdell, Avril. *History in Camera. Wedding Fashions 1860–1980*. Princes Risborough, Aylesbury, Bucks., England: Shire Publications, Ltd. 1983. Monochrome photographs.

Monsarrat, Ann. *And the Bride wore . . . : The Story of the White Wedding*. New York: Dodd, Mead and Company, 1973. Comprehensive text but no illustrations.

Probert, Christina. *Brides in Vogue Since 1910*. New York: Abbeville Press, Inc., 1984.

Morley, John. *Death, Heaven and the Victorians*. London: Studio Vista, 1971. Monochrome and color illustrations, engravings, and photographs.

Stevenson, Pauline. *Bridal Fashions*. London: Ian Allan, Ltd., 1978. 1800 to present day; small section covering the years before 1800. Monochrome and some color engravings, illustrations, fashion drawings, and photographs.

Taylor, Lou. *Mourning Dress: A Costume and Social History*. London: George Allen and Unwin, 1983. Monochrome engravings, illustrations, and photographs.

Zimmerman, Catherine S. *The Brides Book: A Pictorial History of American Bridal Gowns*. New York: Arbor House, 1985.

Costume Design, Theatre, and Film

Anderson, Cletis and Barbara. *Costume Design*. New York: CBS College Publishing/Holt, Rinehart and Winston, 1984. Comprehensive textbook.

Bailey, Margaret J. *Those Glorious Glamour Years, Classic Hollywood Costume Design of the 1930s*. London: Columbus Books, 1988. Many monochrome photographs.

Bakst, Leon. *The Decorative Art of Leon Bakst*. New York: Dover Publications, 1981. Seventy-seven full-page illustrations, 44 in color.

Barton, Lucy *Historic Costume for the Stage*. Boston: Walter H. Baker Company, 1935. New material added 1961. Line drawings.

Brooke, Iris. *Costume in Greek Classic Drama*. Reprint from 1962. Westport, CT.: Greenwood Press Inc., 1973. Line drawings.

———. *Medieval Theatre Costume: A Practical Guide to the Construction of Garments*. New York: Theatre Arts Books, 1967. Basic scale patterns and line drawings.

Chierichetti, David. *Hollywood Costume Design*. New York: Crown Publishers, 1976. Sketches and photographs.

Duchartre, Pierre Louis. *The Italian Comedy*. Reprint from 1929. New York: Dover Publications, Inc., 1966. Drawings, engravings, and prints from primary sources.

Green, Ruth M. *The Wearing of Costume*. London: Sir Isaac Pitman and Sons, Ltd., 1966. Line drawings. Movement for actors in period costume.

Hartnoll, Phyllis. *The Theatre. A Concise History*. London: Thames and Hudson, 1985. Revised edition. First published in 1968 as *A Concise History of the Theatre*. A good quick reference with excellent monochrome and color photographs, many of costumes.

Kelly, F. M. *Shakespearian Costume for Stage and Screen*. Reprint of 1938 edition with corrections and revisions by Alan Mansfield. New York: Theatre Arts Books, 1976. Line drawings and plates.

Laver, James. *Costume in the Theatre*. New York: Hill and Wang, 1964. Early times to twentieth century. Sketches, engravings, prints, and photographs from primary sources.

Leese, Elizabeth. *Costume Design in the Movies*. New York: Frederick Ungar Publishing Co., 1977. Sketches and photographs of costumes by selected designers.

Lewis, Jac and Miriam Streizheff. *Costume: The Performing Partner*. Colorado Springs, CO: Meriwether Publishing, Ltd. 1990. A book for actors about costumes.

Maeder, Edward. *Hollywood and History: Costume Design in Film*. Los Angeles, CA: Los Angeles County Museum/Thames and Hudson, 1987. Published in conjunction with exhibit. Well documented and informative.

Marly, Diana de. *Costume on the Stage 1600–1940*. Totowa, NJ: Barnes and Noble Books, 1982. Engravings, prints, and photographs from primary sources.

McConathy, Dale and Vreeland, Diana. *Hollywood Costume: Glamor! Glitter! Romance!* New York: Harry N. Abrams, Inc., 1976. Monochrome and color photographs. Published in conjunction with an exhibit at the Metropolitan Museum of Art.

Molinari, Cesare. *Theatre Through the Ages*. New York: McGraw-Hill Book Company, 1975. Ancient times to twentieth century. Monochrome and color illustrations from primary sources. Useful for costume.

Motley. *Designing and Making Stage Costumes*. New York: Watson-Guptill Publications, 1965. Plates of monochrome and color sketches and line drawings.

Newton, Stella Mary. *Renaissance Theatre Costume and the Sense of the Historic Past*. New York: Theatre Arts Books, 1975. Monochrome illustrations from primary sources. A scholarly work.

Russell, Douglas A. *Costume History and Style*. Englewood Cliffs, NJ: Prentice Hall, Inc., 1983. Monochrome photographs and line drawings.

———. *Period Style for the Theatre*. Boston: Allyn and Bacon, Inc., 1980. Monochrome photographs and illustrations of costumes, furniture, architecture, etc.

———. *Stage Costume Design: Theory, Techniques and Style*. Englewood Cliffs, NJ: Prentice-Hall, Inc., 1973.

———. *Theatrical Style: A Visual Approach to the Theatre*. Palo Alto, CA: Mayfield Publishing Company, 1976. Monochrome illustrations and photographs.

Strong, Roy A. *Festival Designs by Inigo Jones: Drawings for Scenery and Costumes*. International Exhibits Foundation, 1967–8. Catalogue of a touring exhibit of drawings from the Devonshire Collection, Chatsworth, England. Monochrome and some color plates.

Toshio, Kawatake. *Kabuki: Eighteen Traditional Dramas*. San Francisco CA: Chronicle Books, 1985. Beautiful color illustrations and photographs of the Danjuro Kabuki Dramas.

Van Witsen, Leo. *Costuming for Opera*. Bloomington, IN: Indiana University Press, 1981. Line drawings and photographs.

Decorative Design

Audsley, W. & G. *Designs and Patterns from Historic Ornament*. New York: Dover Publications, Inc., 1968.

Baldauski, Karen and Gos, Francois. *Alpine Flower Designs for Artists and Craftsmen*. New York: Dover Publications, Inc., 1980. Art Nouveau.

Christie, Archibold H. *Pattern Design: An Introduction to the Study of Formal Ornament*. New York: Dover Publications, Inc., 1969.

D'Addetta, Joseph. *Treasury of Chinese Motifs*. New York: Dover Publications, Inc., 1981.

D'Avennes, Prisse, ed. *Arabic Art in Color*. New York: Dover Publications, Inc., 1978.

Loeb, Marcia. *Art Deco Designs and Motifs*. New York: Dover Publications, Inc., 1972.

Markrich, Lilo. *Oriental Iron-On Transfer Patterns*. New York: Dover Publications, Inc., 1980.

Meyer, Franz Sales. *Handbook of Ornament*. New York: Dover Publications, Inc., 1957.

Mucha, Alphonse, Verneuil, Maurice, Auriol, Georges. *Art Nouveau Designs in Color*. New York: Dover Publications, Inc., 1974.

Proctor, Richard M. and Lew, Jennifer F. *Surface Design for Fabric*. Seattle, WA, and London: University of Washington Press, 1984. Dyeing, printing, and needlework techniques. Monochrome process photographs, line drawings, and surface design examples. Some color.

Rhodes, Zandra and Knight, Anne. *The Art of Zandra Rhodes*. London: Jonathan Cape, Ltd., 1984. Drawings, design details, and photographs of garments, mostly in color. Beautiful book.

Seguy, E. A. *Seguy's Decorative Butterflies and Insects in Full Color*. New York: Dover Publications, Inc., 1977.

———. *Full-Color Floral Designs in the Art Nouveau Style*. New York: Dover Publications, Inc., 1977.

Sibbett, Ed Jr. *Pennsylvania Dutch Iron-On Transfer Patterns*. New York: Dover Publications, Inc., 1981.

———. *Peasant Iron-On Transfer Patterns*. New York: Dover Publications, Inc., 1976.

———. *Ready-To-Use Floral Designs*. New York: Dover Publications, Inc., 1981.

Speltz, Alexander. *The Styles of Ornament*. New York: Dover Publications, Inc., 1959.

Verneuil, M. P. *Floral Patterns*. New York: Dover Publications, Inc., 1981. Art Nouveau.

Verneuil, M. P. et al. *Art Nouveau Floral Ornament in Color*. New York: Dover Publications, Inc., 1976.

Weiss, Rita, ed. *Early American Iron-On Transfer Patterns for Crewel and Embroidery*. New York: Dover Publications, Inc., 1975.

———. ed. *Repeats and Borders Iron-On Transfer Patterns*. New York: Dover Publications, Inc., 1977.

Drawing and Color Studies

Allen, Jeanne. *Showing Your Colors: A Designer's Guide to Coordinating Your Wardrobe*. San Francisco, CA: Chronicle Books, 1986. Manipulating color in clothing. Bright color studies throughout.

Birren, Faber. *Creative Color: A Dynamic Approach for Artists and Designers*. New York: Van Nostrand Reinhold Co., 1961.

Edwards, Betty. *Drawing on the Artist Within*. New York: Simon and Schuster, Inc., 1986. All about new ways of seeing.

———. *Drawing on the Right Side of the Brain*. Los Angeles, CA: Jeremy P. Tarcher, Inc., 1989. Revised Edition. Readily accessible text that relates how we see to what we draw. Fascinating and useful.

Eiseman, Leatrice and Herbert, Lawrence. *The Pantone Book of Color*. New York: Harry N. Abrams, Inc., Publishers, 1990. Brief discussion of color theory and over 1000 color standards.

Gerstner, Karl. *The Forms of Color: The Interaction of Visual Elements*. Cambridge, MA:, and London: The MIT Press, 1986. Interesting discussion of color and design with color and monochrome illustrations.

Itten, Johannes. *The Art of Color*. New York: Reinhold Publishing Corp., 1961. Good theory. Beautiful book.

———. *The Elements of Color: A Treatise on the Color System of Johannes Itten, Based on His Book The Art of Color*. New York: Van Nostrand Reinhold Co., 1970. Simplified and condensed version of the above.

Kumagai, Kojiro. *Fashion Illustration*. Tokyo, Japan: Graphic-sha Publishing Co., Ltd. 1984. All aspects of fashion drawing: figures, garments, and details. Monochrome and color.

Loomis, Andrew. *Figure Drawing For All It's Worth*. Cleveland, Ohio: The World Publishing Co., 1943. An excellent book for costume designers. Clear presentation, good illustrations.

Mugnaini, Joseph. *The Hidden Elements of Drawing*. New York: Van Nostrand Reinhold Co., 1974. An interesting investigation of figure drawing.

Penders, Mary Coyne. *Color and Cloth*. The Quiltmaker's Ultimate Workbook. San Francisco: The Quilt Digest Press, 1989. Good color workbook including interesting hands-on exercises. Color photographs and monochrome line drawings.

A Quarto Book. *Mix & Match Designer Colors*. New York: Van Nostrand Reinhold, 1990. Over 600 color swatches, each shown as halftone and with black and with white type.

Raynes, John. *Human Anatomy for the Artist*. New York: Crescent Books, 1979. Male and female anatomy. Clearly presented, illustrated from photographs and drawings.

Sheppard, Joseph. *Drawing the Living Figure*. New York: Watson-Guptill Publications, 1984. Comparison of surface anatomy with underlying bone and muscle structures.

Sloan, Eunice Moore. *Illustrating Fashion*. New York: Harper and Row, 1968. An excellent fashion illustration book full of techniques useful to costume designers.

Stockton, James. *Designer's Guide to Color*. San Francisco, CA: Chronicle Books, 1984. Many colors in many combinations. Beautifully printed.

———. *Designer's Guide to Color 2*. San Francisco, CA: Chronicle Books, 1984. More of the above.

Walters, Margaret. *The Nude Male: A New Perspective*. New York: Penguin Books, 1979. The male figure studied from artists' work over the centuries. Interesting text and very useful illustrations.

Yajima, Isao. *Mode Drawing-Costume*. Tokyo, Japan: Graphic-sha Publishing Company, Ltd., 1987. Costume sketching to capture mood, movement, and activity. Many photographs and the drawings they inspired. Beautiful and useful book.

Dyeing, Painting, Textiles, and Crafts

Baines, Patricia. *Flax and Linen*. Shire Album 133. Princes Risborough, Aylesbury, Bucks., England: Shire Publications, Ltd., 1985. Linen process from plant to woven cloth. Monochrome illustrations and photographs.

Dryden, Deborah M. *Fabric Painting and Dyeing for the Theatre*. New York: Drama Book Publishers, 1982. Beautifully illustrated with photographs and line drawings.

Finch, Karen and Putnam, Greta. *Care and Preservation of Textiles*. New York: Drama Book Publishers, 1985.

Green, David. *Fabric Printing and Dyeing*. Newton Center, MA: Charles T. Branford Co., 1972.

Grey, Robin. *Robin Grey's Batiker's Guide*. San Rafael, CA: DTC Publications, 1976.

James, Thurston. *The Prop Builder's Mask-Making Handbook*. White Hall, VA: Betterway Publications, Inc., 1990. Many monochrome photographs and some line drawings. Good process sequences. Source list and bibliography.

Johnston, Meda Parker and Kaufman, Glen. *Design on Fabrics*. New York: Reingold, 1967.

Joseph, Marjory L. *Essentials of Textiles*. Fort Worth, Chicago, San Francisco, Philadelphia, Montreal, Toronto, London, Sydney, Tokyo: Holt, Rinehart and Winston, Inc., 1976. 4th edition, 1988.

Kleeberg, Irene Cumming, ed. *The Butterick Fabric Handbook*. New York: Butterick Publishing, 1975.

Miller, Edward. *Textiles: Properties and Behaviour in Clothing Use*. London: B.T. Batsford, Ltd., 1984. Distributed in the U.S. by David and Charles, Inc., North Pomfret, VT. Useful reference.

Motley. *Theatre Props*. New York: Drama Book Specialists (Publishers), 1975.

Neumann, Robert von. *Design and Creation of Jewelry*. Revised edition. Radnor, PA: Chilton Book Co., 1972.

Pizzuto, Joseph. *Fabric Science*. New York: Fairchild Publications, 1957, revised 5th ed. 1987. Comprehensive. Monochrome photographs, charts, and line drawings. Very useful.

Ribbon Art Publishing Company. *Old-Fashioned Ribbon Art: Ideas and Designs for Accessories and Decorations*. New York: Dover Publications, Inc., 1986. Abridged version of the 1920s original. Line drawings and monochrome photographs. Excellent.

Rutt, Richard, Bishop of Leicester. *A History of Hand Knitting*. London: B.T. Batsford, Ltd., 1987. Comprehensive history, 1500 to 1980s.

Smith, C. Ray, ed. *The Theatre Crafts Book of Costume*. Emmaus, PA: Rodale Press, Inc., 1973. Collection of articles on costume from *Theatre Crafts*.

Story, Joyce. *The Thames and Hudson Manual of Dyes and Fabrics*. New York: Thames and Hudson, Inc., 1978.

Wiener, Louis. *Handmade Jewelry: A Manual of Techniques*. New York: Van Nostrand Reinhold, Co., 1981. Line drawings and monochrome photographs. Good process sequences.

Wingate, Isabel B, ed. *Fairchild's Dictionary of Textiles*. New York: Fairchild Publications, 1967.

Patterns and Construction

Alcega, Juan de. *Tailor's Pattern Book,* 1589 Facsimile. Carlton, Bedford, England: Ruth Bean, 1979. Reprint, with translations and explanations of *Libro de Geometria* first published in 1589.

Amaden-Crawford, Connie. *The Art of Fashion Draping*. New York: Fairchild Publications, 1989. Excellent instructions for draping women's clothing, also includes a paper pattern for making an arm to attach to the dress form.

Arnold, Janet. *Patterns of Fashion: The Cut and Construction of Clothes for Men and Women c.1560–1620*. New York: Drama Book Publishers, 1985. Detailed drawings with scaled patterns. Monochrome photographs of actual garments, paintings, and engravings.

———. *Patterns of Fashion 1 c.1660–1860: English Women's Dresses and Their Construction*. New York: Drama Book Publishers, 1977. Detailed drawings of period dresses with scaled patterns and construction instructions.

———. *Patterns of Fashion 2 c.1869–1940: English Women's Dresses and Their Construction*. New York: Drama Book Publishers, 1977. More drawings of period dresses with scaled patterns and construction instructions.

Bradfield, Nancy. *Costume in Detail: Women's Dress 1730–1930*. New edition. Boston: Plays Inc., 1980. Line drawings and photographs of extant period garments with construction details.

Burnham, Dorothy K. *Cut My Cote*. Toronto, Ontario: Royal Ontario Museum, 1973. Line drawings with metric scale patterns for shirts, chemises, smocks, surplices, and cotes.

Cabrera, Roberto and Meyers, Patricia Flaherty. *Classic Tailoring Techniques: A Construction Guide for Men's Wear.* New York: Fairchild Publications, 1983.

———. *Classic Tailoring Techniques: A Construction Guide for Women's Wear.* New York: Fairchild Publications, 1986. Both of these tailoring books include excellent pattern adjustment information for many different body types.

Collard, Eileen. *The Cut and Construction of Women's Dress in the 1930s.* Burlington, Ontario: Eileen Collard, 1983. Monochrome illustrations, line drawings, and patterns.

Croonborg, Frederick T. *The Blue Book of Men's Tailoring: Theatrical Costumemaker's Pattern Book for Edwardian Men's Costumes.* New York: Van Nostrand Reinhold, 1977. Reprint from 1907. Line drawings and patterns.

Davis, R.I. *Men's Garments 1830–1900: A Guide to Pattern Cutting.* London: B.T. Batsford, Ltd/ Drama Book Publishers, 1989. Line drawings and patterns. Excellent book.

Devere, Louis. *The Handbook of Practical Cutting on the Centre Point System (1866). Illustrated with nearly 350 Model Patterns or Diagrams.* Lopez Island, Washington: R.L. Shep, 1986. Revised and enlarged reprint of original edition. Pattern drafts for men's tailored garments of the period. Available from the publisher: R.L. Shep, Box 668, Mendocino, CA 95460.

Edson, Doris and Barton, Lucy. *Period Patterns.* Boston: Walter H. Baker Co., 1942. Supplement to *Historic Costuming for the Stage.* Patterns taken from extant garments and period pattern sources and adapted to modern sizes.

Gehret, Ellen J. *Rural Pennsylvania Clothing: Being a Study of the Wearing Apparel of the German and English Inhabitants both Men and Women in the Late Eighteenth and Early Nineteenth Century.* York, PA: Liberty Cap Books/George Shumway Publisher, 1976. Scale patterns, construction instructions, line drawings, and photographs of extant clothing and accessories.

Gibbs, Patricia T. *U.S. Pattern Book: Patterns for the U.S. Fatigue Uniform, 1861–1865.* Fredericksburg, VA: Historians Unlimited, 1980. Scale patterns, construction directions, and drawings of completed items.

Giles, Edward B. *The Art of Cutting and History of English Costume.* Lopez Island, WA: R.L. Shep, 1987. Reprint of original edition published in 1887. Available from publisher (see Devere).

Hansen, James A. *The Frontier Scout & Buffalo Hunter's Sketchbook.* Chadron, Nebraska: The Fur Press, 1980. Line drawings and patterns from extant garments (not to scale) of shirts, leather coats, jackets, trousers, etc.

Hansen, James Austin and Wilson, Kathryn J. *Feminine Fur Trade Fashions.* Chadron, Nebraska: The Fur Press, 1976. Line drawings and patterns as above. Mainly American Indian tools, accessories, and clothing.

———. *The Mountain Man's Sketch Book.* 2 vols. Chadron, Nebraska: The Fur Press, 1976. More patterns and drawings.

Hecklinger, Charles. *Dress & Cloak Cutter: Women's Costume 1877–1882.* Lopez Island, Washington: R.L. Shep, 1987. Revised and enlarged edition of the original, with additional material by R.L. Shep. Available from publisher (see Devere).

Hill, Margot Hamilton and Bucknell, Peter A. *The Evolution of Fashion: Pattern and Cut from 1066–1930.* New York: Drama Book Publishers, 1968. Monochrome drawings and patterns adapted to standard sizes.

Holkeboer, Katherine Strand. *Costume Construction.* Englewood Cliffs, NJ: Prentice-Hall, Inc., 1989. Patterns, draping, sewing techniques, crafts, accessories.

Hollen, Norma R. and Kundel, Carolyn J. *Pattern Making by the Flat-Pattern Method.* New York: Macmillan Publishing Company, 1987 (6th edition).

Hopkins, J.C. *Edwardian Ladies' Tailoring: The Twentieth Century System of Ladies Garment Cutting (1910).* Reprint. Mendocino, CA: R.L. Shep, 1991. Available from the publisher (see Devere).

Hunnisett, Jean. *Period Costume for Stage and Screen: Patterns for Women's Dress 1500–1800.* London: Bell and Hyman, Limited, 1986. Period patterns to scale, many based on original garments. Excellent source.

———. *Period Costume for Stage and Screen: Patterns for Women's Dress 1800–1909.* London, Sydney, Wellington: Unwin Paperbacks, 1988. Continuation of above.

Kidwell, Claudia B. *Cutting a Fashionable Fit: Dressmakers' Drafting Systems in the United States.*

Washington, DC: Smithsonian Institution Press, 1979. Scholarly work on women's nineteenth-and early twentieth-century drafting systems.

Klinger, Robert L. *Sketch Book 76: The American Soldier 1775–1781.* Union City, TN: Pioneer Press, 1967. Sketches, notes, and patterns.

———. *Distaff Sketch Book: A Collection of Notes and Sketches on Women's Dress in America 1774–1783.* Union City, TN: Pioneer Press, 1974. Includes patterns.

Kopp, Ernestine, Rolfo, Vittorina, Zelin, Beatrice and Gross, Lee. *Designing Apparel through the Flat Pattern.* New York: Fairchild Publications, 1960. (Revised 5th edition, 1982) Pattern drafting for women's clothing using basic slopers.

Lawson, Joan and Revitt, Peter. *Dressing for the Ballet.* London: Adam and Charles Black, 1958. Line drawings, scale patterns, and construction instructions. Includes knitting patterns.

Liechty, Elizabeth L., Della N. Pottberg, Judity A. Rasband. *Fitting and Pattern Alteration: A Multi-Method Approach.* New York: Fairchild Books, 1989.

Marshall, Beverley. *Smocks and Smocking.* Sherbourne, Dorset, England: Alphabooks, 1980. Scale patterns and construction instructions for modern and period smocks. Beautifully illustrated.

Mitchell, Jno J. *"Standard" Work on Cutting. (Men's Garments): A Complete Treatise on the Art and Science of Garment Cutting.* Berkeley, CA: Lacis Publications, 1990. Reprint of the 1886 edition.

Moulton, Bertha. *Garment-cutting and Tailoring for Students.* New York: Theatre Arts Books, 1967. Scale patterns for women's garments, line drawings, and tailoring techniques.

Ralston, Margaret C. Edited by Jules & Kaethe Kliot *Fashion Outlines: Dress Cutting by the Block Pattern System. A system of scientific dressmaking explored through the classical styles of the late 1920s and early 1930s.* Berkeley, CA: Lacis Publications, 1990. Reprint of the original edition.

Reader's Digest. *Complete Sewing Guide.* Pleasantville, New York, Montreal: The Reader's Digest Association, Inc., 1976.

Shaeffer, Claire. *Claire Shaeffer's Fabric Sewing Guide.* Radnor, PA: Chilton Book Company, 1989. General guide to fiber content, with particular emphasis on the sewing and care of the various types of fabric available.

Thomas, Michael R. *A Confederate Sketchbook.* Highlands, NJ: M.R. Thomas, P.O. Box 3, Ft. Hancock, Highlands, NJ 07732, 1980. Drawings of garments with measurements and construction notes. No actual patterns.

Thompson, Mrs. F.E. *Garment Patterns for the Edwardian Lady.* Berkeley, CA: Lacis Publications, 1991. Originally published as *La Mode Universelle No. 22, A Book of Pattern Designs, 1905.*

Tilke, Max. *Costume Patterns and Designs: A Survey of Costume Patterns and Designs of All Periods and Nations from Antiquity to Modern Times.* New York: Hastings House, 1974. Garments illustrated flat and in color. Excellent source for ethnic costumes based on geometric shapes.

———. *Folk Costumes from East Europe, Africa and Asia.* London: A. Zwemmer, Ltd., 1978. Similar to the above.

Trautman, Patricia A. *Clothing America: A Bibliography and Location Index of Nineteenth-Century America Pattern Drafting Systems.* New York: The Costume Society of America, Region 11, 1987. (Available from the Costume Society).

Tyrrell, Anne V. *Changing Trends in Fashion: Patterns of the Twentieth Century.* London: B.T. Batsford, Ltd., 1986. Men's and women's patterns to scale, 1900–1970. Formal and informal clothing, including British military uniforms of the two world wars.

Vincent, W.D.F. *Tailoring of the Belle Epoque: Vincent's Systems of Cutting All Kinds of Tailor-Made Garments (1903).* Reprint. Mendocino, CA: R.L. Shep, 1991. 5 parts in one volume: men and women, military, clergy, civil servants, court and academic, servants. Available from the publisher: R.L. Shep, Box 668, Mendocino, CA 95460.

———. *The Tailor and Cutter Academy Systems of Cutting All Kinds of Tailor-Made Garments.* in 5 parts. London: The John Williamson Co., Ltd., 1908–1912. Tailor's patterns.

Waugh, Norah. *The Cut of Men's Clothes 1600–1900.* New York: Theatre Arts Books, 1964. Scale patterns, monochrome photographs of primary sources and excellent commentary.

———. *The Cut of Women's Clothes 1600–1930.* New York: Theatre Arts Books, 1968. Women's version of the above.

Women's Institute of Domestic Arts and Sciences, Inc. *Draping and Designing with Scissors and Cloth: Details and instructions for the creating and developing of garments from cloth without patterns*. Scranton, PA: Women's Institute of Domestic Arts and Science, Inc. n.d. 1920s.

Wright, Merideth. *Put on Thy Beautiful Garments: Rural New England Clothing 1783–1800*. East Montpelier, VT: The Clothes Press, 1990. Scale patterns, drawings, and instructions as well as historical information.

Zamkoff, Bernard, and Price, Jeanne. *Basic Pattern Skills for Fashion Design*. New York: Fairchild Publications, 1987.

Theory and Psychology of Dress

Baines, Barbara. *Fashion Revivals from the Elizabethan Age to the Present Day*. New York: Drama Book Publishers, 1981. Survey of revived styles from all walks of life in England. Sixteenth to twentieth century. Monochrome and some color illustrations from primary sources.

Bell, Quentin. *On Human Finery*. New York: Schocken Books, 1976. 2nd revised edition, first published in 1947. Theories of fashion and clothing. Monochrome illustrations and drawings.

Cremers-van der Does, Eline Canter. Leo Van Witsen, trans. *The Agony of Fashion*. Poole, Dorset, England: Blandford Press, 1980. The pain and discomfort incurred by the fashion-conscious through the ages. Primary source illustrations, some color.

Gattey, Charles Nielson. *The Bloomer Girls*. London: A Femina Book. Macdonald and Co., Ltd., 1967. Clothing reform. Monochrome illustrations.

Glynn, Prudence. *Skin to Skin: Eroticism in Dress*. London, Boston, and Sydney: George Allen and Unwin, 1982. Monochrome and color illustrations and photographs from primary sources of all ages and cultures.

Hollander, Anne. *Seeing Through Clothes*. New York: The Viking Press, 1978. Study of the connection between clothing in the visual arts and real life through the ages. Monochrome illustrations from primary sources.

Lurie, Alison. *The Language of Clothes*. New York: Random House, 1981. Psychology of dress. Monochrome and color illustrations.

Newton, Stella, Mary. *Health, Art and Reason: Dress Reformers of the 19th Century*. London: John Murray, 1974. The movement towards less restricting, more comfortable clothing. Monochrome illustrations from primary sources.

Ribeiro, Aileen. *Dress and Morality*. London: B.T. Batsford, Ltd., 1986. Morality in dress from antiquity to 1980s. Monochrome illustrations from primary sources.

Rudofsky, Rudolph. *The Unfashionable Human Body*. New York: Doubleday and Co., Inc., 1971. An amusing look at fads and fashions and the changing shape of the human body through the ages. Monochrome illustrations from primary sources.

Steele, Valerie. *Fashion and Eroticism: Ideals of Feminine Beauty from the Victorian Era to the Jazz Age*. New York and Oxford: Oxford University Press, 1985. Monochrome illustrations.

Dictionaries, Bibliographies, Encyclopedias, and Reference

Anthony, Pegaret and Arnold, Janet. *Costume: A Bibliography of Costume Books*. London: The Victoria and Albert Museum in association with The Costume Society, 1966. Revised edition, 1974.

Arnold, Janet. *A Handbook of Costume*. London and New York: Macmillan, 1974. A guide to primary sources for costume research.

Cooke, Jean Kramer, Ann and Rowland-Entwistle, Theodore. *History's Timeline: A 40,000 Year Chronology of Civilization*. New York: Crescent Books, 1981.

The Costume Society of America. *A Bibliography of Recent Books Relating to Costume*. New York: The Costume Society of America, 1975.

Cunnington, C. Willett and Phillis, Beard, Charles. *A Dictionary of English Costume*. London: Adam and Charles Black, 1960.

Evans, Hilary and Mary, Nelki, Andra. *The Picture Researcher's Handbook: An International Guide to Picture Sources—And How to Use Them*. Newton Abbot and London, England, Vancouver B.C. Canada: David and Charles, 1975.

Filene, Adele B. *Bibliography*. New York: The Costume Society of America, 1975. Listing of recently published books.

Grun, Bernard. *The Timetables of History: A Horizontal Linkage of People and Events.* New York: A Touchstone Book, Simon and Schuster, 1975.

Huenefeld, Irene Pennington. *International Dictionary of Historical Clothing.* Metuchen, NJ: The Scarecrow Press, Inc., 1967. Information on garments in museums and private collections.

Kesler, Jackson. *Theatrical Costume: A Guide to Information Sources.* Vol. 6 in the Performing Arts Information Guide Series. Detroit, MI: Gale Research Company, 1979. Extensive bibliography of costume books in all categories.

Kybalova, Ludmila, Herbenova, Olga, Lamarova, Milena. *The Pictorial Encyclopedia of Fashion.* New York: Crown Publishers, 1968.

McRae, Bobbi A. *The Fabric & Fiber Sourcebook. A Threads Book.* Newtown, CT: The Taunton Press, Inc., 1989.

Monro, Isabel S. and Cook, Dorothy E. eds. *Costume Index: A Subject Index to Plates and to Illustrated Text.* New York: H. W. Wilson Co., 1937. Supplement published in 1957. Lists books alphabetically and includes an index to costume pictures in the National Geographic.

National Geographic Society. *National Geographic Index 1888–1946.* Washington, D.C.: National Geographic Society, 1967. Listings by subject and author.

———. *National Geographic Index 1947–1983.* Washington, D.C.: National Geographic Society, 1984. Listings by subject and author.

———. *National Geographic Index 1984.* Washington, D.C.: National Geographic Society, 1985. First in a series of supplements to main index.

O'Hara, Georgina. *The Encyclopaedia of Fashion: From 1840 to the 1980s.* London: Thames and Hudson Ltd., 1986. Monochrome illustrations, some colorplates.

Snowden, James. *European Folk Dress: A Bibliography.* London: The Costume Society, 1973.

Trautman, Patricia A. *Clothing America: A Bibliography and Location Index of Nineteenth-Century American Pattern Drafting Systems.* Published by The Costume Society of America, Region 11, 1987.

Wallis, Frank, ed. *Ribbons of Time: World History Year by Year Since 1492.* New York: Weidenfeld and Nicolson, 1988. Similar to *Timetables of History.*

Whalon, Marion K. *Performing Arts Research: A Guide to Information Sources.* Vol. 1 in The Performing Arts Information Guide Series. Detroit, MI: Gale Research Company, 1976. Extensive bibliography covering all aspects of the performing arts.

Wilcox, R. Turner. *The Dictionary of Costume.* New York: Charles Scribner's Sons, 1969.

Wilman, Polly. *Bibliography 1983.* New York: The Costume Society of America, 1983. Lists publications issued between 1979 and 1983.

Yarwood, Doreen. *The Encyclopaedia of World Costume.* New York: Hippocrene Books, 1978.

Miscellaneous

Forty, George and Anne. *They also Served: A Pictorial Anthology of Camp Followers through the Ages.* Speldhurst, Kent, England: Midas Books, 1979. Pictorial record of entertainers, pets, tradespeople, tailors, correspondents, etc., who traveled with armies over the centuries.

History of Private Life. 4 vols. Cambridge, Mass.: Harvard University Press. Vol. 1: Phillippe Aries, et al., ed. *From Pagan Rome to Byzantium.* 1987; Vol. 2: Georges Duby, ed. *Revelations of the Medieval World.* 1988; Vol. 3: Roger Chartier, et al., ed. *Passions of the Renaissance.* 1989; Vol. 4: Michelle Perrot, et al., ed. *From the Fires of Revolution to the Great War.* 1990. All translated by Arthur Goldhammer. Excellent text, lavishly illustrated.

Hodge, Francis. *Play Directing Analysis Communication and Style.* Englewood Cliffs, NJ: Prentice-Hall, Inc., 1971.

Holroyd, Michael. *The Genius of Shaw.* New York: Holt, Rinehart and Winston, 1979. Monochrome and color illustrations and photographs of Shaw, his life, stage productions, etc.

Hornby, Richard. *Script Into Performance: A Structuralist View of Play Production.* Austin, Texas, London: University of Texas Press, 1977.

Stevenson, Sara and Bennett, Helen. *Van Dyck in Check Trousers: Fancy Dress in Art and Life. 1700–1900.* Edinburgh, Scotland: Scottish National Portrait Gallery, 1978. Catalogue of an exhibit at the gallery. Monochrome and some color illustrations and photographs of fancy dress.

Speaight, George. *The Book of Clowns*. New York: Macmillan Publishing Co., Inc., 1980. Color and some monochrome illustrations and photographs tracing the history of clowning from its early development to the present day circus.

Health and Safety

McCann, Michael. *Artist Beware*. New York: Watson-Guptill Publications, 1979. The hazards and precautions in working with art and craft materials.
———. *Lights! Camera! Safety!* New York: Center for Safety in the Arts, 1992. Safety manual for the motion picture and television industry. Available from Center for Safety in the Arts, 5 Beekman Street, New York, NY 10038.
Rossol, Monona. *Stage Fright. Health and Safety in the Theater: A Practical Guide for Everyone in the Performing Arts. The essential information you need on stage, in the shop, or in the front office to ensure health, safety, and compliance with occupational hazard laws.* New York: Allsworth Press, 1986, updated 1991. Covers protective equipment, ventilation, make-up, hazardous materials, and lists information sources.
———. *Artist's Complete Health and Safety Guide. Everything you need to know about art materials to make your workplace safe and comply with United States and Canadian right-to-know laws.* New York: Allsworth Press, 1990. Covers all categories of artist's materials. Deals with toxicity, precautions, ventilation, protective equipment, chemical, and physical hazards, and their control. A comprehensive and invaluable reference.

Booksellers

USA

NEW YORK CITY

Applause Theatre Books
211 W. 71st Street
New York, NY 10023
212-496-7511
Carries books on costume, scenery, and allied subjects.

Barnes & Noble Bookstores, Inc.
105 5th Avenue
New York, NY 10003
212-807-0099
Costume and art books. Sales annex across the street has large selection of remainder books at bargain prices.

Dover Publications, Inc.
180 Varick Street
New York, NY 10014
212-255-3755

Retail store on ninth floor. Mail order catalogues available from:

31 E. 2nd Street
Mineola, NY 11501
516-294-7000

The Drama Book Shop
723 7th Avenue
New York, NY 10019
212-944-0595

Large selection of books on costume, scenery, and allied subjects. Mail orders welcome.

FIT Bookstore
Fashion Institute of Technology
227 W. 27th Street
New York, NY 10001
212-564-4275

Good selection of books on costume, fashion, and construction.

Samuel French, Inc.
45 W. 25th Street
New York, NY 10010
212-206-8990
Scripts. Catalogue available.

Hacker Art Books, Inc.
45 W. 57th Street
New York, NY 10019
212-688-7600
Art books specialists. Good selection of costume
   books. Mail order catalogue available

Military Bookman
29 E. 93rd Street
New York, NY 10028
212-348-1280
Carries some books on arms and uniforms.

Rizzoli International Bookstore
31 W. 57th Street
New York, NY 10019
212-759-2424
Art and costume books.

Shakespeare & Co. Booksellers
716 Broadway
New York, NY 10003
212-529-1330
Carries books on art, costume, and the performing
   arts.

Sky Books International
48 E. 50th Street
New York, NY 10022
212-688-5086
Large selection of books on military uniforms.

The Soldier Shop
1222 Madison Avenue
New York, NY 10028
212-535-6788
Carries some books on uniforms.

Richard Stoddard Performing Arts
18 E. 16th Street Room 305
New York, NY 10003
212-645-9576
Books on theatre, costume, and scenery, mostly
   out of print.

Strand Book Store, Inc.
828 Broadway
New York, NY 10003

212-473-1452
"Eight miles of books." Art and costume books,
   new and used, many at bargain prices.

Tower Books
383 Lafayette Street
New York, NY 10003
212-228-5100
Art and costume books.

BOSTON

Baker's Plays
100 Chauncy Street
Boston, MA 02111
617-482-1280
Plays and theatre books. Catalogue available.

Excaliber Hobbies
63 Exchange Street
Malden, MA 02148
617-322-2959
Military research.

Rizzoli Bookstore
Copley Place
Boston, MA 02116
617-643-0180
Theatre books.

CALIFORNIA

Drama Books
134 9th Street
San Francisco, CA 94103
415-255-0604
Books on theatre, costume, and stage design.

R.L. Shep
Box 668
Mendocino, CA 95460
707-937-1436
Mail order. Catalogue available. Books on textiles,
   costume, and needle arts. Also publishes reprints
   of period pattern and tailoring books.

CHICAGO

Act 1 Bookstore
2633 N. Halstead Street
Chicago, IL 60614
312-348-6757
Theatre books.

WASHINGTON, DC

Backstage, Inc.
2101 P Street NW
Washington, DC 20037
202-775-1488
Books on costume, stage design, and theatre.

CANADA

Theatrebooks
25 Bloor Street W
Toronto, Ontario M4W 1A3
416-922-7175
Good selection of books on theatre, stage design,
    costume, and allied subjects. Mail order catalogue
    available.

Samuel French
80 Richmond Street E
Toronto, Ontario M5C 1P1
416-363-3536
Publishers of plays, musicals, and theatre textbooks.

ENGLAND

Better Books
94 Charing Cross Road
London WC2
01-836-6944
Art books.

Foyles
119 Charing Cross Road
London WC2
01-437-5660

"The World's largest bookstore." Large selection
    of books on art, costume, and theatre.

John Ives Bookseller
5 Normanhurst Drive
Twickenham
Middlesex TW1 1NA
01-892-6265
Scarce and out of print books on costume. Mail
    order. Catalogue available.

Daphne Lucas
28 Addison Way
London NW11 6AP
New and out of print books on costume and allied
    subjects. Mail order. Catalogue available.

Ken Trotman
2-6 Hampstead High Street
London NW3 1PR
01-794-3277
Books on arms, armor, weaponry, and related
    subjects. Catalogues available.

Felicity J. Warnes
82 Merryhills Drive
Enfield
Middlesex EN2 7PD
Out of print books on costume and allied subjects.
    Mail order. Catalogue available.

Peter Wood Bookseller
20 Stonehill Road
Great Shelford
Cambridge CB2 5JL
New and out of print books on the performing
    arts, costume, and allied subjects. Mail order.
    Catalogue available.

Useful Publications

American Theatre
Published 11 times a year. Subscriptions available
    from: Theatre Communications Group, 355
    Lexington Avenue, New York, NY 10017.

ArtSearch
A bimonthly (23 issues) subscription publication
    from TCG (see above) listing jobs in the perform-
    ing arts.

Canadian Theatre Checklist
Annual publication listing Canadian theatres, other useful addresses, and information. York University, 4700 Keele Street, Downside, Ontario M3J 1P3, 416-667-3768.

Cutter's Research Journal
A quarterly publication of the USITT Costume Commission devoted to clothing, accessories, and textiles. Subscriptions available from: Debora Kingston, USITT, 10 West 19th Street, Suite 5A, New York, NY 10011.

Lady's Gallery
Bi-monthly magazine containing articles on antiques, period clothing and accessories. Subscriptions available from: P.O. Box 1761, Independence, MO 64055 or call 1-800-622-5676.

Military Illustrated Past & Present
A monthly publication containing detailed articles on uniforms, weapons, and accoutrements. Information available from: Military Illustrated, c/o Select Subscriptions, 5 Riverpark Estate, Billet Lane, Berkhamsted, Herts. HP4 1HL, England.

Plays and Players
Monthly magazine devoted to British theatre. Subscriptions available from: Plays and Players Subscription Department, Pickwick Papers, Pickwick

House, 995 High Road, London, N12 8BR, England.

Theatre Crafts International
A magazine published ten times a year and devoted to all aspects of the technical side of the performing arts. Subscriptions available from: TCI, P.O. Box 470, Mt. Morris, IL 61054-8027.

Theatre Directory
An annual publication from Theatre Communications Group. Lists LORT Theatres with names of the top management and artistic personnel of each one.

Theater Week
Covers productions on Broadway, off-Broadway, off-off Broadway. Includes interviews and articles on theatre people as well as productions in other parts of the country. Subscription information from: 28 W. 25th Street, New York, NY 10010.

Threads Magazine
An excellent magazine published every two months, it includes articles with instructions for patterns, sewing, knitting, weaving, and embroidery, as well as occasional articles on costume and other subjects of related interest. Subscriptions available from: Taunton Press, Inc., 63 S. Main Street, P.O. Box 5506, Newtown, CT 06470-5506.

Useful Addresses

Actor's Equity Association
1560 Broadway
New York, NY 10036
212-869-8530
Union representing professional actors and stage managers.

Bettmann Archive/Bettmann Newsphotos
902 Broadway
New York, NY 10010
212-777-6200
Picture research (for minimum fee). "Complete resources from ancient cave paintings to this morning's news photos."

Center for Safety in the Arts
5 Beekman Street
New York, NY 10038
212-227-6220

Theatre Communications Group (TCG)
355 Lexington Avenue
New York, NY 10017
212-697-5230

Services nonprofit professional theatres, publishes American Theatre magazine and books on the performing arts.

Theatre Development Fund (TDF)
1501 Broadway
New York, NY 10036
212-221-0885

An audience development organization for the performing arts, also administers the Costume Collection and the TKTS discount ticket booths.

Arts, Crafts, and Theater Safety (ACTS)
181 Thompson Street, 23
New York, NY 10012
A not-for-profit corporation dedicated to providing a variety of health and safety services for artists.

United Scenic Artists (USA) Local 829
16 W. 61st Street
New York, NY 10023
212-581-0300
Union representing lighting, scenery, and costume designers, stylists, and craftspeople.

United States Institute for Theatre Technology (USITT)
10 W. 19th Street, Room 5A
New York, NY 10011
212-924-9088
Membership. Quarterly journal, newsletters. Annual national conference, regional meetings, and costume symposiums.

Costume Societies

The Costume Society of America
55 Edgewater Drive
P.O. Box 73
Earleville, Maryland 21919
301-275-2329

The Costume Society
Membership Secretary:
Miss Anne Brogden
63 Salisbury Road
Garston, Liverpool LI9 0PH
England

The Costume Society of Scotland
Treasurer:
Miss Ethel Geddes
Flat N
23 Grange Loan
Edinburgh EH9 2ER
Scotland

Shopping Guide / Source List

Further information on sources for theatrical supplies can be found in the following publications:

The New York Theatrical Sourcebook
Compiled and edited by The Association of Theatrical Artists and Craftspeople.
Updated and published annually by:
Sourcebook Press, Inc.
To order call 212-496-1310

The Creative Production Source-Book
Published by:
Broadway Press
12 W. Thomas Street, Box 1037
Shelter Island, NY 11964
800-869-6372

TCI Industry Resources
Published annually by Theatre Crafts International and available to subscribers of the magazine.

We highly recommend *The New Theatrical Source-book*. It is updated and new sources are added every year. Some of the sources listed here are to be found within its pages, but it contains a wealth of information, and much more than we have room for in this book.

New York City

ACCESSORIES

Albert's Hosiery
925 Lexington Avenue
New York, NY 10021
212-988-1195
Stockings, tights, leotards.

Brooks Bros.
346 Madison Avenue
New York, NY 10017
212-682-8800
Wing collars, collar studs, cotton shirts, etc.

Stan Novak Co.
115 W. 30th Street
New York, NY 10001
212-947-8466
Canes and walking sticks. Good prices. Brochure available.

Sand & Siman, Inc.
10 W. 33rd Street
New York, NY 10001
212-564-4484
Glove manufacturers. All types in quantity, including white cotton.

F.R. Tripler & Co.
366 Madison Avenue
New York, NY 10017

212-922-1090
Wing collars, collar studs, men's white cotton gloves.

Uncle Sam Umbrella Shop
161 W. 57th Street
New York, NY 10019
212-247-7163
Umbrellas, parasols, canes.

ADHESIVES

H.G. Pasternack, Inc.
151 W. 19th Street
New York, NY 10011
212-691-9555 and
    800-433-3330
3-M agent. Tapes, adhesives. Respirators.

ARMOR AND WEAPONS

Center Firearms Co., Inc.
10 W. 37th Street
New York, NY 10018
212-244-4040
Fax: 212-947-1233
Rentals: firearms, assorted weapons, and armor. Weapon repair service.

ARTIST AND CRAFT SUPPLIES

Adhesive Products Corp.
1660 Boone Avenue
Bronx, NY 10460
718-497-5462
Mold making and casting materials. Latex, rubber, resins, mold releases, etc. Catalogues available. Will ship.

Arthur Brown & Bro., Inc.
2 W. 46th Street
New York, NY 10036
212-575-5555
orders: 575-5552
customer service: 575-5530
Catalogue available. Will ship.

Charette
215 Lexington Avenue
New York, NY 10016
212-683-8822
Sales department:
    212-683-8844
Catalogue and discount membership available. Will ship.

Sam Flax, Inc.
425 Park Avenue
New York, NY 10022
212-620-3060

425 Park Avenue
New York, NY 10022
212-620-3060

12 W. 20th Street
New York, NY 10011
212-620-3038
Catalogue available to purchase. Will ship.

A. I. Friedman, Inc.
44 W. 18th Street
New York, NY 10011
212-243-9000

25 W. 45th Street
New York, NY 10036
212-243-9000
Art and drafting materials. Discount card and catalogue available. Will ship.

Otto Gerdau Co.
82 Wall Street
New York, NY 10005

809-753-3171 and
809-753-3160
Rattan, bamboo, and all
types of reed.

Industrial Plastics
309 Canal Street
New York, NY 10013
212-226-2010 and
212-226-2012
Plastic in all shapes and
forms.

Lee's Art Shop
220 W. 57th Street
New York, NY 10019
212-247-0110
Catalogue available. Will
ship.

*New York Central Art
Supply Co.*
62 3rd Avenue
New York, NY 10003
212-473-7705 and
800-242-2408
Art and drafting materials.
Catalogue available. Will
ship.

Pearl Paint Co.
308 Canal Street
New York, NY 10013
212-431-7932 and
800-221-6845
Large stock. Catalogue
available. Discount. Will
ship.

Sculpture House, Inc.
155 W. 26th Street
New York, NY 10016
212-679-7474 and
212-645-9430
Mold making materials,
tools and accessories.

*Utrecht Art & Drafting
Supply*
111 4th Avenue
New York, NY 10003
212-777-5353
Mail order:
33 35th Street
Brooklyn, NY 11232
718-768-2525
Own and other major
brands. Catalogue
available.

CLOTHING—
ECCLESIASTICAL

Craft Clerical Clothes
247 W. 37th Street, 17th
floor
New York, NY 10018
212-764-6122
Religious clothing and
supplies. Choir robes,
caps, and gowns.
Catalogue available.

Duffy & Quinn
307 5th Avenue
Suite 1509
New York, NY 10016
212-725-0213
Religious clothing and supplies, Catholic apparel,
choir robes, graduation
caps, and gowns.

CLOTHING—MEN'S

Barney's New York
106 7th Avenue
New York, NY 10011
212-929-9000
Men's and women's
designer clothing and
accesories. Also carries
men's big, tall, and hard
to find sizes. Expensive.

Barney's New York
Madison Avenue at 61st
Street
New York, NY 10021
212-826-8900
Studio services:
212-833-2086

Moe Ginsburg
162 5th Avenue
New York, NY 10011
212-242-3482
Men's discount suits, coats,
shirts, accessories, etc. A
good source.

*Imperial Wear Men's
Clothing*
48 W. 48th Street
New York, NY 10036
212-719-2590
Big and tall sizes.

Syms
42 Trinity Place
New York, NY 10006
212-797-1199

Discount designer suits,
shirts, accessories, etc.
Good Source.

Today's Man
625 Avenue of the Americas
New York, NY 10011
212-924-0200
Discount suits, shirts,
accessories, etc.

CLOTHING—RIDING

Kauffman & Sons
419 Park Avenue South
New York, NY 10016
212-684-6060
Riding clothes and
equipment. Catalogue
available.

Miller Harness Co., Inc.
117 E. 24th Street
New York, NY 10010
212-673-1400
Riding clothes and
equipment. Catalogue
available.

CLOTHING—USED
AND ANTIQUE

Alice Underground
481 Broadway
New York, NY 10013
212-431-9067

380 Columbus Avenue
New York, NY 10024
212-724-6682
Men's and women's vintage
clothing and linens.

Andy's Chee Pee's, Inc.
691 Broadway
New York, NY 10012
212-420-5980

16 W. 8th Street
New York, NY 10011
212-460-8488
Used and antique men's
and women's clothing.

*Cheap Jack's Vintage
Clothing*
841 Broadway
New York, NY 10003
212-777-9564
Large selection of men's
and women's vintage
clothing.

Church St. Surplus
327 Church Street
New York, NY 10013
212-226-5280
Antique and used clothing.

Early Halloween
130 W. 25th Street
New York, NY 10001
212-691-2933 and
212-243-1499
Antique clothing and
accessories. Mostly
rentals. By appointment
only. Expensive.

Kasbah
83 2nd Avenue
New York, NY 10003
212-982-8077
Vintage Clothes.

Screaming Mimi
382 Lafayette Street
New York, NY 10003
212-677-6464
Men's and women's 1950s
and punk.

Trash and Vaudeville
4 St. Marks Place
New York, NY 10003
212-982-3590
1950s and punk.

CORSET SUPPLIES

L. Laufer & Co., Inc.
115 W. 27th Street
New York, NY 10001
212-242-2345
Corset bones, corset fabric,
bone casing tape, busks,
etc. Will ship.

Nathan's Boning Co.
302 W. 37th Street, 4th floor
New York, NY 10018
212-244-4781
Continuous steel boning,
tutu wire, and feather
boning.

COSTUME RENTAL
COMPANIES

Abet Rent-A-Fur
231 W. 29th Street, Room
304
New York, NY 10001
212-268-6225

The Costume Collection
601 W. 26th Street
New York, NY 10001
212-989-5855 and
212-989-5856
Rentals to nonprofit
organizations.

David's Outfitters, Inc.
36 W. 20th Street
New York, NY 10011
212-691-7388
Military and civilian uniforms.

Early Halloween
130 W. 25th Street
New York, NY 10001
212-691-2933 and
212-243-1499
Men's, women's, and
children's vintage
clothing and accessories.

Eaves-Brooks Costume Co., Inc.
21-07 41st Avenue
Long Island City, NY 11101
718-729-1010
Fax: 718-243-1499
Rentals, construction, and
alterations.

Odds
231 W. 29th Street, Room
304
New York, NY 10001
212-268-6227
Men's and women's
Victorian to
contemporary.

Rubie's
1 Rubie Plaza
120-08 Jamaica Avenue
Richmond Hill, NY 11418
718-846-1008
Catalogue available.

Stivanello Costume Co., Inc.
66-38 Clinton Avenue
Maspeth, NY 11378
718-651-7715
Opera costumes and scenery
exclusively.

CUSTOM COSTUME COMPANIES

Carelli Costumes
588 9th Avenue
New York, NY 10036

212-765-6166
Construction only.

Eaves-Brooks Costume Co., Inc.
21-07 41st Avenue
Long Island City, NY
11101
718-729-1010
Fax: 718-729-5118
Rentals, construction, and
alterations.

Grace Costumes
244-250 W. 54th Street
New York, NY 10019
212-586-0260
Construction only.

Martin Izquierdo Studio
118 W. 22nd Street
New York, NY 10011
212-807-9757
Costume crafts,
construction, painting,
dyeing, and props.

Donna Langman
39 W. 38th Street
New York, NY 10018
212-382-2558
Construction only.

Barbara Matera
890 Broadway
New York, NY 10003
212-475-5006
Construction only.

*Michael-Jon Costumes,
Inc.*
411 W. 14th Street,
3rd floor
New York, NY 10014
212-741-3440
Construction only.

Parsons-Meares, Ltd.
142 W. 14th Street
New York, NY 10011
212-242-3378
Fax: 212-741-1869
Construction and
alterations.

Studio
322 7th Avenue
New York, NY 10001
212-967-4736

Construction and
alterations.

Studio Rouge
100 W. 25th Street, 3rd floor
New York, NY 10001
212-989-8363
Construction, alterations,
and design studio.

Eric Winterling Costumes
20 W. 20th Street, 5th floor
New York, NY 10011
212-255-6579 and
212-255-5225
Construction and
alterations.

Vincent Costume Inc.
136 W. 21st Street
New York, NY 10011
212-741-3423
Men's theatrical tailoring.

DANCEWEAR

Capezio Dance-Theatre Shop
1650 Broadway, 2nd floor
New York, NY 10019
212-245-2130
Fax: 212-757-7635
Catalogue available.

Capezio in the Village
177 MacDougal Street
New York, NY 10011
212-477-5634

Capezio East
136 E. 61st Street
New York, NY 10021
212-758-8833 and
212-758-8898

Freed of London, Ltd.
922 7th Avenue
New York, NY 10019
212-489-1055 and
212-489-1056 and
212-489-1057
Catalogue available.

S & S Hosiery
135 W. 50th Street
New York, NY 10020
212-586-3288
Stockings, tights, leotards.

Taffy's
1776 Broadway, 2nd floor
New York, NY 10019
212-586-5140
Catalogue available.

DECORATIVE ITEMS

Big Apple Sign Corp.
247 W. 35th Street
New York, NY 10001
212-575-0706 and
800-237-5052
Fax: 212-629-4954
Custom iron-on letters and
silkscreening.

*Cinderella Flower & Feather
Co.*
60 W. 38th Street
New York, NY 10018
212-840-0644

Sydney Coe, Inc.
49 W. 37th Street
New York, NY 10018
212-391-6960
Beads and jewels.

Dersh Feather & Trading Co.
62 W. 36th Street
New York, NY 10018
212-714-2806

Duplex Novelty Corp.
575 8th Avenue
New York, NY 10018
212-564-1352
Manufacturers of wooden
buttons, jewelry parts,
belt buckles, and beads.
Catalogue available. Will
ship.

Eastern Findings Corp.
19 W. 34th Street, 12th
floor
New York, NY 10001
212-695-6640
Jewelry findings, chain, etc.
Catalogue available.
Quantities only. Will ship.

40th St. Trimmings, Inc.
252 W. 40th Street
New York, NY 10018
212-354-4729
Laces, appliques, trims.

Fred Frankel & Sons, Inc.
19 W. 38th Street
New York, NY 10018
212-840-0810
Beads, jewels, jewelled and
beaded trimmings,
rhinestone transfers,
sequin motifs, etc. Large
quantities only.
Catalogues available.

*Friedman & Distillator Inc.
(Owl Mills)*
53 Leonard Street
New York, NY 10013
212-226-6400
Call first. Imported
trimmings, antique
braids, ribbons, etc.

Gettinger Feather Corp.
16 W. 36th Street, 8th
floor
New York, NY 10018
212-695-9470
Will ship.

Gordon Button Co., Inc.
222 W. 38th Street
New York, NY 10018
212-921-1684 and
212-921-1685
Good selection at
reasonable prices.

Hyman Hendler & Sons
67 W. 38th Street
New York, NY 10018
212-840-8393
Beautiful selection of
all types of ribbons.
Swatch cards available.
Will ship.

*Hersh 6th Ave. Buttons,
Inc.*
1000 6th Avenue
New York, NY 10018
212-391-6615
Buttons and sewing
supplies.

K. Trimming Co.
519 Broadway
New York, NY 10012
212-431-8929
212-226-3539
Closed Saturday.
Laces, trimmings, elastic,
thread, zippers, buttons,
buckles, etc. Good
source, good prices.

M. & J. Trimming Co.
1008 6th Avenue
New York, NY 10018
212-391-9072
Buttons, trimmings, etc.
Large selection but
expensive.

1014 6th Avenue
New York, NY 10018
212-391-9072
Drapery and upholstery
trimmings.

Penn & Fletcher
242 W. 30th Street
New York, NY 10001
212-239-6868
Custom embroidery.
Laces and trims.
By appointment.

Ben Raymond
545 Broadway
New York, NY 10012
212-966-6966
Laces and trims. Good
selection. Great prices.

Regal Originals
247 W. 37th Street
New York, NY 10018
212-921-0270
Pleating to order.

Roth Imports Co., Inc.
13 W. 38th Street
New York, NY 10018
212-840-1945
Beaded and sequin
appliqués, ribbons, laces,
rhinestone yardage,
metallic braids, cords,
and silk flowers.
Quantities only.

*Ruben Bead Importing Co.,
Inc.*
45 W. 37th Street
New York, NY 10018
212-840-0500
Beads and sequins.

Sheru
49 W. 38th Street
New York, NY 10018
212-730-0766
Beads, findings, trimmings,
and craft supplies.

So-Good, Inc.
28 W. 38th Street
New York, NY 10018
212-398-0236
Ribbons.

*Star Buttonhole & Button
Works Co.*
242 W. 36th Street
New York, NY 10018
212-736-4960

Buttonholes made and
buttons covered to order.

Stitchworks
27 W. 24th Street
Suite 9D
New York, NY 10010
212-255-2573
Custom machine
embroidery. Logos,
names, show jackets,
T-shirts, etc.

Sure-Snap Corp.
505 8th Avenue at 35th St.
New York, NY 10001
212-921-5515
Buckles, snaps, rivets,
grommets, eyelets, snap
tape, dies, etc.

Temptu Marketing Inc.
26 W. 17th Street
New York, NY 10011
212-675-4000
Fax: 212-675-4075
Temporary non-toxic
tattoos. Custom and
professional kits.

Tender Buttons
143 E. 62nd Street
New York, NY 10021
212-758-7004
Beautiful but expensive!

Toho Shoji (New York) Inc.
990 6th Avenue
New York, NY 10018
212-868-7465
212-868-7466
Jewelry findings, beads,
buttons, chains, etc.
Large selection.

Tinsel Trading Co.
47 W. 38th Street
New York, NY 10018
212-730-1030
Antique trims, ribbons,
braids, etc.

DYESTUFFS

Advance
34-06 Skillman Avenue
Long Island City, NY
11101-2396
718-937-6400 and
800-833-7289

Screen printing supplies,
textile inks, equipment.

Aljo Manufacturing Co.
81-83 Franklin Street, 4th
floor
New York, NY 10013
212-226-2878 and
212-966-4046
Manufacturer of dyes for all
types of fabrics.
Information pamphlets
available. Will ship.

Pearl Paint
(*see* **Artist and Craft
Supplies**)
Good selection of various
types of dyes in small
amounts.

DYERS AND
PAINTERS

Fabric Effects Inc.
20 W. 20th Street, 5th floor
New York, NY 10011
212-255-6579 and
212-255-5225
Custom dyeing, costume
painting, and screen
printing.

Martin Izquierdo Studio
118 W. 22nd Street, 9th
floor
New York, NY 10011
212-807-9757
Theatrical dyeing, painting,
custom props,
headdresses, and jewelry.

Master Dyeing Co.
24-47 44th Street
Long Island City, NY 11103
718-726-1001
Fabric dyers.

FABRICS

Upper East Side

Silk Surplus Inc.
235 E. 58th Street
New York, NY 10022
212-753-6511

Silk Surplus Annex
223 E. 58th Street
New York, NY 10022
212-759-1294

Swatches. Will ship.
Drapery and upholstery
fabrics, many in silk.
Beautiful, expensive, but
worth it!

Regent Fabrics
122 E. 59th Street
New York, NY 10022
212-355-2039
Swatches. Will ship.
Woolens, silks, velvets,
brocades, cottons,
imported, and novelty
fabrics. Good selection of
buttons and trimming in
basement. Expensive.

Stroheim & Romann, Inc.
Showroom:
155 E. 56th Street
New York, NY 10022
212-691-0700
Swatches. Will ship.
Drapery and upholstery
fabrics. Expensive but
beautiful selection.

57th Street Between 5th and 6th Avenues

Weller Fabrics, Inc.
24 W. 57th Street
New York, NY 10019
212-247-3790
Swatches. Will ship. Large
selection of silks, cottons,
brocades, woolens, laces,
velvets, metallics,
imported, and unusual
fabrics. Expensive.

Paron Fabrics, Inc.
56 W. 57th Street
New York, NY 10019
212-247-6451
Swatches. Will ship. Silks,
woolens, brocades,
cottons, linens, metallics,
and imported fabrics.
Reasonable prices.

Paron II
56 W. 57th Street, 2nd
floor
New York, NY 10019
212-247-6739
Swatches. Will ship. 50%
off all fabrics.

Jerry Brown Imported Fabrics, Inc.
37 W. 57th Street
New York, NY 10019
212-753-3626
Swatches. Will ship. Silks,
woolens, cottons, etc.
Large selection. Very
expensive. Not
recommended unless you
have a huge budget!

57th Street Between 6th and 7th Avenues

Poli Fabrics
132 W. 57th Street
New York, NY 10019
212-245-7589 and
212-245-7750
Swatches. Will ship. Silks,
woolens, brocades,
metallics, velvets, cottons,
imported, and designer
fabrics. Reasonable prices.

55th Street Between 9th and 10th Avenues

Dazian, Inc.
423 W. 55th Street, 10th
floor
New York, NY 10019
212-307-7800
Swatch cards available. Will
ship. Scenery and
costume fabrics and
trims. Metallics, plastics,
nets, etc. Fairly expensive.

40th Street Between 7th and 8th Avenues

A & S Quality Fabrics
274 W. 40th Street
New York, NY 10018
212-921-2828
Swatches. Will ship.
Woolens, cottons,
brocades, laces, etc.
Good prices.

B & J Fabrics
263 W. 40th Street
New York, NY 10018
212-354-8150 and
212-221-9287
Swatches. Will ship.
Excellent selection of
silks, woolens, cottons,

brocades, metallics, laces,
imported, and designer
fabrics. Reasonable
prices.

Felsen Fabrics
264 W. 40th Street
New York, NY 10018
212-398-9010
Swatches. Will ship. Silks,
woolens, cottons, linens,
brocades, laces, velvets,
metallics, unusual
imported, and designer
fabrics. Expensive.

Art-Max Fabrics, Inc.
250 W. 40th Street
New York, NY 10018
212-398-0755 and
212-398-0756
Swatches. Will ship. Good
selection of silks,
woolens, cottons,
brocades, laces,
metallics, synthetics,
velvets, and imported
fabrics. Reasonable
prices.

Rosen & Chadick
246 W. 40th Street
New York, NY 10018
212-869-0136 and
212-869-0142
Swatches. Will ship.
Silks, woolens, cottons,
brocades, laces, velvets,
metallics, synthetics, and
imported fabrics.
Expensive.

New York Elegant Fabrics
240 W. 40th Street
New York, NY 10018
212-302-4984
Wide selection of
everything. Reasonable
prices.

Discount Fabrics of Burlington NJ
202 W. 40th Street
New York, NY 10018
212-354-9275
Remnants, just a few yards,
but generally several
remnants of the same
fabric. Woolens,
synthetics, blends, some

silks, linens, linings,
prints, etc. Reasonable
prices.

Paron West
206 W. 40th Street
New York, NY 10018
212-768-3266
Swatches. Will ship.
Cottons, woolens, silks,
designer and novelty
fabrics. Good prices.

Trebor Couture
215 W. 40th Street
New York, NY 10018
212-221-1610
Swatches. Will ship.
Good selection of
cottons, woolens, silks,
synthetics, designer and
novelty fabrics. Good
prices.

39th Street Between 5th and 6th Avenues

Horikoshi NY, Inc.
55 W. 39th Street
New York, NY 10018
212-354-0133
Swatches. Will ship.
Wholesale silks.
Minimum purchase of
ten yds.

39th Street Between 7th and 8th Avenues

A & N Fabrics, Inc.
268 W. 39th Street
New York, NY 10018
212-719-1773
Swatches. Cottons,
woolens, linings.
Reasonable prices.

Sutter Textile Co.
257 W. 39th Street
New York, NY 10018
212-398-0248
Swatches. Will ship.
Good selection of
upholstery fabrics,
cottons, woolens,
some silks, brocades,
velvets, linings, lots of
synthetics, and blends.
Good prices.

A K Fabrics
257 W. 39th Street
New York, NY 10018
212-944-5693
Swatches. Woolens, silks, cottons, etc. Good prices.

Trebor Textiles, Inc.
251a W. 39th Street
New York, NY 10018
212-221-1818
Swatches. Will ship. Silks, cottons, linens, woolens, synthetics, imports, etc. Reasonable prices.

K & M Fabrics
250 W. 39th Street
New York, NY 10018
212-354-9360
Swatches. Will ship. Cottons, woolens, synthetics, metallics, upholstery fabrics, etc. Reasonable prices.

A & S Quality Fabrics
250 W. 39th Street
New York, NY 10018
212-921-5072
Swatches. Will ship. Woolens, silks, cottons, synthetics, etc. Good prices.

La Lame, Inc.
250 W. 39th Street
New York, NY 10018
212-921-9770
Swatches. Will ship. Ecclesiastical fabrics and church goods. Brocades, damasks, metallics, etc. Catalogue available.

F & R Fabric Shop, Inc.
239 W. 39th Street
New York, NY 10018
212-391-9038
Swatches. Woolens, cottons, silks, linens. Reasonable prices.

Fabric Citi
214 W. 39th Street
New York, NY 10018
212-768-0433

Swatches. Will ship. Woolens, silks, cottons, synethetics, etc. Reasonable prices.

37th Street Between Broadway and 7th Avenue

Super Textile Co., Inc. (Dana Importing Corp.)
134 W. 37th Street, 4th floor
New York, NY 10018
212-354-5725
Swatches. Will ship. Large selection of silks, cottons, woolens, metallics, laces, synthetics, imported, and designer fabrics. Large cuts only (generally 15yd min. per fabric). Excellent prices.

35th Street Between 10th and 11th Avenues

Rose Brand Textiles
517 W. 35th Street
New York, NY 10001
212-594-7424 and
    800-223-1624
Swatches. Will ship. Primarily scenic fabrics. Muslin in several weights, canvas, tobacco cloth, velours, etc. Good prices. Discount on quantity yardage.

7th Avenue at 25th Street

Trumart Discount Fabrics
261 7th Avenue
New York, NY 10001
212-924-1332
Swatches. Cottons, woolens, linens, designer fabrics. Good prices.

23rd Street Between 6th and 7th Avenues

L.P. Thur
136 W. 23rd Street
New York, NY 10011

212-243-4913
Swatches. Assorted fabrics at good prices.

14th Street

Paterson Silks
36 E. 14th Street
New York, NY 10003
212-929-7861
Swatches from main floor only. Silks, woolens, blends, synthetics, knits, drapery (2nd floor), and remnants. Reasonable prices.

First Avenue

First Avenue Fabrics
180 1st Avenue
New York, NY 10003
212-353-1355
Swatches (limited number). Silks, cottons, linens, knits, stretch fabrics. Small selection but good prices.

Avenue A

S & H Fabrics, Inc.
34 Avenue A
New York, NY 10009
212-254-2235
Swatches. Will ship. 3 floors. Woolens, rayons, cottons, prints, velvets, synthetics, knits, drapery and stretch fabrics. Excellent prices.

Lafayette Street

Hamburger Woolen Co., Inc.
440 Lafayette Street
New York, NY 10003
212-505-7500
Large selection of uniform fabrics. Woolens, blends, and synthetics. Price list available. Samples on request.

Lower Broadway

Ben Raymond
545 Broadway
New York, NY 10012
212-966-6966

Swatches. Cottons, eyelets, laces synthetics, linings, lingerie fabrics. Good prices.

Inter-Coastal Textile Corp.
480 Broadway
New York, NY 10013
212-925-9235 and
    212-925-9236
Closed Saturday and Sunday.
Swatches. Will ship. Large selection of drapery and upholstry fabrics (best selection is in the basement). Antique satins, velvets, cottons, brocades, sheers, etc. Excellent prices.

Long Island Fabrics
521 Broadway
New York, NY 10012
212-925-4488
Swatches. Woolens, silks, rayons, cottons, prints, velvets, synthetics, knits and drapery fabrics. Excellent prices.

Fabric Warehouse
406 Broadway
New York, NY 10013
212-431-9510
Swatches. Trims, knits, synthetics, blends, cottons. Reasonable prices.

Big Four Pile Fabrics
75 Franklin Street
New York, NY 10013
212-966-2466
Swatches. Will ship. Huge selection of fur fabrics.

Lower East Side:

Orchard Street

Kordol Fabrics
194 Orchard Street
New York, NY 10002
212-254-8319 and
    212-254-8364
Closed Saturday.
Swatches. Will ship. Excellent selection of woolens, worsteds, and

suitings, some blends, and synthetics. Excellent prices.

Weiss & Katz, Inc.
187 Orchard Street
New York, NY 10002
212-477-1130
Closed Saturday.
Swatches. Will ship. Woolens, suitings, cottons, knits, synthetics, velvets, etc. Reasonable prices.

European Woolens, Inc.
177 Orchard Street
New York, NY 10002
212-254-1520
Closed Saturday.
Swatches. Will ship. Limited selection of woolens, worsteds, laces, knits, cottons, some metallics. Good prices.

The Woolen Closet, Inc.
167 Orchard Street
New York, NY 10002
212-674-0180
Closed Saturday.
Swatches. Generally will not ship. Suitings, worsteds, woolens. Reasonable prices.

Modern Woolens
129 Orchard Street
New York, NY 10002
212-473-6780
Closed Saturday.
Swatches. Will ship. Good selection of suitings, woolens, worsteds, some velvets. Reasonable prices.

Beckenstein Home Fabrics Inc.
130 Orchard Street
New York, NY 10002
212-475-4887
Closed Saturday.
Swatches. Will ship. Drapery and upholstery fabrics.

Beckenstein's Men's Fabrics, Inc.
121 Orchard Street
New York, NY 10002
212-475-6666 and
   800-221-2727
Closed Saturday.
Suitings, woolens, worsteds, and linings. Swatches. Will ship.

Stanton Street

Belraf Fabrics, Inc.
112 Stanton Street
New York, NY 10002
212-505-2106
Swatches. Silks, cottons, synthetics, linings, drapery, and upholstery fabrics. Excellent prices.

Grand Street

Grand Silk House
357 Grand Street
New York, NY 10002
212-475-0114 and
   212-475-0115
Swatches. Will ship. Good selection of silks, woolens, cottons, knits, velvets, imported, and designer fabrics. Reasonable prices.

Maxine Fabrics Co.
357 Grand Street
   (basement)
New York, NY 10002
212-674-1196
Will ship. Large swatch book available to purchase, cost deducted from large orders. Good selection of silks, woolens, cottons, brocades and imported dress fabrics. Expensive.

Eldridge Street

Leratex Fabrics
110 Eldridge Street
New York, NY 10002
212-925-3678
Closed Saturday.
Swatches. Will ship. Drapery and upholstery

fabrics. Small store, limited selection, but excellent prices.

M. Zupnik, Inc.
113 Eldridge Street
New York, NY 10002
212-226-4669
Closed Saturday.
No swatches. Will ship. Wholesale. Cottons, some woolens, synthetics, blends, prints, linings etc. Excellent prices.

Hester Street

Listokin & Sons Fabrics, Inc.
87 Hester Street
New York, NY 10002
212-226-6111
Closed Saturday.
Swatches. Will ship. Cottons, blends, synthetics, some woolens, laces, silks, velvets, metallics, and trimmings. Reasonable prices.

Mendel Goldberg, Inc.
72 Hester Street
New York, NY 10002
212-925-9110
Closed Saturday.
Swatches. Will ship. Silks, woolens, cottons, velvets, some metallics, printed rayon crepes, imported, and designer fabrics. Good prices.

Allen Street

Harry Zarin Co. Fabric Warehouse
72 Allen Street
New York, NY 10002
212-925-6112
Closed Saturday.
Swatches. Will ship. Large selection of drapery and upholstery fabrics. Good prices.

Harriman, NY

Gladstone Fabrics
P.O. Box 566
Orchard Hill Raod
Harriman, NY 10926

914-783-1900 and
   800-724-0168
Fax: 914-783-2963
Swatches. Will ship. **Mail order only.** Large selection of theatrical fabrics, silks, cottons, sequin and stretch fabrics, etc. Reasonable prices.

FELT

American Felt and Filter Co.
34 John Street
Newburgh, NY 12550
914-561-3560
Industrial felt. Sample card and price list available. Will ship.

Central Shippee
46 Star Lake Road
Bloomingdale, NJ 07403
201-838-1100 and
   800-631-8968
Industrial and decorator felt. Swatch cards available. Will ship.

FOAM

Canal Rubber Supply Co.
329 Canal Street
New York, NY 10013
212-226-7339
Variety of grades and types. Will cut to size.

Foam-Tex, Inc.
150 W. 22nd Street
New York, NY 10011
212-727-1780
Ethafoam rod and foam

FOOTWEAR

Anani Bros., Inc.
34 W. 46th Street
New York, NY 10036
212-869-5335 and
   212-869-5336
Custom footwear and repairs. Men's period lace-up boots to order.

*J. C. Banks Theatrical &
    Custom Footwear*
890 Broadway
New York, NY 10003
212-529-1125

Capezio's
(*see* **Dancewear**)

Freed of London, Ltd.
(*see* **Dancewear**)
Dance shoes and custom
    theatrical footwear.

Lynn Boot & Shoe, Ltd.
16 W. 46th Street
New York, NY 10036
212-819-0092
Western boots. Carries
    wide fittings.

McCreedy & Schreiber
37 W. 46th Street
New York, NY 10036
212-719-1552

213 E. 59th Street
New York, NY 10022
212-759-9241
Men's boots and shoes.
    Good source for
    hard-to-find sizes and
    styles. Expensive.

Montana Leatherworks, Ltd.
47 Greene Street
New York, NY 10013
212-431-4015
Custom theatrical footwear
    and leather work.

Tall Size Shoes
3 W. 35th Street
New York, NY 10001
212-736-2060
Good selection of women's
    large sizes.

FORMAL WEAR

Academy
1703 Broadway
New York, NY 10019
212-765-1440
Sales.

David's Outfitters, Inc.
36 W. 22nd Street
New York, NY 10011
212-691-7388
Rentals only.

Jack Silver
1780 Broadway
New York, NY 10019
212-582-3298 and
    212-582-3389
Rentals and sales.

HANGERS

American Hanger & Fixture
520 W. 27th Street
New York, NY 10001
212-279-5280 and
    800-221-2790
Wire and wooden
    coathangers in quantity.
    Inflatable legs and bodies.
    Wardrobe supplies.
    Catalogue available.
    Good prices.

HATS

Arnold Hatters, Inc.
620 8th Avenue
New York, NY 10018
212-768-3781
Good assortment of men's
    hats.

Hat Corner Corp.
139 Nassau Street
New York, NY 10038
212-964-5693
Excellent selection of men's
    hats

Champion
94 Greenwich Avenue
New York, NY 10011
212-929-5696
All types of men's hats. Will
    also clean and reblock.

Worth & Worth, Ltd.
331 Madison Avenue
New York, NY 10017
212-867-6058 and
    800-HAT-SHOP
Men's hats, including straw
    boaters. Will ship.

LEATHER AND
LEATHER SUPPLIES

A & B Leather & Findings Co.
769 10th Avenue
New York, NY 10019
212-265-8124

Supplies, tools, dyes,
    Magix, etc. Will ship.

Grosz Leather Co.
245 W. 29th Street
New York, NY 10001
212-268-3070
Good selection at excellent
    prices. Will ship.

*Kaufman Shoe Repair
    Supplies, Inc.*
346 Lafayette Street
New York, NY 10012
212-777-1700
Supplies, tools, dyes,
    Magix, etc. Will ship.

Leather Sales Corp.
(*Minerva*)
78 Spring Street
New York, NY 10012
212-925-6270
Large selection of cowhide,
    pigskin, garment suedes,
    etc. Good prices. Will
    ship.

*National Leather & Shoe
    Findings Co.*
617 Sackett Street
Brooklyn, NY 11217
718-797-3434
Supplies, tools, dyes,
    Magix, etc. Will ship.

MAKE-UP

Abracadabra
10 Christopher Street
New York, NY 10011
212-627-5745
Most major brands,
    make-up supplies, wigs
    and misc., theatrical
    goodies. Expensive.

Alcone Co., Inc.
5-49 49th Avenue
Long Island City, NY 11101
718-361-8373
Catalogue available. Will
    ship. Carries most major
    brands, supplies, crepe
    hair, etc.

Bob Kelly Cosmetics, Inc.
151 W. 46th Street, 9th
    floor
New York, NY 10036
212-819-0030

Bob Kelly brand only. Will
    ship.

The Make-up Center, Ltd.
150 W. 55th Street
New York, NY 10019
212-977-9494
Major brands and supplies.

Temptu Marketing Co.
(tattoos)
(*see* **Decorative Items**)

MILLINERY
SUPPLIES

Arden
(*see* **Corset Supplies**)
Bridal glue.

Friedman & Distillator
(*see* **Decorative Items**)
Millinery fabrics—many
    unusual and hard to find.

Gamples Supply Corp.
39 W. 37th Street
New York, NY 10018
212-398-9222
Buckram, sizing, millinery
    wire in all weights.

*Head-quarters International,
    Inc.*
42 W. 39th Street Suite 407
New York, NY 10018
212-840-0990
Bodies, hoods, cartwheels,
    straws and braids. Good
    prices.

Manny's Millinery Supply Co.
26 W. 38th Street
New York, NY 10018
212-840-2235 and
    212-840-2236
Hat blocks, wire, buckram,
    felt, and velour bodies,
    buckram shapes, flowers,
    hat pins, etc. Catalogue
    available. Will ship.

Zeeman Corp.
270 W. 38th Street
New York, NY 10018
212-302-2822
Ribbons, hat elastic,
    supplies. Brochure
    available.

PRESSING EQUIPMENT

Automatic Steam Products Corp.
43-20 34th Street
Long Island City, NY 11101
718-937-4500 and 800-238-3535
Manufacturer of Sussman pressing equipment. Catalogue available.

Ronis Bros. Sewing Machine Inc.
(*see* **Sewing Machines, Parts, and Repair**)

SEWING MACHINES, PARTS, AND REPAIR

AAB American Trading Co.
132 W. 23rd Street
New York, NY 10011
212-691-3666
Industrial sewing machines. Sales, rentals, parts, and repairs.

Fox Sewing Machine, Inc.
307 W. 38th Street
New York, NY 10018
212-594-2438 and 212-594-2761
Industrial sewing machines. Sales, rentals, and repair. New and used.

Hecht Sewing Machine & Motor Co., Inc.
304 W. 38th Street
New York, NY 10018
212-563-5950
Industrial machines. Sales, service, and rentals.

Garment Center Sewing Machine, Inc.
555 8th Avenue
New York, NY 10018
212-279-8774
New and used. Sales and rentals.

Ronis Bros. Sewing Machine Inc.
257 W. 38th Street
New York, NY 10018
212-575-2679
Pressing equipment, dress forms. Industrial sewing machines, parts, supplies. Good prices.

SEWING SUPPLIES

Fox Sewing Machine Co.
(*see* **Sewing Machines, Parts, and Repair**)
New and used dress forms.

Garment Center Sewing Machine Corp.
(*see* **Sewing Machines, Parts, and Repair**)
New and used dress forms.

Greenberg & Hammer, Inc.
24 W. 57th Street
New York, NY 10019
212-246-2835 and 212-246-2836 or 800-955-5135
Fax: 212-765-8475
Excellent source for findings, supplies, thread, interfacings, fastenings, etc. Catalogue available. Will ship.

Hersh 6th Ave. Buttons, Inc.
(*see* **Decorative Items**)
Tailoring and sewing supplies.

Joan's Needlecraft Studios, Inc.
240 E. 29th Street
New York, NY 10016
212-532-7129
Embroidery threads and yarns. Good selection.

Louis Price Paper Co., Inc.
34-40 11th Street
Long Island City, NY 11106
718-728-8993
Pattern and Kraft paper.

Steinlauf & Stoller, Inc.
239 W. 39th Street
New York, NY 10018
212-869-0321 and 800-637-1637
Excellent source for all notions, tools, interfacings, fastenings, wardrobe supplies, threads, etc. Good prices. Will ship.

Superior Model Forms Co.
306 W. 38th Street
New York, NY 10018
212-947-3633
Dress forms.

Supreme Label
109 W. 27th Street
New York, NY 10001
212-255-2090
Custom printed labels. Good prices on small orders.

Sure-Snap Corp.
(*see* **Decorative Items**)
Snaps, snap tape, eyelets, etc.

Wolf Paper & Twine Co., Inc.
680 6th Avenue
New York, NY 10010
212-675-4870 and 212-675-4871
Kraft, pattern, and tissue paper, boxes, tapes, etc. Will ship.

THEATRICAL SUPPLY HOUSE

Alcone Co., Inc.
(*see* **Make-up**)
Synthetic wigs, wigmaking supplies, crepe hair, books, fencing, and stage equipment, etc. Catalogue available. Will ship.

Gordon Novelty Co., Inc.
933 Broadway
New York, NY 10010
212-254-8616 and 212-254-8617
All types of novelties and costume accessories, synthetic wigs, hats, masks, fans, etc. Catalogue available. Will ship.

UNIFORMS/ MILITARY SURPLUS

Academy
(*see* **Formal Wear**)
Waiters and waitresses.

Craft Clothes
(*see* *Craft Clerical* under **Clothing—Ecclesiastical**)
School uniforms, cheerleaders. Catalogue available.

Dave's Army & Navy
779 6th Avenue
New York, NY 10001
212-989-6444
Military surplus and work clothes. Good prices.

David's Outfitters
(*see* **Formal Wear**)
Military, civilian, all types. Rentals only.

Iceburg of Soho Army-Navy
455 Broadway
New York, NY 10013
212-226-8485 and 212-226-8486
New and used military surplus.

Kaufman's Army & Navy
319 W. 42nd Street
New York, NY 10036
212-757-5670
New and used military surplus.

O.K. Uniform Co., Inc.
507 Broadway
New York, NY 10012
212-966-1984 and 212-966-4733
Fax: 212-226-6668
Great source for work clothes, medical, restaurant, and industrial uniforms and accessories. Good prices.

B. Schlesinger & Sons, Inc.
249 W. 18th Street
New York, NY 10011
212-206-8022
Work clothes, postal, medical, and guard uniforms, etc.

Weiss & Mahoney, Inc.
142 5th Avenue
New York, NY 10011
212-675-1915 and 212-675-1367
Military surplus clothing, uniforms, accessories, insignia, etc. Catalogue available.

WIGS AND HAIR SUPPLIES

Alcone Co., Inc.
(*see* **Make-up**)
Synthetic theatrical wigs, wigmaking supplies, crepe hair, etc.

W. & Y. Chung Traders, Inc.
1225 Broadway, Suite 200-201
New York, NY 10001
212-683-2767 and
212-683-2768
Importers. Human hair goods. Men's and women's Elura wigs. Catalogue and price list available. Excellent prices.

De Meo Bros., Inc.
129 W. 29th Street
New York, NY 10001
212-268-1400

Human hair by the pound, wigmaking supplies. Price list available. Will ship.

Elsen Associates
780 Riverside Drive
New York, NY 10032
212-283-7708
Specializes in Opera wigs and make-up. Rentals only.

Paul Huntley Ltd.
312 W. 82nd Street
New York, NY 10024
212-787-5200
Custom wigs for stage and film. By appointment only. Expensive.

Ideal Wig Co., Inc.
37-11 35th Avenue
Astoria, NY 11101
718-361-8601
Synthetic theatrical wigs and facial hair. Catalogue available.

Bob Kelly Wig Creations
151 W. 46th Street, 9th floor
New York, NY 10036
212-819-0030 and
212-819-0031
Theatrical wigs, custom, and rental. Facial hair to order.

Lacey Costume Wig
505 8th Avneue 11th floor
New York, NY 10018
212-695-1996 and
800-562-9911
All types of synthetic wigs. Good prices.

Ray Beauty Supply Co.
721 8th Avenue
New York, NY 10036
212-757-0175
Wig and hair supplies. Excellent prices. Will ship.

Zauder Bros. Inc.
10 Henry Street
Freeport, NY 11520
516-379-2600
Wig supplies.

YARN

Fibre Yarn Co., Inc.
48 W. 38th Street
New York, NY 10018
212-719-5820
All types of yarn and embroidery threads.

School Products Co., Inc.
1201 Broadway
New York, NY 10001
212-679-3516
All types of knitting and weaving yarns, machines, and looms. Will ship.

The Yarn Center
1011 6th Avenue
New York, NY 10008
212-719-5648

Elsewhere in the U.S.

Items included within each category.

Accessories: gloves, canes, jewelry, novelties, shirt collars, studs, etc., tiaras.

Artist and Craft Supplies: adhesives, bronzing powders, fiber optics, findings, foam, mold and sculpting supplies, paints, protective equipment, reeds, caning, weaving supplies.

Clothing—Miscellaneous: Amish, religious, riding, work clothes.

Clothing—Used and Antique: formal wear, thrift shops, secondhand clothing stores, vintage.

Computers: software.

Costumes—Custom and Rentals: formal wear, made-to-order.

Dancewear: clothing, footwear.

Decorative Items: beads, sequins, buttons, buttonholes, chain, feathers, findings, flowers, lace, novelties, pleating, ribbons, trimmings.

Footwear: custom and retail, heels, shoe repair.

Hats and Millinery Supplies

Leather and Leather Supplies: tools, leather dye.

Make-up, Wigs, and Hair Supplies

Sewing Supplies, Machinery, and Equipment: boxes, corset supplies, dress forms, labels, notions, pattern paper, patterns, pressing equipment, sewing machines, parts, and repairs, tailoring supplies, thread.

Uniforms, Weapons, and Armor: badges and insignia, military surplus, work clothes.

Videotapes

ACCESSORIES

Allied Industrial Distributors
2926 West Virginia
   Avenue
Phoenix, AZ 85009
602-269-5981
Pigskin driving gloves by
   the dozen.

Amazon, Vinegar &
   Pickling Works Drygoods
2218 E. 11th Street
Davenport, IO
   52803-3760
319-322-6800
Period accessories, fabrics,
   patterns, books.

Anderson's
4875 White Bear Parkway
White Bear, MN 55110
800-328-9640
Tiaras, homecoming, and
   float supplies.

Dorothy's Boutique
190 Massachusetts Avenue
Boston, MA 02115
617-262-9255
Inexpensive jewelry and
   wigs.

Dutch Guard
P.O. Box 411687
Kansas City, MO 64114
800-821-5157
Beautiful canes and walking
   sticks.

Gibson Lee, Inc.
78 Stone Place
Melrose, MA 02176
617-662-6025
Shirt collars, cuffs, studs.

Gloves by Hammer of
   Hollywood
7210 Melrose Avenue
Los Angeles, CA 90046
213-938-0288
Gloves.

Theatre House
P.O. Box 2090
400 W. Third Street
Covington, KY
   41012-2090
800-827-2414
Novelties, accessories,
   inexpensive hairpieces.

ARTIST AND CRAFT SUPPLIES

Beacon Chemical Co., Inc.
125 MacQuesten
   Parkway S.
Mount Vernon, NY 10550
914-699-3400
Manufacturers of all types
   of adhesives, millinery
   sizings, etc.

Cane & Basket Supply
   Company
1283 S. Cochran Avenue
Los Angeles, CA 90019
213-939-9644
Caning supplies.

Charrette—Main Office
P.O. Box 4010
31 Olympia Avenue
Woburn, MA 01888-4010
617-935-6010 and
   617-935-6000 and
   800-242-7738

95 Mt. Auburn Street
Cambridge, MA 02138
617-495-0250

45 Batterymarch Street
Boston, MA 02110
617-542-1666
Artists and crafts supplies.

Crescent Bronze Powder Co.,
   Inc.
3400 N. Avondale Avenue
Chicago, IL 60618
312-539-2441

1841 S. Flower Street
Los Angeles, CA 90015
213-748-5285
Bronzing powders and
   liquids, glitters, etc.

Dental Supply of New
   England
80 Fargo Street
Boston, MA 02210
617-482-2372
Alginate for life masks.

Dick Blick
P.O. Box 1267
Galesburg, IL 61401
800-447-8192 and
   309-343-6181
Art supplies.

Dick Blick East
P.O. Box 26
Allentown, PA 18105
215-965-6051

Dick Blick West
P.O. Box 521
Henderson, NV 89015
602-451-7662

Douglas & Sturgess, Inc.
730 Bryant Street
San Francisco, CA 94107
415-421-4456
Resin and glass products,
   mold and sculpting
   materials, other craft
   supplies.

Edmund Scientific Co.
101 E. Gloucester Pike
Barrington, NJ 08007
609-547-3488
Fiber optics.

Farnesworth
819 North 2nd Street
Philadelphia, PA 19123
215-925-1335
Thermal plastic for masks,
   hats, accessories.

Foam Craft, Inc.
947 W. Van Buren Street
Chicago, IL 60607
312-243-6262
Filter foam and adhesives.

Haussmann International
   Corp.
132 Ninth Street
San Francisco, CA 94103
415-431-1336
Sprila glazing colors and
   Halotex B2 colors.

Johnson's Artist's Supplies
355 Newbury Street
Boston, MA 02115
617-536-4065
Artist and craft supplies.

Ken-Kaye Krafts Co.
863 Washington Street
Newton, MA
617-526-1206
Craft supplies.

Lab Safety Supply
P.O. Box 1368
Janesville, WI 53547-1368
608-754-2345 and
   800-356-0783

Respirators, protective
   gloves, etc.

Lambert Co., Inc.
71 Innerbelt Road
Somerville, MA 02143
617-628-8150
Silk screen supplies.

Ohio Travel Bag
   Manufacturing Co.
811 Prospect Avenue
Cleveland, OH 44115
216-621-5963
Rivets, clasps, luggage
   hardware, and findings.

Pearl Arts & Crafts
579 Massachusetts Ave.
Cambridge, MA 02139
617-547-6600
Artist and craft supplies.

Perkins Co.
10 South Bradley Road
Woodbridge, CT 06525
203-389-4011
Reeds, cane, and cane
   webbing.

Rogers Foam Corp
3580 Main Street
Hartford, CT 06120
203-246-7234
Scotfoam.

Rosco Laboratories, Inc.
1135 North Highland
   Avenue
Hollywood, CA 90038
213-462-2233
Craft products, fabric dyes,
   and paints.

Sculptural Art Coating
P.O. Box 13113
Greensboro, NC 27415
919-621-7379 and
   800-743-0379

Solomons Group
P.O. Box 54
Newark, NJ 07101
201-623-0909 and
   800-645-3660
Sobo glue by the gallon,
   four gallon minimum.

Spectra Dynamics
415 Marble Street NW
Albuquerque, NM 87102
505-843-7202
Phlex-Glu and plasticizer.

Straw into Gold
3006 San Pablo Avenue
   (Ashby)
Berkeley, CA 94702
415-548-5241
Natural fibers and hair,
   spinning supplies.

Swift Adhesives & Coatings
Box 1546
3100 Woodcreek Drive
Downers Grove, IL 60515
708-971-6800
Adhesives.

Textile Resources
10591 Bloomfield Street
Los Alamitos, CA 90720
213-431-9611
Fabrics, fabric dyes, and
   paints.

Tri Ess Science
1020 West Chestnut Street
Burbank, CA 91506
818-247-6910
Zap a gap adhesive, special
   effects, flames, smoke.

Unnatural Resources, Inc.
14 Forest Avenue
Caldwell, NJ 07006
210-228-5384
Thermoplastics.

Utrecht's
333 Massachusetts Avenue
Boston, MA 02115
617-262-4948
Artist and craft supplies.

Waldo Brothers
202 Southhampton Street
Roxbury, MA
617-445-3000
Molding plaster,
   Hydrostone, Ultracal 30.

Warren Electric &
   Hardware Supply
470 Tremont Street
Boston, MA 02116
617-426-7525
Craft supplies, hot glue.

Yaulden's
563-569 High Street
Westwood, MA 02090
508-326-1305
Art and craft supplies.

CLOTHING—MISCELLANEOUS

Almy & Son, Inc.
P.O. Box 2628
10 Glenville Street
Greenwich, CT
   06836-1618
203-531-7600
Clerical outfitters.

Gohn Brothers
Box 111
Middlebury, IN
   46540-0111
219-825-2400
Amish and plain clothing.

Harry the Greek
1136 Washington Street
Roxbury, MA 02119
617-338-7511
Men's work clothes.

State Line Tack
Route 121
Plaistow, NH 03865
603-382-4718
Riding clothes.

Walker's Riding Apparel
122 Boylston Street
Boston, MA
617-423-9050
Riding clothes.

Wippell & Co., Ltd.
13-00 Plaza Road
P.O. Box 456
Fair Lawn, NJ 07410
201-796-9421 and
   201-796-9422
Clerical outfitters.

CLOTHING—USED AND ANTIQUE

Aardvark's Odd Ark
7579 Melrose Street
Los Angeles, CA 90046
213-663-2867
Antique clothing.

Arsenic & Old Lace
1743 Massachusetts Ave.
Cambridge, MA 02140
617-354-7785
Secondhand and antique
   clothing.

Cafe Society
131 Cypress Street
Brookline, MA 02146
617-738-7186
Old clothes.

Crystal Palace
8457 Melrose Street
Los Angeles, CA 90069
213-653-6148
Antique clothing and
   accessories.

Deborah's Attic
719 S. Limestone Street
Springfield, OH 45505
513-322-8842
Vintage clothes.

Donna's Olde Clothes
1523 N. Le Brea Avenue
Hollywood, CA 90028
213-874-8119

Forever Flamingo
285 Newbury Street
Boston, MA 02115
617-267-2547
Vintage 1930s to 1950s.

The Garment District
200 Broadway
Cambridge, MA 02139
617-876-5230
Shoes, boots, vintage, and
   children's clothing.

Keezer's
140 River Avenue
Cambridge, MA 02138
617-547-2455
Formal wear, formal wear
   accessories, shoes.

Morgies
Elm Street, Dave's Square
Somerville, MA 02144
617-628-3618
Old clothes.

Odeon
558 Tremont Street
Boston, MA
617-542-4412
Used clothing.

Oona's
1796 Massachusetts
   Avenue
Cambridge, MA 02138
617-491-2654
Vintage clothing, leather
   jackets.

Reddog
1737 Massachusetts Ave.
Cambridge, MA 02138
617-354-9676
1930s, 1940s, 1950s men's
   and women's clothing.

RFG Antiques
195 Harvard Street
Brookline, MA 02146
617-734-2226
Vintage clothing.

Rick's Fashion Americain
330 Selma Road
Springfield, OH 45505
513-322-7766
Men's vintage suits and
   accessories 1930s to
   60s. Supplies movie
   companies.

Salvation Army
209-233 Broadway
Boston, MA 02215
671-231-0803

Second Time Around
1169 Walnut Street
Newton, MA 02161
617-964-4481
Contemporary clothing in
   excellent condition.

Strutters
11 Paul Sullivan Way
Boston, MA 02118
617-423-9299
Vintage clothing,
   accessories, and shoes.

Taylor Trust
111 Marion Street
Brookline, MA 02146
617-566-8126
1920s to 1950s, jewelry,
   clothing, and accessories.

Tuxedo Wholesaler
7750 E. Redfield Road
Scottsdale, AZ 85260
800-828-2802
Used formal wear.

Vintage, etc.
1796 Massachusetts
   Avenue
Cambridge, MA 02140
617-497-1516
1930s, 1940s, 1950s.

COMPUTERS

Computer Tools for Costumers
c/o M.L. Baker
1932 Portland Avenue
Tallahassee, FL 32303
904-385-6750
Producer and distributor of
Body Block Basics, a
computer program that
plots individualized
pattern blocks.

Preferred Theatrical Software
525 Conifer Way
Ashland, OR 97520
503-488-2748
Producer and distributor of
Wardrobe Master, a
computer program to
organize wardrobe
information.

COSTUMES—
CUSTOM AND
RENTAL

Boston Costume
169 Tremont Street
Boston, MA 02111
617-482-1632
Rentals.

Broadway Costume Co.
954 W. Washington
Boulevard
Chicago, IL 60607
312-829-6400

186 South Street
Boston, MA 02111
617-426-3560
Rentals.

But-a-Tux
545 Roosevelt Road
Chicago, IL 60607
312-243-5465
Rentals.

Chicago Costume Co., Inc.
1120 W. Fullerton Street
Chicago, IL 60614
312-528-1264
Custom and rentals,
dancewear, and make-up.

*CTG/Center Theatre Group
Costume Shop*
3301 E. 14th Street
Los Angeles, CA 90023
213-267-1230

Custom costume
construction and rental.

Eastern Costume
2000 Universal Studio
Plaza, Suite 500
Orlando, FL 32819
407-363-1353
Men's and women's
uniforms. Rentals only.

Farrell's Costumes, Ltd.
1525 South Front Street
Wilmington, NC 28401
910-343-0044
Fax: 910-343-1777
Rentals for film, TV and
commercials.

Hooker-Howe Costume Co.
46-52 S. Main Street
Bradford, MA 01835
508-373-3731
Custom and rental.

J. & M Costumers
P.O. Box 5426
North Hollywood, CA
91616
818-760-1991
Custom and rental.

Norcostco California Costume
5867 Lankershim
Boulevard
North Hollywood, CA
91601
818-760-2911 and
213-461-6555
Rentals.

Norcostco, Inc.
3203 N. Highway 100
Minneapolis, MN 55411
612-533-2791

2089 Monroe Drive NE
Atlanta, GA 30324
404-874-7511

373 Route 46 West
Fairfield, NJ 07006
201-575-3503

2607 Ross Avenue
Dallas, TX 75201
214-953-1255
Rentals.

Paramount Pictures Corp.
5451 Marathon Street
Hollywood, CA 90038
213-468-5000

Rentals: costumes, furs,
jewelry.

Production Values, Inc.
331 Elizabeth Street NE
Atlanta, GA 30307
404-584-5529
Custom costume
construction and rental
for nonprofit
organizations.

Salt Lake City Costume Co.
1701 S. 11th Street
Salt Lake City, UT 84105
801-467-9494
Rentals.

Sonnenberg Studios
515 Washington Street
Boston, MA 02111
617-451-2833 and
617-451-2907
Design and/or production
of costumes and
softgoods; alterations.

Tuxedo Center
7360 Sunset Boulevard
Hollywood, CA 90046
213-847-4200
Top hats, spats; will rent
parts of period tuxedos.

Western Costume Co.
11041 VanOwen Street
North Hollywood, CA
91605
818-760-0900 and
818-760-0902
Rentals.

DANCEWEAR

Apparel Warehouse
2089 Westwood Boulevard
Westwood, CA 90025
213-475-1400
Dancewear.

Capezio
59 Temple Place
Boston, MA 02111
617-482-5825

1777 N. Vine Street
Hollywood, CA 90028
213-465-3744 and
213-465-9704
Dancewear.

Dance Plus
85A Mt. Auburn Street
Cambridge, MA 02138
617-547-0263
Dancewear.

*Leo's Advance Theatrical
Co.*
1900 N. Narragansett
Street
Chicago, IL 60639
312-889-7700
Dancewear and shoes.

Taffy's
200 D Linden Street
Wellesley, MA 02181
617-237-5526
Dancewear.

Taffy's-By-Mail
701 Beta Drive
Cleveland, OH 44243
216-461-3360
Dancewear.

*Weissman's Designs for
Dance*
1600 Macklind Avenue
St. Louis, MO 63110
314-773-9000

DECORATIVE ITEMS

A & S Button Co.
503 Lyons Avenue
Irvington, NJ 07111
201-923-0999
Buttons and buckles.

A-1 Pleating Co.
8426-1/2 W. Third Street
Los Angeles, CA 90048
213-653-5557
Pleating, covered buttons,
and buckles.

*Acme Buttonhole and
Pleating Co.*
404 S. Wells Street
Chicago, IL 60607
312-922-0096
Custom buttonholes and
pleating.

Am-Can Feather
8344 Beverly Boulevard
Hollywood, CA 90078
213-653-1508
Boas, specialty feathers;
will custom dye.

Berger Specialty Co., Inc.
413 E. Eighth Street
Los Angeles, CA 90014
213-627-8783
Beads, sequins, rhinestones,
  and other glitz.

Buttonholes
99 Chauncey Street, Suite
  412
Boston, MA 02111
617-426-9327 and
  617-482-5693
Custom buttonholes.

Central Pleating Co.
1007 Washington Street
St. Louis, MO 63101
314-421-1577
Custom pleating.

*Chicago Progressive
  Mercantile Co.*
625 W. Jackson Boulevard
Chicago, IL 60606
312-454-1706
Metal buttons in gross lots.

Colby Feathers, Inc.
7923 ½ W. 3rd Street
Los Angeles, CA 90048
213-653-3054

Floral Supply Syndicate
P.O. Box 15837
1145 Wall Street
Los Angeles, CA 90015
213-747-7496
Silk flowers, floral supplies.

G. Kagan & Sons, Inc.
750 Towne Avenue
Los Angeles, CA 90021
213-627-9655
Trims, buttons, beads,
  feathers, etc.

Hollywood Fancy Feathers Co.
512 S. Broadway
Los Angeles, CA 90013
213-625-8453

*Hyman Hendler & Sons,
  Inc.*
1440 Santee Street
Los Angeles, CA 90015
213-749-6022
Trimmings.

*International Importing
  Bead and Novelty Co.*
17 N. State Street
Chicago, IL 60602

312-332-0061
Beads and other trims.

Isaacson & Kater Button Co.
2530 Superior Avenue
Cleveland, OH 44110
1-800-426-3526
Wholesale buttons.

Klein Bead Box
314 N. King's Road
Los Angeles, CA 90048
213-651-3595

Koplow Trimming Co.
35 Temple Place
Boston, MA 02111
617-426-8549
Large selection of trims in
  bulk and by the yard.

Lace Broker
252 Newbury Street
Boston, MA 02116
617-267-5954
Lace.

M and D Company
Box 11551
St. Paul, MN 55111
612-699-1644
Imported metallic braids
  and trimmings. Great
  selection. Mail order.

Nick-The-Tailor
33 Harrison Avenue
Boston, MA 02111
617-383-9055
Custom buttonholes.

Ornamental Resources Inc.
P.O. Box 3010
1427 Miner Street
Idaho Springs, CO 80452
303-279-2102
800-876-6762
Beads, jewelry, E6000
  adhesive, aluminum
  chain mail, etc.

Progress Feather Company
657 West Lake Street
Chicago, IL 60606
312-726-7443

Rainbow Feather Dyeing Co.
3210 N. San Fernando
  Boulevard
Burbank, CA 91504
213-842-3107

All types of feathers,
  boas.

San Francisco Pleating
425 2nd Street
San Francisco, CA 94107
415-982-3003
Pleating to order.

S.A. Feather Company
5852 Enterprise Parkway
Billy Creek Commerce
  Center
Ft. Myers, FL 33905
813-693-6363 and
  800-226-8698

Southern Importers
4825 San Jacinto Street
Houston, TX 77004
713-524-8236
Display items, theatrical
  materials, specialty items.

State Pleating Co.
582 E Street
Boston, MA 02210
617-426-1986

*Whiting & Davis
Metal Fabric Division*
23 W. Bacon Street
Plainville, MA 02762
617-699-4411
Metal mesh.

Williams Costume Company
1226 S. 3rd Street
Las Vegas, NV 89107
702-384-1384
Showgirl feathers.

Windsor Button
35 Temple Place
Boston, MA 02111
617-482-4969

Shopper's World
Framingham, MA 01701
508-872-8410
Buttons, trim, fabric; some
  millinery and fabric
  painting supplies.

Wolfe/Myrow
Aleppo Street
Providence, RI 02909
401-331-2921
Warehouse: beads, baubles,
  findings, etc.

DYES, DYEING EQUIPMENT AND SUPPLIES

Advance
400 N. Noble Street
Chicago, IL 60622-6383
800-678-1900

6480 Corvette Street
City of Commerce
Los Angeles, CA
  90040-1793
213-685-3400 and
  800-999-1912
Screen printing supplies,
  textile inks, equipment.

Other locations in:
  Atlanta, GA, Bay
  Area/Hayward, CA,
  Cincinnati, OH,
  Cleveland, OH,
  Houston, TX, Kansas
  City, MO, Miami, FL,
  Milwaukee, WI,
  Pennsauken, NJ.

Almore Dye House
4422 S. Wentworth Street
Chicago, IL 60609
312-268-5000

Brooks and Flynn, Inc.
P.O. Box 2639
Rohnert Park, CA 94927
800-822-2372
Dyes and dyeing supplies.

Cerulean Blue, Ltd.
P.O. Box 21168
Seattle, WA 98111-3168
206-323-8600
Fabric dyes, paints, and
  supplies.

Createx/Colorcraft, Ltd.
14 Airport Park Road
East Granby, CT 06026
203-653-5505
Nontoxic fabric paints,
  especially metallics,
  iron-on foil.

Cushing, W. & Co.
P.O. Box 351
Kennebunkport, ME
  04046
207-653-5505
Fabric dyes and disperse
  agents.

Dharma Trading Co.
P.O. Box 916
San Rafael, CA 94915
800-542-5227
Fabric dyes and paints

Dri-Dek
Kendall International
    Centre
2706 S. Horseshoe Dr.
Naples, FL 33942
800-348-2398
Drainage floor tiles for dye
    rooms and laundry areas.

Fabdec
3553 Old Post Road
San Angelo, TX 76904
915-944-1031
Procion dyes, tools, fabrics.

Groen
1900 Pratt Boulevard
Elk Grove, IL 60007
708-439-2400
Dye vats.

Inko
1199 E. 12th Street
Oakland, CA 94606
415-451-1048
Fabrics dyes and supplies.

Naz-Dar Co.
1087 N. North Branch
    Street
Chicago, IL 60622-4292
312-943-8338 and
    800-736-7636
Screen printing inks and
    supplies.

Naz-Dar/KC Coatings
15555 W. 108th Street
Lenexa, KA 66219
913-492-2600
Other locations in:
    Teterboro, NJ, Norcross,
    GA, Troy, MI, Garden
    Grove, CA, St. Louis,
    MO, Overland Park, KS.

Pro Chemical & Dye, Inc.
P.O. Box 14
Somerset, MA 02726
508-676-3838
Textile inks and dyes, dye
    chemicals, technical
    advice.

Rupert, Gibbon and Spyder
P.O. Box 425
Healdsburg, CA 95448
707-433-9577 and
    800-442-0455
Natural fabrics for dyeing,
    fabric paints, dyes, and
    supplies.

*Special Products/CPC
    International*
P.O. Box 21070
1437 W. Morris Street
Indianapolis, IN 46221
317-621-5321
Rit wholesale; minimum
    order required.

Textile Resources
10591 Bloomfield Street
Los Alamitos, CA 90720
213-431-9611
Fabrics, fabric dyes, and
    paints.

FABRICS

American Felt & Filter Co.
34 John Street
Newburgh, NY 12550
914-561-3560
Industrial felt.

Baer Fabrics
515 E. Market Street
Louisville, KY 40202
505-583-5521
Specialty fabrics, metallic
    braids.

Bargain Center
6 Washington Street
Quincy, MA 92169
617-472-1414
Fabrics.

Britex Fabrics
146 Geary Street
San Francisco, CA 94108
415-392-2910

Central Shippee
46 Star Lake Road
Bloomingdale, NJ 07402
201-838-1100 and
    800-631-8968
Industrial and decorator
    felt.

Chicago Sanitary Rag
2170 South Canal Port
Chicago, IL 60608

312-226-3040
Cheesecloth.

Clement Textiles
54 Kneeland Street
Boston, MA 02111
617-542-9511

Dazian's Inc.
1758 N. Newcastle Avenue
Chicago, IL 60635
312-622-1888

165 S. Robertson Boulevard
Beverly Hills, CA 90211
213-657-8900 and
    213-655-9691
Fabrics.

DeCarlo Fabrics
15 Temple Place
Boston, MA 02111
617-426-5749
Natural fibers, woolens.

*Donna Salyer's Fabulous
    Furs*
680 Northland Boulevard
Cincinnati, OH 45240
513-851-8936
Fake fur.

F. & F. Fabric
403 E. 9th Street
Los Angeles, CA 90015
213-488-0909

Fabric Place
136 Howard Street
Framingham, MA 01701
508-872-4888
Decorator fabrics, craft
    supplies, foam.

Fabric Showroom
319 Washington Street
Brighton, MA 02135
617-782-3169 and
    617-783-4343
Decorator and designer
    fabrics.

Fishman's Fabrics, Inc.
1101 S. Desplaines Street
Chicago, IL 60607-4495
312-922-7250

G. Street Fabrics
11854 Rockville Pike
Rockville, MD 20852
301-231-8998
Fabrics, trims, notions,
    books, patterns.

General Rubber Fabric Co.
131 Portland Street
Boston, MA 02114
617-523-0958
Upholstery fabrics and
    supplies.

George B. Tewes Co., Inc.
2619 E. 8th Street
Los Angeles, CA 90023
213-269-0435
Felt.

Gladstone Fabrics
P.O. Box 566
Orchard Hill Road
Harriman, NY 10926
914-783-2963 and
    800-724-0168
Theatrical fabrics, silks,
    cottons, sequin, and
    stretch fabrics.

Harrison/North End Fabrics
31 Harrison Avenue
Boston, MA 02111
617-426-2116

11 Parmenter Street
Boston, MA 02114
617-723-7082

Home Silk Shop
330 S. La Cienga
    Boulevard
Los Angeles, CA 90048
213-655-7513

House of a Thousand Fabrics
611 S. Fairfax Street
Los Angeles, CA 90036
213-938-2311

*International Silks &
    Woolens*
8347 Beverly Boulevard
Los Angeles, CA 90048
213-653-6453

Jerome Fabrics
1750 W. 95th Street
Chicago, IL 60643
312-238-5560
Fabrics and trim.

Left Bank Fabrics Co.
8354 W. 3rd Street
Los Angeles, CA 90048
213-655-7289

Levine Bros., Inc.
530 S. Los Angeles Street
Los Angeles, CA 90013
213-624-6541
Woolens, linings, tailor's supplies.

Michael Levine, Inc.
930 S. Maple Avenue
Los Angeles, CA 90015
213-622-6259 and
    213-622-6316
Fabrics, notions.

New England Textiles
50 Essex Street
Boston, MA 02111
617-426-1965

Oriental Silk Import & Export Co.
8377 Beverly Boulevard
Los Angeles, CA 90048
213-651-1212 and
    213-651-2323

Osgoods Textile Co., Inc.
30 Magaziner Place
Springfield, MA
413-737-6488
Warehouse, large selection.

Ralph Jordan Textiles
332 Washington Street
Brighton, MA 02135
617-254-5852

257 Great Road
Acton, MA 01720
617-263-0606

S. & S. Fabrics
700 S. Los Angeles Street
Los Angeles, CA 90014
213-623-6828

Sewlow Discount Fabrics
473 Cambridge Street
Cambridge, MA 02141
617-661-8361 and
    617-492-9091
Fashion and decorator fabrics.

Slesinger
30 Chauncy Street
Boston, MA 02111
617-542-1805
Fabrics.

Standard Felt Co.
115 S. Palm Avenue
Alhambra, CA 91801
213-282-1106

Industrial and decorator felt.

Stanley Mill Store
P.O. Box 307
140 Mendon Street
Uxbridge, MA 01569
617-278-2451
Mill outlet.

Supreme Felt & Abrasives Co.
4425 T-James Place
Melrose Park, IL 60160
312-344-0134
Industrial felt.

Supreme Novelty Fabrics
913 W. VanBuren Street,
    Suite 1-D
Chicago, IL 60607
312-666-6446
Bridal fabrics, lace, net, and illusion.

Sureway Trading Enterprises
826 Pine Avenue #5
Niagara Falls, NY 14301
716-282-4887
Specializes in silks.

Testfabrics, Inc.
P.O. Box 420
200 Blackford Avenue
Middlesex, NJ 08846
908-469-6446
Specializes in white, untreated fabrics, all fibers.

Thai Silks
242 State Street
Los Altos, CA 94022
415-948-8611

Utex Trading
710 9th Street, Suite 5
Niagara Falls, New York
    14301
416-596-7565, ext. 38.
Silks.

Velvets, Inc.
Box 165
Short Hills, NJ 07078
201-379-4272
Cotton velveteen, full color range.

Vogue Fabrics
621 W. Roosevelt Road
Chicago, IL 60607
312-829-2505

Winmil Fabrics
Woburn Mall
Route 3
Woburn, MA 01801
617-935-3627

111 Chauncy Street
Boston, MA 02111
617-542-1815
Discount fabrics, patterns.

FOOTWEAR

Century Heel Co.
1708 N. Tyler Avenue
South El Monte, CA
    91733
213-283-8238
Custom heels.

Chernin's Shoes
606 W. Roosevelt Road
Chicago, IL 60607
312-922-4545 and
    312-966-4080
Discount footwear.

The Folk Motif
P.O. Box 14755
Long Beach, CA 90803
213-439-7380
Eastern European footwear, costumes, and jewelry.

Foot Connection
123 E. 6th Street
Los Angeles, CA 90014
213-622-4446
Stacy-Adams boots and shoes.

G. Gedney Godwin, Inc.
Box 100
Valley Forge, PA 19481
215-783-0670
Eighteenth-century shoes for men and women.

John Hiatt, the Bootmaker
942 Greenwood Terrace
Salt Lake City, UT 84105
801-581-1983
Custom-made boots.

John Shrader, Bootmaker
1508 San Anselmo Avenue
San Anselmo, CA 94960
415-459-6576
Custom-made footwear; boot and swordhanger kits.

Kling Theatrical Shoes
218 S. Wabash Street
Chicago, IL 60604
312-427-2028
Dance shoes.

Pasquale DiFrabrizio
8216 W. Third Street
Los Angeles, CA 90048
213-655-5248
Custom boots and shoes.

Santa Cross Shoe Repair
10 Temple Place
Boston, MA 02111
617-426-6978
Dance rubber, taps, lifts, general repairs.

Whistle's Clown Shoes
8510 Round Lake Road
Laingsburg, MI 48848
517-651-2042
Custom-made clown shoes.

HATS AND MILLINERY SUPPLIES

Allyns Bridal & Millinery Supplies, Inc.
2306 East Sixth Avenue
Denver, CO 80106
303-377-4969

California Millinery Supply Co.
721 S. Spring Street
Los Angeles, CA 90014
213-622-8746

Hand the Hatter
20 Lagrange Street
Boston, MA 02116
617-338-8496

Hat/Cap Exchange
P.O. Box 377
Betterton, MD 21610
410-348-2244
Wool, cloth, straw hats, caps; wholesale.

Hatcrafters
20 N. Springfield Road
Clifton Heights, PA 19018
215-623-2620
Theatrical hats.

Henry the Hatter
530 Washington Street
Lynn, MA 01901
617-592-9621

Krieger Top Hats, Inc.
3 Taft Avenue
Lynbrook, Long Island,
NY 11563
516-599-3188
Manufacturers of collapsible
and noncollapsible top
and opera hats.

*Leon Berlin Milliners
Supplies*
707 S. Broadway
Los Angeles, CA 90014
213-622-7064

Milliners Supply Co.
911 Elm Street
Dallas, TX 75202-3199
214-742-8284

Nader the Hatter
340 Worthington Street
Springfield, MA 01103
413-736-8081

Parrot Hatters
73 Middlesex Street
Lowell, MA 01853
508-453-4622

Washington Millinery Supply
P.O. Box 5718
Derwood, MD 20855
301-963-4444 and
800-363-2753
Millinery supplies, lace.

LEATHER AND
LEATHER SUPPLIES

Beacon Leather
106 South Street
Boston, MA 02111
617-542-7158
Leather dyes

Berman Leather
25 Melcher Street
Boston, MA 02110
617-426-0870

Chicago Tanning
1500 Courtland Street
Chicago, IL 60622
312-486-8180
Leather.

Fiebing Co., Inc.
P.O. Box 04125
516 S. 2nd Street
Milwaukee, WI 53204
414-271-5011
Leather dyes, finishes,
polishes.

Macpherson Leather Co.
200 S. Los Angeles Street
Los Angeles, CA 90012
213-626-4831
Leather, leather dyes,
findings, etc.

S-T Leather Company
P.O. Box 15152
333 E. Long Street
Columbus, OH 43215
614-224-5443

P.O. Box 78188
17th and Papin Street
St. Louis, MO 63178-8188
314-241-6009
Leather and leather
supplies.

*Tandy Leather Corp., Head
Office*
1001 Foch Street
Fort Worth, TX 76107
817-335-4161

922 Main Street
Waltham, MA 02154
617-899-6215
Leather, tools, dyes,
findings.

MAKE-UP, WIGS,
AND HAIR
SUPPLIES

A & A Beauty Supply
12555 River Street
Hyde Park, MA 01960
617-361-6606
Make-up.

Ben Nye Make-Up, Inc.
5935 Bowcroft Street
Los Angeles, CA 90016
310-839-1984
Theatrical make-up.

California Merchandise Co.
2133 S. Harbor Boulevard
Anaheim, CA 92802
714-971-9447 and
213-924-6686
Wigs of all types.

California Theatrical Supply
132 Ninth Street
San Francisco, CA
94103-2603
415-863-9236 and
800-866-1329
Wigs and make-up.

Chicago Hair Goods Co., Inc.
428 S. Wabash Avenue
Chicago, IL 60605
312-427-8600
Make-up and inexpensive
wigs.

Columbia Drug Co.
1440 N. Gower Street
Los Angeles, CA 90028
213-464-7555
Theatrical make-up, wig-
making tools, supplies.

*Custom Wig and Hair
Creations, Inc.*
1141 Waterloo Road
Berwyn, PA 19312
610-296-4243
Custom wigs, hairpieces,
facial hair for rental or
purchase.

Elsen Associates
845 Maolis Way
Pittsburgh, PA 15233
412-321-1231
Specializes in wigs and
make-up for opera.

Franklin Fashions
103 E. Hawthorn Street
Valley Stream, NY 11580
800-556-0034
Inexpensive wigs.

*Jack Stein Make-Up Center,
Inc.*
186 South Street
Boston, MA 02116
617-542-7865
Jack Stein and other
brands.

Joe Blasco Cosmetics
1708 Hillhurst Avenue
Los Angeles, CA 90027
213-222-5537 and
213-667-0722
Make-up.

Kryolan Corp.
132 Ninth Street
San Francisco, CA
94103-2603

415-863-9684 and
800-866-1329
Make-up and hair color
sprays.

The Make-Up Place
P.O. Box 155
1147 E. Broadway
Glendale, CA 91205
213-669-1161
Make-up and foam latex,
prosthetic supplies.

Mehron, Inc.
100 Red Schoolhouse
Road
Chestnut Ridge, NY 10977
914-426-1700 and
800-332-9955
Manufacturer of stage
make-up and supplies.

Richard Stead Enterprises
555 Fulton Street, Suite
107
San Francisco, CA 94102
415-431-1235
Wigs and hairpieces,
custom built, and rental.

Wig World
27 Temple Place
Boston, MA 02111
617-542-5511
Synthetic and some human
hair wigs.

Wilshire Wigs & Accessories
13213 Saticoy Street
North Hollywood, CA
91605
213-875-2260 and
818-983-0874
Wigs and hairpieces.

Zauder Bros. Inc.
10 Henry Street
Freeport, NY 11520
516-379-2600
Wig supplies.

SEWING SUPPLIES,
MACHINERY, AND
EQUIPMENT

Alder Leonard & Co.
190 N. State Street
Chicago, IL 60601
312-332-5454
Dress forms, tailoring
supplies.

Atlanta Thread & Supply Co.
695 Red Oak Road
Stockbridge, GA 30281
800-847-1001
Sewing supplies,
   equipment, and
   machinery.

Automatic Steam Products
5244 W. Adams Boulevard
Los Angeles, CA 90016
213-857-0411
Pressing equipment.

B. Black & Sons
548 S. Los Angeles Street
Los Angeles, CA 90013
213-624-9451
Sewing supplies.

Banasch's
2810 Highland Avenue
Cincinnati, OH 45212
513-731-2040 and
   800-543-0344
Supplies and equipment for
   the apparel, tailoring,
   and drycleaning trades.

BDS Laundry Supply
7901 12th Avenue
Minneapolis, MN 55420
800-328-1974
Laundry equipment and
   supplies.

Burgess Manufacturing
3600 Windsor Park Drive
Suwanee, GA 30174
404-932-1111
Grommet setters, and dies,
   button-makers.

C & H Distributors, Inc.
P.O. Box 04499
400 South 5th Street
Milwaukee, WI 53204
414-271-2250 and
   800-558-9966
Storage shelves,
   Kee-Klamps for stock
   racks, rolling ladders,
   desks, chairs, etc.

Clotilde, Inc.
2 Sew Smart Way B8031
Stevens Point, WI
   54481-8031
800-772-2891
Mail order sewing supplies,
   notions, patterns, etc.

Crown Foundations, Inc.
225 Federal Street
Bridgeport, CT 06606
203-333-4144
Corset supplies.

Cutter's Exchange, Inc.
3033 Supply Avenue
City of Commerce, CA
   90040
213-726-1907

P.O. Box AD
55 Snowdrift Road N
Allentown, PA 18106
215-395-7177 and
   800-322-9574

P.O. Box 1108
627 19th Avenue N
Nashville, TN 37202
615-329-4931 and
   800-251-2142

P.O. Box 13428K
2585 Chantilly Drive
Atlanta, GA 30324
404-636-0305 and
   800-282-0197

P.O. Box 47383
2939 Irving Boulevard
Dallas, TX 75247
214-638-2700 and
   800-492-9663

P.O. Box 16763
145 Industrial Avenue
Greensboro, NC 27406
919-273-3481 and
   800-632-1068
Industrial sewing machines,
   parts, supplies,
   equipment.

Elliot Sewing Machine
327 Broadway
South Boston, MA 02127
617-268-5667
Sales and repairs.

Fine Brand
3720 S. Santa Fe Avenue
Vernon, CA 90058
213-588-3228
Corset bones, corset
   supplies.

Handy Button Machine Co.
1315 S. Maple Street
Los Angeles, CA 90015
213-747-5349

Grommets, snaps, dies,
   setting machines, etc.

Henry Stuart Co., Inc.
P.O. Box 551
108 W. Main Street
Milford, CT 06460
203-878-0648
Corset boning, tipping
   fluid.

Hi-Steam Corp.
610 Washington Avenue
Carlstadt, NJ 07072
201-460-9333
Naomoto steam irons and
   pressing equipment.

Jiffy Steamer Co.
P.O. Box 869
Route 3
Union City, TN 38261
901-885-6690
Portable pressing
   equipment.

The John Belmont Co.
P.O. Box 411178
4511 W. Belmont Avenue
Chicago, IL 60641
312-282-2882 and
   800-858-0960
Steam irons and steaming
   equipment, sales and
   repairs.

John Danais
50 Tufts Street
Somerville, MA 02145
617-625-7110
Dry cleaning bags and
   hangers.

Kagan & Sons, Inc.
750 Towne Avenue
Los Angeles, CA 90021
213-627-9655
Sewing supplies and
   findings.

*Keiffer's Lingerie Fabrics and
   Supplies*
P.O. Box 7500
Jersey City, NJ 07307
201-798-2266

*Kennedy Sewing Machine
   Co.*
106 E. 17th Street
Los Angeles, CA 90021
213-748-3192

Levine Bros., Inc.
530 S. Los Angeles Street
213-624-6541
Tailor's supplies.

*Mor Real Sewing Machine
   Co.*
128 High Street
Waltham, MA 02154
617-892-5333
Sales and repair.

National Steel Co.
128 Pacella Park
Randolph, MA 02368
508-961-1050
Spring steel for hoops, $1/2''$,
   1075 gauge.

Newark Dressmaker Supply
P.O. Box 20730
6473 Ruch Road
Lehigh Valley, PA
   18002-0730
610-837-7500
Mail order sewing supplies.

Pacific Paper Products
0 Broadway
Lawrence, MA 01842
508-683-8771
Dotted pattern paper.

Pam Tailor Supply
625 Adams Street
Dorchester, MA 02122
617-265-8500

Past Patterns
P.O. Box 7587-TC94
Grand Rapids, MI 49510
616-245-9456
Period clothing patterns,
   including corsets.

Perry Packaging Corp.
Powder Mill Road
Maynard, MA 01754
508-897-5002
Boxes made to order.

Professional Sewing Supplies
P.O. Box 14272
Seattle, WA 98114-4272
206-324-8823

R.S.C. Threads
13711 Camino Del Sol
Sun City, AZ 85375
602-546-1496
Thread on cones.

Reliable Sewing Machine
378 Page Street
Stoughton, MA 02072
617-341-3991
Pressing equipment,
   machines, sales, service.

Richard the Thread
8320 Melrose Avenue
West Hollywood, CA
   90069
213-852-4997 and
   800-473-4997
Sewing supplies.

Sachs
637 W. Roosevelt Road
Chicago, IL 60607
312-666-0091
Speed hooks, grommets,
   and setters.

Schreiber & Goldberg, Inc.
7400 Woodstream Drive
Charlotte, NC 28210
704-376-1228
Industrial sewing machine
   parts, equipment, tools.

*Seidel's Sewing Machine
   Repair Shop*
1412 Dorchester Avenue
Dorchester, MA 02122
617-825-0746
Sales and repair.

*Sewing Machine Exchange,
   Inc.*
1840 S. Michigan Avenue
Chicago, IL 60616
312-842-3700 and
   800-621-1640
Industrial sewing machines,
   rental, and sale.

*Singer Customer Service
   Center*
Singer Lane
Murfreesboro, TN 37130
615-893-6493
Industrial machines and
   parts.

Singer Sewing Center
280 Elm Street
Somerville, MA 02144
617-625-6668
Sales and repair.

Solo Slide Fasteners, Notions
166 Tosca Drive
Box 528
Stoughton, MA 02072

617-341-2770 and
   800-343-9670

Stoddard's
50 Temple Place
Boston, MA 02111
617-426-4187
Scissors and sharpening.

*Uncommon Conglomerates,
   Inc.*
287 East 6th Street
St. Paul, MN 55101
612-227-7000 and
   800-323-4545
Manufacturers of Fresh
   Again, enzyme action
   deodorizing spray for
   uniforms and costumes.

William Wawak Company
2235 Hammond Drive
Shaumburg, IL 60195
312-397-4850
Sewing supplies, buttons,
   linings.

Wolf Forms Co. Inc.
P.O. Box 510
17 Van Nostrand Ave.
Englewood, NJ 07631
212-255-4508
Custom dress forms.

UNIFORMS,
WEAPONS, AND
ARMOR

AAA Police Supply
900 Providence Highway
Dedham, MA 02026
617-326-8846
Police uniforms.

*American Fencer's Supply
   Co., Inc.*
1180 Folsom Street
San Francisco, CA 94103
415-863-7911
Epees, foils, rapiers, hilts,
   blades, etc.

Bay State Uniform Co.
51 Melcher Street, 2nd
   floor
Boston, MA 02210
617-542-2231

Boston Uniform
803 Summer Street
Boston, MA 02127
617-269-8685

Central Surplus
433 Massachusetts Avenue
Cambridge, MA 02139
617-876-8512
Army/Navy surplus.

*The Collector's Armoury,
   Inc.*
P.O. Box 59
800 Slaters Lane
Alexandria, VA 22313
703-684-1111 and
   703-684-6133
Prop weapons.

Costume Armour, Inc.
P.O. Box 85
2 Mill Street
Cornwall, NY 12518
914-534-9120
Vacuum-formed armor
   pieces; swords and
   weapons.

Dixie Gun Works
P.O. Box 130
Reelfoot Avenue
Union City, TN 38261
901-885-0561
Firing guns, gun parts,
   military equipment.

Don Post Studios, Inc.
8610 Milliken Avenue
Rancho Cucamonga, CA
   91730
909-944-3559
Plastic armor, masks.

*George A. Petersen
National Capital Historical
   Sales Inc.*
Fullerton Industrial Park
7721 "D" Fullerton Road
Springfield, VA
   22153-2820
702-569-6663
Rents and sells historical
   and contemporary
   military uniforms,
   including headgear,
   medals, badges, insignias,
   flags, field equipment,
   weapons, books, and
   printed materials, etc.

Kaufman's West
1660 Eubank Street NE
Albuquerque, NM 87112

505-275-1441
Army/Navy surplus.

Massachusetts Army/Navy
Boylston Street
Boston, MA 02116
617-496-1250

Harvard Square
Cambridge, MA 02138
617-497-1250
Army/Navy surplus.

Santelli
465 S. Dean Street
Englewood, NJ 07631
201-871-3105
Fencing equipment and
   swords.

Tobins Lake Studios, Inc.
7030 Old U.S. 23
Brighton, MI 48116
313-229-6666
Vacuum-formed armor
   pieces.

Unique Imports, Inc.
Dept. DMC-2 ABC
610 Franklin Street
Alexandria, VA 22314
703-549-0775
Militaria, WWII uniforms,
   etc.

Wearguard
21 McGrath Highway
Somerville, MA 02134
617-776-1010
Uniforms and work
   clothes.

Wesrow Uniform
810 Massachusetts Avenue
Boston, MA 02118
617-442-1048

VIDEOTAPES

Theatre Arts Video Library
174 Andrew Avenue
Leucadia, CA 92024
619-632-6355
Producer and distributor of
   *The Pattern Development
   Video.*

Canada

ACCESSORIES

Atlas Umbrella
(Murray Sibulash)
176 John Street
Toronto, Ontario M5T 1X5
416-598-4747
Will cover umbrella shapes
and parasols.

William Cline Shirt Co.
5 Michael Street
Kitchener, Ontario
519-743-4118
Cotton shirts.

Firchuk's
Ottawa Street
Hamilton, Ontario
416-549-2005

610 Queen Street W
Toronto, Ontario
416-364-5036
Russian shawls, black lisle
hose.

Huck Glove Co.
120 Victoria Street S
Kitchener, Ontario
519-743-6365

ARTIST AND CRAFT SUPPLIES

Lewiscraft
40 Commander Boulevard
Scarborough, Ontario M1S
3S2
416-291-8406
Mail order. Branches
throughout Canada.
Craft supplies, beads,
findings, etc.

Rosco Laboratories, Ltd.
1271 Denison Street #66
Markham, Ontario L3R 4B5
416-475-1400
Bronzing powders, textile
paints, fabric dyes, craft
supplies.

Swift Adhesives
(Division of Eschem Canada
nc.)
383 Orenda Road
Bramalea, Ontario L6T 1G4
416-791-1744
Adhesives and tapes.

CLOTHING— MISCELLANEOUS

Walter Beauchamp
145 Wellington Street
Toronto, Ontario
416-595-5454
Formal wear, dress shirts,
and wing collars.

Cluett, Peabody, Canada,
Inc.
112 Benton Street
Kitchener, Ontario N2T
4A9
519-734-8211
Formal wear.

CLOTHING—USED AND ANTIQUE

Courage My Love
14 Kensington Street
Toronto, Ontario
416-979-1992
Good used clothing.

Frankel Clothing Exchange
123 Church Street
Toronto, Ontario M5C
2G5
416-366-4221
Good used clothing.

COSTUMES— CUSTOM AND RENTALS

Costume House
284 King Street W
Toronto, Ontario M5V 1J2
416-977-3113
Custom, rentals, and
make-up.

Costume Rentals
2250 Midland Avenue,
Unit 11
Scarborough, Ontario M1P
4R9
416-299-0645
Custom, rentals,
accessories, and
make-up.

Malabar, Ltd.
14 McCaul Street
Toronto, Ontario M5T 1V6
416-598-2581
Custom, rentals (opera
specialists), dancewear,
wigs, and make-up.

DANCEWEAR

Azim-Zim
84 Yorkville Avenue
Toronto, Ontario M5R
1B9
416-921-6543
Footwear, clothing,
accessories, make-up.

Malabar Studio
(Dance Supply)
1234 Yonge Street
Toronto, Ontario M4T
1W3
416-925-4409

Toronto Dancewear
530 Wilson Avenue
Toronto, Ontario
416-630-2292

730 Yonge Street
Toronto, Ontario
416-961-2292

DECORATIVE ITEMS

Better Pleating & Button
545 King Street, 5th floor
Toronto, Ontario M5V
1M1
416-596-1917
Pleating, belts, and buttons
covered.

H. Brown Ribbon
530 Adelaide Street W
Toronto, Ontario M5V
1T5
416-364-4397
Ribbons, flowers, feathers.

Capitol Buttons
399 Adelaide Street W
Toronto, Ontario M5V
1S4
416-366-2723 and
416-366-2474
Factory/warehouse.
Buttons, buckles,
ornaments, antique
items.

Eli David's & Co.
21 Mayfair Avenue
Toronto, Ontario
416-787-5422
Good junk.

Domcord
617 Denison Street
Unionville, Ontario
416-475-9330
Braid, ribbons, lace,
trimmings, appliques.

Dominion Regalia
1550 O'Connor Drive
Toronto, Ontario M4B
2X3
416-752-2382
Military braid, buttons.

Dressmaker's Supply
1325 Bay Street
Toronto, Ontario M5R
2C5
416-922-6179
Buttons, buckles, feathers,
beads, trimmings, etc.

F & F Trading Stone Co.
173 Spadina Avenue
Toronto, Ontario
416-596-6800
Antique findings, stones.

C.M.C.
5485 Tomken Road
Mississauga, Ontario
800-268-2073
Flowers.

Majestic Lace, Ltd.
140 Tycos Drive
Toronto, Ontario
416-783-4296

National Button & Trim
379-C Adelaide Street W
Toronto, Ontario
416-366-6611

Wm. E. Wright Co. of Canada, Ltd.
130 Crockford Boulevard
Scarborough, Ontario
M1R 3C3
416-752-9955
Trimmings, ribbons, tapes, braids, appliques, elastic, etc.

DYES

Advance
133 Rivalda Road
Weston, Ontario M9M 2M6
416-743-3311 and 800-387-2894

445 Boulevard Guimond
Longueil, P.Q.Montreal
J4G IL8
514-879-9000 and 800-363-0596
Screen printing supplies, textile, inks, equipment.

Knomark of Canada, Ltd.
71 Newlin Circle
Downsview, Ontario
416-630-3722
Tintex dyes.

FABRICS

Artex Woolens
42 Dufflaw Street
Cambridge, Ontario
416-256-6188

H. Brown Silks
(*Division of Kingsley Textiles, Ltd.*)
38 Orfus Street
Toronto, Ontario
416-787-0351
Drapery fabrics.

Designer Fabric Outlet
1360 Queen Street W
Toronto, Ontario
416-531-2810

Great source for all types of fabric. Imported silks, linens, and wools. Designer ends, drapery, upholstery, linings, trimmings, etc.

European Textiles
432 Queen Street W
Toronto, Ontario M5V 2A8
416-366-3332
Unusual fabrics.

Archie Fine & Sons
424 Queen Street W
Toronto, Ontario
416-596-6633

Gibson Textile Dyers
1171 Queen Street W
Toronto, Ontario
416-533-8565
Canvas and cotton in quantity.

G.A. Hardie & Co.
3 Dorchester Street
Toronto, Ontario M8Z 4W2
416-259-8461
Factory cotton and sheeting.

Maryan's Fabrics
3213 Yonge Street
Toronto, Ontario M4N 2L3
416-488-6111

Milan's Sari Shop
1418-1443 Gerrard Street E
Toronto, Ontario
416-465-8365

Nash James International
26 Duncan Street, 5th floor
Toronto, Ontario M5V 2B9
416-977-6274
Silks.

The Rumpel Felt Co., Ltd.
P.O. Box 1283
60 Victoria Street N
Kitchener, Ontario N2G 4G8
519-743-6341
Manufacturers of all types of wool felt.

Sherman Tailors
462 College Street
Toronto, Ontario

416-922-3852
Suitings.

Stitsky's
754 Bathurst Street
Toronto, Ontario M5S 2R6
416-537-2633
Dress fabrics.

Sureway Trading Enterprises
111 Peter Street
Toronto, Ontario M5V 2H1
416-596-1887
Silks, thread, dyes.

FOOTWEAR

Michael Bolubash
615 College Street W
Toronto, Ontario M6G 1B5
416-537-2986
Custom theatrical footwear.

Frederick Longtin/The Shoemaker
RR 2 Box 2094
Granville Ferry
Nova Scotia B0S 1K0
902-532-2233
Custom theatrical footwear.

Singer Shoes
903 Bloor Street W
Toronto, Ontario
416-533-3559

HATS

Biltmore Hats
139 Morris Street
Guelph, Ontario N1E 5M6
519-836-2770

The Hatter
137 Yonge Street
Toronto, Ontario
416-366-8195

LEATHER AND LEATHER SUPPLIES

Capital Findings
580 King Street W
Toronto, Ontario M5V 1M3
416-363-8563

Leather, shoe dyes, findings.

Moore Pearshall Leather
47 Front Street E
Toronto, Ontario M5E 1B3
416-363-5881

Perfect Leather
1928 Spadina Avenue
Toronto, Ontario
416-368-4215
Garment leather. Will install straps.

B.B. Smith
37-39 Sherbourne Street
Toronto, Ontario M5A 2P6
416-364-8551
Leather skins.

MAKE-UP

The Make-up Place
72 Carlton Street
Toronto, Ontario M5R 2C3
416-961-1300

SEWING SUPPLIES, MACHINERY, AND EQUIPMENT

Rose E. Dee
76 Miranda Street
Toronto, Ontario
416-785-1400
Corset and lingerie fabrics and supplies.

Dressmaker's Supply
1325 Bay Street
Toronto, Ontario M5R 2C5
416-922-6179

Reliable Sewing Machine
69 Wingold Street
Toronto, Ontario
416-785-0200

MacDonald Faber, Ltd.
Tailor's & Costume Supplies
952 Queen Street W
Toronto, Ontario M5V 2A9
416-534-3940

Neverens Tailor Supply
451 Queen Street W
Toronto, Ontario M5V
    2A9
416-368-4136

Gibbs Wire & Steel Co.,
    Ltd.
120 Walker Drive
Brampton, Ontario
416-791-6811
Steel hoops.

UNIFORMS, WEAPONS, AND ARMOR

Costume Armor, Inc.
2250 Midland Avenue,
    Unit 11
Scarborough, Ontario M1P
    4R9
416-299-0645
Theatrical armor and
    weapons.

Gobles Firearms, Ltd.
410 3rd Street
London, Ontario N5W
    4W6
519-455-4277
Weapons. Sales and
    rentals.

Hercules Army Surplus
577 Yonge Street
Toronto, Ontario
416-924-7764

Stokes Cap & Regalia, Ltd.
11 Canadian Road, Unit 3
Scarborough, Ontario
    M1R 5G1
416-755-5283
Military and civilian
    uniforms hats, badges,
    regalia, etc.

Index

A

Accessories, 175, 176–177
Acrylic paints, 110–112; gel medium, 111; gesso, 111; matte medium, 111; modeling paste, 111; polymer medium, 111; retarding medium, 111
Action charts, 29–30, 33–34, 40, 47
Actors, 159–165; consideration towards, 171–172; disagreements with, 164–165; measurements, 161; rehearsal clothes, 161–164. *See also* Fittings
Actor's Equity Association, 23, 128, 159
Adhesives. *See* Tapes and adhesives
American Catalogue of Books, 59
American Fabrics and Fashions (periodical), 61
Arnheim, Rudolph, 76, 88
Arnold, Janet, 63, 66
Art and Visual Perception (Arnheim), 76, 88
Art equipment, 117–119; magnifying glass, reducing glass, and mirror, 119; mat cutters, 119; paper cutter, 117; rulers, 117–118; stapler, 117; tracing table, 118–119. *See also* Work spaces
Art Index, 61
Art of Using Color, The (King), 78
ArtSEARCH (periodical), 191
Art Students' League (New York), 71
Art supplies and materials, 94–117; brushes, 115–116; color media, 106–115; papers and boards, 100–106; pencils, pencil sharpeners, and erasers, 94–97; pens and inks, 97–100; tapes and adhesives, 116–117

B

Barton, Lucy, 56
Beard, Charles, 66
Beckerman, Bernard, 13, 50
Bevlin, Marjorie Elliott, 78
Blausen, Whitney, 142, 195
Boards. *See* Papers and boards
Book of Costume, The (Davenport), 66
Book Review Digest, 59
Books in Print, 59
Boucher, Francois, 66
Brushes, 111, 115–116; cleaning, 111, 116; sable, 115

Budget breakdown, 42–43, 47, 130–136; cutting corners, 133–136; estimating, 133; starting point, 133

C

Calendars, 43, 47
Character doubling, 39
Characters' attitudes, 20–21
Characters' function, 21–24; antagonist, 22–23; crowds, 24; leading, 23–24; protagonist, 22; stereotypical, 24; supporting, 23–24
Characters' identification and description, 18–20, 40–41; beliefs, 18–20; date or season, 16, 40; geographical location, 16; government, 18–20; relationships and socio-economics, 18–20; religious environment, 18–20; silhouettes, 50–51, 73; textural references, 16, 40
Charcoals, 114; compressed, 114; papers, 102; pencils, 114; stick or vine, 114
Charlestown Museum (South Carolina), 63
Colonial Williamsburg (Virginia), 57
Color displays, 83–84; attaching color samples, 84; incorporating stock and rental costumes, 86; using fabric samples, 84
Color elements, 77–87; display, 83–84; form, 83; perception, 78; properties, 79–80, 83; responses, 78–79; vocabulary, 82–83; wheel, 80–82
Color layout. *See* Preliminary sketching and color layout
Color media, 107–115; acrylic paints, 110–112; charcoals, 114; gouache, 110; inks, 113; markers, 112–113; oil paints, 107; paints, 107; pastels, 113–114; pencils, 114–115; watercolor and gouache 110; watercolors, 107–108
Color properties, 80; warm and cool, 83
Color responses, 78–80; in design, 79–80; love, 79; red and blue, 79; royalty, 79; traffic light, 79
Color vocabulary, 82–83; hue, 82; intensity, 83; shades, 83; tints, 83; values, 82–83
Color wheels, 80–82; afterimage, 80–81; analogous harmony, 81, 82; complementary colors, 80, 82; monochromatic harmony, 81, 82; near complements, 82; neutral colors, 80;

Color wheels, *(continued)*
  primary colors, 80; schemes, 82; secondary
  colors, 80; split complements, 81, 82; tertiary
  colors, 80; triad harmony, 81–82
Contracts, 206–209
Corsets and Crinolines (Waugh), 62, 66
Corson, Richard, 56, 153
Costume bible, 122, 157
Costume Collection, The (New York), 142–143,
  144, 195
Costume design business, 188–211; entering,
  188–196; first professional design jobs,
  196–211
Costume design jobs. *See* Jobs
Costume plots, 34–35, 47, 154; finished, 34–35;
  revised, 125–126; rough, 33, 34, 40
Costume rental assistants, 195
Costume research, 49–68; accuracy, 52;
  comparisons, 53–54; contemporary, 68;
  historical background, 49–50, 64; history books,
  65, 66; impressions, 50–51, 65; libraries, 56–62;
  museums, 62–63; outlines, 54–55; painters, 68;
  primary sources, 65; record and document
  research information, 63–64
Costumer's Handbook, The (Ingham and Covey), 179
Costumes for the Theatre (Barton), 56
Costume shop. *See* Costume technicians
Costume stock, 43, 86, 133, 139–141, 170–171.
  See also Finding, pulling, renting costumes
Costume storage, 140–141
Costume technicians, 42–43, 126–128, 165–182;
  complimenting, 168, 187; costume designers as,
  170, 190–191; as cutters, 166; design guides,
  167–168; as drapers, 166–167, 172; as dyers,
  173–174; jobs, 190–191; as shaders, agers, and
  distressers, 178–179; as stitchers, 168;
  volunteer, 169–170; workload and priorities,
  172–173. *See also* Dress parades; Fittings
Crowds, 24, 39
Cumulations of the Cumulative Book Index, 59
Cumulative Book Index, The, 59
Cunnington, C. Willett and Phillis E., 66
Custom costume designers, 195
Cut of Men's Clothes, 1600–1900, The (Waugh), 66
Cut of Women's Clothes, 1600–1930, The (Waugh),
  66
Cutters. *See* Costume technicians

D

Davenport, Milia, 66
Design conferences: casting considerations, 39,
  40–41; character and script considerations,
  39–41; with directors, 32–34, 35–36, 86–87;
  with directors and actors, 159–160, 164–165,
  170, 175; first, 35–41; with lighting designer,
  44, 45, 184; period and style considerations,
  36–37; preparations, 32–34, 41; with set
  designer, 44–45, 184
Designer color. *See* Gouache
Designing and Making Stage Costumes (Motley),
  49
Designing and Painting for the Theatre (Pecktal),
  83
Designing for the Theatre (Mielziner), 158
Design Quarterly (periodical), 61
Design through Discovery (Bevlin), 78
Dialogue mode, 25–29; ambiguity, 27–29;
  literacy, 25–26; naturalistic, 25; poetic, 26;
  sound and grammar, 26–27
Dictionary of English Costume (Cunnington,
  Cunnington and Beard), 66
Directors, 32–34, 35–36, 86–87, 159–160,
  164–165, 175
Dramatic Imagination, The (Jones), 5
Drapers. *See* Costume technicians
Drawing on the Right Side of the Brain (Edwards),
  70
Drawing papers, 75, 102, 112; butcher, 102;
  layout, 102, 112; newsprint, 102; sketching,
  75, 102
Drawing People (Hogarth), 70
Dress parades, 180–182
Dress rehearsals. *See* Rehearsals
Dyers. *See* Costume technicians
Dynamics of Drama (Beckerman), 50

E

Eaves-Brooks Costume Company (New York),
  142
Edwards, Betty, 70
Enoch Pratt Free Library (Maryland), 56
Erasers, 96–97; art or gum, 97; putty or
  kneadable, 97

F

Fabrics, 84–86, 122, 134, 144–149; attaching to sketches, 84, 122; dipping down, 174; dyeing, 173–174, 177; estimating costs, 133; shading, ageing, and distressing, 178–179; swatching trips, 84–86, 119; washing, 169; wrapping and shipping, 147–149
Facial hair. *See* Wigs and facial hair
Fashions in Hair (Corson), 56
Faulkner, William, 90
Finding, pulling, renting costumes, 137–144; finding, 137–139; pulling, 139–141; renting, 47, 141–144, 179
Fittings, 128, 164; final, 177–178; first muslin, 171–172; for modern or pulled costumes, 170–171; second, 174–176
Free-lance design assistants, 196
Free-lance designers, 197–198

G

Gouache, 110; and watercolor, 110
Grun, Bernard, 64
Gummere, Amelia Mott, 56

H

Hair designers, 154
Halls, Zillah, 56
Handbook of Costume, A (Arnold), 63, 66
Handbook of English Costume (Cunnington and Cunnington), 66
Harper's Bazaar (periodical), 60
Hat list, 47, 140
Hodge, Francis, 21, 29
Hogarth, Paul, 70
Hollander, Anne, 124
Huenefeld, Irene Pennington, 63
Humanities Index, 61

I

IBPAT. *See* International Brotherhood of Painters and Allied Trades
Idea sketching. *See* Preliminary sketching and color layout
ILGWU. *See* International Ladies Garment Worker's Union

Inks. *See* Pens and inks
International Brotherhood of Painters and Allied Trades, 205
International Directory of Historical Clothing (Huenefeld), 63
International Ladies Garment Worker's Union, 195
Interviews, 203
Ives, Herbert E., 80

J

Job market, 188–196
Jobs, 190–211; contracts, 206–209; in costume rental houses, 195; in custom costume shops, 195; as free-lance design assistant, 196; as free-lance designer, 197–198; interviews, 203–205; letter and resume, 199–201; portfolios, 201–203; in regional theatres, 190–195, 209; as resident designer, 197; taxes, 210–211; as teacher, 190; with United Scenic Artists, 205–207, 209
Jones, Robert Edmond, 5, 9

K

King, John L., 78

L

League of Resident Theatres (New York), 128, 191–195
Letters and resumes, 199–201
Libraries, 56–62; books and what else, 57, 59; call numbers, 57–58; catalogues, 57–58; college and university, 56; Dewey Decimal System, 57, 58; interlibrary loans, 59–60; Library of Congress System, 57–58; newspapers, clippings, and pictures, 61–62; open and closed stacks, 58–59; periodicals, 60–61; photocopying, 60; public, 56; research, 56–57
Library of Congress Subject Headings, 58
Life (periodical), 60, 61
Lighting design, 44, 45, 184
Look (periodical), 60
LORT. *See* League of Resident Theatres

M

Marias Museum of History and Art (Montana), 63
Markers, 112–113. *See also* Pens and inks

Materials budget breakdown. *See* Budget breakdown
Maude Reading (Whistler), 114
Measurement charts, 41, 47, 71, 161
Men's Costume 1750–1800 (Halls), 56
Mielziner, Jo, 26, 158
Military Historians and Collectors, Society of, 68
Motley, 49
Mounting techniques, 120–121; window mats, 121
Museum of History and Industry (Washington), 63
Museums, 62–63; where to look, 62–63. *See also* Libraries

N

National Geographic, The (periodical), 60
Newton, Sir Isaac, 78
New York Public Library (New York), 56, 62; at Lincoln Center, 62
New York Times Index, The, 62
19th Century Readers' Guide to Periodical Literature, 61
Notions and trim, 134, 149, 176
Nutley Historical Society Museum (New Jersey), 63

O

Official Museum Directory, The, 62–63
Off-Off Broadway theatre designers, 196, 208
Oil paints, 107
Old Salem Village (North Carolina), 57
Opaque watercolor. *See* Gouache
Outlines: costume research, 54–55; playscript analysis, 15

P

Painters, 68, 113–114
Paints, 107
Papers and boards, 75, 100–106; Bristol boards, 104–105; charcoal and pastel papers, 102, 114; colored papers, 101; drawing papers, 102, 112; frosted or matte acetate, 106–107; illustration board, 105; mat boards, 105; pad sizes, 101; poster and railroad board, 105; protective papers, 105, 121; rice papers, 105–106; tracing paper and vellum, 102–103; transfer papers, 103; watercolor papers, 103–104; weights and tooth, 100, 103–104

Pastels, 113–114; papers, 102, 114
Pecktal, Lynn, 83
Pencils, pencil sharpeners, and erasers, 94–97, 114–115; automatic mechanical pencils, 95; colored pencils, 114–115; drafting or clutch lead pencils, 95; drawing pencils, 94; erasers, 96–97; pencil sharpeners and lead pointers, 95–96; sketching pencils, 95
Pens and inks, 97–100; drawing pens, 97–98; felt and nylon tip pens, 99–100, 112; fountain pens, 98; inks, 99, 113; technical or drafting pens, 98–99. *See also* Markers
Picasso, Pablo, 70
Picture Collection, The (New York), 62
Planning, 125–137; budget, 130–136; costume plot, 125–126; costume shop, 126–127; lists, 125–126, 136–137; schedules and deadlines, 128
Play Directing, Analysis, Communication and Style (Hodge), 21
Playscript analysis, 15–31; characters' attitudes, 20–21; characters' functions, 21–24; dialogue mode, 25–29; outline, 15; play's action, 29–30; play's background, 20; play's theme, 31
Playscripts, 5–31; analysis, 13–15; designer's analysis, 10–11; fact finding, 11–12; films and television, 7–9; outline, 15–31; readings, 6–7, 9, 10
Portfolios, 201–203
Preliminary sketching and color layout, 69–87; attaching color samples, 84; color elements, 77–87; details, 75; drawing, 70; incorporating stock and rental costumes, 86; pencil and paper, 75–76; people, 70–71; period line, 73; proportion, 73–75; showing, 86–87; stock figures, 71–73; thumbnail, 77, 119
Pre-production period, 124–157; finding, pulling, renting costumes, 137–144; planning, 125–137; recording, 154–157; shopping and buying, 144–154
Production book, 45–47, 154–156, 164; action chart, 47; addresses and telephone numbers, 45; calendar, 45; cast list, 47; costume plot, 47; hat list, 47; materials budget breakdown, 47; measurement chart, 47; rental lists, 47; tax exemption number, 45; wig and beard list, 47
Production period, 158–187; actors and directors, 159–165; costume shop, 165–182; dress

parade, 180–182; dress rehearsals, 182–186; handling disagreements, 164–165; read through and design presentation, 159–160; stage management, 164

Productions, 32–48; book, 45–47; characters and script, 39–41; design conferences, 35–41, 44–45; period and style, 36–37; preparations, 32–34; rough costume plot, 34–35; realities, 42–43

Professional design jobs. *See* Jobs

Property items list, 137

Publisher's Weekly (periodical), 59

Pulling costumes. *See* Finding, pulling, renting costumes

Punch (periodical), 60

Q

Quaker, The (Gummere), 56

R

Reader's Guide to Periodical Literature, 61

Reciprocal rentals, 143–144

Record and document research information, 63–64; bibliographic citations, 63–64; sources, 63–64

Regional theatre designers, 128, 190–195, 195–196

Rehearsals, 161–164, 182–186; between, 164, 185; clothes, 161–164; dress, 182–186; first technical, 182; preparations, 182–184; previews as, 186; read through, 159–160; watching, 164

Renting costumes, 141–144, 179; companies, 142–143; lists, 47; reciprocal basis, 143–144. *See also* Finding, pulling, renting costumes

Resident designers, 42–43, 195–196

S

Seeing Through Clothes (Hollander), 124

Set designs, 44–45; basic construction, 44–45; color, 44; furniture, 45; stage floor surface, 45

Sharpeners. *See* Pencils, pencil sharpeners, and erasers

Shipping services, 149

Shopping and buying, 144–154; fabric, 144–149; new clothes, 151–152; notions and trim, 149; old clothes, 150–151; spirit, 154; wigs and facial hair, 152–154

Show bible. *See* Costume bible

Show reference book. *See* Production book

Sightlines (periodical), 191

Sketches, 69–77, 88–123; art supplies and materials, 94–119; covering, 121; information included, 119–120; media used, 93–94; mounting, 120–121; pen and ink lines, 100; photocopying, 45, 121–122, 203; place and time, 90–92; preliminary, 69–77; sizes, 92–93; swatching, 119, 122

Smithsonian Institution (District of Columbia), 57

Social Sciences Humanities Index. See Humanities Index

Stage Makeup (Corson), 153

Stage management, 164, 181, 182

Stitchers. *See* Costume technicians

Sturbridge Village (Massachusetts), 57

Swatches, 84–86, 119, 122, 147; attaching to sketches, 84, 122; buying, 84–86, 119, 147

T

Tapes and adhesives, 116–117; brown paper tape, 117; masking tape, 116–117; rubber cement, 117; Scotch Magic Transparent Tape, 117; white glue, 117

Tatler, The (periodical), 60

Taxes, 45, 210–211

Teaching designers, 190

Textile Museum Quarterly, The (periodical), 61

Theatre Communications Group (New York), 191, 201

Theatre Crafts (periodical), 179

Theatre Development Fund, The (New York), 142

Theatre Directory (periodical), 191, 201

Timetables of History, The (Grun), 64

Town and Country (periodical), 60

Trim. *See* Notions and trim

20,000 Years of Fashion (Boucher), 66

U

Unions. *See* Actor's Equity Association; International Ladies Garment Worker's Union; United Scenic Artists

United Scenic Artists, 196, 205–207, 209

United States Catalogue, The, 59

United States Institute for Theatre Technology (New York), 191

USA. *See* United Scenic Artists

USITT. *See* United States Institute for Theatre Technology

V

Vellum, 102–103, 106–107; multi-media, 106; plastic, 106–107

Vogue (periodical), 60

Volunteers, 169–170

W

Warburg and Cortauld Institutes, Journal of the (periodical), 61

Wardrobe supervision, 181, 182–183, 184, 185

Watercolor techniques, 108–110; dry brush application, 109; dry on dry, 108; flat wash, 109; gouache, 110; graduated wash, 109; line and wash, 109; papers, 103–104; scumbling, 109; stippling, 109; variegated wash, 109; wash, 108–109; wet into wet, 108; wet on dry, 108

Waugh, Norah, 62, 66

Western Costume Company (California), 142

Whistler, James McNeill, 114

Wigs and facial hair, 134, 152–154; lists, 47

Work charts, 128

Work hours, 92, 172–173

Work spaces, 90–92; creative designs, 92; drawing table, 91; lighting, 92; seating, 91

Also by Rosemary Ingham and Elizabeth Covey --

THE COSTUME TECHNICIAN'S HANDBOOK
A Complete Guide for Amateur and Professional Costume Technicians

Here is the classic work on costuming for professionals and amateurs. This is a true handbook for a complex subject, and everyone from costume designers and costume technicians to costume lovers and sewing enthusiasts will find it fascinating and endlessly informative.

Features include:

+ a completely updated chapter on how a costume shop works, the equipment and layout required, and what each job in a shop entails,
+ a new and extensive chapter covering health and safety practices in the costume shop,
+ chapters on pattern drafting and sewing operations have been tripled in length to include much greater treatment of details and procedures, including expanded directions for the draping of the basic body sloper.
+ an expanded section on alterations
+ nearly 500 black and white photos and drawings,
+ an 8-page portfolio of color plates,
+ completely revised and updated list of sources for every sort of material, property, and equipment.

0-435-08610-3   470 pages   illustrated   Paperback

Order your copy of *The Costume Technician's Handbook* from your favorite bookstore.